Anyone Can Landscape!

Joel M. Lerner

Anyone Can Landscape!

Joel M. Lerner

Ball Publishing

Batavia, Illinois, U.S.A.

Ball Publishing
335 N. River Street
Batavia, IL 60510
www.ballpublishing.com

Concept by Richard C. Levy
Front cover design by Tamra Bell. Back cover design by Christine Victor.
Interior design by Carlisle Communications Ltd.

Library of Congress Cataloging-in-Publication Data
Lerner, Joel M., 1947-
    Anyone can landscape! / Joel M. Lerner.
        p. cm.
    ISBN 1-883052-27-0 (alk. paper)
    1. Landscape architecture. 2. Landscape architecture—Designs and
plans. 3. Landscape gardening. 4. Landscape gardening—Designs and
plans. 5. Landscape plants. I. Title.
    SB473.L467 2001
    712'.6—dc21   2001000757

Printed in Italy.
07 06 05 04 03 02 01 9 8 7 6 5 4 3 2 1

CONTENTS

ACKNOWLEDGMENTS

A great number of people are responsible for seeing through to completion an idea for a book. I greatly appreciate the efforts of everyone involved. Many people have given this project their undivided attention, but I especially want to thank the following contributors without whom there would be no *Anyone Can Landscape!*

In the developmental stage, my parents, Matilda "Toby" and Elmer Lerner, put in innumerable hours of research on the Internet and in libraries, reading articles on landscape trends and the latest gardening practices. The material they fed me, thanks to their curiosity, education, knowledge, love, and candor, was invaluable. I could not have been blessed with better parents.

One of my business partners and wife of thirty-one years, Sandra Leavitt Lerner, generated graphics, created documents, shot hundreds of photographs, checked facts, cleared intellectual property rights, applied her art background, made sure that we met deadlines, and did whatever it took. Frequently investing sixteen hours a day, her work was a selfless act of devotion. What she coordinated and accomplished was truly amazing, but it was no less an effort than she puts into every aspect of the business. I thank and love her.

There is a great deal more to book publishing than meets the eye, and nothing escapes the eye of Richard C. Levy. Richard, our other business partner and a close friend, is a brilliant fellow who used his creativity, marketing genius, entrepreneurial business acumen, and sixth sense to conceptualize this book, find the perfect home for it, Ball Publishing, and guide us to ensure its success. His sage counsel and showmanship are appreciated as much on this project as on everything we do at Environmental Design.

I turned to veteran journalist and good friend Randi Henderson to help me pull together, write, and organize content. Author of numerous books, hundreds of articles, and a features writer at the *Baltimore Sun* for twenty years, Randi was never daunted by the enormity of this assignment. She graciously endured many meetings, by phone and in person, as we developed the ideas and text and researched what people wanted to know most about the landscape.

Rick Blanchette, my editor, did a Herculean task of editing, writing, culling slides and scanned images, overseeing all the components and molding them into a book. His enthusiasm for this project was the amino acid that gave life to *Anyone Can Landscape!* Rick was our champion inside Ball who made it happen. I very much appreciate his help, intense focus, and the good cheer he displayed as he fielded phone calls from Sandy, Richard, and me.

They and many others have made this a work I am proud of.

Happy gardening!
Joel M. Lerner

INTRODUCTION

Knowledge is power, but experience rules. That's where knowledge originates. This book is the culmination of my thirty years of experience as a landscape professional—or you could say forty-two years of experience, since landscape gardening has been my passion since I began working.

I have done my utmost to design this book to impart more than just gardening information. I have tried to give you another aspect to gardening and landscape design, one that puts you in the mental zone, sensitized to the art form, one that will help you to think of the form of your landscape as a whole, not just a random collection of trees, flowers, lawn, and structures.

I hope you'll discover, within these pages, many wow factors, little gems of information that cause you to say, "Wow! That's good to know," and, "I can do that myself."

But it will take more than this book to keep your ideas fresh. You have to open your eyes and mind to the smorgasbord of free landscape ideas that you are exposed to daily. Every time you take a stroll, jog, drive to work, visit a friend, go to the market, etc., landscape concepts abound. Look at what people have done with trees, shrubs, flowers, design, maintenance, composting, and other practices around the landscape. Jot down ideas on paper. They will be like money in the bank towards your property's landscaping budget.

People use the terms *garden* and *landscape* interchangeably, but consider them differently. When I use *landscape*, it refers to the big picture, the combination of permanent plants and structures that enhance a yard, park, or community. The term *garden* refers to a plot or smaller scale space for flowers, fruits, and vegetables, or to small sections of an overall property, as in a meditation or water garden.

How you perceive the landscape deserves considerable thought and reflection because this sets the tone for your designs. Please pay special attention to the section on Lernscaping. Fill out the checklist, even if you only intend to plant one tree. You should consider the results of this analytical exercise before you turn one spade of soil or drive a single nail. By following this self-help design program, you'll be able to organize your goals and dreams and solve landscape problems on paper before investing one dollar or one minute of unnecessary time and labor to execute an idea that might not work or satisfy you.

Lernscaping is a system I created to put you in touch with your property and assure that it reflects the essence of your personality and needs. Lernscaping is a simple process that will translate your requirements into a language that can be understood by landscape architects, designers or nurserymen. If you opt to do the job yourself, Lernscaping will provide the road map.

Having a great landscape design for your property will enhance your life overall. Studies show that plants have a therapeutic effect. People who live among plants feel better and are happier and more relaxed. In the workplace, they contribute to higher morale. Psychological studies have shown that the color green induces peace and serenity. There is extensive documentation of the therapeutic value—both physical and psychological—of gardening and the tasks involved in maintaining attractive grounds. These activities offer good calorie-burning exercise and good escapism from the pressures and pace of daily life. Landscaping is important, not just for the value of being surrounded by green space, but for the opportunity it offers for active participation in it as well. This means participation from idea conception through the continuing growth and necessary maintenance that is required for any landscape.

The right landscape will also increase your property value. The appeal of a well-landscaped private home increases its value by at least 15 percent. In fact, landscaping is the only home improvement you can make that increases in value with time.

I encourage you to dig into this book and use it as a reference. You don't need to read it cover to cover, in sequence, for it to be useful. Take the information in bits and pieces, and put your own spin on it. The tips offered here—organized around themes that run the gamut from initial stages of design to execution of complex ideas—are practical, hands-on suggestions. Some are general; some are quite specific. They will guide you through the planning and installation of a landscape that reflects your personality and will offer comfort and esthetic delights to you, your family, and friends for years to come. With little or no prior knowledge of landscape design, you will be able to employ the principles of design described here to make an artistic statement and create an area of interest and physical comfort in your life.

I hope this book holds the answers to most of your questions and proves invaluable for creating a tremendously successful design for your landscape or garden space.

I accept full responsibility for the points of view, the opinions, and the conclusions presented. They are entirely my own.

Joel M. Lerner

The Beginning Landscape

THE BEGINNING LANDSCAPE

You're a neophyte. You feel you don't know anything about landscape design. Don't worry. We all felt that way. Everything you've ever done in your life was new to you at some point, and look how well you do those things now. Landscaping is no different.

I started in the landscape business in 1970 with a lawnmower and pickup truck. People were always asking me questions: What can I plant here? What can I plant there? What should I replace that dying tree with? How do I enhance my entry? How can I screen out my neighbors? Where should I put the patio? How big should I make it? What about the walkway? Before I knew it, I found myself doing seat-of-the-pants landscape design.

Everyone who works in landscape professions—the grounds manager, the landscape contractor, the nurseryman, the landscape architect, the landscape designer, the arborist, the drainage engineer—is being asked these questions. But the fact is, no one can tell you what will work best for you and your property. You have to do this for yourself.

The tips supplied here will help you figure out what to do and how to do it. They will give you a path to travel, and guideposts and options to consider each step of the way. These tips—used in conjunction with the checklist in chapter 2—are the tools you need to figure out what works best for the landscape design of your property. The tips will be illustrated with examples, both specific and general, including possibilities for plantings. Some may sound very familiar, and some may be more obscure, and they should be used only as examples or suggestions of the diverse and extensive plant possibilities that are available.

DESIGN BY CONCEPT

You are the best person to decide what you want for your landscape design. Don't be limited by your plant knowledge. Decide on a size, shape, color, or effect, such as screening or shade. Then determine the characteristics of the right plant for your needs. For example, for screening you might say, "I want a plant that will grow eight feet tall, be evergreen, and have flowers." Or you can tell the plant expert, "I'm looking for a shade tree with brilliant fall color, a clean growth habit, and good disease resistance." The expert can offer suggestions. There are 300,000 plants in nature and more than 100,000 that have been identified, so be wide open to the full range of plant possibilities.

The basic principles of design are the rules that will govern the use of the landscape design tips in this book. Which came first—the principles or the designs? It's a chicken-or-egg quandary. There is evidence that the principles that we still apply today were used in the earliest recorded instances of landscaping. Probably the principles and the applications grew simultaneously, building upon each other. People planted what they felt comfortable with and what pleased their senses, and through the years theorists came along and identified why something looked good and then set the rules accordingly.

ARTISTIC PRINCIPLES OF DESIGN

The five basic principles to be applied to landscape design are the same that all artists use in any medium: balance, repetition, sequence, proportion, and contrast. The application of these principles in landscaping creates interest and will make you feel more comfortable, physically and psychologically.

BALANCE AND SYMMETRY

Most of us have understood balance since we first sat on a seesaw and realized that the person on the other side had to be of an approximate size and weight. Balance is a part of every single aspect of our lives, and that's probably why we look for it in our properties.

Identify a Central Axis

To achieve balance in landscaping, establish a strong central axis, then enhance the right and left sides of it by using plantings that are of an equivalent mass. The central axis could be the house, the

A walk edged with candytuft (*Iberis sempervirens*), *Liriope*, and impatiens offers symmetry to an otherwise asymmetrical entry.

front or back door, a shed, fountain, or any other structure that has visual impact on your property.

In a symmetrical landscape design, the right and left sides are equally weighted with the same elements, a mirror-like repetition on either side of a vertical axis. In an asymmetrical design, the right and left sides are equally weighted with different elements. Symmetry implies formality. The following tips illustrate this principle.

Symmetrical Entry

Establish symmetrical design in front of the house by enhancing the entry with two matching shrubs, such as slow-growing dwarf conifers (evergreens), one on each side. Edge them with a row of low growing plants, such as germander (*Teucrium*), lavender, or lily-turf (*Liriope*), that can be sheared into a formal hedge and kept about eight to ten inches in height. The tight-needled habit of dwarf conifers and the low hedge effect of sheared edging plants create a formal design. Edge with lavender or santolina, and shearing them will be a scent-sational experience. Choose Montgomery blue spruce (*Picea pungens* 'Montgomery') or Blue Star juniper (*Juniperus squamata* 'Blue Star') for your conifers, and they will blend well with the blue-green leaves of lavender or silver-colored foliage of santolina.

Symmetry in Backyard Gardens

For an effective use of symmetry in a sitting garden, center a fountain, relief, or other feature on a wall as a focal point. Use boxwood (*Buxus*), dwarf hinoki falsecypress (*Chamaecyparis obtusa* 'Nana'), or another plant with a compact growth habit on either side of the feature and border the shrubs with low-growing, long-blooming

Balancing plantings on both sides of a sculptural element lends symmetry. (Bishop's Garden, Washington National Cathedral, All Hallows Guild)

perennials, such as moonbeam coreopsis, gaillardias, and verbenas. Add a stone or English garden bench directly across from and centered on the fountain. Match the plantings on each side of the bench with those at the fountain.

Asymmetry

While it is somewhat simpler to envision and illustrate symmetry, asymmetry is more commonly found. Plants grow this way in nature. And asymmetry implies informality. Today's architectural styles generally do not have a formal colonnaded front door, for example, or symmetrical windows. More often in modern architecture, the door is on one side, a window on another, or a kitchen window on one side and picture window on the other. A garage and driveway to one side of the property also creates asymmetry. Since most homes are asymmetrical, the architectural designs dictate this style in landscape design.

Always Consider Balance

Even if it's an asymmetrical property, don't sacrifice balance. Objects equally weighted on the right and left of your house will give you a balanced design, even though they are not the same type. For example, plant a hinoki falsecypress (*Chamaecyparis obtusa* 'Nana') to the right side of your front door and a couple of weeping English yews (*Taxus baccata* 'Repandens') to balance it to the left. With the deep, forest green color and needled habit of both plants, this is a balanced attractive informal arrangement. Edge with lily-turf (*Liriope*) on both sides.

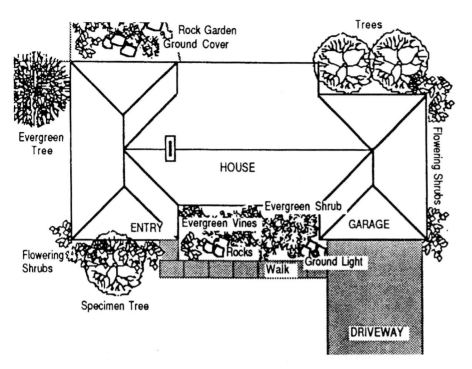

Radial Symmetry

Radial symmetry is employed when you need to enhance an area all around. In a design of this type, all the landscape design elements are distributed around a central point and there is a circular focus, such as a water garden, swimming pool, or playground.

A well-balanced water garden.

Design a water garden with radial balance. For example, arrange three water lilies equidistant around the perimeter of the pool. About five feet from the water's edge, plant a Japanese black pine (*Pinus thunbergii*), cut-leaf Japanese maple (*Acer palmatum* var. *dissectum*), or another tree with a graceful or windblown growth habit, where stems can arch near the water's edge. Place an arrangement of low informal shrubs next to this, such as nandina (*Nandina domestica*) or dwarf fothergilla (*Fothergilla gardenii*), which are quite disease resistant. Nandina is deep pink in the spring, coloring red in the fall, with red berries that can be dried for dried flower arrangements. Fothergilla has fragrant white flowers in spring, a compact growth habit, and beautiful fall color. Plant irises around the edges on each side, and azaleas will overhang the edge in a protected area of the water garden.

REPETITION

Repetition—repeating the same or similar elements in a design—is one of the basic laws of architecture as well as landscape design. It gives meaning to variety and introduces a sense of order in viewing the landscape. A single repeating theme is the strongest technique you can employ to unify a garden. Using repetition in a design tends to promote harmony as well as reduce confusion. Repetition can—and should—be applied to form, color, texture, and size. The one-of-each approach is the common error of the amateur designer.

Let's take a look at how repetition can be used in each of these contexts.

Repeat Plant Form

With trees, the habit of the branches dictates the form. A row of conifers installed for screening along the rear border of your property will have a uniform, strictly pyramidal (Christmas tree shaped) habit. Repeat that form throughout the plantings of your landscape to blend and give cohesion to the various elements. For a shade tree, use a pin oak (*Quercus palustris*) or katsuratree (*Cercidiphyllum japonicum*), which have a conical shape, particularly in youth (first twenty-five to thirty years). Continue the repetition of form with hinoki falsecypresses or American hollies (*Ilex opaca*) on the other side of the yard. Like the conifers, they have a strong single leader.

Repeat Textures

In general, coarse texture is associated with an informal, woodland look, and fine texture with a more formal and manicured look. In the example above, the fine texture of needled habit of the conifer is repeated in the falsecypress. Here is another example: Plant leatherleaf viburnum on the west side of your property as a shield between you and your neighbor's playground. Mimic the large leaves (and coarse texture) of the viburnum with rhododendron, which will also be protected by the viburnum. Complete the area with a coarse-leafed flowering tree such as a magnolia and several fragrant-leafed spicebushes (*Lindera benzoin*).

Plant Size

When massing plants together for form and texture, always determine the mature size of a tree or shrub. The most common error of amateur and professional designers alike is planting plants too close together. It is human nature to make the area look full at the moment of planting. This will create problems in the landscape because a plant that will eventually grow ten feet in height and spread is only two feet tall when installed. Design for the size a plant will become in ten to fifteen years, which is about two-thirds of the mature size. So a plant that will have a mature twelve-foot spread should be considered to grow to at least eight feet. Plant so that the centers of the plants are as far apart as the spread, so the plants will touch but not grow into each other when fully grown. In our example, since we figure on the plants growing to an eight-foot spread, plant them eight feet apart. A landscape professional would state it as "those plants should be planted on at least eight-foot centers."

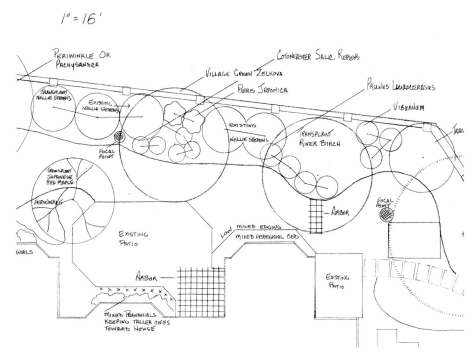

Plant Spacing This hand-drawn plan shows proper plant spacing. Note that measurements are from the centers of plants.

EXAMPLES OF COARSE- AND FINE-TEXTURED PLANTS

Plant texture is determined by leaf size. Coarse-textured foliage (large leaves) advances toward the viewer (above). Fine-textured foliage (small leaves) recedes from the viewer (below).

While many different sizes of plants are important for a complete landscape design, within each level, ground vertical and overhead, know how big a plant will grow and match it with plants of similar sizes. In some cases, another plant is intended to stand above or below a planting to act as a foil or canopy. Match those sizes as well.

Repetition of Colors

Color is the first thing to be noticed in a landscape, making it one of the most important elements to repeat. Color gets noticed and should not be haphazard or arbitrary. However, colors are often used incorrectly, and you are apt to see the one-of-everything approach. Splashes make a bigger impact than sprinkling color.

Pick one color and stick with it. This can be difficult because you have every color of the rainbow available to you, but be selective. Use one color in a mass (except in a cutting garden, where you will want a variety of colors). When you do introduce variation, use colors that flow and harmonize. In a rose garden that is planted for its outdoor ornamental value (as opposed to a cutting garden), plant a mass of three to five rose bushes of the same color, perhaps with a backing of linden viburnums (*V. dilatatum*) that have white flowers in spring and red berries in summer as roses are blooming and are maroon in fall when the roses are fading. Edge roses with white sweet alyssum for a low flowering border that will further enhance the rose fragrance.

Keep color selection simple. Wax begonias make a nice flowering annual border, but don't give in to the temptation of the many

Black-eyed Susans and maiden grasses (*Miscanthus sinensis* 'Gracillimus') in repetition increases their appeal. The crapemyrtle flowers offer a contrasting element to the design.

color combinations that are available. Just buy one color. Begonias are available in different forms: green leaf with white, pink, or red flowers; pink leaf with pink, white, or red flowers; and red leaf with pink, white, or red flowers. If you want two colors, use repetition of color to create the design—for example, alternating rows of white and pink begonias.

SEQUENCING

Sequencing adds a third dimension to your garden. Sequencing means movement, either the movement of the eye of the person using the landscape or the movement of the person himself through the landscape. The use of sequencing is seen in the pedestrian circulation pattern, or it can be employed in the arrangement of plants so the viewer of the landscape will look from one point to another—for example, from the low point to high point in a bed.

Eye Movement

For effective sequencing, make your beds at least ten feet wide. A layering in height of three to four plants, low ones to the front and taller to the rear, is necessary for proper sequencing.

To sequence visual movement, arrange plants from a low to high point. Begin a bed with a low edging variety (twelve to eighteen inches; see sidebar for examples). Behind that, put in a mass planting of a taller perennial (about twenty-four inches) such as

LOW EDGING PLANTS

Candytuft (*Iberis* species)
Corsican mint (*Mentha requienii*)
Germander (*Teucrium chamaedrys*)
Japanese painted fern (*Athyrium nipponicum* 'Pictum')
Joseph's coat (*Alternanthera versicolor*)
Lanceleaf coreopsis (*Coreopsis lanceolata* hybrids)
Lavender (*Lavandula angustifolia*)
Lily-turf (*Liriope* species)
Magic Carpet spirea (*Spiraea* x *bumalda* 'Magic Carpet')
Mondo grass (*Ophiopogon*)
Pinks (*Dianthus allwoodii*)
Plantain lily (*Hosta*)
Sedge (*Carex*)
Threadleaf coreopsis (*Coreopsis verticillata* hybrids)

Make beds wide enough, at
least ten feet, to allow for
effective sequencing of plants.
(bottom: Bishop's Garden,
Washington National Cathedral,
All Hallows Guild)

long-flowering daylily or astilbe, or a low mounded shrub such as
Helleri holly (*Ilex crenata* 'Helleri') or cranberry cotoneaster (*C. apiculatus*), azaleas, or dwarf rhododendron such as PJM. Behind
that, place the next taller planting, such as Koreanspice viburnum
(*V. carlesii*) or dwarf fothergilla. Finally, behind that, plant a taller
level of background shrubs such as lilac or doublefile viburnum or
a taller holly, using this back row to repeat elements of design that
have appeared in the front rows.

A curved pathway facilitates appreciation of your garden. (Ladew Topiary Gardens, Monkton, Maryland)

Traffic Flow

Certain psychological principles govern moving the user through the landscape. We know that curved lines tend to make people want to meander, while straight lines imply rapid movement and intersecting lines imply hesitation.

Put a curved pathway through your flower garden to encourage viewers to take their time and appreciate the beauty of the flowers. Intersecting paths and changes in paving imply hesitation, making these spots good places to put seating. (See Seating, chapter 19.)

The path to get the trash out or any other purely utilitarian task taking you from the house to the back gate should be laid straight. The goal of these paths is function, not decoration. While you will still design to make these areas attractive and to blend with the rest of your landscaping, you do not want to linger while toting heavy objects or trying to get from point A to point B.

For efficient entry into the house, even if you want a curved path, make sure that the line of circulation is clear and straight enough that you walk efficiently from the drive or street to the front door.

CONTRAST

The basic rule for the use of contrast in landscape design is to not overdo it. Use it in moderation—a little can go a long way. The contrasting element is the object that becomes the focal point of a design, so it must be selected judiciously. It is often what creates the

This entry is both interesting and efficient.

impact of the garden. Remember, however, that too much contrast becomes confusing and will cause you to lose sight of the contrasting element.

Consider grouping several trees together of a species that has very colorful bark, such as paperbark maple (*Acer griseum*). It is distinguished by a cinnamon russet-red exfoliating bark. Planted within a grouping of more conventional hardwoods, the paperbark or other tree with a colorful bark contrasts with the deep furrowed gray, brown, or black barks of the surrounding trees.

If you have a stone wall, place a single rose bush or flowering vine so it will climb against the wall. This touch of color and splash of greenery against the stone is the perfect way to accentuate both the wall and the vine.

To introduce a contrasting element into a lush green woodland setting, place a single piece of statuary to be discovered along a path, tucked into the natural plantings.

PROPORTION

Given the vastness of the physical world, it is not surprising that we are always trying to reduce a landscape to people-size proportion. We feel more comfortable, more at home in a setting that has been proportioned in some way to the human dimension. Garden spaces feel friendlier when the user can fathom the size of the area. There are a number of techniques that are employed to achieve this effect in various settings.

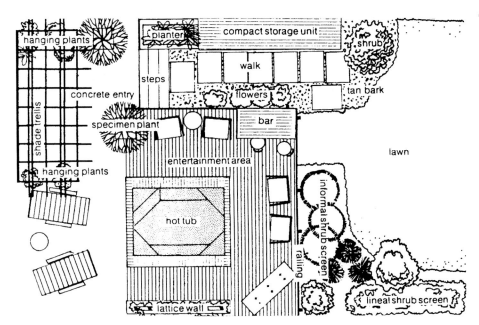

Rooms in a Landscape   One yard has successfully been divided into several areas, enhancing the beauty and function of the space.

Lower the Canopy

Since the most expansive element in a landscape is the sky, look for ways to bring it down. A canopy of trees or installation of overhead structures is the best way to do this. Use shade trees to get the people-sized proportions you want. Or put in shade trellises or other outdoor structures with overhead beams, such as arbors, belvederes, bowers, gazebos, and pergolas. For more on these structures, see chapter 25, Shelters, and chapter 26, Trellises.

Break into Small Spaces

Break your property into smaller, more accessible pieces by deciding what activity takes place in each area. Some of the finest gardens in the world are composites of smaller spaces. Kew, Kyoto, Versailles, and all botanical gardens are broken into smaller usable areas. But a townhouse with a twenty-by-forty-foot yard can also become two garden spaces.

CREATING COMFORT THROUGH DESIGN

The landscape design that works best is the one that combines the artistic principles described above with the elements you need to create maximum comfort in your garden and on your grounds. These are very personal considerations for each home owner and designer—one person's level of comfort is not necessarily another's. But there are some basic psychological principles that rule our comfort, and anyone can apply these to their home.

DESIGN FOR USE

For total outdoor living, design your landscape to create the maximum use for the maximum number of people. Determine what activities you want to do, how many people will be using the space, and how it will be used. If you would like an informal gathering area, this could be as simple as including a sitting wall where five or six people can sit along the edge of a patio. If you host large formal cocktail parties, you will need a larger patio space that has room for tables and chairs.

DESIGN FOR SPATIAL ENCLOSURE

We tend to feel more comfortable in our own personal bubble of space. Most people would find it more appealing to sit at a picnic table within the confines of a grove of trees rather than in the middle of a football field.

There are a number of ways to create spatial enclosures. One option is with hedgerows. Tall evergreen hedges using plants such as arborvitaes, hollies, or yews will give yearlong tight spatial enclosure. (See chapter 16, Screening and Noise Abatement.) Large conifers are also a way to create an enclosure. As they mature, they will create private space where you can put a bench for a small, hidden sitting area.

You can create spatial enclosure with fences. And this does not necessarily mean enclosing an entire property. Small sections of fencing can be used effectively to screen unpleasant views or to separate an area from the rest of the garden. (See chapter 27, Fences and Walls.)

DESIGN FOR VIEW

Look around the area you are designing—in every direction—as far as you can see. It could be forty feet to your neighbor's brick wall, down an alley, a bay or ocean, or snow-capped mountain. Identify the pleasant and unpleasant views. Then screen the unpleasant views and frame the pleasant ones with plants, fences, or a combination of both.

Plant large conifers to screen unpleasant views. Vines on trellises are often used for narrow spaces, but tall evergreen shrubs such as arborvitaes, junipers, yews, viburnums, and hollies are commonly used on residential properties. A twist on this is to frame attractive views. Framing, in effect, is actually screening less attractive views in order to direct attention to the more aesthetically pleasing focus. Frame an attractive view by planting to the sides and leading the eye toward the open vista. Use tall plant masses, either shade-tolerant plants such as hollies, viburnums, and rhododendrons or screening plants for sun, such as yews, junipers, boxwoods, and hollies. For framing a distant vista, Norway spruces, white pines, and other conifers are effective.

DESIGN FOR INDOOR-OUTDOOR HARMONY

Another element of designing for comfort is the importance of making it easy and comfortable to get from the house to the garden and vice versa. A smooth indoor-outdoor relationship will enhance your enjoyment of your garden and give you incentive to spend more time in it.

When building a deck, have your deck open onto the garden with a tiered descent or low wide step, as opposed to a steeper flight of stairs that serves to separate rather than unite the deck and garden. And if you intend to use a patio with any regularity, place it in close proximity to your house for ease of access.

Similarly, think of this if you have the option of designing a driveway. A circular driveway will take guests right to the front door of your house in their cars with little exposure to the elements. Compare that to parking on the street or on a long driveway and walking up the front walkway. You will also welcome the convenience of a driveway around to the front door when you get out of your car and your arms are loaded with bags of groceries.

DESIGN FOR YOUR ENVIRONMENT

Your landscape design can also enhance your personal comfort by moderating environmental extremes and ameliorating environmental problems. Identify your environmental problem areas from a design standpoint. For example, the hottest part of the day is when the sun is in the southwestern sky. Therefore, a southwestern or western exposure of a house needs shade. This area should be planted with deciduous shade trees to keep the house shaded and cool in the summer. Deciduous trees will lose their leaves in the fall and allow the warming rays of the sun through to help heat the house in winter.

If soil erosion is a problem on your property, you can minimize that by planting groundcover. Low plantings offer your best protection for stabilizing the soil. Groundcovers are discussed in greater detail in chapter 37.

"Your landscape design can also enhance your personal comfort by moderating environmental extremes and ameliorating environmental problems."

Wind and noise can also be dealt with effectively with screening. Identify where the prevailing winds blow from and use tough evergreen trees or shrubs—such as spruces, junipers, and arborvitae—as wind breaks for prevailing winter winds. (See chapter 13, Energy Efficiency and Physical Comfort.)

Another frequently encountered environmental problem is noise from a nearby highway (see chapter 16, Screening and Noise Abatement). Planted berms, which are mounded areas of soil, can help with this problem. Build your berm as high as possible—at least eight feet tall and twenty feet wide, wrapping it around the area you wish to make quieter. Plant it with a mix of deciduous and evergreen low and high plants. The more you plant, the more noise you will be able to abate. A wide berm with a mix of plants can cut noise 70 to 80 percent. Highway noise is very difficult to screen, but sometimes a psychological barrier, while not completely masking the noise, will help. For example, a thick planting to shield the sight of the highway can imply noise screening—out of sight, out of mind—even if traffic sounds still filter through.

SUSTAINING INTEREST THROUGH DESIGN

Of course, all of the tips that are suggested throughout this book will have a role in sustaining interest in your landscape design. In this section, I will introduce some of the basic principles that contribute to an interesting design, with some tips for achieving them. These subjects will be expanded in later chapters.

TWELVE-MONTH INTEREST

Design for year-round interest (see chapter 48). Look at plants or groups of plants for their ornamental characteristics all year long. The leaf, for example, might give you colorful new growth in the spring and color again in fall. The flower may be showy and fragrant, with a long season that goes from spring into summer. The fruit may be showy, edible, or bird-attracting. The bark could be colorful, striped, checked, exfoliating (peeling), or lacy. Taking all of these characteristics into account when designing is the way to offer twelve months of interest.

Many plants offer four seasons of interest all by themselves. Kousa dogwood (*Cornus kousa*) is an example of a small flowering tree with twelve-month interest. It flowers for a long period from May well into June. The large, red, ornamental fruit is edible. Autumn leaf color is maroon, and the bark displays a lacy texture that makes the tree a focal point in winter.

THE OTHER SENSES

Design for all of your senses—hearing, touch, smell, taste—not just sight. We generally think of landscape design as primarily visually oriented, but your experience on your property and in your garden goes far beyond visual appreciation.

Hearing

Design for your sense of hearing. This can be done for a cacophony, as explained above, to screen out sounds. But a more positive use of sound in the garden adds a sophisticated touch to landscaping. Water, as in a bubbling fountain or a gently lapping pool or rain drumming the roof of your gazebo, is the most obvious way to add sound to the garden. Other possibilities include rustling branches, such as the thick evergreen leaves of longstalk holly, which make a rustling sound all year round. Or you can hang wind chimes, which are available in a wide range of materials and prices. Other elements that add sound to your landscape include bird feeders and berry bushes—both will attract birds, which will bring their song to your garden.

Touch

Design for your sense of touch. The pleasure of plantain lily (*Hosta*) or lavender brushing against your ankle as it spills onto a walk is subtle but distinct. I love to rub the furry foliage of lamb's ears between my fingers, and its silver foliage makes it an outstanding plant for perennial borders. You can use the sense of touch in a less pleasing way by installing prickly or thorny plants in an area where you wish to discourage foot traffic.

Smell

Design for your sense of smell. This is an instinct as old as gardening. Aromatic flowers and plants and their oils have been used as ornament, medicine, and food throughout history. Plant woolly thyme in spaces in a flagstone patio laid on stone dust or sand. When you walk, you'll bruise it, and it will emit a fragrance. Many herbs will add fragrant aroma to your garden, including mint, thyme, basil, rosemary, and sweet bay. Lilac, sweetshrub (*Calycanthus*) or Koreanspice viburnum in bloom will accent your garden with an unmistakably pleasant fragrance. Brush against an edging of herbaceous lavender, rosemary, or thyme, and it will fill the air with its sweet aroma, or try a hanging basket or window box of sweet alyssums, fragrant geraniums, or sweet Williams (*Dianthus barbatus*).

Taste

Design for your sense of taste. Use tomato vines to grace a walk, for example, or train pole beans or peas onto a trellis to create privacy around a porch in summer. Purple basil, cilantro, oregano, and mint in containers are ornamental and tasty. The term *gardening* originally referred chiefly to cultivating edible plants. Integrate this original sense by incorporating fruits, vegetables, and herbs into your visual landscape. (For more on edible landscaping, see chapter 44).

PLANT FORM

Other ways to sustain interest in your landscape combine artistic and practical considerations. Consider plants for form, size, texture, and color; design for ground, vertical, and overhead planes; and create a sense of mystery in the garden with the technique of progressive realization.

Shape

Use the form of a plant to make it more interesting. The habit of the branches dictates a plant's form, so do something unusual to shape the plant's form. Train a weeping plant on a shade trellis and allow the branches to weep down across a walkway for an interesting curtain effect. Or train a weeping tree, such as weeping beech, spruce, or white pine to arch over the entry to a garden.

Mature Size

As stated earlier, always ascertain the growth rate and mature size of the plants you want to use. Place your plants in a space that is appropriate for their size—not just for the moment of planting, but for the long term, thus ensuring more interesting growth habits, less maintenance, and a greater longevity for your design.

Texture

Use plant textures for a number of different psychological effects. Coarse-textured plants such as rhododendrons and leatherleaf viburnums (*V. rhytidiphyllum*) seem to advance toward the viewer, creating the feeling of an introverted, enclosed environment. They make a space seem smaller. Fine-textured plants such as Japanese hollies or yews recede from the viewer, making a space seem larger.

Color

Design colors into your landscape scientifically. Bright, warm colors—reds, oranges, and yellows—advance toward the viewer. Greens, blues, and violets recede and are the first colors to disappear in the evening as darkness falls. White, the last color to disappear, is good for the evening garden.

DESIGN ON ALL PLANES

When you design, think of all planes: ground level, vertical, and overhead. The ground level, of course, is what covers the ground. The vertical plane, the area at eye level, is the most noticeable and is usually comprised of shrub masses and small flowering trees, which provide the garden's screening and privacy. The overhead plane is created with a canopy of shade trees and overhead structures. Consideration of all three of these is critical for the well-designed landscape.

When looking at the ground level, don't overlook unleveled ground. Add interest to the design by turning slopes or grade changes into garden spaces. Retaining walls are one way to claim garden space and create stability in your design. And slopes planted with groupings of trees and masses of shrubs and perennials will add an extra expanse to a garden. Once you see the effect, you will want to introduce mounded beds and rolling hills to your level yard. (See chapter 17, Slope Enhancement.)

This steep slope has been enhanced by creating planting beds with groupings of trees, shrubs, and perennials.

A hint of what's to come draws people through a garden space to satisfy their curiosity.

MYSTERY

Progressive realization is a design technique in which elements are developed one after another, with one leading to the next. This sense of mystery, the need of the viewer to move beyond a bush to see what else is there, to move closer to examine something more closely, is rooted in landscape history. It probably originated in Oriental gardens and was perfected by the British, with the classic path that leads away to the secret garden. Mystery is one of the greatest draws in the garden, playing on human nature by giving just a hint of what's beyond to make people want to move past a point to what they can't see.

To bring a sense of mystery to your design, don't show the whole view at once. Instead, tease the viewer into the landscape with hints of views to come. For example, allow just a glimpse of water or a sculptural element through a copse of small trees, or plant a Japanese black pine to wisp across an entry so that the viewer wants to move closer and see what is beyond. Or plant huge ornamental grass that hides an area and makes the viewer want to part the grass and move through to the other side.

PLANNING BEFORE PLANTING

Once you know the rules and principles of design explained in chapter 1, the next step in planning is to figure out, working within these design parameters, what you want in your landscape. Planning before planting is the essence of landscape design. The checklist starting on page 29 is your road map for planning, your guide for organizing your ideas and focusing on what you want your landscape to include. With a few more tips in mind, you will be ready to fill out the checklist.

KNOW YOUR ZONE

Hardiness zones have been determined by the U.S. Department of Agriculture to give you a guide to the lowest temperature ranges at which a plant will survive. The USDA took into account the many different conditions that are responsible for making a plant thrive, such as temperature, humidity, rain, snow, elevation, wind currents, and light.

Use the USDA Plant Hardiness Zone Map as a guideline to determine how specific plants will grow in your area. The map shows eleven different zones. Each zone represents an area of winter hardiness for plants. Hardiness zones are determined by cold, not warmth; in other words, the zones indicate the lowest the temperatures reached, not the highest. Zone 1 is designated for areas that have average annual minimum temperatures below −50°F; Zone 11 is for areas that have average annual minimum temperatures above 40°F, thus frost-free year-round.

Knowing what zone you are in will be invaluable if you are planning on ordering plant material from mail-order catalogs or online. While your local garden centers will usually sell only plants that will

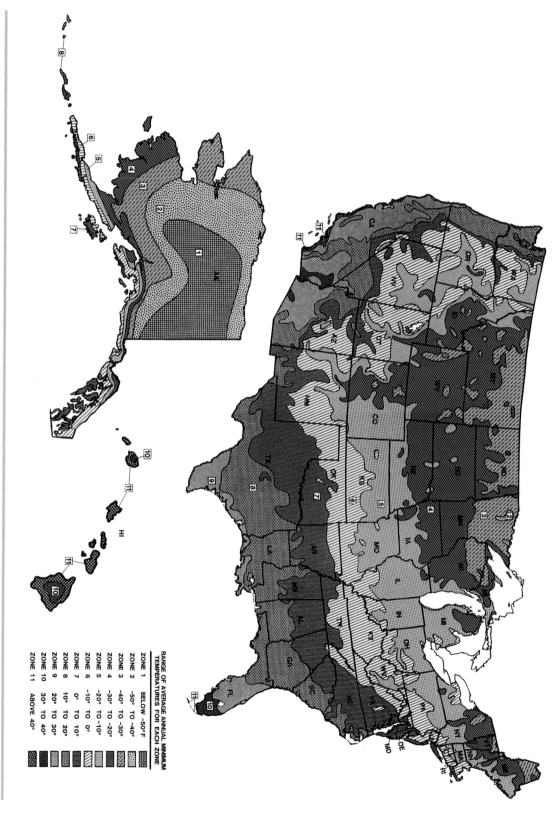

RANGE OF AVERAGE ANNUAL MINIMUM
TEMPERATURES FOR EACH ZONE

ZONE 1	BELOW -50°F
ZONE 2	-50° TO -40°
ZONE 3	-40° TO -30°
ZONE 4	-30° TO -20°
ZONE 5	-20° TO -10°
ZONE 6	-10° TO 0°
ZONE 7	0° TO 10°
ZONE 8	10° TO 20°
ZONE 9	20° TO 30°
ZONE 10	30° TO 40°
ZONE 11	ABOVE 40°

24

perform in your area, mail-order and Web businesses ship all over the country. If you live in Minneapolis, you would not want to order a plant that is suited for Zones 8 through 9; that plant wouldn't survive your winter. So know your zone, and check the zone on anything you order.

Remember that the Hardiness Zone Map is just a guideline. Don't be afraid to use a plant that isn't in your specific zone. For example, if something you particularly like is suited for a zone one step warmer than the one you live in, give it a try. Microclimate—the weather in your immediate local space—has a great deal of impact on whether a plant will survive or not. Philadelphia is in Zone 6, yet you can grow Zone 7 plants such as crapemyrtles, and even camellias will thrive in a protected courtyard or on the warm wall of the house. You never know until you try a plant. Try growing an orange tree in San Francisco. Try growing gardenias in Atlanta. They may not make it, but gardening is an ongoing process in which you learn from your experimentation.

DESIGN WITHIN A BUDGET

As I said in the introduction, landscaping will increase the value of a home by at least 15 percent and is the only home improvement that increases in value over time. It gives a 100 to 200 percent return on investment, contrasted to an 80 percent return for a new kitchen or a 75 percent return for a new bathroom, both of which start depreciating as soon as they are installed. Landscaping is the most important home improvement you can make.

Therefore, do not look at landscaping costs as expenses but as investments in your home. A benchmark I like to follow is to budget 10 percent of your property value for landscaping, including hardscaping, such as a fountain, sculpture, patio, and lighting. It could cost less, or more, depending on the maturity of the plants you use and who does the landscape installation (see Acquiring Plants and Materials, chapter 6, and Meeting a Budget, chapter 8). If you do the planting yourself, there will be more money in your budget for bigger, showier plants or for the tools you'll need to maintain the garden (see Tools and Maintenance, chapter 5). Hiring professionals to do the work will increase your cost, but you will save yourself time and labor (see the section Hiring the Professional at the end of this chapter).

Don't be frightened—you don't have to spend this all at once. Most people will not have a lump sum of fifteen to twenty thousand dollars or more to spend on improvements, especially after just having purchased a new home. Spread the work and costs out over several years, working in stages to complete the design you really want, rather than skimping and finishing quickly a landscape you are not happy with.

DESIGN BY CONCEPT

Think conceptually. I like to tell my clients that you don't have to know botanical names to design. Don't start out thinking about plants; start out thinking about concepts—I want screening here. . . . I want a walkway there. . . . I need a groundcover here. You've got hundreds of possibilities for design ideas and thousands of plant ideas are possible. Don't begin your design with an agenda that focuses on specific plants. The design should come first, then you can specify the plants to fill it.

Your next task, as you go through items on a checklist, is to match your personality to your landscape. The landscape you plan and design should bring you aesthetic pleasure, utility, and comfort—and only to the degree that it accomplishes that will it be a success. To give you an idea of how to come up with the most comfortable fit for your personal needs, consider the following tips.

Early Stage of Design   In this design, generic plant descriptions are used instead of specific plants, which would be named later.

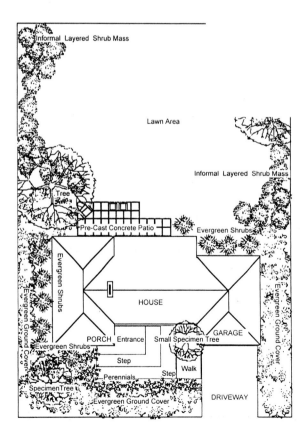

DETERMINE YOUR PERSONALITY

Look around your home and determine your own personality. If you're an eclectic home decorator, then your garden will reflect a similar diverse mix of features that interest you. If you're the fastidious type, you will want your plants all in a row. If your home is clean but not manicured, then your garden should show the same characteristics.

THE BUSY PERSON

If you are a very busy person, you want a garden that can be easily maintained. To accomplish this, you can use a pre-emergence herbicide in your planting beds in early spring to control annual grasses such as crabgrass; in fall, use one that will keep broadleaf fall and winter weed seed, such as speedwell, from germinating. Mulch the beds with two inches of compost and a one-inch veneer of ornamental mulch on top. Install shrubs that have low pruning requirements, and keep the area to be mowed small. A natural way to control weeds is by lightly cultivating them and hand pulling, which makes the most sense for small areas.

THE GARDEN LOVER

If you love gardening and nothing makes you as happy as being surrounded by plants and working in the ground, you want a garden that will always have new flowers, providing a sense of renewal and seasonal change. With this plan come the maintenance tasks of regular planting and transplanting, dividing every two to five years, deadheading, and cutting back foliage. But since you love gardening, you don't shirk the tasks. Employ the busy person's herbicide and mulching programs, or use weeds as just another reason to get into the garden and work among the plants. Add the excitement of more exotic bulbs and perennials, and add annuals and vines that give a lot of flower but must be planted every year. In other words, have a garden that makes you want to take every opportunity possible to be in it.

THE PART-TIME GARDENER

As a part time gardener with only one day a week to spare, choose a plan that will allow you to do what you enjoy most in the garden. For example, if you like mowing the lawn, you won't want to install extensive bedding areas. If you enjoy pruning but dislike mowing, you'll want larger bedding areas, a smaller area of lawn, and lots of trees and shrubs.

DETERMINE YOUR HOME'S PERSONALITY

Just as every person has a personality, every home has its own personality. We've already talked about matching your garden to your personality. Likewise, you should match your home's personality to your garden. Your landscape, to a certain extent, should match the architectural style of your home. For an English Tudor, for example, you will want an English-style country garden. With a Williamsburg-style home, use rectangular squared-off parterre areas, herb gardens, boxwood, and tightly clipped hedges. This is not a rigid rule, however. Other elements are possible if they are thought out in advance and blend the house with the landscape.

THE CHECKLIST

Use the following checklist of over eighty considerations to decide what you want for your personal landscape design. It is part of a program I developed called Lernscaping that gets you in touch with what you want for your property so you can make it reflect the

A wonderful match between home and garden. (Ladew Topiary Gardens, Monkton, Maryland)

essence of your personality. For example, if you are a person who is interested in comfort, you will want a comfortable garden. You'll want to plan for patio space, an area for relaxing, perhaps a porch swing, and another area with the cooling flow of water.

Go through this checklist of considerations for your property, concentrating on areas that are relevant to you. All categories won't apply to everyone, so use what you need and ignore the rest. By the time you're finished, you should have a better idea of what you really want your landscape to look like.

Please feel free to photocopy this list so you can mark in your answers without feeling that you are defacing this book. The checklist is only helpful if you are really able to use it.

The Lernscaping™ Checklist

This checklist contains many landscape features and considerations. Each category has a wide variety of items from which to choose. Utilizing this list will help you to gain a better understanding of what your needs are.

The Planted Space (Softscape)

Plants

Check all that you would like to include:

- ☐ Shade trees (40 to 100 feet)
- ☐ Small flowering trees (under 40 feet)
- ☐ Specimen trees (under 40 feet)
- ☐ Evergreen trees (15 feet and over)
- ☐ Deciduous hedges (5 to 15 feet)
- ☐ Evergreen hedges (5 to 15 feet)
- ☐ Deciduous/flowering shrubs (3 to 10 feet)
- ☐ Evergreen/flowering shrubs (3 to 10 feet)
- ☐ Deciduous groundcover
- ☐ Evergreen groundcover

- ☐ Vines
- ☐ Perennials
- ☐ Annuals
- ☐ Vegetables
- ☐ Herbs
- ☐ Bulbs
- ☐ Fruit trees and shrubs
- ☐ Flowers/cutting
- ☐ Other:

Favorite plants: _____
_____
_____

Unfavorable plants: _____
_____
_____

[continued]

Plant Use

Intended goal to be achieved through plants used:

☐ Privacy
☐ Fragrance
☐ Attract birds/butterflies
☐ Wildlife habitats
☐ Hypoallergenic
☐ Edibles
☐ Herbs for cooking
☐ Climbing for children

☐ Site enhancement
☐ Energy efficiency
☐ Pollution reduction
☐ Noise reduction
☐ Wind reduction
☐ Erosion control
☐ Shade
☐ Other: _____

Style

☐ Informal (natural)
☐ Formal (manicured)
☐ Curved rows or edges
☐ Linear rows or edges

☐ Inward orientation
☐ Outward orientation
☐ Other: _____

Favorite Colors

☐ _____
☐ _____
☐ _____

Favorite Seasons

☐ Spring
☐ Summer
☐ Fall
☐ Winter

Time(s) of Day Garden Will Be Used

☐ Early morning
☐ Mid-morning
☐ Noon

☐ Mid-afternoon
☐ Early evening
☐ After dark

Your Ideal Planted Space

Plants: _____
_____
_____

Style: _____

Use: _____
_____
_____

[continued]

The Structural Space (Hardscape)

Design Theme

Note: There is no need to choose one theme unless there is a particular style that you wish to adhere to.

- ☐ Oriental (strong symbolism, simplistic, use of sand and gravel aggregates, stone sculptural elements)
- ☐ English (colorful, naturalistic, mixed perennials, topiary, whimsical, eclectic)
- ☐ Early American (practical, symmetrical, hedged in, mixed herbs and vegetables
- ☐ New American (asymmetrical, colorful, twelve-month interest, mixed woody/perennial)
- ☐ Contemporary (single specimen plant or several trees, simple, uncluttered)
- ☐ Other:

Motif

Overall shapes you prefer and style of installation.

- ☐ Curves
- ☐ Rectangles
- ☐ Squares
- ☐ Crescents
- ☐ Natural
- ☐ Tiered/Stepped
- ☐ Mortared
- ☐ Dry
- ☐ Sunken
- ☐ Raised
- ☐ Hidden
- ☐ Formal
- ☐ Informal
- ☐ Rustic
- ☐ _____
- ☐ _____
- ☐ _____

Landscape Structures

Features you would like to include.

- ☐ Decks
- ☐ Patios
- ☐ Walks/Paths
- ☐ Seating
- ☐ Table(s)
- ☐ Athletic courts
- ☐ Swimming pool
- ☐ Hot tub
- ☐ Jacuzzi
- ☐ Sauna
- ☐ Play gym
- ☐ Arbor
- ☐ Portico
- ☐ Pergola
- ☐ Gazebo
- ☐ Retaining wall(s)
- ☐ Planter(s)

- ☐ Pond
- ☐ Fountains
- ☐ Steps
- ☐ Trellis
- ☐ Fence
- ☐ Barbecue
- ☐ Lighting
- ☐ Statuary
- ☐ Greenhouse
- ☐ Driveway
- ☐ Irrigation
- ☐ Ramp(s)
- ☐ _____
- ☐ _____
- ☐ _____

[continued]

Utility Structures

What you need and/or would like to include.

- ☐ Clothesline
- ☐ Storage
- ☐ Parking
- ☐ Garage
- ☐ Pets
- ☐ Firewood
- ☐ Potting Shed
- ☐ Compost
- ☐ Maintenance shed
- ☐ Trash/recycling bins
- ☐ Service
- ☐ _____
- ☐ _____
- ☐ _____

Building Materials

Check all those that appeal as possibilities.

- ☐ Brick
- ☐ Flagstone/slate
- ☐ Rock
- ☐ Pavers
- ☐ Lumber
- ☐ Concrete
- ☐ Textured, colored, and patterned concrete
- ☐ Asphalt
- ☐ Gravel
- ☐ Mulched paths
- ☐ Interlocking block
- ☐ Epoxied gravel
- ☐ Stabilized aggregate
- ☐ Fiberglass
- ☐ Steel
- ☐ Rubber
- ☐ Reed or fabric

Your Ideal Structural Space

Motif: _____

Landscape structures: _____
_____
_____

Utility structures: _____

Building materials: _____
_____
_____
_____

The Functional Space

Your Ideal Functional Space

Functions: _____
_____

Mood: _____
_____

[continued]

Design Functions

Outdoor activity's spatial needs

- ☐ Dining
  - ☐ How many? _____   ☐ How often?
- ☐ Entertaining
  - ☐ How many? _____   ☐ How often?
- ☐ Children
  - ☐ How many? _____   ☐ Ages?
- ☐ Athletic activities
- ☐ Reading
- ☐ Listen to music
- ☐ Sunning
- ☐ Dancing
- ☐ Dry laundry

Design Mood

What mood or feeling would you like your outdoor space to convey?

- ☐ Relaxing
- ☐ Private
- ☐ Social
- ☐ Open
- ☐ Other:

Maintaining Your Outdoor Environment

Caring for the Environment

Maintenance you plan to perform yourself	Estimated hours/week/task
☐ Mow lawn	_____
☐ Rake leaves	_____
☐ Fertilize and treat lawn and shrubs	_____
☐ Prune shrubs	_____
☐ Prune trees	_____
☐ Irrigate	_____
☐ Weed and edge beds	_____
☐ Mulch beds	_____
☐ Paint/preserve/repair structures	_____
☐ Plant trees and shrubs	_____
☐ Plant perennials and annuals	_____
☐ Install landscape structures	_____
Total hours required for working in the garden	_____
Hours you intend to spend working in the garden	− _____
Hours you will require assistance from professionals or other helpers	= _____

[continued]

Your Property's Vital Statistics

Measurements of design areas: _____
_____
_____

Geographic orientation and hours of sun: _____
_____
_____

Prevailing winds:_____
_____
_____

Sloping areas and percentage of grade: _____
_____
_____

Pleasant views: _____
_____
_____

Unpleasant views: _____
_____
_____

Drainage pattern and/or problems: _____
_____
_____

Location of underground utilities:_____
_____
_____

Features worth retaining:_____
_____
_____

Other property characteristics: _____
_____
_____

Additional notes: _____
_____
_____

Overall Budget

$ _____ $ _____

WHERE TO GET DESIGN IDEAS

When you take an idea from one resource and publish it, it's called plagiarism, but when you take ideas from multiple sources, it's called research. Design ideas come from a multitude of sources, so do your research.

CHECK GARDENS EVERYWHERE

The best way to get ideas is to just look around you. Go outside, pay attention to your surroundings, and take notes. Look at what is planted and how it is arranged at neighbor's properties, shopping centers, office buildings, hospital grounds, government buildings, even median strips down the highway. Cemeteries are an excellent source for seeing mature landscapes that have been maintained for many years.

Don't just look—but notice what is going on in a landscape. Take note of what's flowering, how people have treated their slopes, how they screened, how they planted in the shade, what they did for color. You must have the right mindset to find landscape design ideas. It is amazing what we miss by not noticing our surroundings.

Incorporate noticing the landscape into your daily routine, such as driving, riding public transportation, or biking to work. While drive-by plant identification is difficult for most laypeople and even

This is a great idea for a very limited space.

You can easily integrate this island bed at a town entry into your own backyard.

for professionals, you can develop concepts and ideas by seeing them this way. For example, the shapes and colors of trees and large plantings are evident, as are the ways plants were used: "I saw evergreens that blocked the view of the scrap yard from the interstate. They had brilliant red tops and were about eight feet tall and six feet wide." Describe this to a landscape professional, who can help you with identification. (The hedge might be *Photinia,* a massive shrub that grows twenty by twenty feet, with red new growth and cold hardy to Zone 7 and warmer according to the USDA Hardiness Zone Map.)

In addition to your normal daily routines, drive through the grounds of large institutions. Look at elaborate landscape designs for possibilities you want to consider for your own property. Institutions are composites of numerous landscape design concepts and configurations. There are acres that must be covered, many buildings to be enhanced, and every imaginable vehicular and pedestrian circulation pattern possible. I've gotten quite a few ideas for private homes while jogging through the grounds of the National Institutes of Health in Bethesda, Maryland.

Great sources of inspiration are botanical gardens and arboreta. These are plant collections that are often arranged in a wide variety of designed settings. Put a botanical garden or two on the agenda of every vacation. One of the finest arboreta in the nation is on the grounds of the U.S. National Capitol in Washington, D.C., where some of the trees were planted more than a century ago, and all specimens are clearly labeled.

"Design ideas come from a multitude of sources, so do your research."

You can incorporate ideas from arboreta, such as this sunken garden design at the U.S. National Arboretum in D.C.

EXTRACTING IDEAS

As you get around and see what others have done, realize that the grand-scale designs you are looking at can often be reduced to something you can use on your property. Design extraction—just picking out one element of a large design—can be very effective. A blue spruce against a large lava rock (volcanic rock weighing much less than regular stone) might grab your attention, for example, or a flower arrangement of pink geraniums, an annual, that is backed by *Liatris*, a native perennial with spikes of pink flowers. A lion's head mounted on the wall of a large ornate fountain that spews a stream of water into a basin below might give you the idea for a water feature in your sitting garden. These ideas come from extracting little pieces from larger designs. Collect enough pieces, and you can create your perfect garden.

MEDITATE ON YOUR SITE

For another strategy, try a contemplative, meditative approach—the Frank Lloyd Wright method of design. When the brilliant architect got a commission, it is reported that before one spade of soil was turned, he would take a chair and sit at the site for days, developing a concept of what the building he was designing should look like. Live with your property. Get to know your plants. Look to the horizon.

Take as much time as you need to develop your design. Follow your property for a couple of years. Learn how you use it, where you walk and how the sun moves across the horizon.

Observe and Experience the Real Thing

Finally, while I—and most who write about landscaping—have tried to use pictures to give a visual impression of some of the concepts I am describing, I don't recommend using pictures as a major method of getting ideas for your landscape. Instead, as the above tips suggest, go beyond the two dimensions of photographs to observe and experience real landscapes in order to put together the most applicable ideas for your own property.

Free Information

There are a variety of sources where you can get more information for designing your landscape. Many of these can give you valuable facts that are localized for your area—and many are free.

Garden Centers

Check out your local garden centers. Many provide free information in the form of handouts, educational programs, and an informed staff to answer questions.

Cooperative Extension Service

Every state university has a Cooperative Extension Service. Extension specialists range from trained master gardeners to Ph.D.s, and they are dedicated to providing thorough, reliable, unbiased information about every aspect of landscaping. Extension services are generally run at the county level, but they may also provide information at the university. They are excellent sources for publications that cover the full spectrum of horticultural topics—from disease diagnosis to plant design suggestions. Please call them; many are funded on the basis of how much they are used, and they're an invaluable free service for do-it-yourselfers. They can be found in the state or county listings of your phone book.

U.S. GOVERNMENT PRINTING OFFICE

Reliable free information is available through the U.S. Government Printing Office (GPO). The GPO publishes books, pamphlets, and fact sheets on a wide range of subjects: pruning, fertilizing, historic gardens, hardiness zones, lists of plant materials, lists of native plants, plants for certain conditions—these are just a few examples. There may be a nominal charge for some of these publications. You can get a GPO catalog by writing to Superintendent of Documents, P. O. Box 371954, Pittsburgh, PA 15250-7954, or by calling (202) 512-1800.

NATIONAL AGRICULTURAL LIBRARY

The National Agricultural Library in Beltsville, Maryland, is an excellent U.S. government source. This library, an agency of the U.S. Department of Agriculture, has public service and reference divisions and will fax you information about a variety of subjects related to landscape design. You can contact them at (301) 504-5755.

PROFESSIONAL/TRADE ASSOCIATIONS

There are professional or trade associations representing every landscape discipline. Everything you wanted to know about any landscape profession is at your fingertips, including landscape architects, contractors, designers, arborists, grounds managers, growers, and others. (See pages 42 and following.)

SOCIETIES AND ASSOCIATIONS

Societies and associations exist for virtually every plant you know. Any of these groups will be happy to provide you with a wealth of literature about their specific interests. For example, if you go to an azalea society plant sale, you'll get more information about azaleas from the people who really know what they're talking about than you could find from any other source (see next page).

PLANT SALES

Plant sales are wonderful places to learn about and acquire flowers and plants. Learn when they're being held through the local botanical gardens and plant societies.

PLANT SOCIETIES

Here is a sampling of the many societies across the country. They are listed alphabetically by subject, with general plant societies coming first, followed by specific plant societies. This is not a complete list, however. If you want information on a plant not represented here, your local library or botanic garden should be able to help you find the association you're looking for.

American Horticultural Society
7931 East Boulevard Drive
Alexandria VA 22308-1300
(800) 777-7931 or (703) 768-5700
www.ahs.org

Aquatic Gardeners Association
www.aquatic-gardeners.org

Azalea Society
www.azaleas.org

American Bamboo Society
www.halcyon.com/abs

American Begonia Society
www.begonias.org

American Bonsai Society
ABS Executive Secretary
P.O. Box 1136
Puyallup, WA 98371-1136
www.absbonsai.org/abs_home.html

International Camellia Society
www.med-rz.uni-sb.de/med_fak/physiol2/
camellia/home.htm

National Chrysanthemum Society Inc.
www.mums.org

American Conifer Society
www.conifersociety.org

American Daffodil Society
www.daffodilusa.org

International Geranium Society
Dept. WWW
P.O. Box 92734
Pasadena, CA 91109-2734
www.geocities.com/RainForest/2822

Heather Society
www.users.zetnet.co.uk/heather

American Hemerocallis Society
AHS Executive Secretary
Department WWW
P.O. Box 10
Dexter, GA 31019
www.daylilies.org/daylilies.html

Herb Society of America
9019 Kirtland Chardon Road
Kirtland, Ohio 44094
(440) 256-0514
www.herbsociety.org

American Hibiscus Society
c/o Executive Secretary
P.O. Drawer 321540W
Cocoa Beach, FL 32932-1540
(407) 783-2576
americanhibiscus.org

Holly Society of America Inc.
11318 West Murdock
Wichita, KS 67212-6609
www.hollysocam.org

American Hosta Society
www.hosta.org

American Iris Society
www.irises.org

Dwarf Iris Society
The Dwarf Iris Society of America
9130 North 5200 West
Elwood, UT 84337-8640
www4.net/dwarfiris.soc

Society for Siberian Irises
w3.one.net/~wilsonjh/ssimemb.htm

American Ivy Society
www.ivy.org

International Lilac Society
lilacs.freeservers.com

American Orchid Society
6000 South Olive Avenue
West Palm Beach, FL 33405
(561) 585-8666
www.orchidweb.org

American Penstemon Society
www.biosci.ohio-state.edu/~awolfe/
Penstemon/Penstemon.html

American Primrose Society
www.backyardgardener.com/aps.html

American Rhododendron Society
Executive Director
11 Pinecrest Drive
Fortuna, CA 95540
(707) 725-3043
www.rhododendron.org

North American Rock Garden Society
www.nargs.org

American Rose Society
P.O. Box 30000
Shreveport, LA 71130-0030
(800) 637-6534 or (318) 938-5402
www.ars.org

International Water Lily and Water Gardening
Society
Suite 328-G12
1401 Johnson Ferry Road
Marietta, GA 30062-8115
www.iwgs.org

Lady Bird Johnson Wildflower Center
(formerly the National Wildflower Research
Center)
4801 La Crosse Avenue
Austin, Texas 78739-1702
(512) 292-4200
www.wildflower.org

New England Wild Flower Society
180 Hemenway Road
Framingham, MA 01701-2699
(508) 877-7630.
www.newfs.org

LIBRARIES

Not only should you check with your local library, which is an excellent resource, many gardens have libraries. And there is usually someone there eager to help you with their collection of books, handouts, and other information.

HIRING THE PROFESSIONAL

It is my experience that just turning your work over to a team of professionals will not give you the landscape that works best for you. You need to be involved. But even the most involved home owner can benefit from professional help. Take advantage of the experience of others. Sometimes just a tip or two from an expert may bring your ideas to life.

Pros are available for as much or as little help as you need. Hire a designer to give you ideas for you to create the garden, or have one generate a drawing for you. Hire a landscape contractor to tell you how to install your design or to actually do the work. You can hire a grounds management professional to lay out diagnostic and preventive maintenance procedures for you or to assume complete care for your property. Support by landscape professionals can be a big help in implementing your landscape design. Your personal interest and the time and funds that you have available will determine how much involvement you will want to have with them.

If you hire some work out, remember that everyone coming to your property to perform any work must be insured. Any damage or other liability that might be incurred on your property should be covered by your contractor's policy. If there is any doubt, ask for a certificate. Any landscape professional can have the insurance company send or fax it directly to you. Insurance questions can be directed to your state's insurance commission.

Landscape-associated professions overlap and are not precisely defined, but here is an idea of what you can expect from each one.

LANDSCAPE ARCHITECTS

Landscape architects, whose training qualifies them as the structural engineers of the landscape industry, oversee the design of large areas, such as regional plans, subdivisions, cluster housing, and commercial projects. They also work on private homes.

Landscape architecture is usually taught through schools of architecture and design, and they face the strictest licensing requirements of any landscape professional in approximately forty states. To obtain information about where to locate a registered landscape architect and how to learn more about this profession, contact the American Society of Landscape Architects (ASLA), 636 Eye Street, N.W., Washington, DC 20001-3736; (202) 898-2444; www.asla.org.

LANDSCAPE DESIGNERS

The landscape designer is the professional who brings the horticultural aspects to the landscape. Designers work on residential or commercial landscape projects or on planting designs for public spaces. Most landscape designers have an academic and practical background in horticulture and are well trained in the use of ornamental shrubs, trees, and perennials for the garden. But individuals using the title landscape designer are not required to have training in the profession.

One way to know a landscape designer's expertise and experience is through a nationally recognized certification program. Ask if the designer is a certified professional landscape designer. And, of course, ask for references and to see examples of work. Information about finding a certified professional landscape designer is available by contacting the Association of Professional Landscape Designers (APLD), 710 East Ogden Avenue, Suite 600, Naperville, IL 60563; (630) 579-3268; www.apld.com.

GROWERS/NURSERYMEN

Turn to the growers or nurserymen for plant expertise and guidance. These professionals represent the source of our plant material. They may or may not be the primary grower, but they are generally current with the latest information in the plant world. You can contact them through local nurseries and garden centers. In fact, many garden centers and nurseries offer a full line of services that cross over all the professions.

For names of nurseries, garden centers, and landscape companies that offer "soup to nuts" design, installation, and care, contact the American Nursery & Landscape Association (ANLA), 1250 Eye Street, NW, Suite 500, Washington, DC 20005; (202) 789-2900; www.anla.org.

LANDSCAPE CONTRACTORS

The landscape contractor is the person who will actually install your landscape. These professionals have broad responsibilities overseeing a range of projects, from landscape architecture to grounds management.

Licensing is required in many states, but it can range from basic registration, such as a home improvement contractor, to many different sorts of testing procedures. For more information, contact

the Associated Landscape Contractors of America (ALCA), 150 El-
den Street, Suite 270, Herndon, VA 20170; (800) 395-2522 or (703)
736-9666; www.alca.org.

GROUNDS MANAGERS

Hire a grounds manager for pruning, fertilizing, mowing, seeding,
and other lawn services. This is the person who will maintain your
landscape after it is installed. There may be overlap between the responsibilities of the grounds manager and the landscape contractor, such as in the rapidly growing field of lawn treatment.

Professional grounds managers are employed to care for trees,
shrubs, flowers, and lawns. Ways to certify expertise in this field are
through the Professional Grounds Management Society (PGMS),
the Professional Lawn Care Association of America (PLCAA), or by
investigating a firm's qualifications yourself. PGMS can give you
names of certified grounds managers and certified groundskeep-
ers. PLCAA, in a program with the University of Georgia, offers a
certified turfgrass professional rating.

To locate certified grounds professionals, contact the Professional Grounds Management Society (PGMS), 720 Light Street, Baltimore, MD 21230; (800) 609-7467 or (410) 223-2861; www.pgms.org.
To find a certified lawn care specialist, contact PLCAA, 1000 Johnson
Ferry Road, NE, Suite C135, Marietta, GA 30068; (800) 458-3466;
www.plcaa.org.

ARBORISTS

Arborists and consulting arborists are the tree experts of the nation.
They, more than anyone else, are best trained to protect and work
with the largest, oldest, and most venerable members of our plant
community. They will prune, diagnose, treat, and remove trees or
advise you how to care for them. There are people other than arborists who will prune trees. Anyone who is not afraid to climb with
a chainsaw in his or her hand can offer tree pruning services, but
because of the severity of damage that can be caused to the tree and
surrounding structures, make sure that you call a professional.

To locate a consulting arborist who does not perform pruning
services and, therefore, will offer you unbiased information on all
aspects of tree care, you can contact two associations: For names of
consultants in your area, contact the American Society of Consulting Arborists (ASCA), 15245 Shady Grove Road, Suite 130, Rockville,
MD 20850; (301) 947-0483. For the names of certified arborists, contact the International Society of Arboriculture (ISA), P.O. Box 3129,
Champaign, IL 61826; (217) 355-9411; www.isa-arbor.com.

TREE AND LANDSCAPE APPRAISERS

There are also tree and landscape appraisers, who are trained to assess damage and estimate the value of mature plant material, which can be handy for insurance purposes or just for your information. You can find a tree and landscape appraiser by contacting the ASCA at the address and phone number on page 44.

DRAINAGE EXPERTS

Drainage might rank as the number one problem for home and grounds. Virtually all wetness problems on your property can be solved without a sump pump or waterproofing your basement walls. If you can't solve the problem, consult with a civil engineer trained in matters of drainage. Civil engineers can be found in the Yellow Pages. Soil conservation specialists also handle water and drainage issues. Contact a city, county, state, or federal soil conservation office to find one of these experts. For additional information, you can contact the American Society of Civil Engineers (ASCE), 1015 15th Street, N.W., Suite 600, Washington, DC 20005-2605; (800) 548-2723.

DRAFTING YOUR DESIGN

3

Once you have filled out the Lernscaping checklist (starting on page 29) and have developed your ideas, your next step is to begin drafting your design. Getting ideas down on paper is a critical part of the design process. Once you draw something on paper, it will be much easier to go out and plant or build it in the garden.

Don't begin any planting until your design is drawn. The paper draft will provide an overall concept of what you're doing in the garden. It is much easier to move plants around on paper than it is to move them around in the garden. And you should move them over and over, using more eraser than graphite. Then if it looks good on paper, it's worth a try. It generally will look good in the garden too.

When you begin drafting, put the ideas on scratch paper without specifically mentioning the name of a single plant. Think of what you want in terms of style, size, shape, color, and use of plant material. The specifics will come later.

The first fact you need to know is how your property is laid out.

> "Now is the time to let your imagination take you where it wants. Don't hold back."

USE YOUR TAX PLAT

Start the drawing with a copy of your tax plat. This will show you the property lines, how your house is situated on the property, and what direction you are facing. This shows only the property that you own and building restrictions, easements, right-of-ways, and other details. The amount of setback on your property (land owned by the city, township, county, or state) is not shown on a tax plat, even though it may look like the rest of your property. And you might not be allowed to plant trees or build structures in this area. Check with the department that maintains your thoroughfare. Since the setback is not shown on your plat, check the exact measurement from your house to the street. Compare it with the measurement from your tax plat. The difference between the two measurements is the setback.

BASIC DRAFTING SUPPLIES

Gather a few drafting supplies. You'll need:

- Sheet of graph or good-quality vellum (a durable, translucent drafting paper), eighteen-by-twenty-four inches or larger, that can handle erasures
- A twelve- or eighteen-inch ruler
- Pencil (a mechanical pencil stays sharp), preferably one with a medium-soft lead so it erases without leaving marks but won't smudge
- Eraser
- A way to draw circles; either a compass, template, or round object to trace
- Tracing paper
- A set of triangles (30-60-90 degrees and 90-45-45 degrees)—optional but very helpful for drawing straight, perpendicular and parallel lines

CREATING YOUR DRAFT

SCALING YOUR DESIGN

Begin your design by converting the outline of your property on the tax plat to your piece of paper. Convert the plat to a scale that is easy to read and will work with an inch ruler. For example, one inch could equal four feet (a quarter-inch equals one foot) or one inch could equal eight feet (an eighth-inch equals one foot). These are easy scales to work with, if you can fit your property onto the paper at these dimensions. Note the scale on the paper for consistency in future use.

Another advantage of using the plat is that you must have an overhead view of your property and the landscape. This is the only way to know how to locate your plants. The bird's-eye view will show you the distance your plants are from the house, from the road, from each other. This layout gives you the ability to generate a design that you will be able to install.

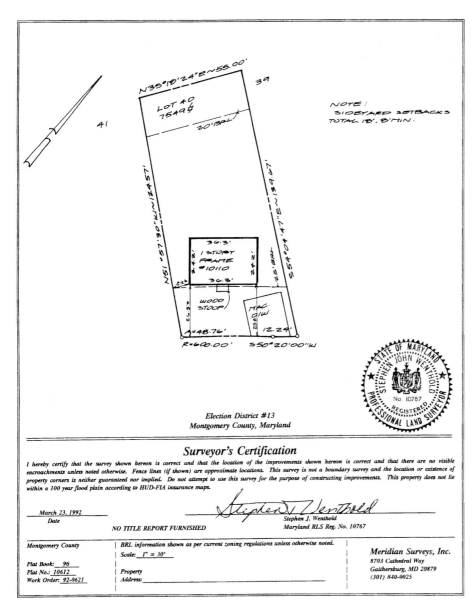

Election District #13
Montgomery County, Maryland

Surveyor's Certification

I hereby certify that the survey shown hereon is correct and that the location of the improvements shown hereon is correct and that there are no visible encroachments unless noted otherwise. Fence lines (if shown) are approximate locations. This survey is not a boundary survey and the location or existence of property corners is neither guaranteed nor implied. Do not attempt to use this survey for the purpose of constructing improvements. This property does not lie within a 100 year flood plain according to HUD-FIA insurance maps.

March 23, 1992
Date

Stephen J. Wenthold
Maryland RLS Reg. No. 10767

NO TITLE REPORT FURNISHED

Montgomery County	BRL information shown as per current zoning regulations unless otherwise noted.	
Plat Book: 96	Scale: 1" = 30'	Meridian Surveys, Inc.
Plat No.: 10612	Property	8703 Cathedral Way
Work Order: 92-0621	Address:	Gaithersburg, MD 20879
		(301) 840-0025

Tax Plat   Your plat or survey should look similar to this one. Use it as the basis for your landscape draft.

LOCATE EXISTING STRUCTURES

On the piece of vellum with your house laid out on your property, locate and draw the existing structures that are to remain in your landscape design. This will include the hardscape such as the house, garage, deck, shed, driveway, and walkways. Also locate the existing softscape that will remain—perennials, shrubs, and trees, for example.

Plan with Existing Hard- and Softscape

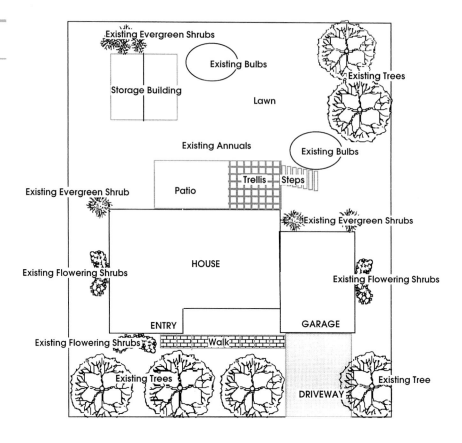

LOCATE NORTH

From the tax plat or using a compass, locate north. This determination is important because it helps you follow the path of the sun and know where winter and summer winds might blow from, where to put outdoor sitting areas, and how to match plants to the proper exposure so they will survive and thrive.

LOCATE UTILITY LINES

Indicate the location of all utility lines on your design so that you don't disturb them with your landscaping. These lines run across county right-of-ways onto your property. Most are underground, and it is the law in many areas that you locate the lines before you dig. If you don't know where the utility lines are, utility companies have free line locating services. Use them.

Finding and marking utility lines will save you aggravation and possibly an explosion. I've cut phone lines. One of my excavators hit

Utilities & Depths*

Utility	Minimum Depth
Electric	Minimum of 18″, 36″ preferred
Gas	No standard depth, 24 to 36″ is preferred (gas lines are plastic and puncture easily)
Sewage	24 to 30″ in most parts of the country
Water	36″ is the national standard. Can be any depth if not subject to freeze.
Telephone	If line is in conduit, can safely be placed at any depth. Without conduit, should be at least 24″.
Cable TV	Can be located at any depth, even just under the surface.

*Note: These are general guidelines. Confirm with local utilities. Grade changes performed after line was laid may alter depth.

a gusher when he lifted a water line with his backhoe. My mason cut a gas line that records showed had been disconnected years ago—and the gas was on and flowing! Know where to dig, and then dig with care.

CHECK BUILDING CODES

Some of what you do around your home will be governed by zoning regulations and building codes set by your municipality, county, or sometimes state. These considerations can affect your landscape design as much as climate conditions. You must understand these regulations and the required permits and other procedures.

Ascertain local municipality, county, or state zoning requirements, especially for fences, steps, decks, retaining walls, sheds, county right-of-way, and other building restrictions. Be sure to find out whether you need a permit for the work you are doing. Even if the job seems insignificant to you, you may need to get approval from your local or county officials. For example, in Montgomery County, Maryland, a permit is required just to erect a small section of fence for screening a utility area or even for keeping animals out of a vegetable garden. Chevy Chase, Maryland, requires an application to cut a tree on your property. Knowing what these codes are can help you determine whether you want to plant a hedge instead of installing a fence or build a patio instead of a deck.

Mark Slopes and Contours

Mark on your design the slopes and contours of your property, especially if there is something extreme. This is particularly important if you are going to contract to have the work done; the workers will not be as familiar with the personality and special features of your property as you are. A surveyor generates contour maps; it would be difficult to do your own. You can lay tracing paper over a contour map to design your property.

Use Tracing Paper

All the space that remains open within your property lines on the piece of vellum is a blank canvas, where you can start figuring out what you want and where to put it. Place a piece of tracing paper over the basic plot plan that you laid out. With the tracing paper as an overlay, you can begin to draw the pieces you want to add—the plants, the new deck, your new walkway, for example. Use tracing paper because you can erase it, smudge it up, or throw it away. You can change things freely and always have the clean framework of the design underneath.

Draw whatever you think you might want in the lifetime of your garden. Now is the time to let your imagination take you where it wants. Don't hold back. Try out ideas on paper; you have nothing to lose but a sheet or two of paper and some eraser rubber. If you don't know what you want in an area, circle it. Write in the activities you wish to perform there and come back to it.

Draw Plants at Mature Size

Draw plants the size they will be at maturity, so they will be properly spaced. Draw the garden as it will be in three to five years, not at planting, so that you don't overplant and end up taking things out. For example, don't plant a three-foot-high Christmas tree five feet from the house because eventually it will grow to twenty feet around. Check with your garden center or nursery for correct information on how far apart the plants should be placed.

Draw Canopies

A tree can have a very large impact on a property. When you draw an existing tree, draw it not by how big the trunk is but by how big the canopy spreads at its widest point. Something that grows forty feet across at the top must be shown as a large circle in order to appreci-

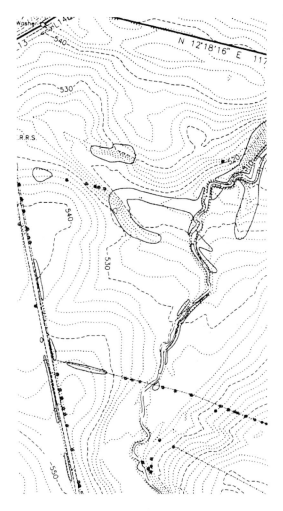

Contour Map   Contour lines with numbers representing feet above sea level. The closer the lines, the steeper the grade.

ate the impact it has on the property. You can indicate plants under the tree by adding elements within the circle of the tree's expanse.

USE VELLUM FOR FINAL DESIGN

With your house and property layout already drawn onto quality vellum (sixteen to twenty pound), transfer your ideas using the tracing paper. Vellum is translucent enough so that you can place your tracing paper under the plan and trace all your roughed-out ideas onto your final design.

LABEL EVERYTHING

Label every element that you place on the landscape design. You might want to use numbers or letters and have a corresponding key for the trees, shrubs, and other plantings. You can easily label the house, driveway, walks, lawn, pool, or other larger features, but filling in names for a perennial border, herb garden, or mixed shrub mass would be tedious without a key. You should also show lines for the planting beds.

Drawings for Permits

If you are building a structure for which you need a permit—a deck or shed, for example—you may be required to submit a drawing of your plans. This will be an elevated view (elevation) of what you're planning, not the bird's-eye view used for your landscape design. An elevation shows the cross-section of a structure so you can see footings, walls, supports, and roofline. It is handy to have a drawing such as this in advance of construction to show how all the parts will fit together.

Perspective Drawings

A tip for doing perspective drawings (artist's renderings) of your house and property is to hang a piece of paper on the wall and project a slide of your home onto it. Then trace the house, property, and plants onto the piece of paper. This will ensure accuracy of design and proper proportion.

Deck & Step Detail

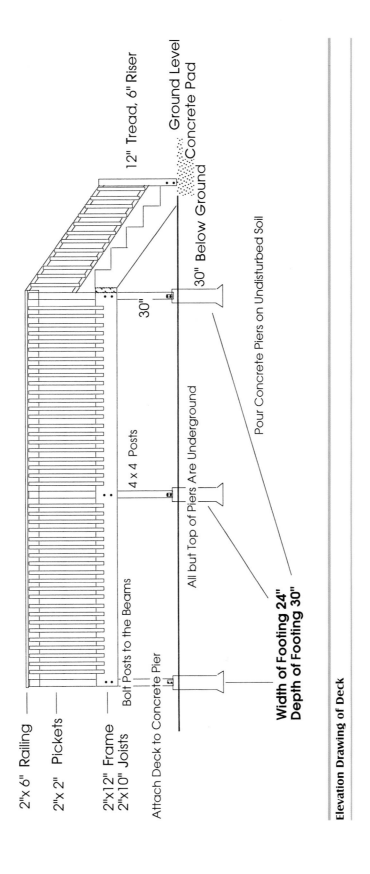

2"x 6" Railing

2"x 2" Pickets

2"x12" Frame
2"x10" Joists

Attach Deck to Concrete Pier

Bolt Posts to the Beams

4 x 4 Posts

All but Top of Piers Are Underground

Pour Concrete Piers on Undisturbed Soil

Width of Footing 24"
Depth of Footing 30"

30"

30" Below Ground

Ground Level

Concrete Pad

12" Tread, 6" Riser

Elevation Drawing of Deck

SITE PREPARATION

4

Your landscape begins with your site—specifically, the soil that makes up your site. You only get one go-around with the soil before the plants go in the ground and you can't get to the root zone again. The soil provides the nutrients to feed growing plants and the structure to hold air and moisture for the plants without becoming waterlogged. More than any other factor, the soil dictates the success of a plant. Poor soil preparation is the primary reason that plants do not survive.

It takes one hundred years for nature to make an inch of topsoil and a thousand years to create a full soil profile. But you can do it in a day with the right materials. Topsoil is subsoil with organic material added. Most topsoil I've checked contains 1 to 5 percent organic material, and plant scientists say at least 20 percent composted organic material is necessary.

TEST SOIL

Use a quick and dirty method of checking the organic material content of your soil by volume. Take a cup or two of soil from a three- to four-inch depth in your yard. Put clean soil into a quart jar of water. Shake up the soil water mix and let stand overnight. The profile of the settled soil generally reflects the sand, silt, clay, and organic content of the soil—sand on the bottom, the silt layer next, and clay on top with a dark layer of organic material covering the clay or floating. If you measure the layers, you may find, like I did, that virtually no organic material exists in soil that has not been amended.

For the most scientific approach, have your soil tested before you do anything to it. Most counties have an extension service that provides soil testing through a state university agricultural department. Testing will tell you the pH, phosphorus, and potash levels and, perhaps, some trace elements. Take a composite soil sample, mixing several cups of soil taken from about an inch or two below the surface from several spots in the garden. Usually about one cup of this mixture is all that is needed for testing.

pH LEVELS

The desirable pH—the acidity-alkalinity index—depends on what you are planting. pH runs from 1 (most acid) to 14 (most alkaline). A pH of 7 is neutral. Most garden plants do best at a pH of 6 to 7, although sun-loving flowering shrubs such as abelia, deutzia, weigela, lilac, and forsythia prefer "sweet" soil (above 6.6) and woodland shrubs such as blueberries and rhododendron prefer a more acidic environment (below 6.0).

To correct over-acidity, add ground limestone to the soil. Broadcast at a rate of fifty pounds per thousand square feet, it changes the pH reading approximately one-tenth (0.1) of one pH. So, if the pH is 6.2, you take it to 6.3. To correct over-alkalinity (which is most likely to be found in semi-arid regions and may cause yellowing in plants), add sulfur or iron sulfate according to labeled instructions.

PREPARE YOUR BEDS

Create the best medium for planting trees, shrubs, flowers (annuals and perennials), and grasses by preparing your beds with at least three inches of well-composted organic material dug eight to sixteen inches (depending on plant size) into the soil over as wide an area as you can cover.

COMPOST SOURCES

There are a variety of sources for compost. In some areas, composted sewage sludge and leaf mold (composted leaves) are available commercially. The compost that is made from your own yard debris is the best material to enrich your soil, but using any of these materials is great for the environment and the secret to a lush healthy landscape. (Compost is covered in detail in chapter 10.)

Another way to enhance the soil is to use compost as a mulch on the surface. Just lay it over a bed to a depth of about two inches;

don't work it in, but let gravity do the job. This can make a tremendous difference in plant health in just one growing season.

ROTOTILLING

My tool of choice for digging up the soil to make it loose and friable is a rototiller. For one-time site preparation, you can rent a tiller. Plan on having it for at least a half-day, particularly if you are breaking previously untilled sod. The manual alternative to the rototiller is a pointed digging spade. Both can be used efficiently to turn the soil, but the tiller will save time and labor. Take care when you are tilling near existing plant roots; the tiller will do as effective a job of tearing them up as it does turning the soil.

PREPARE YOUR NEW LAWN

For planting a new lawn, dig in a one- to two-inch layer of compost and fifty pounds of pulverized agricultural limestone per thousand square feet to a depth of three to five inches. Rake out rocks, level the area, and spread grass seed. Do not dig in lime if a soil test shows your pH to be 6.8 or higher. Lawn planting and maintenance are covered more fully in chapter 38.

SITE CONSIDERATIONS

How your land is graded and prepared dictates the health of a plant as much as the sun, wind, or rain. If the water stands, for example, and the plant doesn't like wet feet, it will die. Preparing the soil as described above will lighten it to the point of being a much better-drained medium with more nutrients, more moisture holding ability, and more air to the roots.

In addition to soil, consider other physical characteristics of a site when installing plant material. These include wind exposure, surface drainage, slopes with over a 20 percent grade, and possible plant damage due to wounding by animals, equipment, or plant vandals.

GOOD DRAINAGE

A slightly graded soil surface will drain water away from a planting site, unless the wet spot is caused by an underground spring surfacing. In which case, you would use plants that like boggy conditions.

SLOPES

Slopes with more than a 20 percent grade (a one-foot rise over five feet) are candidates for a retaining wall or groundcover. Mowing lawn on steep slopes is dangerous and to be avoided. See chapter 17, Slope Enhancement, for more information.

PROTECTING PLANTS

Protect plants from mower damage and soil compaction by putting beds around all of them. Screen tender plants from the wind with a couple sections of fence or a planting of wind-tolerant spruces or firs. You can protect a young trees with a product called a tree tube. This tube must be removed within a few years, as soon as the bark gets rough, or it holds moisture against the trunk and promotes decay. Protection against vandals may have to be a locked garden gate.

CHOOSING PEOPLE PLACES

Plants are not the only residents you prepare a site for. There are a number of considerations to keep in mind to prepare your site for people too. Human needs can be very different than plant needs.

When you're picking a site to prepare where people will be spending time, look for a southeastern orientation. The most pleasant orientation for relaxation and enjoyment is southeast with protection from the southwestern sun. An elevated setting on a slope will enhance the pleasant vistas and keep you warmer since cold air rolls down hill. A site that is designed for people traffic needs soil that has a good weight-bearing ability. Clay and shale are generally good surfaces to build on or walk on.

TOOLS AND MAINTENANCE

5

Landscape design and grounds maintenance are inextricably connected. Plants must be installed and maintained properly or the design is lost. So for the perfect landscape, you need the right tools. They are an integral part of all landscape-related tasks.

Mowing, spreading, spraying, pruning, clipping, cutting, digging, edging, elevating, grading, hauling, manicuring, planting, raking, skimming, and transplanting could be prohibitively difficult to perform. With the right tool, these tasks can be relatively simple.

CHOOSING A LAWN MOWER

Most properties have a lawn. For a groomed appearance, there is no substitute for a manicured lawn defining a large, sharply edged planting bed. To achieve this, one piece of equipment is a necessity: a lawn mower. Gasoline (two- and four-cycle, walk-behind and riding), electric (cord or battery), and people-powered mowers are available at lawn and garden equipment dealers or hardware stores. The size of your property and how much effort you are willing to put into mowing will determine what type of mower you use. Larger lots require a gasoline mower.

GASOLINE MOWERS

Gasoline (two- and four-cycle) mowers are available at lawn and garden equipment dealers or hardware stores. All mowers cut grass, but your choices are mind-boggling. The cutting action of most power mowers is achieved with a blade that spins horizontally; they are called rotary mowers. The exact type that you need

> "For the perfect landscape, you need the right tools. They are an integral part of all landscape-related tasks."

61

should be determined by the size of your property and your penchant for exercise and bipedal locomotion.

Any brand of gasoline-powered mower will give good service for years. Keep the blade sharp and change the oil and clean the air filter every twenty to twenty-five hours of operation. (Two-cycle engines burn a mixture of gas and oil; they don't require oil changes.) Change the spark plug every hundred hours. Lubricate wheels with #2 multipurpose lithium grease if they have fittings, and winterize a gasoline-powered type according to manufacturer's recommendations. And be very careful not to mow over rocks or heavy surface roots.

The more features the mower offers (e.g., grass catcher, self-propelled, ride-on, easy-adjust variable heights, multiple speed gearbox, etc.), the more expensive and, candidly, the more opportunity for problems. I prefer basic mowers with the emphasis on safety (e.g., toe guard, rear deflector, extended discharge chute, lower rpm, automatic shut-off whenever your hands leave the mower, etc.).

ELECTRIC MOWERS

Consider an electric mower for a small, compact lot. It requires very little maintenance beyond blade-sharpening. Electric mowers get their power from a house outlet or a rechargeable, onboard battery. In the case of AC-powered units, purchase a long enough extension cord to reach the outermost boundaries of your lawn, and be very careful not to run over it while you are mowing.

REEL MOWERS

Don't overlook the exercise benefits of the old-fashioned reel mower. New versions of the reel-type push mower do an excellent job if a lawn is mowed regularly. There are only a few manufacturers of reel-type push mowers (the largest is the American Lawn Mower Company/Great States Corporation), and most models sell for less than a hundred dollars. A reel-type mower is fun and easy to use, and you don't have to winterize it.

SPREADERS AND SPRAYERS

Use spreaders and sprayers for applying nutrients to your lawn and garden. There are a number of different types of spreaders and sprayers, and they each have a distinct function in the part they play in your landscape design. Whichever you choose, always thoroughly clean sprayers and spreaders after every use. Rinse at least three times to ensure the material is thoroughly flushed from the equipment.

DROP SPREADERS

The only way to assure accuracy and even distribution of dry fertilizer, weed killer, or insect control is to use a drop spreader. As you push it from behind, a drop spreader drops material through holes in the bottom of a hopper.

BROADCAST SPREADERS

A broadcast spreader throws material six to ten feet in a circular pattern, and is perfect for grass seed, lime, gypsum, fertilizer, fine-textured compost, and even ice-melting salts in winter. However, don't use a broadcast spreader for weed killer or insecticide because of the inaccuracy of the spread, and these materials cannot be allowed to go into your beds.

SPRAYERS

Use sprayer tanks to apply liquid nutrients and pesticides. I prefer a two-gallon plastic pump sprayer because it is lightweight to carry and the plastic is noncorrosive.

If you are doing the maintenance yourself, the best-maintained design may require two to three sprayers: one for total brush killer (nonselective herbicides) and one or two for lawn weeds, fertilizer, and insecticide. Foliage sprays with nutrients are popular to make shrubs look healthier and fuller, but make sure there's no residual weed killer in the tank when spraying.

PRUNERS

Even if you're not doing the work yourself, if you have a landscaped property, you need a pruner. There are a variety of situations when they will be handy, such as cutting flowers, taking branches and limbs out of your way, keeping shrubs off the house, even cutting limbs on the Christmas tree. The most versatile tool that will cut from fairly large (three-quarter-inch) to small stems is a hand pruner, which you hold with one hand. There are several different varieties. Anvil pruners have a single blade that cuts onto a flat surface set into the jaw of the tool. Bypass pruners cut like scissors. Long-handled lopping shears, which cut by either an anvil or bypass method, will cut thicker tree limbs and shrub stems. Pruning is discussed in greater detail in chapter 49.

PRUNING SAWS

Keep the integrity to your landscape design by keeping limbs of deciduous shade trees pruned at least six to eight feet above the ground. To cut big branches, you need a saw. Folding pruning saws will cut branches up to three or four inches thick and fit in your pocket. If you cut more than an occasional branch that is three or four inches in diameter, a bow saw is a good idea. A bow saw will cut firewood-sized wood if necessary.

HEDGE SHEARS

An optional pruning tool is a hedge shear. If there are a lot of shrubs or hedges in your design, they may have to be sheared because it might not be practical to prune that many plants any other way. A good quality pair of scissors-type hand shears works fine, once you learn the rhythm of using them. If you have a lot of shearing to do, you might be happier with electric hedge shears.

GARDEN TOOLS

SHOVELS

It takes a decade to install the perfect garden. You will need to move shrubs around, divide perennials, and possibly discard some plants. The best shovel for general digging, dividing, making holes, and turning the soil is a round-point spading shovel with a forty-eight-inch handle.

SPADES

A useful multipurpose digging tool needed to perform a great deal of tasks in order to have a finished looking landscape design is a straight-edged garden or nursery spade with a twenty-seven-inch handle with a D-grip. It is ideal for manicuring a bed edge, skimming sod and weeds, dividing perennials, and transplanting trees and shrubs. A heavy-duty blade and an all-steel or full-steel reinforced handle will withstand slamming through rocks and roots.

MATTOCKS

A helpful item to create your design features is the mattock. It is an excellent tool for planting bulbs and perennials, chopping out small trees, trenching for irrigation or lighting, and digging a hole for a water feature, especially if there are rocks or tree roots. Look for a cutter or pickax type with a thirty-six-inch handle.

PITCHFORKS

A pitchfork is the tool of choice to turn the compost pile, spread mulch, or lift tangles of lawn debris. Buy a five- or six-tine manure fork with a fifty-four-inch handle. A heavy-duty model is worth the investment.

LEAF RAKES

In autumn, a leaf rake will save the life of the lawn by keeping leaves off of it and will keep your patio usable. It is also the ultimate design tool in spring for cleaning up yard debris. I recommend a spring steel wire rake because it is more versatile than bamboo or polypropylene for raking debris such as leaves, twigs, trimmings, and weeds out of lawns and beds.

GARDEN RAKES

The finish work may require a garden rake. This is the tool to use to finish backfilling the hole or trench you dug with your mattock. Use the hard steel kind for raking off rock and sod. It is also the tool used to make the soil level in order to plant a lawn.

BROOMS AND ACCESSORIES

To fill out your tool collection for the perfectly maintained design, add a coarse-textured push broom, a flat scoop shovel, and a wheelbarrow or lawn cart. These make gardening easier; however, you can use a household broom, a dustpan, and plastic tarpaulin almost as effectively.

MAINTENANCE GUIDELINES

Maintenance is the key to a successful landscape. It's all the tasks of maintenance—deadheading, trimming, weeding, mulching, pruning, mowing, fertilizing, spraying, controlling pests—that create the perfect garden. You could install $100,000 worth of fabulous plantings, but without adequate maintenance your field of dreams will become a field of weeds or dust during a single growing season.

The most important thing you can know about landscape maintenance is that slow and steady wins the race. Take a preventive approach. Trim a branch before it's in your face. Pull one weed before it goes to seed and increases exponentially.

The key to low maintenance is doing the correct garden activity at the correct time. If you want a low-maintenance garden, do your activities regularly. In this way, you will keep ahead of the weeds, the bugs, and the out-of-control growth.

Establish a maintenance schedule as a guide for getting things done at the right time. To schedule your maintenance, you need to inventory your grounds and determine what needs to be taken care of, in what area, and when. Put each specific scheduled maintenance activity on your calendar at the time it has to be done, as if it was an appointment with a person. Then keep the appointment.

Use the following general maintenance chart as a guide to help you determine the specific activities that need to be done for your property.

Maintenance Chart

Category	Activity	Interval
Lawns	Mow	Weekly
	Edge paving	Monthly
	Rake leaves	Spring and fall
	Fertilize	Spring and fall
	Apply weed killer	Spring and fall
	Test soil	Every two to four years
Shrubs (deciduous and evergreen)	Shear hedges`	One to four times per season
	Prune selectively for shape	One to five times per season
	Prune selectively for flowers	Specific to variety
	Prune dead wood and weed bed	Monthly
	Clean out leaves and debris	Spring and fall
	Fertilize	Annually
Trees (deciduous)	Prune inside crossings and branches	Annually
	Prune suckers	As necessary
	Prune dead wood	Monthly
	Shape (don't top)	Every two to five years
	Prune lower limbs	Annually
	Hire tree service to clean out large shade trees	Every two to five years
	Fertilize	Annually (spread on surface)
Trees (evergreen)	Shear	As needed to keep in bounds
	Shape (don't top)	As necessary
	Prune dead wood	Monthly
	Fertilize	Annually (spread on surface)
Groundcover	Trim edges or unwanted growth	Monthly
	Rake leaves and debris	Spring and fall
	Fertilize	Annually

[continued]

Category	Activity	Interval
Vines	Prune selectively as needed	Two to six times per season
	Prune selectively for flowers	Specific to variety
	Train to a structure	Two to four times per season
	Fertilize	Annually
Perennials and Bulbs	Plant, prune, separate	Specific to variety
	Weed	Weekly
	Fertilize	Specific to variety
Annuals	Plant, trim, water	Specific to variety
	Weed	Weekly
	Fertilize	Specific to variety
Beds	Edge	Monthly
	Mulch	Annually
	Weed	Weekly
	Rake	Spring and fall
Structures	Check for paint, stain, repairs	Annually

ACQUIRING PLANTS AND MATERIALS

6

You have a number of places to turn to acquire plants and materials for your landscape. The three basic categories are mail order (catalog), local garden centers or nurseries, and large home-improvement stores such as The Home Depot, Sears, or Lowe's. Each has its own usefulness, as the following tips will explain, and you might find that you want to use a mix of all three. And while these are the most obvious choices, there are other options that can be just as valuable, such as flower shows, plant sales at botanic gardens, and neighbors.

MAIL ORDER

Catalogs are a good source for seeds, bulbs, and plants. Buying via mail order, whether from a catalog or over the Internet, is an inexpensive way to get plant material, but keep in mind that you get very young plants. From a catalog, you will usually be getting seeds, bulbs, seedlings, and bare-root stock. After all, it's hard to ship a hundred-pound root ball through the mail.

Herbaceous plants are those that usually have soft, fleshy, green stems, such as annuals, perennials, grasses, and bulbs. Purchasing them when they're young will not compromise your landscape design. Whether they are bought in a container from a garden center or as bare-root stock through the mail, perennials will grow to maturity in two to five years, depending on the variety.

Annuals are usually only available by seed when buying through the mail, although I have seen some vegetables that are shipped bare root. To get annuals as started bedding plants, you generally need to get them locally. Bulbs are the same regardless of where you acquire them; they can only be planted as bare-root stock.

You can buy woody plants through a mail-order catalog, but they will not be as large or as attractive (at least in the short run) as those bought at your local garden center. Compare, for example, the flowering cherry whip you would get from a catalog (a single stem, about the thickness of a finger, with a few leaves at the top and minimal branching) to the one you would buy from a garden center (a one- to two-inch-thick trunk with branches on top as thick as the whip you would get in the mail). In three years, the mail-order piece will still be a very young tree, but it will also cost a lot less.

To learn more about ordering plants through the mail and how to find mail-order suppliers, contact the Mail-Order Gardening Association at (410) 730-9713.

GARDEN CENTERS AND NURSERIES

Most garden centers are complete supply sources for tools, plant material—both seedlings and mature specimens—and information. Garden centers are listed in the Yellow Pages of your phone book. Many garden centers serve as middlemen between the nursery and the public, although quite a few have growing facilities of their own.

The nursery is where the plants are grown and is an excellent source for information about growing plants. You can find a list of nurseries that sell directly to the public in your Yellow Pages. A nursery is where your most mature stock will come from, and in establishing a viable landscape, you will want to plant some older trees and shrubs, unless you are very patient in expecting results.

Get to know the nurseries and garden centers in your area because it takes a decade for your garden to be fully developed. That's ten years of planting, replacing, dividing, removing, discarding, having things die and learning where they will and won't survive and thrive. A continuing relationship with your plant supplier and information resource will bode well for you and your property.

Always ascertain warranties for plants. Most garden centers and large chains offer guarantees, which can be extremely valuable. I have seen them range from thirty days up to two years. Remember to ask about a guarantee when you are at the plant supplier. Of course, this won't replace the satisfaction you will receive if the planting is a success and thrives. So always remember proper plant care.

> "Many people don't realize that you can go back to the store with your receipt and the dead plant and get a replacement."

HOME IMPROVEMENT STORES

While large chains and discount stores may offer the best prices, be wary of buying plants from retailers who do not specialize in garden supplies. Certainly, you can find many healthy annuals at these outlets and a selection of trees, shrubs, and perennials. They will do very well for you, if you buy at the beginning of the growing season. But because plants are just one of the many product lines handled by these huge merchandisers, you will find considerably less variety than at a large garden center. You will also be buying plants that may have received less-than-optimal care.

FLOWER SHOWS AND PLANT SALES

Flower shows and plant sales are excellent sources for plants and flowers. Many public gardens and garden clubs conduct plant sales. Flower shows are popular all over the country. Some are sponsored by private entrepreneurs and some by venerable societies, such as: the Philadelphia Flower Show, one of the grandest, run by the Pennsylvania Horticultural Society; the New England Spring Flower Show, sponsored by the Massachusetts Horticultural Society; or the Maymont Flower Show, run by the Maymont Foundation in Richmond, Virginia.

PASS-ON PLANTS

Common Sense Carl (Carl Orndorff), who was a regular on my radio show and has seventy-five years of landscape and nursery experience, believes in gardens for everyone. For him, part of the joy of gardening is its communal aspect, and he coined the phrase "pass-on plants" to describe another way of acquiring plants.

Just about every plant, herbaceous or woody, can be divided or rooted to establish new offspring. Pass-on plants are not only the most inexpensive way to establish a garden, but they also assure plantings that will do well in your area since they were already growing there.

Here's how it can work: When it's time to divide your perennials, go to your neighbor and say, "I'll trade you some daylilies for a peony and some hosta," or "I'm dividing my ornamental grasses. Would you like some, or would you like to trade?" Perennials are an excellent bartering item. A drawback to acquiring woody plants (trees and shrubs) this way is the five to ten years required for them to mature, because they were probably started from cuttings or seeds.

SOURCES FOR FREE AMENDMENTS

Keep your eyes open for natural materials. They are the best soil amendments and often available for free through city, county, or state composting programs. Farmers are happy to give you free manure, if they don't use it. Horse manure must be fully composted; cow manure isn't as rich and can be used in garden and beds without fully composting it. If you live near a zoo or if the circus comes to town, get elephant manure; it's one of nature's best soil enrichments. It is perfectly balanced and does not need to be composted.

The best fertilizer is the one plants make themselves right where they stand—their own composted leaves. The debris from your garden is an excellent fertilizer for you to put back on it. Just let the material lay or compost it, and then dig it back into your garden. For example, when you cut down the tops of your perennials in fall, let the leaves lay; let the foliage that has fallen from your shade tree remain to compost over its own roots. If leaves collect in an area where they will ruin the design or the lawn, compost them in a separate area.

PART

II

The Practical Landscape

THE PRACTICAL LANDSCAPE

Now that you've read part 1, The Beginning Landscape, you have a solid basis for moving ahead with your landscape design. As you do this, you must deal with some of the more practical considerations. The basic philosophy behind designing a landscape includes creating a useful space as well as installing an esthetically pleasing picture.

In this part, I will give you the how-to about many functional and useful aspects of installing a landscape. Starting with the necessary realities of meeting a budget, we will move through lighting, irrigation, where to walk your dog, assuring security, providing shade, and many other practical points of landscape design. You may recognize many of these topics from the checklist, and they are covered further in the chapters of this section.

One practical consideration begins right at the street. It's simple common sense, as are most of these guidelines. Plan for visibility when entering the street from your driveway. Keep a clear line of vision for several hundred feet where you reach the thoroughfare. If you want to screen your property, design the wall or screening shrubs back far enough so that your car clears them before you reach the sidewalk or street. Don't place large shrubs or a tall wall in your line of vision where you need to see pedestrians or other cars.

Illuminate walking surfaces. It doesn't take a bright light. Fifteen or twenty watts, aimed onto the paving and not in your eyes, will offer lots of visibility without losing ambiance. Steps should be lit from above.

Never have a single step in your landscape. Among design professionals, it's known as a "trip step." For a flight of stairs in your garden, don't have more than ten steps without a landing. A thirty-two-inch high railing should be installed along them.

Texture is important on walking surfaces. A pathway must provide traction even when wet. Concrete can have a broom finish for traction; brick and flagstone should have a rough texture. Most concrete pavers that you find at home improvement and garden centers also come with a rough finish for good traction. If you seal asphalt, be careful that the material you use penetrates and doesn't lie on top, giving the asphalt a slick surface. Sealants that are applied in a spray form by installers are better than those you buy and apply with a roller are.

Providing seating is a practical concern. You should have some location to sit, a rock, wall, planter or tree stump, so that you have a sense of place in the garden. There are many different types that you can buy, from a flimsy folding chair to an ornate stone bench, but don't cheapen the surroundings with inferior seating. Place seats in a way that will provide maximum enjoyment and provide incentive to get pleasure from the garden.

There's always a need to stow equipment and supplies. To me, it means a place to safe-keep lawn and garden tools. I want you to look ahead as you design and anticipate your needs. If you consider them now, you'll be able to install necessary storage as a part of your landscape and not as an afterthought. You may find the need to store landscape maintenance and recreational equipment, tools, lawn and garden supplies, and almost anything else that requires protection from the elements or, for aesthetic reasons, must be kept out of view.

If you have a space that you wish to shield from view, such as one that is used for trash cans, a heat pump, gas meter, or other utility, use a storage shed as a screen by positioning it to hide an unsightly area. Use an ornate storage building to create spatial enclosure, to separate a rear garden from a front garden, or to define a small space. Put a small sitting area and some flowers around it to tie it into your landscape design as an ornamental feature. Build a storage shed to look like a cottage, a playhouse, or a rustic log cabin—whatever fits with your design.

Use a shed for triple duty, for storage and to screen and shade your air-conditioning unit or heat pump. This will block the view of these units and help you save money on utility bills by shielding them from the sun's rays. Shading your heat pump can save you 3 percent on your utility bills.

Other utilitarian features that are practical concerns for your landscape design include firewood—namely, a place to stack it. Don't leave it in a heap in the yard. A stacked pile not only looks nicer, but it seasons better, keeps the bottom layer from rotting, and allows air circulation between logs, keeping them dry. I like to use firewood as a design element for spatial definition. A nicely stacked pile can provide a rustic touch and divide rear and front gardens.

A potting table is another object that can be unsightly, but with a little thought, it can have a positive impact on your landscape. Use a little imagination. Rather than just a table, bucket, and hose, for example, use a contemporary potting table, backed by a trellis with a plant trained on it. Build it where it can double as a wet bar during social times.

Parking is a necessity in the American landscape. It can be very difficult and will take innovative thinking to work parking into a landscape design in an aesthetically pleasing way. Driveways provide a harsh expanse of paving, and parking on the grass is unsightly, as well as bad for the lawn. But in the chapter on driveways, along with rules of design, I offer some tips to make your driveway better fit the landscape.

Another challenge is the garage. But, if you consider it as part of your design from the inception, you can make it work. You probably need to consider multiple vehicles since surveys show that the average American family today has 2.3 cars.

With the increasing popularity and environmental good sense of recycling, composting is practical. If you have a good logical space for it, build your entire service sector around the compost area because, from a design standpoint, it's difficult to do anything but screen compost. Even in these times of state-of-the-art compost barrels, bins, and other receptacles, by its nature, yard debris begins as an eyesore.

These are a few of the considerations in this section for the practical landscape. I begin with the most important of all of them in the next chapter: meeting a budget.

Meeting a Budget

8

Most home owners, of course, have to consider the realities of budget and financial limitations as they landscape their property. As noted earlier, a general rule of thumb is to budget 10 percent of the appraised value of your property for landscaping. Budget this out over a period of about twenty-three years. This is because it is estimated that a landscape has a life of about twenty to twenty-three years before it needs to be renewed. However, this does not mean you have to start from scratch again every twenty-three years. Many plants at that age are doing wonderfully, and all you have to do is renewal pruning (see the maintenance chart on page 67)—as in the case of overgrown boxwood or azaleas or the old deciduous flowering shrub border.

Whatever the value of your property, as you begin your design, I recommend that you approach budgeting from an indulgent perspective. Don't let your budget limit your imagination. Put your dreams in your design. Consider everything—the swimming pool, the picnic grove, the tennis court, the run-off pond. Don't leave something out of your design because you think you can't afford it. So what if the tennis court ends up as a woodland garden. Create the design you want—at this point it will cost you only thinking time, graphite, and eraser rubber.

Once you've created the design of your dreams, focus on the bigger ticket items and decide if the cost is worth the return in enjoyment and use. If not, you can redesign—erase a more expensive idea and redesign the space to have a more realistic use. For example, your swimming pool might become an herb, vegetable, or cutting garden. Or you can leave an ambitious element in the landscape design, such as the water garden or a formal fountain and parterre, and be patient. Take it a step at a time. If all you can do is locate and install the trees and some shrubs in the first year or two, do that. Perhaps the water garden could be installed in ten years, or for your retirement. You will be delighted that you left the idea on paper all those years and finally fulfilled your dream. Remember that Rome wasn't built in a day.

You can save money by doing the job yourself with the help of temporary laborers, rather than contracting out the entire project. This way you may be able to afford an item that would be out of your budget if you hired all of the work out. It is impossible for me to quantify the value of your time. In most cases, much of what is performed in landscaping lends itself well to do-it-yourselfers, as long as you get involved in it with a commitment to completing the project and doing it right. If you lose focus in the middle of the job, you can lose everything when you're working with living materials, but successfully installing a project yourself will usually save you money.

BUDGETING PLANTINGS

Give your trees priority over other plantings. They are the slowest growing element and add the most value to your property. Trees are expensive to buy when mature, and there are advantages beyond cost when you buy them younger. Less mature trees are easier to transport, easier to plant, and, if you locate them and prepare the site properly, research shows that they become better established and develop larger trunks when installed young (when trunks are an inch or two in diameter). Planting trees first is also the best way for your landscape to evolve. For example, you might have designed a bed of shade-tolerant plants, such as rhododendron, hosta, hakone grass (*Hakonechloa*), and Japanese yellow waxbells (*Kiringeshoma*), under your large shade trees, but the trees have to be mature enough to provide shade before the shade garden will be successful.

Once your trees are planted, let your budget drive your priorities. When shrubs are on sale, for example, buy them and put them where they have been scheduled on your design. Or, as with trees, shrubs can be started young. This again requires patience, but the savings can be tremendous.

You can order perennials from a catalog or buy them on sale at a garden center, and they will be less expensive. Another option is to divide yours or a neighbor's perennials, and they are free. This is a wonderful way to establish and add diversity to your garden without any cost.

You can also save money by not planting every year. Use fewer annuals and plant perennials, shrubs, and trees over the years. Planting in this manner requires designing a coordination of blooms because few shrubs and perennials will offer flowers throughout the entire growing season (see Year-Round Interest, chapter 48). You should still use a few annuals to complement the rest of the garden and ensure bloom during the inevitable slow time for flowers from the other plantings.

SHOPPING FOR PLANTS

There is no one company that has the cheapest prices across the board for plants. To find the best prices for all your plant material, you have to comparison shop for each item, something that few of us are willing to take the time to do. An exception to this might be the large chain discount stores where you will find every item they stock at competitive prices, but you will be sacrificing variety and possibly quality if you do all of your shopping in these outlets.

But high prices are not necessarily an indication of plant quality. Make sure that certain nursery standards are met for every piece of plant material that you buy: Plants should be well-rooted but not pot bound, with a full symmetrical top coming fairly well out of the container. Trees should have a good, full-branching habit and should not have sharp crotches or ones that are too wide spread, or limb breakage may be a problem in five to ten years, depending on how vigorously they grow. Stems of a multi-trunk plant should come from the ground, not from partially up the main stem.

The price of plants depends on their speed of growth. Annuals cost less than perennials; perennials are cheaper than shrubs; shrubs cost less than trees. A fast-growing shrub like forsythia will cost you considerably less than a slow-growing scarlet oak, for example. The prices are dictated by how long it has taken a plant to get from seed to usable plant. This can be from weeks (as in the case of annuals) to a year to ten years. The longevity of fast growing plants is often shorter than the slower-growing varieties.

BUDGETING HARDSCAPES

The hardscaping or constructed part of your landscape is a major cost item in your design, and there are a number of budget considerations that can be applied here.

DRIVEWAYS

The driveway is the lane to your home. It's an important early budget factor to consider. Keep aesthetics in mind, but they aren't critical as you consider the different budgetary levels of installing a drive. You can pave it for longevity or stone it. Where you live might determine what materials you should use. If everyone has the same driveway paving material, you should too. Otherwise, from a design standpoint, you'll stick out by not fitting the theme set by the neighborhood. You must also determine how big to make the driveway; the smaller it is, the less it will cost.

Stone is the least expensive way to cover your lane; it's about half the price of asphalt. Spend a little more and install a solid base under the stone with larger rock, shale, crushed stone dust, or other material that will pack hard. The cost increases, but so does longevity.

The next level up in expense is asphalt. Asphalt needs far less grooming and usually stays cleaner looking than stone. It is also about one-third the cost of concrete, but isn't as permanent. Even when properly laid, asphalt will crack, will need sealing and repairs, and will have to be replaced sooner than concrete.

Concrete is about three times the cost of asphalt. It is a higher initial investment, but it will outlast asphalt five to one or more. Within the category of concrete paving, there are cost variations. Each addition, such as texture, color, and thickness of pour, will add cost, but these extra touches will also make your driveway stronger, and/or more aesthetically pleasing. Driveways are discussed in greater detail in chapter 32.

> "Create the design you want—at this point it will cost you only thinking time, graphite, and eraser rubber."

WALKWAYS TO THE HOUSE

For the walk or path to your front door, look at different options. If you are operating on a shoestring budget, you might want to lay flagstone, bricks, or concrete pavers right onto soil. For a bit more of an investment in time or money, you can lay paving materials on a level base of stone dust or sand for a more finished look. Flagstones or bricks set in mortar on concrete are the cleanest and possibly the most long-lasting alternative, but also the most expensive. It will cost at least 20 percent more than concrete. If done properly, concrete pavers can be quite permanent if laid without mortar, which would make them an inexpensive alternative to mortar and concrete. (See Installing a Patio or Walk, page 226, for more on this subject.)

OTHER CONSTRUCTIONS

These same choices can be made for every aspect of your design. You can build a tennis court of asphalt, clay, or concrete. A swimming pool can be lined with plastic fabric, shot with gunnite (a cementitious material), or made of poured concrete. Or patios that cost a great deal can be installed more economically if you brainstorm with professionals until the numbers work.

Look for money-saving methods in the way that you do your installations. For example, a deck costs about the same as a mortared and concrete flagstone patio, but it can be far less expensive if the yard isn't level. Patios must be built on level undisturbed soil. So, if you have to fill and build a retaining wall to level your yard enough for a patio, a deck built on the original grade will save you a lot of money.

If your ideal landscape design takes you to a bottom line that is unrealistic, target the costliest elements on the design and consider alternative ways to achieve a similar effect. For example, you might

have wanted to build a flagstone patio in concrete complete with iron railing and lighting and realized that it was way outside of your budget. Go back to the drawing board. Design the flagstone to be installed on stone dust. Wait to install the railing. Use a low wooden fence with an open design in place of iron. And hang a couple low-voltage lights in a nearby tree to blanket the area in soft "moon-light" instead of installing many more ground or patio fixtures.

ATHLETIC ACTIVITIES 9

Athleticism has become a consuming passion for many people in this country. States, counties, municipalities, and private firms spend millions of dollars every year to build and maintain athletic facilities for professional athletes and for children, teenagers, and adults who pursue various activities through schools, recreation councils, and other organizations.

It's no wonder then that many people want to have some sort of athletic facility right in their own backyard. This can range from the simplicity of hiking paths through woodland areas, to an environment in which competitive games are played, to an exterior space specifically planned and artificially constructed for active recreation.

Don't let lack of formally designed athletic facilities limit the use of your property for this purpose. Don't be afraid to improvise. Remember, when our games evolved, it was from a desire to play, and any lack of physical facilities was surmounted by a sense of improvisation.

TYPICAL ATHLETIC FACILITIES FOUND IN HOMES

Children's playground

Swimming pool

Partial basketball court or area for shooting hoops

Volleyball court

Badminton court

Croquet court

Tennis court

Horseshoe area

Golf putting green

PLAYGROUNDS

A children's play area of some sort is often seen in landscape designs for private homes. A few safety tips are important to keep in mind. The playing surface should be soft. Possibilities include lawn, shredded bark, peat moss, ground-up tires, or rubberized paving. If you are installing a play gym, slide, or set of swings, make sure each piece has a smooth surface. Follow all age recommendations and other precautions offered by the manufacturer.

If the athletic facilities are intended for young children now, consider an evolution of design, whereby your playground can eventually turn into a basketball court, and then become a patio later in life.

Liven up your barbecues by incorporating a putting green into your backyard patio/grill setup. (© 2001 Sport Court, Inc. All rights reserved. Used by permission.)

ATHLETIC AREAS

In designing space for athletic activities—particularly competitive sports—it is important that the designer be familiar with the nature of the contest, how the game is played, the rotation of play, and the perspective of spectators.

If you are designating your athletic areas for specific sports, it's a good idea to know the recommended sizes for courts. The world federation for each sport sets these specifications. Of course, you can use these recommendations for guidelines and make your necessary personal modifications to accommodate restrictions such as space and zoning.

- Badminton: Seventeen by thirty-nine feet, with an extra eighteen inches on sides, thirty inches to the rear.
- Basketball: Thirty-seven by eighty-four feet, with a three-foot out-of-bounds zone around edge. Regulation half-court basketball is thirty-seven by forty-two feet.

◎ Croquet: Thirty-seven feet, two inches by eighty-five feet.

◎ Horseshoes: Ten by sixty feet, with forty feet between stakes.

◎ Shuffleboard: Six by fifty-two feet.

◎ Swimming pool: Lap pool is sixteen by thirty-four feet, with a three-foot apron plus pad for pump and filter. Depth must be at least four feet for swimming and eight feet for diving.

◎ Tennis: Singles court is twenty-seven by seventy-eight feet; doubles court is thirty-six by seventy-eight feet; both courts need an extra fifteen feet in back and six feet on sides.

◎ Volleyball: Thirty by sixty feet, with four-foot out-of-bounds area around perimeter.

Maintain a one to two percent grade on all athletic courts to ensure drainage. A poorly drained playing surface cannot be used.

Keep solar orientation in mind when setting up your game areas. For example, place a badminton net on an east-west axis so players will not be looking into the setting sun. An example of the importance of solar orientation was demonstrated in professional athletics. At Oriole Park at Camden Yards, the state-of-the art stadium built for baseball in Baltimore, Maryland, an outfield wall was so reflective of sunlight that fast-growing ivy had to be planted on it so that it didn't bother the batters.

To install an athletic court that will allow flexibility of use in the future, lay two-by-two-foot pavers on at least three inches of leveled gravel, sand, or stone dust to minimize freezing or thawing movement. Lay the pavers tightly against each other so there are no apparent joints. This will give you a "temporary" court that is level and hard enough for basketball or anything else you need a hard surface for, and you can count on it not to move for at least five years.

COMPOSTING AND RECYCLING

10

As explained in chapter 4, the use of compost is an important element in the installation and maintenance of many aspects of your landscape design. In case you are unfamiliar with the term, compost is decomposed plant material: trees, shrubs, vines, flowers, vegetables, etc. Composting takes place when naturally occurring bacteria and fungi in the soil decompose these organic materials. The nutrient-rich substance that results—also called humus— works to bind together the sandy particles of light (porous) soil or to keep apart the clay particles of heavy (dense) soil.

The recycling of organic wastes through composting is the duty of every responsible home owner. Many trash collectors won't even take your yard waste to the landfill. So help out your local landfill and your landscape by composting what you would throw away.

MAKING YOUR OWN COMPOST

The best nutrients and amendments to add to your soil are the materials that are taken from your garden, composted, and returned back to it. Therefore, when the builder clears your land, the vegetation, debris, and branches under half an inch thick that get scraped into piles should be allowed to compost for a year and then reincorporated into your site to enrich the existing soil.

You do not want to compost cooked food materials, grease, or diseased plants. Make sure not to compost animal parts (such as meat, bones, skins) because this will attract dogs and wild animals such as raccoons. Even if you want to create a wildlife habitat, these are not the animals you wish to attract.

Air, heat, and moisture are needed for composting, and you can manage these basic requirements to maximize the efficiency of the process. A compost heap can be as simple as a pile in your yard, or it can be a more elaborately constructed bin surrounded by used railroad ties or lumber.

BUILDING A BIN

You can incorporate the basic function of composting into the construction of a container. Build your compost pile with a border of bales of straw stacked like bricks, about four feet high. The straw actually forms a bin for the compost; in a year or two as the bales decay, they will become compost themselves.

For a more permanent compost pile, construct the frame from blocks. Or use any of a variety of manufactured compost bins that are commercially available. These include barrels that can be turned or cubicles to which you can add water to mix with the compost. Many of these manufactured bins come in dark-colored plastic, which absorbs heat, one of the basic requirements for making compost.

Aeration is key to composting. To get great aeration, you can make your container from wire mesh or wooden slats. Design it so that one side of the container is removable, providing easy access to the compost. Don't use a container with solid sides because air circulation is vital to the bacteria that break down plant material.

Depending on your originality and innovation, a composting bin can be an ornamental part of your landscape, if you design it that way. One such idea is a three-sided bin of brick or stone laid against a larger block backing. Build it in a way that will leave many openings in the brick so the compost can breathe. Plant a vine on the wall, but do not use one that will root into the compost through the openings in the brick, such as trumpet creeper (*Campsis radicans*) or English ivy (*Hedera helix*). Or use a dry stacked stone for the walls of the bin. The stone will create an aesthetically pleasing background for a rose garden.

Whichever type you build or purchase, put your compost pile in full sun. This is the best way to encourage the heat that is necessary to make compost.

It's a wise idea to keep two compost piles going so you can put your spring cleanup into one and your fall cleanup into the other. Use the compost that forms from your fall cleanup for spring planting and soil preparation, and the decayed organic material from your spring cleanup should be ready in time for fall planting and mulching your perennials and tender shrubs for winter.

THE RIGHT MIX

The two basic elements of compost that are subject to decay are carbon and nitrogen. Carbon is the energy source for the bacteria and fungi as they do their breaking-down work, and nitrogen is necessary for protein synthesis by the composting organisms. The ratio of carbon to nitrogen in your pile is important and will affect the speed of decomposition. The following suggestions will give you the most efficient breakdown of organic materials, but all organic material will eventually decay, even if your mix isn't quite right.

The ratio of carbon to nitrogen in your compost pile should be approximately twenty-five parts carbon to one part nitrogen, measured by volume, then mixed well. Carbon comes from dry leaves and wood chips; nitrogen from herbaceous and leafy materials and grass clippings. Too little nitrogen will slow the composting process; too much will generate ammonia gas and the unpleasant odors that come with it.

One way to achieve the appropriate chemical ratio for a compost pile is to add twenty-five bags of leaves and one bag of grass clippings. Then all you need is the organisms, which can be added through topsoil. A good way to stimulate the organisms is by throwing a little fertilizer on the pile. Compost accelerators sold at garden centers will provide all the organisms your pile needs in a small convenient package. Since everything you need is there, it can speed up the process. You only need to buy it one time; once the accelerator is in your compost pile, all of the organisms will remain.

> "A composting bin can be an ornamental part of your landscape, if you design it that way."

MAINTAINING THE PILE

As mentioned above, aeration is an important component of composting. As the decomposition process uses up the available oxygen in the pile, you need to provide more. Building the pile on palettes will help provide the airflow you need. Shipping palettes might be available at no charge from many businesses that receive goods by the truckload. Also, turn the compost for aeration. Use a pitchfork, shovel, or a tool that is designed for this purpose, called an aerator. The more frequently you turn, the faster the decomposition.

Moisture is necessary because organic molecules can be utilized or "eaten" by the microorganisms only if they are dissolved in water. Water the pile weekly, particularly during dry periods. The moisture content of the pile should be from 40 to 60 percent. Determine the moisture content of your compost pile by squeezing a handful of the composting material. It should feel like a well-wrung sponge. If it is too wet, turn it or add dry materials such as leaves.

Compost is ready to use when it is black or dark brown, crumbly, and neutral to musty smelling. Under the proper conditions—full sun, air, and moisture—this can take as little as three months in the hot summer and six months in cooler climates or during winter.

▲▲▲

AMENDING THE SOIL

Now that you've recycled your organic wastes, it's time to take the recycling process one step further and use the compost on your landscape. Applying compost is the ideal method of soil fertility adjustment before planting. Compost is probably the most important element you can add to the soil for the health of your plants. Using compost is one of the best things you can do to keep a plant flourishing and healthy and one of the best ways you can revive one that is having problems.

You can never add too much organic material to the soil. It is the toughest element to keep around the roots of plants, and compost is the best way of adding it. Plants will grow in all compost, and they will thrive. Ideally, soil should be at least 20 percent organic material, although that proportion is rarely seen, except on the richest forest floors.

If you are having a problem with a plant, one of the best practices to revive it is to lay a generous amount—two to three inches—of compost over the root system. Another practice for incorporating compost around an already installed plant is called "vertical mulching." Dig holes or trench around the outside branch spread (drip line) of a plant. Fill the holes or trench with compost. Dig deeply, eight to ten inches, into the soil. The deeper you vertically mulch, the better.

When the compost is ready, lay it over the top of your garden like a blanket. It is important that the materials making up the compost have had an opportunity to partially decompose before they are added to the soil. Make sure that decomposition is well underway before applying compost to the garden. The microorganisms that cause decay use a great deal of nitrogen in the first stages of the process, so the addition of fresh organic waste can cause *temporary* nitrogen deficiency in the soil. If you think you applied the compost before it was ready, use a nitrogen-rich fertilizer.

Compost is a panacea for many root rot diseases and drainage problems. Few nutrients are available to plants until their form has been altered by decomposition, and the decomposed material kills many pathogens. Depending on how much your compost heated up, it will kill *Botrytis, Rhizoctonia, Phytophthora, Sclerotinia,* stem rot, bacterial blight, cyst nematodes, southern root-knot nema-

"Compost is a panacea for many root rot diseases and drainage problems."

todes, and others. Digging liberal amounts of compost into the soil around a plant's roots not only applies the compost as fertilizer, but it also improves the aeration if you are working over a sufficiently broad area. As a general rule, when planting, prepare the area at least eight feet square whenever possible.

Another important reason for preparing the soil with compost in as wide an area as possible is that if you dig into poorly drained clay soil and fill the basin with rich compost, you may create a water-holding foundation for the moisture-rich compost, leading to wet feet for the plant. In this situation, a lot of compost is not good and could lead to the decline of the plant.

GREEN COMPOSTING

Another method of composting—used more effectively for large fields rather than the smaller confines of most home landscaping—is called green manuring because the green grasses that are planted for this purpose break down so rapidly into the soil. This method could also be used for your vegetable garden. Grow a cover crop for the purpose of plowing it under as another source of humus (organic material). Quick-growing crops such as winter rye, buckwheat, rye grass, mustard, and rape are good for this purpose. They should be dug into the soil just before they flower. They will prepare the poorest of soils for the richest landscape of designs.

Certain legumes provide another source of compost. Legumes such as soybeans, vetches (a cattle feed crop), cowpeas, and clovers—all feed crops—have nodules in their roots that collect free nitrogen from the air and store it. This nitrogen source can be utilized by plant material if it is plowed under, and this is the best natural source of nitrogen in the soil. If you plant in this manner for a season or two before installing your landscape design, you will reap the rewards for many years.

DISABLED ACCESS DESIGN

11

Issues such as wheelchair access to a garden or landscape enjoyment for the visually impaired have long been topics of interest for families with disabled members. However, it has only been since 1990 and the passage of the Americans with Disabilities Act (ADA) that these concerns have become institutionalized. This act bars discrimination against individuals with disabilities and provides guidelines for making facilities accessible. It presents a challenge to us from a design standpoint and a challenge to professional landscape designers to learn more about this new discipline.

You are not required by law to make your private garden accessible to the disabled, but any area that is open to the public or is paid for in any way by public funds must be accessible. Equal access was always considered a nice idea, but now it's the law. This has provided the new challenge of creating an environment that is user-friendly for people with disabilities yet still aesthetically pleasing. And the federal guidelines can also provide new sensibilities and a new frame of reference for the home landscaper.

DESIGN FOR ACCESSIBILITY

Take time to think about accessibility for the disabled when you are designing and installing your landscape. Look to the future. Think, for example, of Grandfather, who is not getting around very well and may soon need a wheelchair. Think about your own retirement and the possibility that in your later years your mobility may be limited—but you will still want to enjoy your garden. Where appropriate, design ramps, railings, or walks that will help disabled individuals negotiate the landscape.

> "Texture changes, for example, are an excellent cue that an intersection is approaching or you are getting close to the edge of a walk."

DESIGN FOR VISUAL IMPAIRMENT

To help a sight-impaired person to enjoy your garden, install railings thirty to thirty-four inches in height and kickboards or edges about six inches high along paths so that a blind or visually impaired individual can follow the edge with a cane. The maximum height of edges or kickboards is twenty-seven inches.

Texture changes along a path or across grounds can help a visually impaired person find his or her way. Texture changes, for example, are an excellent cue that an intersection is approaching or you are getting close to the edge of a walk. A textural change could be achieved by designing a cobblestone edging with a smooth paver to designate where it is safe for foot and wheelchair traffic, for example. When going from a secondary to a primary walking surface, change from asphalt to concrete with an exposed aggregate finish.

Visual impairment is no obstacle to enjoying fragrance. For optimal enjoyment of your garden area, provide an array of fragrant plants no higher than six feet tall. Herbs, lilacs, hyacinths, spicebushes—these are just a few of the plants that will fill your garden with fragrance. For a more detailed discussion, see chapter 45.

DESIGN FOR WHEELCHAIRS

In designing your landscape for disabled access, a major feature is likely to be ramps for wheelchairs and the width and grade of paths where wheelchairs will be able to traverse. There should be no more than a 2 percent grade in areas where wheelchairs will be loaded and unloaded from cars. The maximum grade on a walking surface for reasonable wheelchair passage is 5 percent. The ADA specifies that a ramp should have a slope of one foot of ramp length for each inch of elevation (one-for-twelve rule), or about 8 percent. However, I prefer a 5 percent grade; that will meet any requirements and make it easier to navigate. To get a complete listing of the requirements and guidelines of the ADA, please call the Department of Justice, which administers the program, at (800) 514-0301.

If ramping is not a possibility because of space limitations, but you need wheelchair access either now or in the future, leave room

Figuring Percentage Grade
Determining percentage grade of a slope or ramp is as simple as determining rise over run.

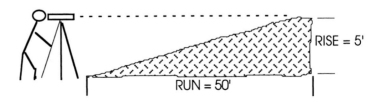

TO DETERMINE PERCENTAGE GRADE PUT RISE OVER RUN AND DIVIDE

in a portion of your construction to accept a lift. The time to think this through is early in the design process. Determine if a lift or elevator is necessary by figuring the percentage grade. If the percent is too high to negotiate the slope, that is when you need it.

The way to determine the percent grade is to divide the rise by the length of the run: % grade = rise ÷ run. For example, if a ramp is fifty feet long and changes grade by five feet, you would figure $5 ÷ 50$, or a 10 percent grade (see illustration). A 10 percent grade is about as steep as you should ever install for wheelchair access and exceeds ADA standards. Some architects have used 12 percent grades for short ramps—a person in a motorized wheelchair would have no trouble with this, nor would someone being pushed, but it might be difficult for a person in a self-propelled wheelchair.

Ramps should have level platforms at top or bottom, at changes of direction, and at doors. They should be a minimum of thirty-six inches wide—but forty-two inches is better. A ramp should have edge protection and handrails on both sides. Handrails should be thirty-four to thirty-eight inches from the ramp surface.

To accommodate wheelchairs, a path must be at least thirty-six inches wide. Gates must have at least a thirty-two-inch opening; a sixty-inch width is needed for a wheelchair to turn around, and passing zones at least sixty inches wide should be placed at reasonable intervals.

Remember that someone in a wheelchair cannot reach down to the ground. Keep this in mind when planting and include plants that can be grasped at wheel level—spicebushes, dwarf fruit trees, rosemary, or many other herbs, for example. Design your garden so that the person in the wheelchair can pinch the herbs, smell the flowers, pull the weeds. A person in a wheelchair can reach from nine inches to about fifty-four inches above ground level. Raised beds are a good option to provide enjoyment of the garden.

DESIGN FOR LIMITED MOBILITY

It is helpful to keep the principles of some of these tips in mind when designing access for areas that may not be used by people in wheelchairs, but by older individuals with a degree of infirmity.

Use a gentle riser height for steps that will be used by anyone with a cane or walker or who has impaired mobility. Never use risers steeper than six inches, as a low riser height is very accommodating to the older person or anyone with reduced mobility. For example, install stepped terraces with low, three-inch steps between lawn areas. This can provide a useful passage to get in and out of the garden and may be more aesthetic than ramping.

Be certain that there are no protruding objects in any pathways that will be used by people with mobility or visual impairments.

Such items could startle or trip them up. Instead, keep structures set back from the pathways, and make sure plants are pruned from the walk.

SOFTENING STRUCTURES

There are a number of ways that you can make the accommodations for disabled access more aesthetic. This can be a big job—we are often talking about a long stretch made of planks or concrete with a railing. It can be aesthetically challenging to change grade with a single ramp without steps. It takes a great deal of innovative thought to design an aesthetically pleasing arrangement without a series of wooden ramps, landings, and more wooden ramps.

If a ramp is already installed, an easy way to soften or screen it is to plant along the ramp. Use a mixed flowering deciduous shrub border to screen and offer a coordination of blooms throughout the growing season. For tighter screening, use needled evergreens, such as yews, or broad-leaf evergreens, such as Japanese hollies. Sequencing plants (a concept discussed in chapter 1) will do a better job of screening or softening the ramp than a single row, which may accentuate it. Consider a mixed flowering border and background shrubs with interesting winter characteristics such as witchhazel (*Hamamelis*) for fall color and winter flowers and winterberry holly (*Ilex verticillata*) for winter berries. Face them with purple coneflowers (*Echinacea*) and black-eyed Susans (*Rudbeckia*) and edge them with verbena and *Liriope*.

If you are putting in a new ramp, consider installing one that uses curves and sweeps rather than straight lines and right angles. Just be sure to keep your curves wide enough so that the wheelchair doesn't have to turn sharply. Or, design and build a ramp from the house with a couple of angles and stages of landings. This can create a nice large planting area wrapped around your entry, with a place for a specimen tree and low, flowering shrubs and perennials. You can also plant an evergreen or flowering deciduous border along the outside of the ramp.

PET AREAS

12

In general, when we speak of pets and the garden, we are talking about dogs. This is in no way meant to be discriminatory toward cats; dogs just spend more time out in the yard than cats do. To be fair, I will offer some tips about cats, as well as some tips for more exotic pets.

DOGS

There is no such thing as a dog-proof plant. The job of a dog-owning gardener is to figure out how to separate the plants from the dog. Generally this means allowing your dog to run in an area that won't impact your plantings. This process is similar to that used to separate humans from plants by providing paths. But dogs are more difficult to train than most people. Train your dog early (as soon as possible) to use a specific area of the yard for its toilet duties.

DESIGNING FOR DOGS

Incorporate your ideas for keeping your dog separated from your plants into your design plan, rather than taking makeshift actions later. This can lead to novel ideas and applications that will be far more attractive than something cobbled together in desperation. Be innovative in separating dogs and the garden. For example, use an ornamental iron or wooden fence to contain the garden or the dog—it can work either way.

Look for other creative ways to separate your dog from your landscaping. It doesn't have to be a fence. Set up your landscape, for

Fences can be an ornamental and efficient way to keep pets in and others out.

DOG PLANTS

If you're a true dog lover, try these dog-influenced plants in your landscape.

Dogwood (*Cornus*)

Dog fennel (*Anthemis tinctoria*)—also called dye fennel

Dogbane (*Apocynum*)—invasive, so beware

Dogmint (*Satureja vulgaris*)

Dog rose (*Rosa canina*)—shrub rose, used as base stock for grafted roses

Dog's tooth violet (*Erythronium dens-canis*)

Dalmatian bellflower (*Campanula portenschlagiana*)

Dalmatian iris (*Iris pallida*)—a variegated form with good foliage through season

Dalmatian laburnum (*Petteria ramentacea*)

Dalmatian toadflax (*Linaria genistifolia* var. *dalmatica*)

example, so that the dog runs in the front and the manicured garden is in the back. Of course, that doesn't mean that you can't take the dog through the garden with you sometimes, but it should not be his regular running space.

The lawn will generally stand up to light dog foot traffic, but a dog running regularly through planting beds or over the grass will probably compact the soil and destroy the garden, just as regular human traffic would. Your dog can run on stones, mulch, gravel, a paved pad, or dirt paths, if you can train it to use those areas. Or, once your pet establishes a path of circulation, follow that and lay in an edging and wood chip path.

Recognize that having a dog may restrict what you can do with your landscape. If your dog likes to run around the edge of a fence—as many dogs do—don't plan on doing any planting around the side of the fence that the dog runs along. Be prepared for higher-than-usual maintenance in all the areas that the dog uses.

LIMITING DOG DAMAGE

When feeding your plants, don't use bone meal as a fertilizer because your dog might eat it. Natural bone meal is crushed bones, which we all know are attractive to dogs. Instead, use a chemical phosphorus. Dogs are less likely to eat or dig up an area where there is no attractant.

An unavoidable part of having a dog is dealing with where they do their business. Try to train your dog not to urinate on the flowerbeds. If it continues, it will eventually destroy the bedding plants and most low perennials. Urine is also harmful to grass. Dog urine, particularly from female dogs, is known to create large patches of dead grass in the lawn. If you are a dog owner, expect that your lawn will require more maintenance than the lawn of someone who does not have a dog. This means more frequent re-seeding. Many a urine spot has been diagnosed as a lawn disease or insect infestation, but it is in reality dog damage, which can be easily repaired. Hose down the dead areas to wash the salts through the soil, then seed and sprinkle regularly until the grass grows. You can also use pregerminated grass patch mixes, which will fill in a spot in the lawn in a couple weeks.

There are landscape design arrangements that might withstand dog traffic. If you prepare the soil well enough and use plants with a tall, leggy habit, such as lilac (in cooler climates) or crapemyrtle (in warmer climates), a dog could certainly run under and around those plants without doing a great deal of damage. Prepare the soil with extra organic material to avoid soil compaction from the dog's trampling and use a wood based mulch that will take the wear and tear of paw prints.

An easy solution has nothing to do with landscaping: Walk your dog off your property. Use park space or city streets, but be thoughtful of where you let them go and clean up after them.

CAT PLANTS

To show how much you love your cat, plant a garden using these "cat plants."

Cat greenbriar (*Smilax glauca*)

Catmint (*Nepeta*)—also called catnip; cats will love this

Cat's whiskers (*Tacca chantrieri*)

Cat's claw (*Macfadyena unguis-cati*)—clawlike tendrils, yellow three- to four-inch flowers

Cattail (*Typha*)

Cat's ear (*Hypocoeris*)—woolly leaves

Cat's ear (*Calochortus coeruleus*)—flowers have hairy petals

Cat's ears (*Antennaria*)

CATS

You can't keep a cat out with a fence—they just climb too well. And you'll be able to tell if your cat (or a neighborhood stray) develops a special feeling in his heart for a certain part of your garden by the strong ammonia smell emanating from those areas.

Prevent a cat from using an area of your garden as a litter box by planting something that would make the cat decide he does not want to be there; for example, cactus. Or apply a scent the cat will not like, such as mothballs or oil-based applications such as Mole-Med and Mole-Away, which are effective in keeping rodents away. This is not an exact science, so try different things until you find what works.

There is another theory that says if the cat wants to play and relax there, it will not use the area as a bathroom. So try planting a bed of catnip (*Nepeta*). Cats are attracted to this hardy perennial herb of the mint family—they eat it, roll in it, and find it highly exciting and attractive.

EXOTIC PETS

Some people may have more unusual pets that they want to be a part of their landscape now and then. There may be the occasional ferret, snake, rabbit, turtle, or other pet that will use the yard at times. This type of recreational use of the property is usually fine; however, it is always best to have an animal in a cage. Many turtles have been lost in the garden. If you don't have a cage, it is a good idea to only put the animal in a fenced area, away from flowerbeds and the vegetable garden. Don't let your pet rabbit roam your vegetable garden if you want to have any lettuce remaining.

ENERGY EFFICIENCY AND PHYSICAL COMFORT

13

A beautiful landscape can do more than provide aesthetic pleasures and sensory delights. A carefully considered landscape design can serve a very practical purpose in making your home more energy efficient and enhancing your physical comfort.

Design your landscape to save energy in both heating and cooling your house and shielding it from winds. There are many different measures you can take that will result in fuel conservation—a benefit to the environment and to your pocketbook.

SUN

Much of your effort will be focused on the sun—providing protection from it in the summer and allowing it to do its warming work in the winter.

If you are building a new home, you can incorporate these considerations when choose a lot or place your house on a lot. In climates where it is necessary to heat in the winter, the ideal setting for a house is halfway up a south or southeastern slope, with the longest walls and roof pitches facing slightly southeast. This allows the maximum exposure to the winter sun's rays.

No matter what the orientation of a home, you should follow the same suggestions for working with the sun. During winter, keep the southeastern, southern, and southwestern sides of the house free of obstacles that will block the sun. Conversely, in the summer you will want to shield your house from the heat of direct sunlight. Conveniently, nature has given us a tool that will serve both the winter and summer purposes: deciduous trees.

Plant large deciduous shade trees on the southern, southwestern, and western sides of your house. Bushy with leaves in the summer

> "Much of your effort will be focused on the sun—providing protection from it in the summer and allowing it to do its warming work in the winter."

and bare in the winter, they will block summer sunshine but allow full penetration in the winter. Don't use evergreens because they will block the winter sun. Do use sturdy oaks, ash, or lindens, which can also prevent wind damage from these exposures. For best effect, plant your trees approximately fifteen to twenty-five feet from the house and fifteen to twenty-five feet apart. Properly placed shade trees can reduce your summer cooling bills by 25 percent or more. If you have outdoor activity areas in your landscape, also plant large deciduous shade trees along their southern, southwestern, and western exposures. This will cool these areas in the summer and provide a canopy for the space.

Deciduous vines can serve a similar purpose as trees and grow more quickly. In as little as five years, some vines, such as trumpet creeper (*Campsis radicans*), five-leaf akebia, or Boston ivy (*Parthenocissus tricuspidata*), will grow large enough to shade a portion of your home. On a brick or masonry house, plant vines so they climb on the southern and eastern walls. For a wood house, train vines on a trellis next to the house walls to prevent the rotting problems caused by vines on wood.

Another thing you can shade to conserve energy is your air-conditioning unit or heat pump. According to the American Association of Nurserymen, shading an air-conditioner can lengthen the life of the compressor by easing the strain on the unit. Plant a flowering tree or shrub near the unit, taking care not to block necessary air circulation. Or build a trellis two to three feet away from the unit and grow a Montana or sweetautumn clematis (*C. montana* or *maximowicziana*).

WIND

Suitable landscaping will also protect your home from harsh winter winds and channel cooling summer breezes. To take advantage of this, track the prevailing winds. Determine where they blow across your property and against the house during the winter months (usually the north and northwest sides), and block them with two or more rows of evergreens. This can reduce fuel consumption by 10 to 35 percent, depending on the height and density of the trees. Evergreen windbreaks will reduce wind velocity for a distance of about ten times the height of the plants, so a continuous hedge ten feet tall and eleven times that in length (110 feet) will provide protection for about one hundred feet behind it.

Dense plantings of evergreen shrubs will also provide insulation against cold air. Evergreen vines on walls or trellises can serve the same purpose. Plant a dense screen of shade-tolerant evergreen shrubs on the north side next to the house. This will provide a dead-air zone adjacent to the external walls of the house, which reduces the infiltration of cold air into the home through doors, windows, and walls.

In many areas, the same hedge that blocks the northwest winter wind can provide a cooling effect in summer by channeling summer winds from the southwest. Check your prevailing winds.

Another important principle to remember is that cold air flows downhill, always seeking its lowest level. Install plant masses, groups of shrubs and trees, so they allow the natural downhill flow of cooler air. Promote air circulation in the summer and prevent the creation of "cold air lakes" near the house in the winter by designing plants along the hills, not across them. Don't trap the air.

IRRIGATION

14

Water is essential to all life, and nothing has a greater impact on plant life. Its effects can be quite dramatic. The addition of water can push up a lawn in a matter of days, and the lack of it can cause plantings to shrivel overnight and keep grass from growing for months.

Providing water is as important as good drainage. While excessive water causes its problems—flooding, erosion, soggy root balls—drought or insufficient irrigation has ruined many more landscapes than an overabundance of water. Irrigation and water-efficient landscaping go hand in hand. Chapter 47, Xeriscape Design, discusses this in greater detail.

Consider your irrigation needs early in your design and installation processes. This is much more efficient than retrofitting after all your plants have been installed—and essential if you are installing underground irrigation.

Proper site preparation with compost can reduce the need for irrigation. (See chapter 4, Site Preparation.) Mulches hold moisture very efficiently—any type will hold the moisture, even sheets of newspaper. This is as important as the actual irrigation. You can facilitate irrigation by leaving a depression around the plant when you install it. Build a low (two-inch-high) wall of soil outside the root zone of the plant so that when it rains or when you irrigate, the plant will water itself more efficiently.

Irrigation can be a boon to establishing and maintaining plants in sandy or clay soils. Water must be added more often to sandier soils because they drain more quickly than most clay soils. Check soil moisture by sticking your finger or other probe, like a screwdriver, into it so you can sense or see the moisture. Soil will feel cool and moist or it will look several shades darker than when dry.

Always be aware of the need for irrigation during dry periods. Water as soon as you sense that the soil is drying and your plants won't know there was a drought. When you use a spray type of irrigation, give plants about an inch of water. Measure this by placing a glass or other measuring device in the area of spray. Run the spray until one inch of water is collected in the glass. This will soak down to a depth of six to ten inches, depending on the soil type. A quick spray does no good at all. Run a slow soaker hose until the soil is watered deeply, seven to ten inches, once a week or more if the temperatures soar.

The other critical period when irrigation is a necessity is during plant establishment. Even if plants are touted as drought-tolerant, they must be watered when they are establishing their feeder roots, during the first several months to a year. The most efficient method of watering is drip irrigation, or you can use soaker hose, sprinklers, or a slow-running hose. Depending on the severity of drought and rapidity of growth, you might have to irrigate for several years. It might take two to three years or more for them to grow enough roots to become self-sufficient in periods of dryness.

There are dozens of variations on two basic methods of irrigation, soaking and spraying. This can range from simple to complex, from laying a slow-running garden hose at the base of a bed and moving it around, to a soaker hose, to a sophisticated underground system with pop-up heads and a timer to turn it on and off.

I recommend the use of drip irrigation in most cases. It is the most efficient soaker system when you need to irrigate. The drip line is plastic hose with small holes along it that release water at a set rate evenly along the entire line. The water saturates the soil

Irrigation systems, such as this in-ground system, protect against plant loss. (© 1997 The Irrigation Association. All rights reserved. Used by permission.)

slowly and thoroughly, and there is virtually no wasted water since it doesn't evaporate into the air or flow away over the soil surface. It can be installed in the soil or just under the mulch.

In-ground systems are the most user-friendly if they are set up properly; make sure you consult with an irrigation specialist. These systems are quite common in the drier areas of the West and Southwest, but they are found everywhere in this country. They can be problematic if they do not receive a high level of maintenance, but they are usually the best-balanced system when working correctly. Unfortunately, when a property changes hands, the schematic of the underground irrigation system usually does not, and the lines will end up cut and chopped by the unknowing new home owner or landscaper. When you install an underground irrigation system, map it and attach it to the plat of your house that will be transferred to any subsequent owners.

When you design an irrigation system, consider the needs of different parts of your property. Shaded areas and those with northern and eastern exposures will require less irrigation than those with full exposure to the sun will. Make sure that systems covering these areas are valved and controlled separately.

Let the character and type of plants help determine the sprinkler heads you will use. For example, for raised planters with low plants adjacent to a front entrance, choose a bubbling or flooding head instead of a spray head that may block the entrance. Lawns are most evenly watered with a spray; trees are best with a drip or slow soaker.

When you water can be as important as how you water. To avoid excess evaporation, try not to water on windy days or at the hottest time of the day. Also, watering on hot, sunny afternoons can burn the plants, as the water beads act as magnifying glasses for the sun's rays. Try to water in the morning so plant foliage will dry by nightfall.

> "Even if plants are touted as drought-tolerant, they must be watered when they are establishing their feeder roots, during the first several months to a year."

Drainage

15

Drainage is one of the most important aspects of any landscape. When the ground doesn't drain properly, you get mud. The only things that grow in mud are bog plants, mold, and algae. Even if you only have a tiny plot of land or a single tree, the area must drain.

There are two different types of drainage necessary for the health of your property—surface drainage and soil percolation.

SURFACE DRAINAGE

Poor surface drainage causes a serious problem experienced by many home owners—water in the basement. This is usually caused by the lack of surface water runoff or runoff in the wrong direction. The first thing to do to troubleshoot the problem of a wet basement is to walk around the house and assess how the water is running. Even if water in the basement is not a problem, check the drainage patterns around your house during a storm to make sure that all water rolls away from the downspouts and walls. An ounce of prevention can save you a gallon of problems.

Don't forget to look behind your plantings. Often the cause of poorly directed runoff is hidden by gardens or shrubs planted close to the side of the house. The source of water leaking into your basement is usually caused by a low spot or a downspout or gutter that doesn't carry the water away from the house, and this may be obscured by a shrub or flower bed.

RECHANNELING WATER

You can correct the problem by rechanneling the water. The best solution is a downhill slope dropping three to six inches per ten-foot run. If a grade slopes down and away from your home and continues slightly downhill to the edge of the property, your basement will stay dry and the area will remain well drained and usable for plantings or picnics. The fill should have a high percentage of clay and a low proportion of rock, sand, or compost. The soil closest to the wall—within approximately two feet—should have as little organic material (e.g. composted leaves, wood chips, straw, etc.) as possible in it. You want the soil to direct water away from the house, not absorb it and percolate it down.

Only build soil up against a masonry wall, and never against siding or wood. If you must drain water away from siding or wood, don't build up the soil. Instead, remove it five to ten feet from the wall of your house, creating a downhill slope from the wall to a swale, a dish-shaped drainage channel. The water that once collected against the wall will flow down through the newly excavated area and off the property.

Once you rechannel the water, be careful not to block the drainage pattern of your property with structures or beds—you could find water in the basement once again.

PATIOS AND SIDEWALKS

I once got a call from a home owner who had designed and installed his own patio and hadn't given careful thought to drainage. It turned out that his patio was blocking the natural flow of rainwater and the dam created by the patio's raised edge turned his backyard into a rice paddy. Eventually the water made its way into his basement.

Don't overlook the need for surface drainage when you work on your landscape. Homemade patios, walks, and mounded beds can cut off existing grades, and puddling can render these areas useless most of the year. When you install paving, always maintain a drainage pattern on your property that moves water from your structures to your property lines.

A common error is laying walks or patios perfectly level. A level surface will hold water and promote growth of fungus and algae. Install walks or patios so they drain. Paved surfaces should drop one to two inches over ten feet. This is less than a 1 percent grade, and it will still appear level to the eye and foot.

ASK AN EXPERT

Some water problems—such as those caused by underground springs, high water tables, or creeks that have been piped underground—are beyond your control and may require correction with subsurface pipes and/or sump pumps.

Consult with your county soil conservation office for unbiased information and help in mapping out a plan. Or you can hire a civil engineer who is trained in drainage matters (see the section Hiring the Professional in chapter 2). Contractors might recommend expensive solutions such as excavation, buying a sump pump, waterproof paint, or a sophisticated underground drainage system. The soil expert or consultant has nothing to gain from your investment and is trained in hydrology, the science that deals with the occurrence, circulation, distribution, and properties of the waters of the earth.

SOIL PERCOLATION

Poor drainage around plants can mean a lack of soil percolation, when water doesn't drain quickly enough from the plant's root zone. This is often referred to as wet feet.

To determine if you have a problem with standing water for planting, dig a hole, fill it with water, and see how long it takes to drain. The exact length of time depends upon the size of the hole, but the water must drain within an hour or two. I've dug holes, filled them, and had water standing twenty-four hours later. In sandy soils, you will find water flowing through as fast as you add it. Then there is every degree up to water-impermeable clay.

Don't plant in hard, undrained soil. Even if you add nutrients and compost, after the first good rain your plants could be floating

A plant community effectively sets off a home. This is more attractive than a single plant would have been in the same cultivated area.

in this watertight basin if you don't improve the drainage over a wider area.

To encourage air and water circulation in previously undrained soil, cultivate as widely and deeply as possible (eight to fourteen inches or more) using this soil recipe:

- Spread two to three inches of compost over the soil surface. Organic material is critical to plant health, and it helps trees, shrubs, and flowers planted anywhere, but especially in poorly drained sites.
- Spread eighty pounds of gypsum per thousand square feet over the compost.
- Dig deeply and thoroughly—as the British say, double dig (two spade depths).

If the area is too large or the soil too hard to dig with a shovel, use a rototiller (a power tool for digging) to break up the soil. If you don't own a rototiller, you can rent one from an equipment rental company.

When tilling a large area in an effort to help water percolate, the entire area becomes a desirable root zone. So you may want to expand your thinking. Even though you might initially have been thinking of putting only one plant in that area, a community or group of plants would lend itself well to the larger space that you should be cultivating.

SCREENING AND NOISE ABATEMENT

16

Screening is one of the most common things people ask for in a landscape design. Screening provides privacy, or at least the illusion of privacy. There are many things you might want to screen: your neighbor's house, a utility area on your property, a highway—especially the noise that comes with it.

SCREENING FOR PRIVACY

There are a number of different ways to screen and to incorporate screening into your landscape. Your screening choices are rather simple—use strategically located hedges, groupings of low-branching trees and shrubs, or fences and other structures. The selection of fence, shrubs, trees, or other plantings that you use for screening will depend on the purpose of the screen. Where a pool may require a fence for safety and protection, a backyard recreation area would be better shielded with tall evergreens. Trees with low canopies will work best against elevated sitting areas such as decks and balconies.

LIVING SCREENS

Hedges and Borders
A hedge is a growing fence and could provide better screening than a wooden structure, with more longevity. If you want to use your hedge for screening, don't shear it into a box or gumdrop shape. Let it grow naturally, and renewal prune it every several years (see Pruning and Training, chapter 49). For a list of shrubs to use for an effective screen, see appendices H, Deciduous Shrubs/Hedges, and L, Evergreen Shrubs/Hedges.

Classic Deciduous Shrub Border

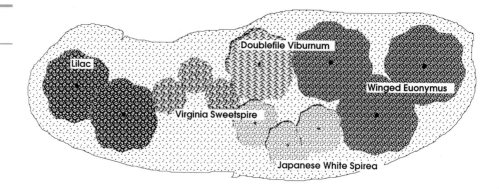

You may want to be subtle; screen things without being obvious about it. I call this "guerrilla screening." If you can make the aesthetics as important as the practicality of screening, you will be ahead of the game.

Create a strong screen with a double wall of plants by bordering a tall background hedge with shorter flowering plants. If the planting is mixed woody plants, this arrangement is called a shrub border, or it could be referred to as a perennial border if the low, flowering plants are perennials. Either one will appear to have been planted there for flowering value as much as for screening.

An option that never goes out of style is the deciduous shrub border. This classic planting style of the 1940s and 1950s consists of a mix of flowering deciduous shrubs that will flower throughout the year.

Or, you can try a border that is also valuable in the kitchen—an herb and berry border. Plant an herb garden with tall shrubs and a few dwarf fruit trees as a background. A grouping of highbush blueberries and one of raspberries with some masses of tall and low herbs mixed in will make a tasty attractive screen with an alluring scent.

Another attractive option is island screens. Plant islands of shrubs—some tall, some lower. Add trees to create a parklike setting. An island might consist of a tree, three to five shrubs, and a grouping of tall, dependable, flowering perennials completely surrounded by lawn. If your shrubs are strategically located, you will get screening value without really noticing that this is the purpose the shrubs are serving.

One thing to remember about using shrubs: Slow and steady wins the race. Be patient. Shrubs do not grow in a day. Therefore, an effective planted screen cannot be achieved overnight, or even in a single growing season.

As they grow over the years, you should be thinking of evolving uses for your screening shrubs. Today's accent shrub or small tree can grow into a screen. When you feel that a shrub may be getting too large, rather than hacking it back, think of how you can take advantage of its size and screening ability. For example, think of a

> "If your shrubs are strategically located, you will get screening value without really noticing that this is the purpose the shrubs are serving."

walkway disappearing behind the shrub into a secret garden. Or plant in front of it with new low flowering shrubs and use the already mature plant as a background.

Trees

Trees, particularly large trees, are one of the most effective elements to use for screening. Consider, for example, the deck that you build eight feet off the ground. You want to screen your deck, but most hedges will not grow that big in a decade. A tree, on the other hand, will reach that height in several years.

Plant a tree to screen that high deck. Even deciduous trees will work because their crown is located at the point where you want your privacy, and they are in leaf during the seasons you are most likely to be using your deck and need the screening.

Take advantage of the other values of the tree you plant for screening. For magnificent fall color, for example, plant a red maple, sugar maple, or dogwood. Use a flowering tree for beauty in the spring, summer foliage, and winter berries. (See appendix I, Deciduous Specimen Trees.)

CONSTRUCTED SCREENS

Fences best made for screening are those with boards that are overlapping or one tight against another. They serve as good screening elements, but they have their limitations. Producing strong enclosure,

This wooden fence on a stone wall provides excellent screening. (© 1997 Walpole Woodworkers. All rights reserved. Used by permission.)

they would be used when you want complete separation between you and an adjoining feature. Many jurisdictions have codes against fences taller than six or eight feet, so they will not screen elements larger than that. One of those taller elements might be the second story of your neighbor's home or a high-rise apartment. You can find more information about fences in chapter 27.

Constructed elements of your landscape can also be used as screening. A shed used for storage can double as screening. An ornamental shed can conceal from your view something that clashes with your landscape or is an eyesore to you. Place a cottage storage shed around your cottage garden, for example, in the line of sight that will shield your neighbor's blue-and-red plastic gym set. See chapter 22, Storage, for more on sheds.

SCREENING NOISE

Think of driving down the highway in your car, and the surge of noise that assaults your ears when you crack open the window just a fraction of an inch. It doesn't take much space for noise to get in, and this illustrates the difficulty of screening your landscape from undesired sounds.

However, this does not mean that you are powerless. As increasing urbanization—and particularly vehicular traffic—has elevated the amount of noise in our environment, the field of noise abatement engineering has grown rapidly. Look at any highway with adjacent residential neighborhoods, and you will see sound walls erected to protect the ears of residents from the highway cacophony. While most of us have to depend on the government to erect these tall, dense barriers, there are smaller steps you can take to abate the noise that reaches your property.

PLANTINGS

Use a mix of plants to absorb and deflect sound waves. How well plants control noise depends on intensity, frequency, and direction of the sound and the location, height, width, and density of the planting. As with the example of allowing noise in by opening the car window a crack, any space in mixed plantings will also allow a lot of sound through. Mixed broadleaf plantings at least twenty-five feet thick and conifer plantings from fifty to one hundred feet thick can give you up to a ten-decibel drop in noise level. This isn't a practical width for most home landscapes, but narrower barriers can give psychological screening—the noise won't seem as loud since you can't see the source.

The mix of plants is important since different types of vegetation reduce noises of different frequencies. For year-round noise reduction, plant a mix of evergreens such as arborvitaes, spruces, pines, and firs mixed with broadleaf evergreens such as viburnums, Southern magnolias, rhododendrons, and mountain-laurels. To be effective sound barriers, all of these trees must have foliage that reaches to the ground. For a good mix, plant an area at least twenty-five feet wide.

Some deciduous plants are also effective for noise abatement, but only when foliage is present. Like evergreens, these must also have foliage from the ground up to really do the job. Thickets of sassafras and pawpaw have been found to be relatively effective for this purpose.

When trying to screen noise, include your lawn or use another groundcover in the shady areas. Turfgrass or other low vegetation has a muffling effect on sound, compared to surface areas of bare soil or paving, which are more likely to bounce sounds off their surfaces.

BERMS

The most effective measure you can take against noise depends less on the actual plantings and more on what you plant them on. Establish a soil berm for your plantings. This is the best way to reduce noise. These large mounds of soil are effective themselves in cutting down on noise. When thickly planted, as described above, this effect is greatly enhanced and they do a very good job of shielding sounds. Make your berm as high as possible—at least eight feet tall and twenty feet wide—and as long as your property line, if it is practical. A well-planted solid berm can cut auto and truck noise 70 to 80 percent and substantially reduce sound from playgrounds or sporting activities.

FENCES

A fence, if it is tall enough and dense enough, can also shield noise—like the barriers you see along the highway. If you can't get the Department of Transportation to do the job, get as close as you can to that type of barrier. It must be solid, with no spaces to let sound through. A tongue-in-groove style of wooden fence constructed of unfinished two-by-ten-inch lumber built as tall as local ordinances allow would serve this purpose. A decorative hedge on either side of the fence would further screen noise, muffling what makes it through the fencing.

SLOPE ENHANCEMENT

17

Some people look at slopes as an impediment to functional landscape design, something to work around. I suggest a different attitude. A slope can add a fair amount of interest to your property, and the nature of the slope alone can give a dimension to your property that a level site would not. Look, then, for ways to enhance your slope and add to the interest of your landscape.

ORNAMENTAL DESIGN

Consider installing a rock garden, a natural treatment for a slope. Plant alpine plants, which naturally occur on mountainsides. These plants are often dwarf specimens because trees don't get very large in these areas. Low firs and other conifers like the cool dry air of the elevations. Heaths and heather are also good rock garden plantings.

If you do not want to go with a full rock garden, try placing several large rock outcroppings, which will add an interesting sculptural element and natural mountainous look to the terrain. When you do this treatment to your slopes, add the same look elsewhere on your property, but just several well-placed stones, not a rock-strewn look, like you might use with a rock garden.

Another option is to cover a slope with several conifers—it's a way to get interest on different levels with the same plant. Plant, for example, a group of spruces together. Install some up and some down the slope. Planting at different levels and using the slope for elevation will give you a very interesting effect—and the slope itself plus the tall evergreens on it will provide a tremendous amount of screening. With a planting of trees, such as conifers, on the slope, you should also plant a groundcover or a low mass of shrubbery if you want to hold the slope against erosion. The trees will anchor it

Crimson pygmy and golden threadleaf falsecypress offer year-round interest to this slope.

deeply against movement, but some low cover on the earth's mantle keeps topsoil from washing away better than any other treatment. See chapter 37 for more about groundcovers.

Slopes lend themselves well to a tapestry of plants, mixed perennials and woodies. The incline sets them off as a lovely picture, a tableau, showing them off to their best advantage. This tapestry of plants will grow together and require less maintenance than a rock garden.

For an interesting mixed planting on a large sun-facing slope, plant a mass of crimson pygmy barberries and three golden threadleaf falsecypress for color. The contrast of the red and gold on the slope will be striking. Add a Japanese maple (*Acer palmatum*) or several hophornbeams (*Ostrya virginiana*) and an evergreen flowering groundcover to tie it together, like periwinkle (*Vinca minor*) or willowleaf cotoneaster (*C. salicifolius* 'Repandens'). The cotoneaster is a nice plum color in the winter and has semi-evergreen foliage.

For a shade-facing slope, try massing hellebore for evergreen and winter flower. Add a grouping of Japanese sedge (*Carex morrowii* 'Aurea Variegata'), and some *Leucothoë* 'Rainbow', a low growing evergreen of the heath family with small white bell-shaped flowers in the spring and colorful variegated foliage all year long. Edge the lower part of the slope with hosta. Narrow-leaved plantain lily (*Hosta lancifolia*) is a good choice because it is slug resistant and is a vigorous grower that leafs out early in the spring.

You do not need to cover the slope with trees or other plantings. Consider the importance of a slope for its recreational value. Use it

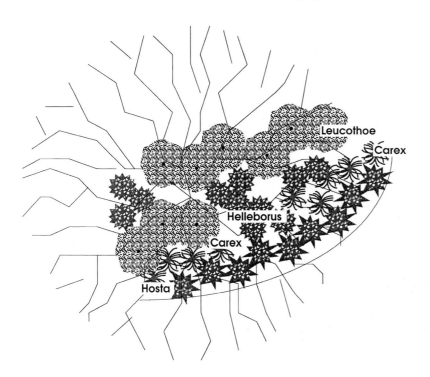

for rolling down or for sledding—skiing might even be a possibility. In all of these situations, find a tough plant that likes compaction and the challenge of constantly having to renew itself. I suggest keeping the area in lawn in preparation for that snowy day when a sturdy piece of cardboard will turn the slope into a winter playground. And, for obvious reasons, don't plant obstacles such as trees and shrubs or place ornamental rocks on the hill in this situation.

No matter how you choose to plant it, you'll want to keep your slope as low maintenance as possible. For lowest maintenance, don't mow it unless you are planning to use it for recreation, and don't mix many different plants. Put in a groundcover meant to mass together as a monoculture to achieve the lowest maintenance. The most popular groundcovers are English ivy, pachysandra, and periwinkle, and any one of these will work in protected areas of sun or shady locations. In full sun, try low-growing groundcovers such as juniper, particularly the very prostrate, blue-foliaged blue rug juniper (*Juniperus horizontalis* 'Blue Rug') or the salt-tolerant blue-green foliage of the shore juniper (*J. conferta*). See chapter 37 for more about groundcovers.

Another common treatment for a slope is a retaining wall. A retaining wall gives a slope a look of stability. The most attractive retaining wall for blending into a residential landscape should be lower than four feet. It would be better yet if the slope were gradual enough to use walls that are two feet or less. A tiered or stepped arrangement in three or four areas will serve to level parts of the

hill, similar to terracing. Low tiers are aesthetically pleasing, and they will still add a tremendous amount of stability to the slope. Chapter 27, Fences and Walls, covers in detail how to install retaining walls.

If you'll be working with slopes, either landscaping or just maintaining them, here are a few suggestions:

- Don't mow more than a 30 percent grade (a three-foot rise over ten-foot run).
- Slopes over a 12 percent grade should have steps if you walk them regularly.
- Retain slopes with walls no higher than four feet.
- Good retaining wall material that doesn't require a footing is pressure-treated six-by-six-inch wooden ties or dry laid rock (without mortar). Preformed concrete retaining wall blocks that stack together and lock in place without mortar are sold at building supply centers.

EROSION CONTROL

One of the most important issues involved with slopes is erosion control. Soil erosion is primarily caused by raindrop splash, the impact of rain hitting the soil. Erosion can be a serious problem, especially in areas where man disrupts the soil, which means much of our modern urbanized and suburbanized world. Studies show that up to twenty-five times as much soil is lost in suburban areas than in forest areas. Most suburban erosion occurs during the building stages.

Erosion washes away the richest part of your soil, topsoil that could have been retained with proper erosion prevention techniques. And that's not all. Besides the wearing away of your topsoil, a major problem caused by erosion is that it deposits sediments in the streams. What is good for the soil, unfortunately, is bad for the stream, and the nitrogen-rich sediment poisons the natural wildlife of the stream. Nitrogen increases the growth of algae and undesirable water plants.

Planted low green spaces are the best hedge against erosion. Plants reduce the impact of rain on the soil. You want to keep the water from hitting the soil at a point very close to the ground. Therefore, something covering the ground at a low height provides that protection, as opposed to a tree or even a shrub. Low green plantings filter particles, consume carbon dioxide, hold the soil that might wash away with their roots, and generally support the ecosystem of the area. A plant density that leaves two-inch bare spots between plants is an adequate protection against erosion. Have no more than two-inch bare spots between leaf surfaces when plants are mature. Grass is the most widely used vegetation for erosion control.

Rock is another method of erosion control. Rip rap is rock laid onto the side of a slope to hold it into place and is very effective in reducing fast surface runoff. Rip rap should be used with landscape fabric underneath, between the rock and the soil. The fabric holds moisture and allows it to penetrate the soil, and it prevents the rocks from sinking into the ground.

Retaining the soil while you establish your groundcover plantings can be a challenge, especially during periods of heavy or frequent rain. Mulch acts as a hedge against erosion while you are establishing your groundcover. Shredded bark not only holds moisture and keeps weeds down, but also protects the roots of the plants. On a slope, mulch also serves to hold the soil in place as the groundcover is established. On a real problem slope with deep-cutting water, use netting materials and heavy-duty straw mats that will decay as the plant material establishes itself. Erosion control blankets are more popular in large commercial situations, but netting, which should be available at your local garden center, is a good idea for planting your slope.

Perhaps the best method of erosion control is to divert the water before it ever hits the slope. Divert flowing water by trenching along the top of the hill and channeling the water so that it flows away before it ever goes over the edge. Or pipe the water beyond the slope entirely.

"Erosion washes away the richest part of your soil, topsoil that could have been retained with proper erosion prevention techniques."

If you are involved in a project that will keep the soil cleared for any length of time, such as putting in a driveway, shed, or working on any other construction project, you may want to consider a sediment control fence. This is a woven fabric on stakes that cordons off an area so that it will catch eroded sediment as it flows against the fabric. These fences are available at your building supply store. Any construction project—for example, a new home development where the area has been cleared and will be for some time, particularly on a slope—should have sediment control fences.

SHADE

18

While we may think of the sun as a necessary accompaniment to most growing things in our landscapes, some great gardens are made in the shade. Woodland gardens, in particular, feature many shade-loving plants and are gaining in popularity.

A shady site is defined as an area that receives less than five hours of direct sunlight per day, or never receives any more than dappled light. If you choose the right plants, you can grow the mature shade trees that you want on your property and still complement them with a variety of other plantings. And unless you are willing to clear-cut your property, you will need to work with areas of shade around your home.

The best way to design for the shade is to think like nature. In nature, shade-tolerant plants are brought in by birds and wind, and they keep trying to grow until they find just the right placement. Then they establish in random groupings where they are happiest. As humans in nature, we take the paths of least resistance and walk in and around the trees, shrubs, and undergrowth. Our foot traffic creates meandering woodland paths. Sometimes a creek is part of the picture, and the path can follow the stream, since water, like people, also takes the path of least resistance.

To recreate this natural woodland garden on your property, locate plants in groupings. Place several mountain-laurels here, a witchhazel and a few spicebushes there, a rhododendron grove at the property line, ferns along the creek, and trilliums and Jack-in-the-pulpits to naturalize through the woods. Let the leaves lay and play around with other shade-tolerant perennials, bulbs, and grasses to see what will do well and what needs to be moved elsewhere. For example, we made the mistake of planting bergenia and Japanese painted ferns in too much shade on our property, so my

This columbine blooms well in the shade of this woodland garden.

wife moved them into an extra hour or two of sunlight. Within months, they became robust and full, signaling satisfaction in their new site. Pay attention to plants' needs and accommodate them for a successful woodland garden.

Look to the future and create the perfect canopy for a woodland garden by planting shade trees—American and European beech, katsuratree, October glory maple, red sunset maple, scarlet oak, and red oak are all good choices for shade trees. Prepare the site deeply, and the roots will stay down in their zone where they belong so that the trees can be under-planted with shrubs and perennials.

Proper attention to your shade trees is an important part of achieving beautiful gardens in the shade. Prior to planting new plants, walk through the shady area with a pruning saw. Prune lower limbs on the mature trees so they are at least eight feet above the ground. Prune them back to within three-quarters of an inch of the main trunk or an intersecting branch. This will give enough clearance so that you can determine where to place the lower plantings. Elevating lower limbs also lets in more sun, and even shade-tolerant plants need some light to photosynthesize.

Don't expect fruits, vegetables, or herbs to thrive in the shade. While some varieties may survive, it is unlikely that they will flourish, flower, and be productive. So don't include edibles in your plans for planting in the shade.

You can keep a lawn green and growing in partial shade (at least four to five hours of sun), but it will require special attention. This

After trimming low-hanging branches from established trees, placing newer plantings is an easy task.

may mean aerating, top-dressing, fertilizing, and reseeding every spring and fall. See chapter 38 for more details.

SHADE-TOLERANT PLANTS

Use the suggestions below to familiarize yourself with some shade-tolerant plants that are grown on the ground plane (one to two feet tall), the vertical plane (four to ten feet tall), or the overhead plane (fifteen to twenty feet tall). Always check your zone against the plant's hardiness (see USDA Hardiness Zone Map on page 24).

GROUND PLANE

- Barrenwort (*Epimedium*)—The early pink or yellow flowers and fall leaf color are attractive features of this disease-free, versatile, long-lived perennial. Several species are available, and you can't go wrong with any of them. This is a plant that, once established, is happy in shade, sun, moisture, and drought. Zones 4 through 8.
- Big blue lily-turf (*Liriope muscari*)—This is a tough plant that does well in sun or shade. It forms a tight clump, stays green in winter, and has lavender, grape hyacinth–looking flowers in summer. Zones 5 through 10.

- Christmas or Lenten rose (*Helleborus*)—This European hellebore has large leaves and stays green year-round. Blooming from February to April, the whitish purple flowers will show through late-winter snow. Zones 3 through 10.
- Hardy begonia (*Begonia grandis*)—Establish this pink, late-summer and fall bloomer in the fall. Its reddish green foliage emerges from the ground in spring, and the new leaves are shaped like angel wings. Zones 6 through 10.
- Plantain lily (*Hosta*)—Also get this early-leafing plant in the ground in the fall for a head start on spring. There are hundreds of varieties to chose from. Two hosta species I like are gold variegated 'Montana' and fragrant-flowered 'Honeybells' with its light green leaves and fragrant white flowers. Zones 3 through 9.
- Silver variegated Japanese sedge (*Carex morrowii*)—This variety presents silver-edged foliage, which colors a woodland garden throughout the growing season. Zones 5 through 9.

VERTICAL PLANE

- Bugbane (*Cimicifuga*)—The white flowers of this herb, named for its tendency to repel insects, will brighten a shady site in summer, and it is a good companion when installed with ground plane plants in front of it. Zones 3 through 9.
- Dwarf winged euonymus (*Euonymus alatus* 'Compacta')—This is an excellent low-maintenance shrub that is nicknamed "burning bush" for its almost fire-engine red fall leaves. Zones 4 through 8.
- Fothergilla (*Fothergilla*)—Here is another dependable shrub with fragrant flowers and showy yellow/red fall foliage. It is a nice complement to azaleas and rhododendrons. Zones 4 through 8.
- Japanese yellow waxbells (*Kiringeshoma palmata*)—This perennial grows four feet high, and its large maple-shaped leaves lend a shrublike appearance. Several waxbells planted together can define a sitting area, and planting them in a grouping gives the yellow nodding flowers more impact when they bloom in late summer. Zones 5 through 9.
- Chinese witchhazel (*Hamamelis mollis*)—Depending on how you prune it, this plant could qualify as a shrub or a tree. The yellow fragrant flower that opens in late winter is an ex-

citing sneak preview of spring. Fall leaf color is an outstanding orange-red. Zones 5 through 8.

OVERHEAD PLANE

- American redbud (*Cercis canadensis*)—This native American member of the pea family has small budlike pink flowers in March and April. An interesting characteristic of this tree is that it flowers profusely through its bark as well as at the branch tips. Plant in the fall for spring blooms. Zones 4 through 9.
- Kousa dogwood (*Cornus kousa*)—This plant offers year-round interest. It has wide, white, long-lasting flowers in spring, large red edible fruits in summer, a lacy bark, and deep red fall foliage. It is extremely disease resistant. Zones 5 through 8.
- Japanese maple (*Acer palmatum*)—There are numerous varieties of this small, graceful tree, but I recommend the species Japanese maple because it is typically less expensive and serves the purpose in shade as well as hybrids, which can cost many hundreds of dollars. The species foliage may not be as full, colorful, or interesting as cultivated hybrids that are planted in full sun, but it will still grow into a handsome specimen. Zones 5 through 8.

Snowdrops naturalize and will provide bright spots in the early spring landscape. (© 1997 Brent Heath, Brent & Becky's Bulbs. All rights reserved. Used by permission.)

SPRING BULBS

Use early-blooming spring bulbs for your woodland garden. Some of my favorites are crocus, glory-of-the-snow (*Chionodoxa*), winter aconite (*Eranthis*), and snowdrop (*Galanthus*). These are varieties that will naturalize, which means they will come back year after year. They flower early enough to make food for next year's bulb crop just as the trees overhead leaf out.

Plant spring-flowering bulbs in the fall, about three times as deep as the size of the bulb. Plant them in groups of at least six to ten of all the same type. Do not mix varieties. For more details about bulb planting, see chapter 39.

Seating

19

Take a seat and enjoy the pleasures of your garden. Anything can serve as a seat in a garden or around your landscape—a rock, a wall, a planter, or a tree stump. Plan ahead in your design for double duty so that some of these decorative and functional elements will also serve as a comfortable place to sit down.

A comfortable seating height for most adults is from seventeen to twenty inches. This guideline applies to wherever you are sitting—on a chair, a wall, a rock, or even a dock where you want to sit and dangle your feet. A comfortable depth for a seat is a bit more flexible—from twelve to twenty-four inches.

This ornate iron bench surrounds this tree, combining to become a focal point of the garden. (Ladew Topiary Gardens, Monkton, Maryland)

AESTHETIC SEATING

While seating is a very functional element of landscape design, don't overlook its aesthetic features. Seating can be much more than chairs and benches in the landscape. Make seating the sculptural element of your design. Place a bench along a bed of flowering shrubs on the edge of a patio or in a grove of small trees. A well-placed, nicely designed bench can sometimes create the aesthetic of the garden, so match the seating style to the style of other elements in the garden. For example, use an informal rustic bench on a wood chip path through the woods tucked into some shrubbery, or a wooden picnic table and chairs on a flagstone patio and barbecue area, but in a formal space with balanced fountains, you would use a stone or wrought-iron table and bench.

Another aesthetic purpose seating can serve is to screen a view you want to avoid. Design your seating so that the area to be screened is behind you, screened just by the implication of the positioning of the seat. To further enhance the screening, place a trellis behind it. Lattice with small openings will serve to block views without the need for a vine. Add a planted element in the form of a wisteria or trumpet creeper (*Campsis radicans*) if you have a sturdy support and at least six to seven hours of sun, or plant an annual vine that will grow on a lighter trellis. If given enough sunlight, hy-

This rustic bench is at home along a wooded path. (Brookside Gardens, Wheaton, Maryland)

The enchanted forest look to this stone table-and-chair set blends the brick together with the surrounding plantings. (Ladew Topiary Gardens, Monkton, Maryland)

acinth bean (*Dolichos lablab*), morning glory (*Ipomoea*), or Dutch-man's pipe (*Aristolochia*) can be trained on any type of support, even chicken wire.

Meadows are lovely places in which to have a seat and relax. Tuck a bench into the taller flowers, such as cosmos or *Cleome*, both

A lattice screen provides a high degree of privacy.

annuals that will seed themselves and come back every year. Mow a walking path through the wildflowers to this sitting area. Plan it so that your seat commands a view across your meadow, off into distant hills or some other pleasant vista. Benches built of wood, stone, iron, or concrete would all be possible to use in a space such as this.

A seating element can be used to give a sense of place in your garden. Set a curved stone bench on a couple of carved supports to provide an ingredient of excitement for someone to discover as he or she is winding around a curve in the walkway. An ornamental stone bench can turn a well-beaten path into a garden walk and make you feel like you belong there. Place seats at intersecting lines to encourage people to linger. Or place a bench or couple of chairs in a separate seating area off the path. This seat gives you a destination in your garden.

If you have installed a water garden or a fountain, put seating near the water feature, on the patio or adjacent to the patio, where you can sit and possibly get a cool spray from the water. The bench can fit the water by matching the concrete or stone of the feature, or it could be constructed with fish, water plants, or a likeness of the Greek water god Neptune molded right into its design.

For a more subtle effect, place your seating by a fragrant plant. Make it a special place to go. For example, site a bench next to a fragrant, spiked *Elaeagnus pungens.* You can't see its flower because the insignificant tiny white blooms are hidden under its semi-evergreen leaves, but in October and November, when you least expect it, the floral fragrance completely drenches the area. In the

Garden Seating   A sitting area tucked in off the path makes your garden a destination to enjoy, not just to pass through.

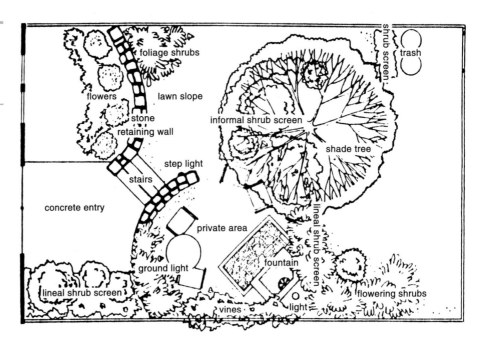

spring, a Koreanspice viburnum (*Viburnum carlesii*) or lilac (*Syringa*) will provide the same fragrant effect, as will roses in June.

TYPES OF SEATING

There are many different types of seats that you can buy for your landscape, from a flimsy folding chair to an ornate stone bench. Try to keep your seating congruous with the tone of your garden, and don't cheapen the surroundings with inferior seating. Place your seats in a way that will provide maximum enjoyment and provide incentive to get maximum pleasure from your deck, patio, or garden.

BUILT-IN DECK SEATING

If you are building or refurbishing a deck, incorporate into your railing the framing for permanent seating on your deck. Lay planks at a height of seventeen to twenty inches, using the railing for the back of the seat. If you're going to use a cushion, make sure you take that into account in calculating the height of the seat, which will be raised by the cushion. In other words, if the cushion is three inches thick, the planks for the seat should be fourteen to seventeen inches from the deck floor. To further increase the utility of your built-in bench on the deck, put doors under the seat and use the space for storage.

Recliners

You can place a recliner on your patio or deck. There are a variety of garden recliners available today constructed of many different materials, including various woods, metals, fabrics, recycled plastics, and many of them are very nice products. The places to find these would be garden centers, specialty furniture stores, and home improvement centers. Many mail-order companies specialize in fine-quality garden furnishings and other landscape amenities. Some of these are Country Casual, (800) 284-8325; Heritage Casual Furniture, (888) 639-6406; Smith & Hawken, (800) 981-9888; and Walpole Woodworkers, (800) 343-6948.

Adirondack Chairs

Use Adirondack chairs on a porch with a vista, in a rustic setting, or along a pond or lake. The Adirondack is a large, high-backed, slatted, wooden chair that you can lose yourself in. This is not a chair that you want to jump in and out of, but one you can relax in—an easy chair for the outdoors.

Stone Chairs

When you are placing heavy stone chairs, be sure you know where you want them. These chairs, sometimes more ornamental than practical, can weigh seventy-five pounds or more and are not easily moved around. However, they are a wonderful sculptural addition to the landscape and can turn a private, enclosed area into a sitting garden.

Colonial Benches

Place a colonial bench against the wall in a kitchen garden. A simple wooden bench such as this or a squared-off, ladder-backed chair will give the garden character and give you a place to sit among your herbs or to ready supplies for planting.

Patio Furniture and Lawn Chairs

You can find quality garden furniture for a patio, deck, or screened-in porch. The same stores and catalogs that offer chaise lounges usually offer patio sets. These range from steel to wrought-iron to cast aluminum, which is very nice since it will not rust. Tables are available with solid metal, wire mesh, or glass tops, and chairs can have fabric seats and backs or cushions.

Folding lawn chairs are not the most attractive form of seating, but they serve the important function of adding seating on the deck or patio for a family get-together or for extra company. They don't have to make a fashion statement since they are often used temporarily. Some are made to fold; others are molded from plastic and stack for easy storage. You can get lawn chairs in a variety of styles and materials, many of which are made well and are very attractive. They can be made of nylon, canvas, or plastic webbing with tubular aluminum, wooden, and plastic frames. Some even come with pillows.

HAMMOCKS

Nothing quite says summer like a hammock. Lash it between two trees for the classic picture of summer laziness. Or tie it to a free-standing frame so you can move it around from patio to perennial garden, for the maximum in design flexibility.

SWINGS AND GLIDERS

Swings and gliders are a part of Americana and can fit in almost any setting. Use a swing for seating on your porch. The swing, which needs a place to hang from, is fairly stationary, unless you want to build a portable frame so that you can also use your swing on the patio. A swing in a tree will have the same effect for adult and child—it will reach out and say, "Come on and try me!" Make sure the rope is strong and well secured to a strong living branch.

Be creative with the placement of a glider. A glider is a portable self-contained unit, and it can provide attractive, comfortable seating throughout your landscape, not just on the front porch. Place it in a flowerbed or tuck it into some azaleas or under a Japanese maple, somewhere that will invite you to sit down and glide. The feeling can be mesmerizing.

LIGHTING

20

Lighting the outside of your property is a necessity. You need to light the walkways and doorways for safety. You will most likely use the outdoors in the evenings or at night to relax and enjoy the wonders of nature. And you may even consider security lamps that will keep your home and family from harm.

You don't have to spend big bucks or have a degree in electrical engineering to install lighting. Low-voltage (twelve-volt) landscape lighting can be inexpensive and safe to put in by yourself. And what a wonder of difference this lighting can make to your overall design. Use lighting to change the mood of your garden. You can make your property look like a Victorian garden by lighting many objects, a carnival using strings of lights, an island paradise with torches, a romantic getaway with a full moon by washing the area with lights from above, or any other treatment you might want to achieve.

LIGHTING TECHNIQUES

In recent years, landscape lighting has developed into a discipline in its own right, borrowing many of the principles of theatrical stage lighting and adapting them to the outdoors. There are several different functions of lighting your landscape, and they are achieved using different techniques. There are three basic ways to light a plant or an object: front-lighting, backlighting, and side-lighting, and you can use variations of these techniques.

FRONT-LIGHTING

Use front-lighting so you can see the color, the foliage, and the flower of a planting. If you are planting a shrub with colorful leaves and flowers, such as forest pansy redbud (*Cercis canadensis* 'Forest

Front-light to see the colors of the plant and foliage. (© 1997 Bruce LaPierre. All rights reserved. Used by permission.)

Pansy'), front-lighting will show off the deep pink flowers in early spring and maroon foliage throughout the growing season.

Up-lighting, a form of front-lighting, is a dramatic way to highlight your plantings or other aspects of your landscape. Use either surface or direct buried fixtures mounted in the ground and aimed upward to illuminate trees, walls, sculpture, facades, etc. It mimics the only other natural light that comes from the ground, which is fire.

Up-lighting can create a wonderland year-round, and especially in winter. (© 1997 Bruce LaPierre. All rights reserved. Used by permission.)

BACKLIGHTING

Backlight an object to display its silhouetted form. This is a good way to accent trees, shrubs, or statues with interesting shapes, such as weeping or contorted plants or a contemporary sculptural form. It is especially effective with a wall or building facade for a background that will reflect the light off the wall. Place a fixture between the focal point and the wall, and illuminate the wall to frame and outline the shape of the object.

Backlighting this sculpture makes it fill the wall, creating dramatic impact. (© 1997 Bruce LaPierre. All rights reserved. Used by permission.)

SIDE-LIGHTING

Use side-lighting to cast shadows and create interest and influence the mood of your garden. With this type of lighting, you can make the shadow of a small plant fill an entire wall or cast the shadow of a tree across the expanse of a lawn. This can cause an eerie effect or an effect comparable to moonlight if you aim the light down through the tree and onto the ground. Side-lighting along a wall, or facade lighting, also adds an element of security to your garden, since you'll more easily detect movement on your property with a swath of light brushing across it. Changing the intensity of the light and the distance from the object will change the size of the shadow.

Use another lighting technique called "grazing" to bring out the interesting texture or contours of a stone wall, brick facade, tree bark, or other surface. For the grazing effect, position a fixture just a few inches from the surface to be illuminated and shine it along the wall or over a low planting. The shadows are cast by the textural changes in a wall or bed of groundcover.

SPOTLIGHTING

Spotlighting is an effective way to highlight a particularly interesting element in your landscape. Shine a spotlight on a piece of sculpture, a tree with an intriguing shape, a trellis, or an entranceway. Or use smaller fixtures to feature an individual planting. Be selective with spotlighting, highlighting only a few dramatic points in your landscape.

DOWN-LIGHTING

With down-lighting, you can illuminate paths, driveways, stairs, slopes, and other elements of your landscape by placing your fixtures high in trees and casting light down through the branches. This form of lighting, which simulates moonlight, is very natural looking and not only lights paths and stairs for safer walking, but also lends a romantic feeling to the garden.

PATH LIGHTING

Path lighting is another method of lighting your walkways, patios, and plant beds. These fixtures—generally low wattage, less than three feet high, and available in a number of shapes, styles, colors, and sizes—come in two types. In a "spread" path light, the bulb is hidden under the top of the fixture so that it acts as down-lighting. With a "glow" path light, the bulb is housed in a globe or glass-sided fixture, throwing light in a full circle. The spread light will be less likely to shine in your eyes, but the glow path light is more likely to light steps and walks with fewer fixtures.

A pitfall of path lighting is overdoing it and installing too many lights too close together. The light only needs to illuminate the walk. Use restraint—you don't want your garden to look like an airport runway. You can alternate them from side to side or place them

LIGHTING FIXTURES AND THEIR FUNCTION*

Now that we've discussed the principles of lighting design, let's put those principles into action. There are numerous low-voltage lighting fixtures from which to choose in this relatively new develpoment, which dates from the late 1950s.

Type	Function
Cylinder, box, and bullet-shaped	These designs help focus and direct the light beams. Some also cut off glare and protect the lamp and socket from debris and moisture.
Spread and diffused	These low-level units are designed to cast illumination in a broader pattern for flowerbeds, perimeter plantings, driveways, steps, and paths.
In-ground and well	Burying these fixtures flush with the ground conceals the light source. Use for up-lighting trees and shrubs and for grazing textured walls.
Spot and accent	Versatile and adjustable fixtures used for lighting, cross-lighting, accenting, and grazing. When mounted high up, they provide focused down-lighting and moonlighting.
Wall bracket, ceiling close-up, and chain-hung lantern	Mounted at entry doors, garage doors, and on porches, these stylish units cast direct or diffused light outward.
Bollard and post lights	These standing fixtures light pathways, steps, garden walks, and deck and pool areas. They also provide attractive light patterns for driveways.
Swimming pool and fountain lights	Installed in sides and at ends of swimming pools and bottoms of fountains. Wet niche fixtures can be removed for lamp changes, while dry niche fixtures require access to the back of the pool shell. Colored lighting is popular for these fixtures.
Timers, transformers, and other accessories	Automatic timers, photocells that turn lights on at dusk and off at dawn, or motion sensors that turn on when movement is detected make landscape lighting convenient and energy efficient.

*Reprinted with permission from the American Lighting Association.

These lights are recessed into riser light treads for safety and to keep glare out of your eyes. (© 1997 Bruce LaPierre. All rights reserved. Used by permission.)

all on one side. Plan it out first and decide which requires less maintenance and looks better in your design.

Decks can be lit in several ways. Light your deck and steps with an even, soft glow and avoid hot spotlights or glare. A number of specialty lights are on the market for lighting decks and steps for safety and nighttime use. Recessed lights flush mounted into stairs

Lighting placed under handrails add a touch of class to a deck and light a pathway without glare. (© 1997 Bruce LaPierre. All rights reserved. Used by permission.)

or walls will provide a safe, soft illumination. Or mount fixtures under the handrails of your deck to provide light with no visible fixtures. Disk lights are relatively new. These are a series of lights that are surface-mounted on the railing support posts and wash a deck with soft light.

LIGHTING WATER FEATURES

An area of illumination that employs a different set of techniques is lighting water features on your property. You can do this with underwater fixtures, overhead light, or low-level side-lighting. Your pond, fountain, pool, or any other water feature can be enhanced with appropriate lighting.

To up-light focal points in the water, use freestanding underwater fixtures with an adjustable yoke for aiming. This will give you the flexibility to move it around if you change the focal point or need to make minor adjustments to the beam.

Use underwater glow lights to illuminate the water itself. Be careful, though—if your water is murky, it will look dirty through these lights. But glow lights can provide a very attractive effect, especially on moving water that appears to ripple with dancing lights.

Lighting above the water can also be impressive. For a moonlit effect on your water, illuminate from above with fixtures in trees and structures. Lights above the lower tree branches will cast shadows of the lower branches on the water. You can use path lighting to illuminate the top of the water and the plants and sculpture around its edge. The fixture should be tied in so that it's light on the feature or path is all that you see. Or for a dramatic effect in lighting water features, use mirror lighting, which will reflect surrounding plantings or structures into the water. Achieve this effect by up-lighting the object on the opposite side of a dark pool or pond, and the image will be mirrored across the water to the viewer.

Water lighting entails another set of safety considerations. Mixing electricity and water can be dangerous, so be sure to only use approved equipment and keep these safety tips in mind.

- Low voltage (twelve volts) is the safest power source in illuminating water. Always use a ground fault circuit interrupter (GFCI) receptacle when combining water and electricity.
- Don't put free-standing underwater lights in areas where people swim. Only install lighting that is recessed into pool walls for swimming areas.
- Don't use copper underwater lights in fish ponds because the copper sulfate corrosion will kill the fish.

- @ Make your wire connection outside of the actual water whenever possible.
- @ Protect your fixtures by placing grills or grates over them so that debris or traffic does not damage them.

SECURITY

For a more practical purpose, use lighting to provide security and/or safety to your property. Put the brighter lighting on separate switches so the security lights don't washout the aesthetic value of your landscape lighting. The more functional lighting might involve different techniques and will probably operate on a 110-volt line, not the low 12 volts of the garden lighting that you're installing as much for aesthetics as safety. See the following chapter for more on security.

PLACE CAREFULLY

Go into your yard—in the dark—and move the lights to your satisfaction to create the effects you're seeking. Become a master of your own lighting design and create a tapestry on your property, balancing light and dark areas. Light a walkway and a tree, for example, but let a shed disappear into the darkness. Walk around your property looking at the design from every angle to make sure that you like the scene you have created; move the fixtures around until you do. Look for creative ways to generate different lighting effects—hang lights in trees or shine lights along walls.

Also, make sure that the lights don't shine in your eyes. While you're playing around with the lights, that is the time to ensure that you keep down on the glare in your garden. There are fixtures made with shields or covers that keep the beam aimed in the right place. They should illuminate the plants, not you.

Pay attention not only where the light shines, but also where you place the lights themselves. Keeping fixtures out of the grass is one of the best pieces of advice you can follow. Invariably, they will be hit and cut during routine tasks. Always try to put them into beds to blend with the plantings and to be as unobtrusive as possible.

Finally, while you are lighting for the security, safety, and artistic enhancement of your landscape, remember that what is aesthetically pleasing to you may just be an annoyance to your neighbor. When installing and aiming fixtures, make sure that the light will not flow over onto your neighbor's property. Some jurisdictions are developing codes to enforce this concept, but be a good neighbor and do it without being told.

SECURITY AND SAFETY

21

We live in an era when security is as much a practical concern for our landscapes as where we plant the vegetable garden. There are techniques we can use so that our landscapes enhance the security of our homes, and you don't have to sacrifice beautiful gardens to do this. Happily, security and aesthetics can work hand in hand.

THORNY THICKETS

Achieve security with a classical method that has been used through the ages—plant a thorny thicket of shrubs to create an impenetrable hedge. Use a thorny thicket for a barrier or for security at the edge of your property or in a dark corner when you may have occasion to walk at night to take the trash out. Keep it pruned low for clear visibility. It's doubtful that someone would be lying in it. Plants serving this purpose well include hardy orange (*Poncirus trifoliata*) and barberry (*Berberis julianae*), which will always hurt an intruder. But be careful: They can also draw blood from whoever prunes them. Rotunda Chinese hollies (*Ilex cornuta* 'Rotunda') have a similar effect—you won't find someone hiding in one.

Consider the growth patterns of the plant as you design your thicket. A single row of hardy orange might suffice where you might need a double row of barberry to achieve the same degree of impenetrability because the barberry has more flexible branches. Check the growth habit of the plants you use for your thicket in case you have to prune them. The rotunda Chinese hollies should not need pruning, but if necessary, they, as well as all others, will perform better if they are selectively pruned, which means cutting about one-third of the oldest wood out of the plant and leaving the low younger growth (see chapter 49, Pruning and Training). Always wear thick gloves to trim these plants.

The orange berries on thorny pyracantha grab your attention in fall.

Remember, also, that a thorny plant is by its very nature a trash and leaf catcher. The best rake to use for leaf cleanup is a wire one. Make sure that you wear gloves if you reach in to pull out a piece of paper or a cup that is being held captive in the thorns.

Get double duty from your security thicket with its aesthetic value. Birds are attracted to the berries on the barberry and flit through the leafless hedge in the winter. The hardy orange takes on a twisted thorny characteristic when it loses its leaves, giving it a very interesting winter habit. Likewise, the red berries in the holly are very attractive in winter. Pyracantha is another attractive choice for a thorny shrub, with its bright red-orange berries.

WALLS

Consider security issues when you erect walls in your landscape. Security may dictate where you put them and how high they are. For a secure area, you would need complete enclosure and eight-foot walls. To minimize the possibility of a section of wall or fence concealing an intruder, use see-through fencing, such as lattice or pickets, or walls with an open pattern. Be sure to check local ordinances about fence height and construction.

Make sure your gate latch is lockable. This can be with a padlock, a deadbolt, or be innovative and discover other possibilities.

I've seen latches that were like puzzles that needed to have a bar slid and a pin pulled or some other configuration. If there is a dog on the inside of the fence, no stranger will stay around to figure out your latch. As a general rule, homes with dogs are often passed over by burglars.

LIGHTING

Tie garden security into landscape design with lighting for security. Lighting can be used for aesthetic purposes (see previous chapter), but also to keep your home and property safe from burglars and vandals. You can set up your existing light fixtures with motion sensors to turn lights on when movement is detected, timers to turn on and off lights at preset times to give the appearance that the residence is occupied, or photocells to go on at dusk and off at dawn. Most home-improvement and lighting stores sell decorative lights with these security features built right into the fixtures, concealing the sensors for a more attractive appearance. You can also use supplemental security lighting, which affords an occupant a complete view of the grounds after dark. These high-wattage (five-hundred-watt) floodlights will have no aesthetic value and should be turned off except when needed for security purposes.

PROTECTING PLANTS

Sometimes security must be addressed to protecting not the humans in the landscape, but the plants themselves. Unfortunately, in some urban areas, plantings sometimes have a way of disappearing. There are preventive measures to address plant vandals.

To keep newly installed plants from being stolen, tie them to each other, locking several together with a network of cables and a padlock and stakes set into the ground. I have seen this in a public garden in Greenwich Village in New York City. In spite of an ornate eight-foot iron fence with points on top and a padlocked gate, plants were stolen immediately after installation. The cabling and staking has stopped this.

Protect your garden with steel, iron, or barbed-wire fencing. While barbed wire is a bit drastic, if you have a rustic, split rail, Old West look to your property, it might fit. Iron can be quite ornate. There is nothing ornamental about chain-link fence, although it is an affordable, see-through product that works quite well to secure an area.

OTHER MEASURES

Don't plant shrubs that grow up to cover your windows. This creates the opportunity for an intruder to get into the window without being seen. It's a misconception that covering your windows from the outside keeps others from seeing in. In fact, you create a security risk for yourself because you cannot see out.

The use of shrubs, especially large masses, is often not wise where there might be potential problems with people hiding in them. For example, in urban parks it's necessary for civil authorities to monitor activities to ensure the safety and protection of those using the park. While shrubs provide privacy, they also have the potential to provide a screen for criminal activity. Move shrubs from areas where you believe criminals could hide, such as in dark corners or near doorways. Or use thorny shrubs, as discussed at the beginning of this chapter, which will keep people from hiding in them.

SAFETY

Besides security, there are personal safety issues you should be aware of in your landscape.

Fireproof your mulch if there is any chance that someone will thoughtlessly toss a glowing cigarette butt into it. Good, aged, moist mulch will not ignite from a lit cigarette, but dry, neglected, poorly prepared tanbark or shredded wood will catch on fire. I saw it happen to an apartment complex in beds adjacent to their swimming pool. Thoughtless patrons would throw lit cigarettes over the wall onto the mulch. A lot of birches, dwarf winged euonymus, and junipers burned before the fire department extinguished the blaze. In these days of smoke-free indoor atmospheres, smokers will congregate outdoors, so be sure to fireproof mulch in high-traffic areas with fireproofing chemicals that are available through companies listed in the Yellow Pages under "Fire Protection." Theatrical supply stores are also a source for fireproofing agents.

Illuminate the walking surfaces for safety. Texture is also important on walking surfaces so the pathway will provide traction, even when wet. Concrete should have a broom finish for traction; brick and flagstone should have a rough finish. Be careful when you seal your asphalt driveway that the material will penetrate the driveway and not lay on top, causing a slick surface. Most commercially produced concrete pavers are made with a rough enough finish for good traction.

Where your path or driveway reaches a thoroughfare, plan for visibility. Don't place large shrubs or a tall wall in the line of vision where you must see pedestrians on a sidewalk or oncoming vehicles. Try to keep a clear line of vision for several hundred feet in each direction from the end of your driveway and sidewalk.

Any water feature on your property demands attention to safety issues. Remember that a person can drown in a small amount of water and that children are particularly attracted to water. Make sure you locate your pond or swimming pool in a place where people are not likely to stumble into it or where people can wander by when you are not home. It may be necessary to install a fence, depending on your pool's location and local ordinances. Water safety is discussed in greater detail in chapter 33, Swimming Pools and Water Gardens.

> "Fireproof your mulch if there is any chance that someone will thoughtlessly toss a glowing cigarette butt into it."

STORAGE

22

Storage is a necessity that most of us never seem to have enough of. We need to store tools, landscape maintenance and recreational equipment, lawn and garden supplies, and almost any other item that might need protection from the elements and be kept out of view. The classic storage facilities are the woodshed to keep firewood dry and the carriage house for buggies. The twenty-first century versions are the backyard shed and the garage for the car.

If you look ahead as you plan your landscape, you will find many ways to anticipate your storage needs. Consider them when you design your patio and garden. Then you can install storage areas as an integral part of your landscape.

CONCEALED STORAGE

If you already have an area that you wish to avoid or screen, such as your trash can area or air conditioner, this is a natural place to locate your other storage if possible. If you plan ahead, you could use the storage unit to screen the utility and service area.

Include some camouflaged storage areas in your plantings. Mass large shrubs or small trees around a storage container, and it can be tucked away and out of sight but very accessible for gardening tools or other outdoor utensils.

Use a mature tree trunk or evergreen shrub to screen a storage rack. I designed this for a client once by attaching tool holders onto a section of fence behind a very mature tree trunk. Hooks were attached to the fence to hold a variety of tools, and the thirty-six-inch diameter tree trunk screened the tools from easy view. You can use different kinds of hooks or large galvanized nails on the fence to hold tools.

Fence as Storage   Hooks and hangers on this fence are screened by a mature tree.

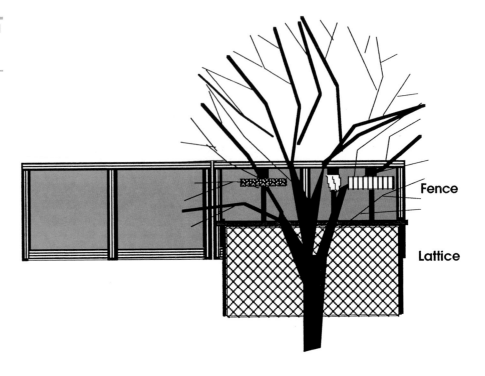

Fence

Lattice

SHEDS

Work a storage shed into your landscape as an ornamental feature. Build a shed to look like a cottage, a playhouse, a rustic log shed—whatever fits with your design. Or use your ornate storage building to create spatial enclosure, to separate a rear garden from a front garden, or to define a small space. Put a small sitting area and some flowers around the shed to tie it into your landscape design. If your storage shed is a pleasing-looking structure, a building looking like a spring house, for example, locate it at the rear of the garden. It could be planted with shrubs and perennials and serve as a focal point that you can see from other parts of your landscape.

Or use a shed for triple duty: for storage and to screen and shade your air-conditioning unit or heat pump. This will block the view of these units, plus you will save money on utility bills by blocking the sun's rays—shading your heat pump can save you up to 3 percent on your utility bills.

Prefabricated storage sheds range in size from four-by-six feet to twelve-by-twelve feet, and even larger. These utilitarian structures are usually not very attractive, so to minimize their intrusion upon the beauty and serenity of your garden you will usually want to hide them in some way. Set the prefab shed, also called a tool house, off in a service area that you might also use for a doghouse,

Hiding a Prefab Shed   An unattractive prefab shed can be hidden in a utilitarian area, with the right amount of plants and a little creativity.

Shelving on a deck can add useful storage and display space.

gas grill, firewood, compost pile, or other utilitarian purposes. Screen the area with a row of evergreens or a border of mixed flowering plants.

DECK STORAGE

Decks are one of the most popular additions to a landscape, and you can take advantage of unused space and have your deck double as storage space. Build cabinets under the benches of your deck. Place your storage under a bench or padded outdoor hassock. Build shelves as part of your lattice screening to create even more surface area for display or storage.

Take advantage of the wasted space under low decks. This is an excellent spot for storage. Put finish work around the outer edge to block the sight of the storage area. Doors can be fashioned that look like exterior wooden siding, or you can use a heavy-duty pressure-treated lattice, with small openings, mounted in a frame.

OTHER STORAGE

There are other utilitarian features in your landscape that can provide storage space. A potting shed can have a cabinet underneath, or a covered outdoor bar for entertaining can have storage on top and on the bottom.

Some storage ideas have evolved out of the necessities of life, particularly farm life, and can still serve a practical purpose. Use underground cold storage to hold winter vegetables such as potatoes and turnips. This can be in the form of a basement room or an underground stone or wood structure that has historic as well as utilitarian value, giving a rural or small-town style.

Sometimes living plants need storage. You may have some material that you didn't get around to installing. To store plants over a season, heel them in. This means putting the plants in a shady location, throwing mulch around their bases, and keeping them moist. Most plants that are fully hardy will overwinter well that way. You can also create a shelter for the plants by stapling burlap to two-by-two-inch stakes tall enough to shield the plants from prevailing winds.

Utility and Service Areas

23

As a rule, utility and service areas are generally separated in some way from the landscape. Think, for example, of an estate garden design, where service areas are approached by using a separate driveway than the one that serves the home. While you may not have an estate garden and two driveways, you will find that your landscape is more comfortable if you locate utilitarian structures away from your garden as much as possible. Don't try to hide all of the utilitarian aspects of your landscape with shrubbery, but place them where they will be out of the way, tucked into corners, not intruding into the garden.

Locating Utilities and Utility Lines

Locating utilities is one of the first steps in preliminary design work. Look ahead and design your utility areas before you even begin to build your house. Conceptualize the entire plan. You don't want to stick your air conditioner or heat pump in the spot that would be perfect for your patio and outdoor eating area. And show these utility lines on a piece of paper that should be filed for posterity with your tax plat and other records.

Pay attention to the location of all the underground utility lines on your property whenever you undertake any project involving digging the soil. This includes building a wall, putting in a patio, even planting. Sometimes you can disturb more soil putting in a shrub than putting in a patio. Once I was putting in a shrub and didn't bother to locate utility lines because it was only one shrub and I didn't think I would do any damage. I ended up cutting a bundle of phone lines that supplied service for several homes in the neighborhood.

Before you start any project involving any subsurface excavation, find the number for the utility locating service in your area and call them. Nearly every region in the country has a free service, such as Miss Utility in the Baltimore/Washington, D.C., area. Many jurisdictions have laws requiring notification of the utility-locating service before any digging is begun. Once you have notified the locating service, they will contact any utility companies that have underground lines in your area and the utility company will work with you to ensure that your digging doesn't disturb the lines. For a referral to a utility locating service in your area, contact North American One Call Referral System, (888) 258-0808.

SCREENING UTILITIES

A utility box on the side of a house is something that most home owners must deal with, especially as more and more electric and gas meters are being located outside the home for ease of meter reading. If you are building your own home, locate the utility box in a location where it will be easy to screen with some sort of planting, such as a large evergreen shrub. Mount it on a completely out-of-the-way wall of the house. Design gardens and recreational areas on other parts of the property.

If you are landscaping to screen utilities, consider techniques that mask the area without calling attention to it. Often a hedge can accentuate what it was planted to hide if it perfectly outlines the object.

CLOTHESLINES

There are other utilitarian structures around your home that require some consideration from a landscaping point of view. For example, clotheslines were once a staple of the American landscape. Many people still want their laundry air-dried, but clotheslines are now perceived as unsightly and even banned in some areas by neighborhood covenants.

Install a tube in the ground, where you can insert a pop-up umbrella-type clothesline. Or use free-standing drying racks. They can be found as antiques, which can actually enhance a 1930s, heirloom-style garden. With either method, you can hang your clothes on laundry day, then fold up the line and put it away. Or use a retractable clothesline that you can pull from a starting point across your yard to an anchor where you can attach it, perhaps between two trees. When the clothes are dry, put the line away. You can also hang your clothes indoors. Whatever arrangement you decide on for a clothesline, keep it away from the ornamental part of your garden and in a designated service area.

A clothesline designed into a garden space.

DRIVEWAYS AND PARKING

Parking is a utilitarian feature that has become a given in the American landscape. It can be very difficult and takes innovative thinking to work parking into a landscape in a way that is aesthetically pleasing, but here are some tips that will help. (For more detailed information about driveways, see chapter 32.)

When possible, expand the driveway into a utility area, because you want to keep both of them out of view from your more ornamental garden spaces. But if your driveway comes from the street to the front or back or your house or into a carport or garage, as most driveways do, it may be difficult to separate it from the landscape. Consider installing a curved driveway to break up the harsh expanse of paving. If your property is sloped, with the house banked into the hillside, bring your driveway down the hill out of view of the front of the house and to an entry at the basement level. Put your parking area here and screen it from the rear garden area.

Parking cars on the grass is unsightly as well as bad for the lawn. Avoid this whenever possible. However, there is a variety of materials you can use to provide parking areas and still grow grass. One such product is open-cell pavers such as Grass Rings and Grassy Pavers. They are made of concrete or heavy-duty plastic and consist of a honeycomb-like structure capable of bearing considerable weight. The honeycomb is filled in with soil that you can grow

Sloped Driveway   By taking the driveway down a slope and to a garage below the house, the parking area and garage itself are screened from the front, allowing for a more attractive front yard.

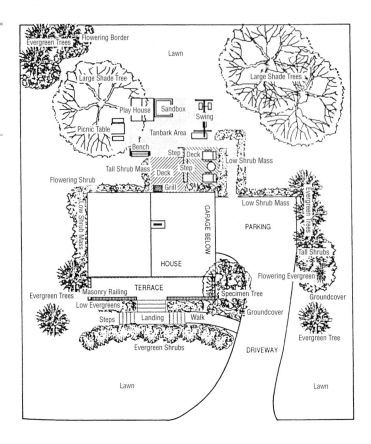

grass in, and the structure prevents a vehicle from compacting the soil. They are useful for establishing and maintaining turf in areas of high foot traffic or other difficult growing situations.

GARAGES

Another challenge for the landscape designer is the garage. One of my clients is a car collector and needed an eight-car garage. That can be tough to fit into any design, but if you consider it from the inception, you can make it work. While you might not need an eight-car garage, you probably need to consider multiple vehicles, since surveys show that the average American family today has 2.3 cars.

If you are building your home, include the garage in your original landscape design, just as you should do with all utility features. Try to keep it from facing front or dominating the front of the house. Design the garage so that it fits the landscape and the style of your house. Provide a way to comfortably go between the house and the cars, especially when carrying groceries or moving other items in and out.

For an existing garage that does not add architecturally to the landscape of your home, install trees and shrubs to set it apart from your front door or to screen it as much as possible.

PETS

As discussed in chapter 12, pets and plants usually don't mix and there is no such thing as dog-proof plants. It's all right to stroll through the garden with your dog, but it becomes a problem when you give your pet the run of a garden space everyday. As much as possible, incorporate your pet's needs into your utility area. You can upgrade a pet area aesthetically by turning the well-beaten path where the dogs run along a fence into a mulched path. Plant shrubs and perennials that will screen the path, such as crimson pygmy barberries (*Berberis thunbergii*), blue princess hollies (*Ilex* x *meserveae*) and black-eyed Susans (*Rudbeckia*).

FIREWOOD

While few of us use firewood exclusively for heating these days, many homes have fireplaces and woodstoves for supplemental heat, and the firewood supply is another utilitarian concern that must be considered in the landscape.

Stack your firewood; don't leave it in a heap in the yard. A stacked pile not only looks nicer, but it seasons better, keeps the bottom layer from rotting, and allows for air circulation between the logs, keeping them dry. Leave your wood uncovered during the summer so moisture is not trapped within. However, during the months that you are burning firewood, you will want to keep a portion covered so that you have a supply untouched by rain or snow. A covered lean-to or shed is another excellent way to keep firewood dry.

You can use firewood for spatial definition. A nicely stacked firewood pile can divide the rear and front garden, or a shed or clothesline from a sitting area, for example, and provide a rustic touch to the landscape.

POTTING TABLES

A potting table is another utilitarian object that can be unsightly, but with a little thought can have a more positive impact on your landscape. You need the potting table to store your tools, and you need a hose to reach it to supply water. Beyond that, use a little imagination. Use a contemporary potting shed, backed by a trellis or open louvered slats on the backing, rather than just a table, bucket and hose, for example, and use your potting table as a wet bar during social occasions.

Compost Areas

Finally, with the increasing popularity and environmental good sense of composting, a compost site is a given for your utility area. It you have a logical place for your compost area, build the service area around this. From a design standpoint, it would be difficult to do anything but screen the composting area. For more information about composting, see chapter 10.

The Constructed Landscape

THE CONSTRUCTED LANDSCAPE

24

When you think of beautiful gardens, you think of stately trees and lovely flowers and lush shrubbery—what landscape professionals call softscape. But equally important to the success of your landscape is the other half of the equation—the hardscape.

The landscape is 50 percent hardscape and 50 percent softscape. The hardscape is the constructed part of your garden, and you can't have a garden without it. A plant won't survive if a person repeatedly walks on it, much less if it is exposed to vehicular traffic. Plants need friability, the aeration and drainage necessary for growing things to flourish. Hardscape provides the complementary alternative so that people can enjoy the garden without destroying it. It solves the problem of people and plants being mutually exclusive.

Hardscape should be an inclusive concept that encompasses your driveway, patio, flagstone path, swimming pool, gazebo, and even dirt footpaths. Through the years, I have worked with many home owners who were not convinced of its importance in the garden, but felt that something was missing from their landscape. If you think something is missing, it could be a functional path, a comfortable sitting area, or a piece of sculpture, which can create a focal point and appeal for a garden.

The aesthetics of the hardscape, more than any other feature, play into the basic philosophy of landscape architecture and design—to create objects that are both functional and aesthetically pleasing. As you design and live in your landscape, these should be ongoing considerations and a back-and-forth relationship. Is it functional? Does it look good? Here's a sweeping path, but does it get me to my door?

Hardscape is also the part of your landscape where you are most likely to incur liability, as I have learned in my years in the field. Concern over public health, safety, and welfare comes from items like overhead structures that are not supported properly, decks not attached to houses properly, walking surfaces that are too smooth and slippery for traction, walkway grades that are too steep—the list goes on and on. This is why many states and other jurisdictions are requiring that building contractors be licensed and the industry maintains strict codes and guidelines for construction.

The following chapters will guide you through the different types of structures that comprise the hardscape, from trellises to sculptures to driveways.

SHELTERS

25

Shelters in the landscape allow us to live closer to plants and enjoy them in their natural setting. Dating back to the caveman, shelter is one of the most basic human needs—to get in out of the rain or the sun or the wind.

Planning and placing shelters is an important part of landscape design and helps determine the relationship you will have with your garden. You have a broad spectrum of choices when it comes to choosing them, and they can be built in myriad sizes, shapes, colors, and materials. Essentially, any structure in the garden with beams or a roof is a shelter. In this chapter, I will describe an assortment of shelters and suggest ways they can enhance your landscape.

Before you plan and construct a shelter, get to know a little bit about the varieties that are available. Each has a name, such as arbor, belvedere, bower, casino, gazebo, loggia, pergola, portico, shade trellis, or screened-in porch, but there is considerable overlap in terminology, so make sure you use pictures or models to guide your choice.

Get ideas for your shelter by looking at public gardens in your area. Sometimes you can scale down designs from large public gardens to suit your residential space. Check your local library for books on the subject of garden shelters and look in magazines. *Architectural Digest, Country Living Gardener, Fine Gardening,* and the *Better Homes and Gardens'* publication *Garden, Deck & Landscape Planner* will have articles and display ads illustrating a variety of garden structures.

Hiring a licensed architect or landscape architect is an option if you wish to have a custom-designed structure. The professional you hire should provide you with a ready-to-build drawing of your concept. Check your Yellow Pages under the listing "Building Contractors" for other builders.

TYPES OF SHELTERS

You can build a shelter yourself, hire a professional, or buy a prefabricated structure that will be brought in on a truck. Kits are also available to build garden shelters.

PREFABRICATED

Some national firms that supply prefabricated structures (but by no means a definitive list) are Amish Country Gazebos, (800) 700-1777; Dalton Pavilions, (800) 532-5866; Leisure Woods Inc., (888) 442-9326; and Vixen Hill Manufacturing Company, (800) 423-2766. To find prefab structures locally, check your Yellow Pages and call garden centers, home improvement contractors, outdoor furniture suppliers, and companies listed under sheds and building materials suppliers. Establishments will have shelters built on site or pictures in brochures.

Now let's look at some of the variety of shelters available and how they might fit into your landscape.

COVERED SHELTERS AND BELVEDERES

If you are interested in a shelter with a solid roof, build a belvedere, a gazebo, a loggia, or a portico. These are open-sided structures with a solid roof for protection against the elements. A belvedere is the name

A covered pavillion is one of many variations on the covered garden structure. (Anderson Pavillion at Brookside Gardens, Wheaton, Maryland)

given to any garden structure that commands a beautiful view. For a getaway, consider a gazebo. Developed for English gardens, the word *gazebo* is derived from a combination of English and Latin meaning "I shall gaze," and gazebos are designed to be retreats with a view.

PROMENADES

If you have a courtyard, install a loggia. A loggia is a covered open area overlooking a courtyard and is generally attached to a house. A portico is similar and is simply a covered promenade. It was popularly used around pools in the Moorish gardens of Spain and was decorated with mosaic tiles, carved pillars, fountains, and formal rows of shrubs.

ENCLOSED SHELTERS

Use an enclosed garden shelter to serve as a summerhouse or guest dwelling. These include bowers, casinos, or screened-in porches. You might consider attaching it to the house if you will be entertaining guests there.

Use a bower in a woodland garden or other natural setting. A bower is a rustic structure often covered with branches and vines twined together.

For a formal garden setting, a casino might be appropriate. The casino was introduced in Italian landscape design as a formal entry onto an estate, usually a level down from the main house. Traditionally, it is sculpturally very ornate and usually low and colonnaded, with a flat roof. From the casino, which doubled as guest quarters, the visitor could enter the garden.

In the American-style garden, a more suitable shelter might be a screened-in porch. A screened-in porch makes eating and relaxing outside both practical and enjoyable.

PERGOLAS AND OTHER OPEN-ROOF STRUCTURES

The pergola is a formal structure, generally with three walls and pillars for support along an open front. A pergola is an open-roof shelter that is good for training a woody vine around. Pergolas are often used near a pool or a water feature. A more informal open roof structure is a shade trellis or arbor. A shade trellis consists of overhead joists that rest on beams and form an open overhead structure, usually without sides. It is very decorative, even without plants growing on it and can grace a house or garden entry, patio, or deck. It can offer shade over your patio or deck and add interest on the overhead plane. An arbor consists of open rafters or lattice

overhead. Arbors are usually freestanding, a simple arrangement of poles and overhead netting of some sort. Arbors may be decorative or strictly utilitarian.

SPECS

Regardless of style or construction method, a garden shelter should meet certain size requirements to ensure that it is comfortable. Use these measurements to ensure that your shelter fits human proportions:

- Total area: Fifty square feet per person.
- Roof: Eight feet to beams, more if design requires.
- Doorway: Thirty-two-inch width is a minimum.
- Table height: Twenty-nine to thirty-one inches.
- Seating height: Seventeen to twenty inches.
- Steps: Six-inch risers, fourteen-inch tread.

SMOOTH INDOOR/OUTDOOR RELATIONSHIP

It's not necessary to attach a shelter to the house. Some are better in the "lower pasture" or the "upper meadow," such as a gazebo or belvedere. Whether in close proximity to the house or on the "lower

A stone planter is included as part of this gazebo. (Brookside Gardens, Wheaton, Maryland)

forty," a garden shelter can give the landscape a more designed look.

The placement of your garden shelter depends upon usage. For the most pleasant orientation, situate it slightly elevated on a south-eastern slope away from the lowest point of the property. I also like to design them near enough for a smooth indoor/outdoor relationship. A casino, patio, pergola, porch or shade trellis designed to match your existing architecture will integrate the structure with your property, even if it's across the garden.

Several garden shelters are most effective when completely separated from the house. Locate a belvedere, gazebo, or bower in a private or separate part of the garden to make you feel like you are getting away from the workaday world. The design of these freestanding structures can be completely independent of the design around your house.

One way to integrate structures into your landscape is to incorporate softscape and hardscape. This can even apply to utility structures. Wherever they are located, many shelters can double as a trellis for training plants. Install flower boxes on the windows of a structure such as a tool shed or other enclosed structure. A beautiful option is to build a gazebo with a stone planter for its lower wall.

TRELLISES

26

A trellis is defined as an ornamental structure of sticks, rods, or poles crossed to form a lattice, a geometric pattern, and is used to support vines or trained plants. I use the term more loosely to mean any support on which plants are trained. While trellises don't provide shelter from the elements, they offer implied shelter and often privacy and wind protection. Trellises are usually decorative and can serve a number of functions.

Custom-build a trellis to match the style of your home and garden. In a woodland garden, for example, use rough-hewn posts made of the weatherproof rot-resistant woods, such as pressure-treated lumber, redwood, cedar, or locust. A wooden or brick colonial home might need a formal trellis of painted lumber, iron, or brick, and there are some plastic trellises that are very sturdy and ornamental.

Tailor the use of a trellis to suit a situation in your landscape. For example, if you have a rose that has been trained to the height of a wall but you wish to make it a taller specimen, design a trellis to hold it, perhaps one that could stand in front of the wall and grow with the rose.

If you are locating your trellis to stand independently, pay attention to where the prevailing winds come from. Most prevailing winds come from the west. It could blow over if it's top-heavy with plants. To avoid a kite effect, keep the wind from hitting a trellis broadside. Place it so that wind hits its narrow side, creating a few inches instead of a few feet of surface area.

FUNCTIONS OF TRELLISES

FOR PRIVACY

Use trellises for screening around decks and patios or against homes. They could be built in as an integral part of a deck or house, or they can stand as separate structures in a garden along a patio or defining your property line. When you don't have much room between you and your neighbor and want to screen the view and achieve some privacy, use a trellis. It will fit the thickness of any space. As long as you have enough room to plant a vine, this is as narrow a planting as can be installed. You can use a trellis in conjunction with a shelter to further enhance privacy and enclosure and create more interest and beauty. Trellises afford an opportunity to create ornamental plant arrangements on a narrow vertical scale.

A TROMPE L'OEIL

Use a trellis to create a false illusion of space, a *trompe l'oeil* (trick the eye). Build a small trellis within a larger one and make it look like the smaller one is off in the distance. Give a sense of space by painting the walls behind the trellis to highlight it. Or you may want to paint the walls sky blue to make them seem to disappear or give a false perspective with another type of mural. To see some

An ornate trellis sets off plants and divides parking from patio. (© 1997 Walpole Woodworkers. All rights reserved. Used by permission.)

examples on the Web, go to: http://bridge.skyline.net/illusions and http://users.senet.com.au/~rfrancis.

TO MAKE ROOMS

Break up a long narrow property by installing a planted trellis across it, making the property feel larger. The division provided by a trellis can not only make the property seem wider and more comfortable, but also give a sense that there is a beyond. Being able to see through the trellis gives a sense of perspective. A hedge, fence, or wall would make it look like the end of your property. Place a low stone table and an English garden bench by a water feature on the other side and plant the trellis with one of the plants from the list of vines on page 183.

TYPES OF TRELLISES

Companies that handle prebuilt ornamental landscape structures will usually sell or build trellises. Trellises are made of pressure-treated lumber, redwood, cedar, iron, or plastic. A wide variety of prefabricated trellises are available, ranging from flimsy to solid and beautifully constructed. Expect the price to reflect the quality. Look for them in catalogues of garden amenities, and check at your local garden or home improvement center, or surf the Web.

Trellises are also a good project to create yourself, and many different trellis constructions are possible. The following are just a few examples.

WOODEN TRELLISES

Building a trellis involves two components: the main structural framing and the internal webbing. For the framing, rot-resistant black locust, cedar, and redwood, as mentioned above, all make long-lasting wooden posts. Pressure-treated lumber is available in any size you might need, for framing or support.

HEAVY-DUTY TRELLISES

Plan ahead if you are training large plants that will develop heavy wood as they grow. You'll need strong supports on your trellis, such as steel pipe, and heavy lumber, such as two by fours for trellis and four by fours for supports. Trumpet vines (*Campsis radicans*) or

wisterias, for example, will train themselves on anything they touch and need heavy-duty trellises to support their weight.

HOMEMADE IRON TRELLIS

Use galvanized pipes or rebar stakes (reinforcing rods used by contractors) for a trellis alongside the house. Set the pipes in the ground two feet apart and extend them up to the eaves of the house or garden shelter. String wires across the bars and create a ladder effect if you are using plants that require tying.

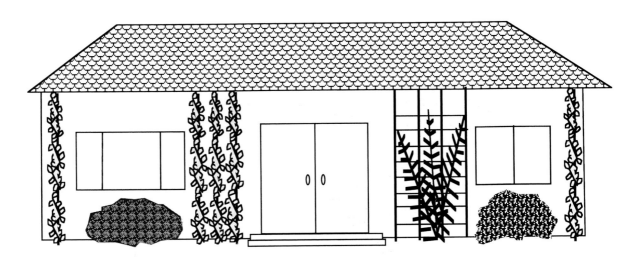

Galvanized Pipes or Rebar Used as Trellises

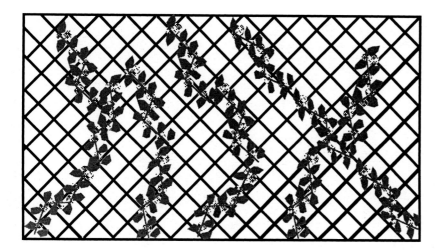

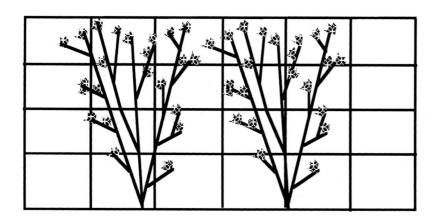

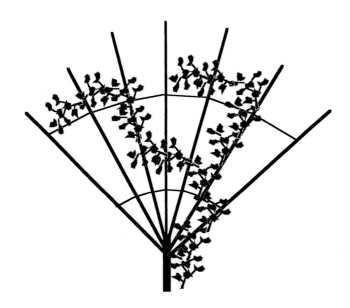

Trellis Lattice   Three different styles of trellis lattice: diamond (top), ladder (middle), and fan (bottom).

Wire Mesh

If you are looking for a versatile material to use for training plants, try wire mesh. Plastic-coated or galvanized reinforcing wire can be attached to a fence or wall. The wire mesh that comes in six-inch squares works well. If you are attaching the wire to a wooden structure, make sure you leave air space between the wall and structure so that moisture does not hold against the wall.

Lattice

Use lattice for lighter-stemmed plants. Look for a variety of materials that are used to construct lattice, including wood, plastic, fiberglass, metal, and combinations. Popular lattice patterns are diamond, ladder, and fan, or variations of these. You can experiment with the patterns of your trellis.

Plants and Trellises

While we usually think of vines or roses climbing on a trellis, a wide variety of plants are excellent for training on them. Use the growing patterns of the plant (how it climbs) to determine the design of your trellis. For example, morning glory climbs by entwining around a structure, so there should be lots of openings for the plant to grow up and around; Boston ivy climbs by attaching a pad type of structure to the wall, so it must have a solid surface to grab onto. The type of planting also determines the amount of work necessary to train the plants onto the structure. Climbing roses must be tied, properly pruned, and might need protection, but honeysuckle will take care of itself. Chapter 49 explains specifically how to train plants on trellises.

Plants for Training on a Trellis

Shrubs and Trees

Apple/crabapple (*Malus*)
Cherry (*Prunus*)
Corneliancherry (*Cornus mas*)
Cotoneaster (*Cotoneaster*)
Crapemyrtle (*Lagerstroemia*)
Devilwood (*Osmanthus*)
Euonymus (*Euonymus*)
Firethorn (*Pyracantha*)
Forsythia (*Forsythia*)
Hawthorn (*Crataegus*)
Holly (*Ilex*)
Juniper (*Juniperus*)
Southern magnolia (*Magnolia grandiflora*)
Amur maple (*Acer ginnala*)
Mock orange (*Philadelphus*)
Pear (*Pyrus*)
Photinia (*Photinia*)
Podocarpus (*Podocarpus*)
Flowering quince (*Chaenomeles speciosa*)
Rose (*Rosa*)
Rose of Sharon (*Hibiscus syriacus*)
Rosemary (*Rosmarinus*)
Rhododendron (*Rhododendron*)
Silver berry (*Elaeagnus commutata*)
Viburnum (*Viburnum*)
Weigela (*Weigela*)
Yew (*Taxus*)

Vines and Trailing Plants

Bittersweet (*Celastrus*)
Boston ivy (*Parthenocissus tricuspidata*)
Clematis (*Clematis*)
Grape (*Vitis*)
Honeysuckle (*Lonicera*)
Climbing hydrangea (*Hydrangea anomala*)
Ivy (*Hedera*)
Japanese star jasmine (*Trachelospermum asiaticum*)
Carolina jessamine (*Gelsemium sempervirens*)
Climbing rose (*Rosa*)
Silver lace vine (*Polygonum aubertii*)
Trumpet creeper (*Campsis radicans*)
Virginia creeper (*Parthenocissus quinquefolia*)
Wintercreeper (*Euonymus fortunei*)
Wisteria (*Wisteria*)

FENCES AND WALLS 27

Fences and walls serve many valuable roles, both functional and decorative. Fences mark property boundaries, provide privacy from neighbors, keep young children and pets safely inside, protect wildlife, and provide comfort. Walls serve many of the same functions and can also supply a barrier to erosion. Optimally, you can use your fences and walls to add both utility and beauty to your landscape.

Fences or walls can be inviting or forbidding, depending upon style and size. Use a low barrier (three to four feet) to imply privacy, but still impart an inviting feeling. On the other hand, a tall fence or wall (six to ten feet) is foreboding and says "keep out," as does a tall narrow gate. If you desire variation from a level fence line, an

This dipping, or concave, pattern is friendlier, inviting conversation at the low points in the fence.

185

arched or dipping pattern is eye-catching. The arched pattern says private, while the dipping pattern (lower in the center than at the posts) is more inviting.

Generally, fences between the house and the front of the property must be no higher than forty to forty-eight inches. This height is required for safety because clear lines of sight are crucial in order to see pedestrians and vehicular traffic. If rear fence heights are regulated, maximum allowable height typically ranges from six to seven feet. Many prefabricated fences are available in six-foot-high sections. Use support posts that are eight feet long (two feet in-ground). Before beginning to install any fencing, check with your local government to find out maximum heights allowed for fences and any other rules and regulations applicable to fencing. Many jurisdictions require a building permit before fencing can be erected.

STYLES OF FENCING

The style and construction material used for a barrier can make it look like it belongs in the landscape. Here are a few examples of how to coordinate your fencing with your property.

Use a white, wooden picket fence around a colonial-style home, and split rails around the cabin in the mountains. Use a bamboo or reed fence to define the boundaries of a Japanese garden. Ornamental iron fits in well with a Spanish or New Orleans style, as do stucco and old brick. To give your property the feel of an estate, a country home, or summer getaway, use brick for a wall, or brick or stone pillars for uprights as fence posts supporting boards. A stone wall is a beautiful feature to have on any property, but it should still look like it belongs there. Several natural or installed rock outcroppings (see chapter 34, Rocks in the Landscape) would make the stonework fit the property. And rather than letting a fence dominate your property, design it in a way so that it unobtrusively flows with the contour of the landscape. Don't let it cut your vistas.

CHAIN LINK

I admit to a prejudice against chain-link fences. While chain link is probably one of the more economic, versatile, and secure types of fencing you can install, I'll often look at a property and feel that I can make the most positive impact on it by getting rid of the chain-link fence. So don't be afraid to pull out a chain-link fence when you are redesigning your landscape, or to take it back from the front yard to the corners of your house. This will add an open, expansive feel to your property.

Fence Styles

Lattice

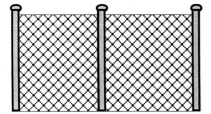

Board on board

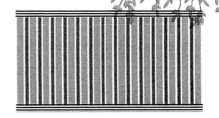

Picket

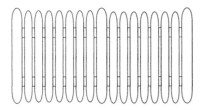

Privacy

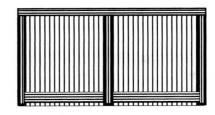

Hurdle

Split rail

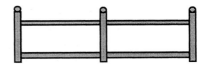

Dipping

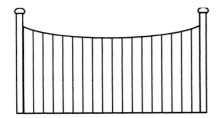

Arching

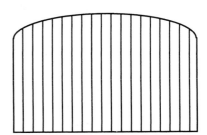

If you feel that chain link is the only material that suits your purposes (and pocketbook), there are several ways to make it more compatible with the landscape. Chain link is available in green, brown, or black mesh. On a level terrain, use black vinyl-coated chain link, which will blend with the background as it picks up shadows. Black is also most effective against the shadows of shrubbery. Against a grassy slope, green chain link will be barely visible.

Plant the fence to both sides if you can, and treat the chain link as though it were invisible. Place the shrubs in a staggered pattern, disregarding the fence line. The links of the fence are excellent for growing vines, including cucumbers, grapes, and honeysuckle, to name a few. This treatment accentuates the fence line, so plant a vegetable and/or flower garden to the front of the vines to bring them into your landscape design.

PARTIAL FENCING

My preference is to use fencing as an accent. While the most common conception of a fence is as a continuous run around a property, if it is not being used as an enclosure (as for dogs or around a swimming pool), fencing can be used very effectively in sections. Use a fence section as a background for a garden. For example, run a six- to eight-foot section of white picket fence through a perennial border with low plants to the front and taller ones behind it, or use it to back up a rose garden. It sets roses off beautifully.

A section or two of ornamental fencing around a patio or other private space may be enough to offer a feeling of privacy and enclosure, to add contrast and an element of interest.

Use sections of fence to screen unpleasant views or for privacy. Then install plantings in front of the fence to create an aesthetically

---

FENCING MATERIALS

There is a range of fencing styles and materials available, custom built or ready to install. You can use these alone or in any combination, whichever works better with your property and design.

Aluminum	Picket
Bamboo	Plastic
Board-on-board (vertical and horizontal)	Reed
Brick	Split rail
Canvas (windbreak on patio or deck)	Stone
Chain link	Wire
Louver	Wrought iron

Planted Fence   Plantings around fences can screen the fence, and fencing can make a nice background for a garden area.

pleasing arrangement that makes it look like it was designed as a planted fence not a screen. When fencing and plantings are combined as a screen (for example, to shield a heat pump from view), repeat the elements in several areas of the property. Then you will not draw undue attention to what you are trying to hide.

Fences can screen wind from a small sitting area, water garden, or other feature, but their use for this purpose is limited because of height restriction. Shrubs, which can grow to fifteen or twenty feet high, are more useful to block prevailing winds.

INSTALLING FENCES

POSTS

Once you've settled on design and checked the regulations, there are two ways of installing fences. A note of caution: As with any planting or construction, be sure to always locate underground utility lines before digging any postholes.

Crushed Gravel

Using a crushed gravel base is the best method of do-it-yourself fence installation in most parts of the country because it is done dry, without concrete, and can hold the fence post firmly. Wooden fences are especially susceptible to rot at ground level, and crushed gravel for a base is a useful alternative to concrete, which can hold moisture around the post and encourage decay.

To set a wooden post, put a pressure-treated four-by-four-inch or six-by-six-inch post two feet into a hole you've dug with a posthole digger or auger. Use a level to make the post plumb, that is, perpendicular to the ground. Tamp crushed gravel firmly in the hole around it. This should keep the area well drained, hold the pole solidly in place, and keep it from rotting for at least twenty years, especially if the lumber is pressure treated.

Concrete

There are times when it isn't practical to use stone because it will not set the post securely enough. If that is the case, use concrete. With the advent of pressure-treated lumber, wooden posts are no longer as susceptible to decay when set in concrete footings. For a chain-link fence, the metal poles must be anchored in concrete because chain link is installed by tightly stretching the mesh between the posts. Only concrete will hold the steel poles. Wrought iron also needs a permanent, unmoving concrete support. Posts should be set in concrete about two feet deep in the Middle Atlantic States, deeper further north.

Chain link and iron are best installed by a professional. But if you choose to install your own fence, pour the concrete the thickness and depth of the hole. Always use a level and set the posts plumb—you'll only get one opportunity to do it right.

Footings

Walls require more solid construction. Masonry walls mortared together must not move or lean. They need to be perfectly plumb if they are to stand for any length of time. This is true for any mortared material, which is why you need footings for a wall. Start the wall on concrete footings, which should be poured on undisturbed soil below the freeze line. The average depth of footings is twenty-four to thirty-two inches. Check with your county or city government for exact building codes.

CROSS-MEMBERS AND PANELS

Now that the support posts are installed and have been firmed, you can attach the cross-members. The crossing parts that create the actual enclosure can be virtually any material. If you have an innovative idea, like tires bolted together or reinforcement bars or other construction iron wired into a pattern, try it. Build a small section and see if it's a viable structure.

Here's some good advice for all fence projects: Carefully measure and layout the posts and cross-members on paper before one shovel of soil is dug. Then install one section and take a measurement to make sure that the posts and fence section are correctly spaced to fit the way that you laid it out on paper. You want to find that out before you've dug every hole and planted every post!

Fence builders will install all of the posts first and build the fence onto them, but when they are building it, they cut the lumber in exact lengths to span the distance as they go. If you install all of your posts at one time, make sure to measure the cross-sections for each span as the pros do. Cutting all the cross-sections at one length will guarantee wasted lumber and a world of headaches.

In situations where it is important that post and fence match exactly, such as with the prefabricated sections that you can get at home improvement centers, install the posts for each section one at a time. Measure the entire length of the run to know how many to get and if fence sections will fit evenly. You might need to shorten one section by sawing and rebuilding it to reach the end of the intended fence run.

Fences that are built for visual screening are most effective if you keep the upper edge level as you install it. Prefabricated sections are built to be installed square on top. On slopes, step the fence down or up and keep the top level.

Regardless of the fence you decide to install, it must be attached to support posts. There are many methods, depending on the type of fence you use. Here are attachment procedures for a few of the ones you might be inclined to install as a do-it-yourself project.

Nails or screws are the way to attach a prefabricated wooden privacy fence to supports. Stockade fences made with narrow two-inch slats and board fences constructed of lumber four-inches or wider are built so that you can nail or screw the fence section to the post. Nails or screws often need to be put into the crossbeam, or stringer, and then into the fence post at an angle, a process called toenailing. Some fences can be nailed straight in from the front if they are built to be installed across the front of the post.

A three-inch, flathead, galvanized screw is about the right size for most fence sections. Drill holes for screws to avoid splitting the wood. Nails of about ten- or twelve-penny size usually work well, but it depends entirely on the size of the wood. Use galvanized nails with an annular ring or spiral pattern to the shaft for extra holding power. The nail or screw should be of a size that will go almost halfway into the post, but no further. Quarter-inch galvanized bolts drilled through the fence and supports are often used for fences with heavier lumber. Stove bolts have heads that mount flush with the surface and offer more aesthetic appeal, especially for hinges on gates. They will also best support the weight of a gate.

Some types of open wooden fences are meadow, split rail, and picket.

Split rail is rustic and simple to install with a handheld clamshell posthole digger. The rails run directly through the center of the posts, so there is no need for nails or screws. The support posts come with the holes already cut into them, and the rails are

> "Cutting all the cross-sections at one length will guarantee wasted lumber and a world of headaches."

tapered at the ends so they slip right into the openings that were made for them. You must make sure that you install this fence one section at a time to ensure that the rails will fit properly into the uprights.

A meadow fence is the type used for pastures to contain livestock. It has three or four boards attached horizontally across posts. These can be attached by simply nailing the boards onto the front of the post with no extra preparation. For a more finished appearance, you could chisel a notch into the front of the post so boards will fit flush. You can cut notches into the sides of the post, so it looks like the boards go directly through the center of it. For this configuration, you will need to attach the boards by toenailing them. These types of open fences do not need to be kept level with the horizon. They look good following the contour of the land. Just follow the line that you make with the posts and keep the boards equally spaced from top to bottom and horizontal with the ground.

Picket fences are prefabricated, or you can nail a stringer, or support beam, from one post to another and nail each picket on individually. This might be best accomplished with six or eight-penny size nails, depending on the thickness of the lumber used to make the pickets. The posts will usually be notched to accept the stringers so they lay flush along the entire run of fence.

PLANTING FENCES

Already touched upon earlier in this chapter, planting around and on fences adds beauty to the landscape, either by the plants screening the fence (especially important if you have a chain-link fence) or by the fence providing a background for a garden.

Let your fence double as a trellis for flowers on the vertical plane. Train roses, pyracantha, honeysuckle, clematis, trumpet creeper, or one of many other plants that can be grown as vines. See chapter 26 for information on trellises and plantings you can use on a fence.

Hang planters on your fences in the form of window boxes or hanging baskets. Specially designed planters are manufactured for this purpose—look for them at garden or home improvement centers. Design them to blend with your planting beds, and try several planter arrangements. Place them at varying heights; have someone hold them in place to determine exact placement before permanently attaching them. Then you'll have to play around and try planting flowers, herbs, vegetables, and vines until you get just the right mix for your planted fence.

RETAINING WALLS

When landscape architect Frederick Law Olmstead was commissioned, around 1870, to come up with a design for the hill on which the U.S. Capitol building stands, he devised a system of walls and terraces that provided a feeling of stability to the landscape that was not there before.

Retaining walls are used to hold back soil on banks and slopes and add strength to your design. They allow a steep drop from one level to another in the landscape and give you the ability to level areas that would have been slopes. They can allow you to turn slopes into multilevel terraces. They can also help reclaim level yard areas for sitting, croquet, or other activities requiring a flat surface.

Retaining walls require a more complex approach than building a freestanding wall. A retaining wall must be able to withstand hundreds of pounds of pressure from elements beating down on the soil. Several different types of construction are available to you.

BLOCK WALLS

Specialized concrete blocks that are designed to stack and lock together using fiberglass pins work well to build retaining walls because they come in large individual units. These retaining wall systems are built without mortar or a footing. The finished product will automatically step into the soil it is retaining. There are many companies that offer concrete block retaining wall systems under myriad brand names. One that I have used successfully is Keystone Retaining Wall System. Call a garden center, building supply house, or landscape contractor for more information.

BRICK WALLS

Brick is an aesthetically pleasing material for a retaining wall, but the small units and dense material require a footing, rear drainage, and weep holes. Brick will hold up much longer if a concrete wall is poured first. The concrete can be faced with brick, stone, or any material.

WOODEN TIES

You can build a retaining wall with pressure treated six-by-six to eight-by-eight-inch ties. In six- to eight-foot lengths, these very

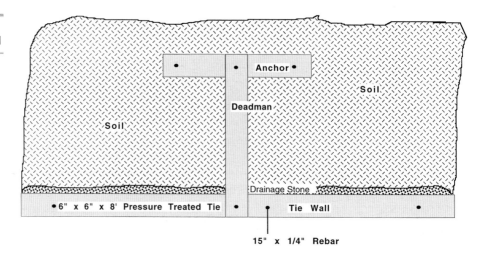

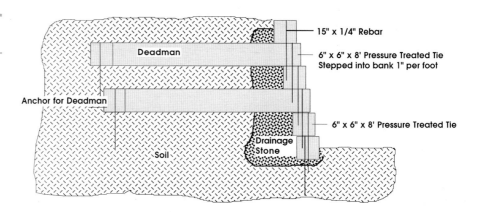

effectively retain a bank of soil. To level the ties, begin the first course on a layer of crushed gravel. Drill and stake the ties with twelve-inch spikes as they are laid into place. Step or batter (lean) the wall into the bank. Use "deadmen" to secure the wall over two feet tall. A deadman is a tie attached to the retaining wall that runs perpendicular into the bank. It is attached to a crosspiece set four to five feet into the bank and then buried in soil.

Stone Walls

Dry rock or stone walls are easy to maintain. If rocks fall down, the pieces can easily be picked up and put back together, contrary to the Humpty Dumpty theory. Rock or stone, stacked without mortar,

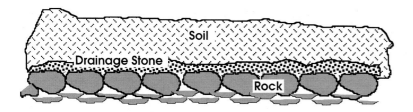

Battered Retaining Wall   A battered retaining wall without mortar, plan view (top) and cross section (bottom).

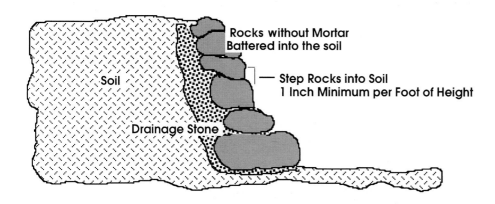

is versatile. It fits the landscape and offers natural weep holes that can be planted.

Native stone is usually the most cost-effective rock to use. Most rocks or stones will work well as non-mortared wall materials, as long as they can be stacked. Use rocks of a similar shape, and take time to assess how each one will fit. Their shape is the most important consideration for a dry stack wall. Take care when laying rock walls, and the effort is noticeable in the finished product.

Start with a two- to three-inch layer of gravel for leveling, and use larger, sturdier rocks on the bottom courses. Keep the rock in each course about the same size as the others in that level. If the color varies from rock to rock, even slightly, spread out the variations evenly over the entire wall. Step or batter rocks into the bank just as you would for any other retaining wall material laid dry.

When building a retaining wall without mortar, batter it, or step it into the bank, making it lean against the soil that it is retaining. Dry walls, battered or stepped into the bank one inch per foot of height, make the best retaining walls.

Because dry walls aren't mortared, there are plenty of natural weep holes, openings for water to flow through. You should also put a layer of stone behind the wall to drain it. Water pressure is what makes walls topple. The best drained retaining walls are the ones that will stand the longest.

ENTRIES

28

An entry could be a gate to a garden, a back or side door to a house, or the most obvious entry, the front door. Entries are thought out and designed, whether on a grand scale—the *Arc de Triomphe* in Paris comes to mind—or more modestly for your home. In my years of landscaping private homes, I have developed a general rule about entries: Keep it simple. Your entry should make a statement that this is a well-cared-for property. Save the showiness for the garden or inside the house. If you start out showy and then become drab, you are setting the visitor up for disappointment. A general rule of thumb is to proceed from simple to ornate as you move further onto your property.

A simple yet ornamental entry sets a nice tone for the rest of the house. (© 1997 Walpole Woodworkers. All rights reserved. Used by permission.)

Another consideration is how you want others to perceive your home. Low wide entries—think of the traditional white picket fence with a wide swinging gate—are inviting while tall narrow openings are more forbidding. A dip in the center of a gate or fence lends a hospitable tone to your entry. Or you might not care to convey any image other than that of a practical, functional way to get to and into the house. If that's the case, you'll be keeping your plantings and hardscapes to a minimum.

Entries in different locations will require different treatments. Most people won't want to meander through a perennial garden to get to your front door, but if you're going from a side door out to the yard, a perennial border leading from the entry would be more appropriate.

ENHANCING THE FRONT ENTRY

The best way to set off the entry is to use unifying plant material, repeating plantings, and keeping your design very simple. Think in terms of all your plantings working toward a common cause—enhancing the entry. You do not wish to create a sitting area, water garden, or any spot that is pretty in and of itself, unless it also sets off the entrance. It is important not to lose that focus.

Don't make the mistake of trying to put too much in your front yard. This is not usually the place for your botanical wonderland or meditation garden, unless there is nowhere else to put it. These types of gardens usually don't serve to set off an entry.

There are many ways, however, in which you can use plantings to enhance your entry. For instance, try a low planting of something like verbena, a perennial in some zones and an annual in others. Let it roam over the low areas of the beds and spill over onto the entrance walk. Use several taller shrubs and perennials, but keep to one low unifying element, such as the verbena.

If you plant entrance shrubs, mass the same varieties. For example, use low-mounded spireas or hollies, but pick one type. The same would apply for using shrubs as a tall background for flowers. Pick one variety, and keep the design simple.

A single shrub or tree can enhance an entry if it is planted for exceptionally showy qualities, such as dwarf hinoki falsecypress (*Chamaecyparis obtusa* 'Nana Gracilis') or paperbark maple (*Acer griseum*). The decorative plant will draw the eye in that direction. Place the specimen tree or shrub near the front door or entry, where it won't ever grow to block it. An exception would be a weeping pine, spruce, or cedar, which could be trained to arch over the entrance to a house or garden.

This tree makes an exceptional entryway.

Flowers are a natural to plant around an entryway, to enhance color and maybe add a pleasing aroma. A bed of perennials and annuals is often an attractive way to set off an entry, and you can use more than one variety of flower. We have a bed of bright black-eyed Susans, sage (*Salvia*), sweet alyssum, and lily-turf (*Liriope*) around the front entry to our home, but we have repeated the plants in the design and massed them together. The front door is also an excellent place to put your container plantings. It sure is handy having them close to the house when it's time to water them. See chapter 43 for more about container planting.

Fences can be an attractive treatment for entries. Some entries offer the perfect place to set a partial fence. Use just a couple of sections of low pickets, for example, to each side of the front walk to define planting beds.

Sculpture, carefully selected to match the style of the home, has a very real place in the entry garden. Sculpture can provide the unity and continuity you want and set off the entry, saying, "Here, come this way to the house." See chapter 29 for more about how to use sculpture in your landscape.

I encounter a fair amount of debate regarding my philosophy of keeping entries simple. People will want to put a Japanese garden at their entrance, for example, but I find this the antithesis of the serenity and privacy that the Japanese garden is supposed to suggest. Or I'll see a water garden and think, *What's that doing at the front door?*

A few sections of fence perfectly define this entry. (© 1997 Walpole Woodworkers. All rights reserved. Used by permission.)

However, there are some innovative ways these ideas can be incorporated. Let's look again at that water garden. Use water as a unifying element and make your pathway to the house over a wooden bridge, with a fountain and big carp pool to one side. If you have the resources, designing the water, fish, and plants to flow under a formal concrete stoop and walkway would fit with a contemporary style of architecture. You can even get whimsical and replicate a castle entrance with a moat and drawbridge.

You always want to set off your front entry in some way to provide curb appeal and let your visitors know exactly how to get into the house, but sometimes space limitations make it difficult to grow the other types of plants you might want. For example, when your entry is the only place on the property where you get enough sun for a cutting garden or a vegetable garden, you should incorporate them with ornamental plantings. Peppers are a handsome plant to incorporate into the ornamental garden, and squashes are an excellent annual groundcover.

You may want to come up with a design for an entry that is simple and inviting enough to look good, yet leaves you room for these other types of plants. Think innovatively. Use utilitarian herbs and vegetables as you would ornamental plants. For example, plant an edging of marigolds, an insect-repelling plant, in front of a mass of pepper plants. The smooth bright foliage and colored fruit of various sweet and hot pepper plants in late summer and fall can make a very attractive bed. On a hillside, plant squash instead of a groundcover. Squash plants used in mass make a terrific groundcover. Use lavender as a sunny edging and clip the lavender buds and bring them in for sachets. Plant cherry tomato vines in a pot on your front porch, providing an attractive, cheery, and edible accent to the entry.

If the size of your yard makes in impractical to use multiple plants for ornamental effect, find a way to separate the garden and the entry. Use a low hedge or a picket fence to make it look like the kitchen and cutting garden is off to the side. Give it its own separate entry and curve the walk in from a main walk that goes to the front door.

This gated fence clearly separates the front lawn from the vegetable garden. (© 1997 Walpole Woodworkers. All rights reserved. Used by permission.)

GARDEN ENTRIES

Moving from your house to your garden gives you other entries to incorporate into your landscape design. Keep the same simple-to-ornate principle in mind when designing an entry for a garden to provide a sense of being contained in a place.

Arbors make a wonderful passageway to create entries for front or rear gardens, as was discussed in chapter 25. Or for an Asian flavor, mark the entrance to your garden with a torii. A torii is the name used for the gateway at the entrance to a Japanese garden.

This structure consists of two upright posts supporting a curved beam with a straight crosspiece under the curved beam.

Historically, entries have featured a fence and gate or an overhead structure, something that imparts a sense of screening. I'm thinking of the walled gardens of New Orleans, for example, where a gate and fence give a sense of privacy yet also have a place where you can clearly see to enter. Every botanical garden has formal gates of some sort which usually serve as a focus for entering the garden. Formal entries such as these often illustrate a principle I emphasize: Repeat design elements on both sides of the entry for a formal look. For example, place matching pillars, shrubs, and flowers on both sides, rather than introducing a number of different elements.

Formal Entry Plantings

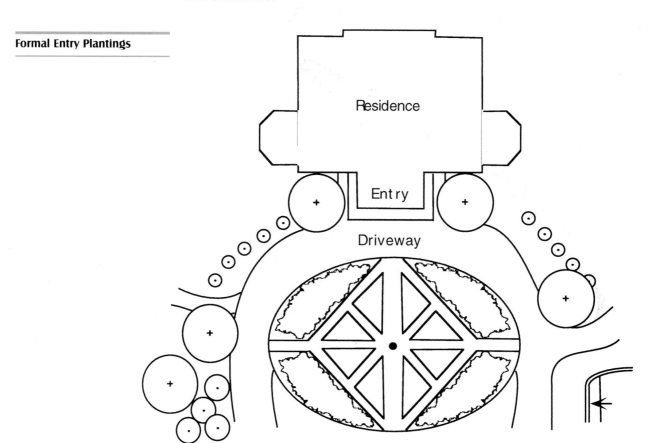

RAMP AND STEPS

A common feature of many entries is steps. Stairs imply that you are moving from one area to another, and they make more of an entry statement than a ramp. A ramp can be more confusing and round-about. Sometimes ramps even need to be switchbacked to have enough distance so that the percentage grade stays low enough to be accessed by people with disabilities. But if you require a ramp for a wheelchair or for someone with limited mobility, you will need to put one in, regardless of the design challenges. Thus, landscape design is more important than ever when designing an entrance with a ramp. See chapters 11 and 31 for thorough treatments of this subject.

SCULPTURE

29

There's no question about it—sculpture can make your landscape. The trick is to do it with style and class. If you have just a single piece of sculpture in your front yard, located in a planting bed in reference to your front entrance, and you keep the plants looking good and the bushes trimmed, you can have an attractive landscape. On the other hand, I've seen too many properties littered with pieces of sculpture in a way that detracts from the landscape and becomes merely concrete, stone, glass, and plastic debris. Chose your sculpture carefully and with restraint, and coordinate a sculptural element with the rest of the landscape.

This sculpture is tasteful and gives the garden a focal point.

USING SCULPTURE

Look around and you'll see many places where you can use sculpture to enhance a garden or a patio, the house, swimming pool, or tennis court. The key is to find something fitting for the particular space.

Incorporate your sculpture into the landscape. It can be used anywhere, but it is usually not a good idea to place it standing without a background, where it doesn't relate to anything. Rather, tuck the sculpture in somewhere, into a planting of trees, around the base of shrubbery, into a bed of groundcover. Place a piece of sculpture—for example, a sundial—as the central axis of an herb garden. A formal sculpture can stand alone better than a whimsical piece, but even the formal piece will look out of place if is not integrated.

You can use sculpture to add perspective to the garden. A big piece and a small piece of similar style at different ends of the garden may create an illusion of additional space. A small statue placed at a low level will make its surroundings appear larger.

The size of a sculpture depends on its use and the size of the landscape. Life-size is rarely practical, especially in most home

Stone sculpture is most effective when tucked into some greenery. (Como Ordway Memorial Japanese Garden, Saint Paul, Minnesota)

This small statue of a little girl adds a nice touch to this garden path.

gardens, and it would be very expensive. Most figures are in the three- to four-foot range. You can add to the impact of a sculpture by placing it on a twenty-four- to thirty-inch pedestal. A scaled-down figure standing on a pedestal brings it to eye-level and makes it more affordable. Or, elevate a small statue on a hillock or promontory to increase its visibility. Use a large element judiciously. Remember, a large structural element will reduce the importance of nearby features and could become the sole focal point.

Not all sculpture needs to be large and easily visible. A fun thing to try is to create an element of surprise in the landscape. It can add so much to the interest and fun of the garden to discover something, to happen upon a ceramic turtle peeking out from the edge of a fern in your garden or an imp, pixie, or wood nymph hiding under your hosta.

TYPES OF SCULPTURE

A variety of materials are used to make sculptures for our landscapes: concrete, stone (marble or granite), glass, plastic, fiberglass, molded stone, and stone particles. If you want inexpensive sculpture, look at concrete pieces. Pressed stone is a bit more expensive, then granite and marble. Bronze is very expensive, but it weathers well.

> "Whimsical elements can also play a part in the well-designed landscape."

Steel, which is often used for modern pieces, will sometimes be allowed to rust on purpose. Steel will oxidize to an ornamental russet color. Copper will develop a greenish patina. To take advantage of the ornamental qualities of rust, use discarded farm equipment for pieces of sculpture. A wheelbarrow, a plow welded into a form—these can fit rustic and certain contemporary styles of landscape. Just remember that the sculpture should conform to the style of your architecture and landscape.

Admittedly, every type of sculpture exists, but to simplify your choices, classify sculpture in four categories—classic, modern, rustic, and pieces of junk, which we talked about above. Pick just one type for your home. Classical sculptures are generally recognizable figures, such as a fish cutting water or a cupid with a bow and arrow. Often figures from Greek mythology are used in classic statuary—Diana returning from the hunt or Eros, the god of love. Or sculpture can be classified as formal or whimsical, such as a trimmed hedge or topiary of a horse and rider chasing a fox, jumping a shrub.

Whimsical elements can also play a part in the well-designed landscape. The mother duck with baby ducklings following, the woman gardener bending over with exposed bloomers, the "Marlboro man" with his foot on a barn or a shed and holding a cigarette—these commonly seen sculptures are whimsical elements that can highlight a garden if used with restraint in an informal setting.

Another world of garden art can be found in the kitschy pieces that can be seen in gardens everywhere—pink flamingos and gazing balls, the colored glass globes that sit on a pedestal and reflect the garden around them. Used with taste and whimsy, these pieces can also add to the landscape. One possible use of pink flamingos is to place one in a southern landscape, perhaps under a banana tree and sited so you can see it from your "Florida room."

The most ubiquitous of garden sculptures, the lawn jockey, has become an antique collectible, and some of these have great value. These have been the brunt of criticism because they were often misused, but they too can have an appropriate place around your home. Use the lawn jockey at an entry to convey a greeting. The jockey, with his outstretched arm suggesting a place to tie a horse, can be very effective just outside a white picket fence surrounding a colonial home.

Use any of a variety of components to establish a sculptural element in your landscape. A sculpture can be a bench, a self-standing water feature, a birdhouse or birdbath, or an actual statue. It can be realistic; it can be abstract.

You can get sculpture from people who specialize in producing ornamental garden sculpture. High-quality products are available at garden centers. Often artisans and craftsman produce and sell

original garden art directly from their studios or make it available to the public through art galleries or in quality landscape amenity shops. Try calling around to landscape professionals; they may keep a listing of garden artists. Some high-quality manufactured materials are also available through international dealers.

DECKS

30

Decks are popular, perhaps because they're reminiscent of the great American tradition, the porch. They're the most versatile types of structures to put in the landscape. I've designed many brick and stone patios because decks didn't match the architecture of the house, but masonry must be laid on level ground and drained. With decks, it doesn't matter. I have designed them on hillsides, over tree roots, in barren desert, and into almost every soil, sand, loam, or clay.

By the nature of their construction, decks are raised above ground level. Spaces between planks allow rain to flow through, so drainage isn't a problem. Taller decks also stand above any possible cold air sinks, which form in low spots when we get an arctic blast. This will extend the useful season of a deck. And to capture the morning sun, design your deck, if possible, with a southeastern orientation.

BENEFITS

Decks are wonderful because their design is flexible, to allow for many uses and configurations. You extend your living space tremendously by being able to walk right out onto the deck from the dining room, living room, den, bedroom, or kitchen. For something different, design it as a two-tiered structure, one level to eat on and the other for relaxing. Or, hang a deck overhead off a second story. It can come off a bedroom and serve the purpose of a balcony without the need for the sophisticated tie-in of iron and concrete required for a traditional balcony.

A question many people have concerning decks is what to do underneath them. For decks six feet high and above, plant with a shade-tolerant groundcover, such as sweet box (*Sarcococca hookeriana*), yellow archangel (*Lamium*), lily-turf (*Liriope*), or mondo grass (*Ophiopogon*). Or consider turning the area into a shaded sitting section with pavers, a couple of swinging chairs bolted into the deck above, a bird bath, and other site amenities.

If your home allows for this, place a deck off your living room above the entrance to your walkout basement. This is a common arrangement that offers the dual advantage of the deck above for living space as well as shelter over the basement entry.

You can also install a deck in conjunction with a patio. Located several feet above a brick, flagstone, or other masonry paving, the deck will enclose and add privacy. If you plant flowers, shrubs, and trees, the garden will have interest on two levels. This is an opportunity to create a "sunken garden." Even if it's only slightly elevated, a deck offers a wonderful view from which to look down on the plantings below. Add a lower seating area in the garden, and you can sit among your plantings and enjoy them from below.

If the deck is low to the ground (three to four feet), lattice or other panels can screen the bare ground underneath decks. If you attach the screening with hinges, you can use the area for storage (see pages 158–159).

SOMETHING DIFFERENT

You probably have a pretty standard image of a deck in your mind, but you can be innovative and try a design that does more to enhance your landscape than the conventional rectangle on stilts.

Design curves into your deck, as you would for a patio. This can be a challenge, and you may run into a carpenter who tells you he can't do it. My advice here is to find another carpenter because it can be done. It may cost more, but breaking up the strong straight line of a deck is well worth considering. With a straight deck, you'll accentuate the straight line of the house and create another mass of square corners that needs to be softened by the landscape.

Another way to distinguish your deck and make it more interesting is with the planking arrangement. A great deal of variety can be achieved by laying the planks of the deck in different directions. Try diagonals, for example, like rays of the sun around a central circular piece or to give a herringbone effect.

The design challenge in building decks is managing to screen them so that people using them have some privacy. This is a particular problem for decks off a second story, where they are elevated well above most screening elements. Shrubs or conventional screening won't work. How do you screen a deck that comes off your house eight feet above ground level?

Install lattice along the edge of the deck, and establish quick-growing vines. Put containers with small shrubs planted in them

around the perimeter of your deck, or just on the side you want to screen. Planters on the deck can give you some interest, and while it may not be total, there is implied screening. If you get a deep freeze in winter and want to plant containers with shrubs and trees that will overwinter, choose plants that are hardy to Zone 2 or 3 (−40 or −50°F). Several plants I use are Siberian pea shrubs (*Caragana*), hedge maples (*Acer campestre*), burning bushes (*Euonymus alatus*), and northern bayberries (*Myrica pensylvanica*). The best time to plant them is in spring. (See chapter 43.)

Think ahead in planning and design and locate your deck where there is already a large tree that will screen it on one side. Or plant a fast-growing evergreen tree whose crown will reach deck level within a few years of planting, such as eastern white pines or Norway spruces. Another method of screening high decks is using tall, low-branching trees such as beeches, birches, columnar maples, or fastigiate English oaks. You can purchase them at the size you need, depending upon your budget. They're deciduous but have leaves when you need them—in summer.

CONSTRUCTION

In order to ensure longevity, talk with a pro before installing a wooden deck. Decks can be more susceptible to wind lift, warping, and rotting than forms of paving. Setting the footings, connecting all the pieces, and attaching it to the house correctly are all crucial,

"If you skimp and use nontreated lumber in contact with the soil, you'll be replacing your deck before you can really start to enjoy it."

so much so that you're often required by your local jurisdiction to get a building permit to construct one.

I'll now give you some guidelines for building your own deck. But remember, this is just an overview—you may want to consult a professional carpenter, and even if you are an adept do-it-yourselfer, consulting a specialized book on wooden deck installation is probably a good idea.

First, use No. 1–grade, kiln-dried pressure-treated pine, fir, redwood, or cedar to build your deck. Kiln-dried lumber is the least likely to shrink and warp, and it will hold a more finished appearance after installation. If you skimp and use nontreated lumber in contact with the soil, you'll be replacing your deck before you can really start to enjoy it.

To start, dig a hole below the freeze line and pour a concrete footing, or use precast concrete piers. The footings should stand on undisturbed soil. Use special feet called Simpson post bases to set in the concrete when you are pouring. These footings will support the legs, or uprights, up out of the ground.

Set uprights on the concrete footings as supports for the beams or joists. Attach the beams to the uprights using straps or nailing plates. Specially made nailing plates should be used to attach the crossbeams or joists to the uprights. If you can't find these plates, bolt the pieces together or use a strap to screw the two pieces together. Never nail the joists (beams) to the uprights, because wind lift could work them loose over time.

Lay out all the planks across the beams. Before you nail them down, consider other possible ways they can be laid. A professional can help you get innovative with the pattern. Lay the planks tightly against one another, with little or no spacing between them, or else the joints will become too large as they weather. The spaces you see between decking planks usually form as the lumber weathers and shrinks.

If your deck is more than three feet high, install a thirty-four-inch-high railing around the entire perimeter. The rails should be attached to the banister on five-inch centers so nothing can slip through. Of course, you will need stairs if the deck is built more than a few inches off the ground. For guidelines, see the discussion of stairs in the landscape on page 218.

While pressure-treated lumber, especially a wax-coated type, will stand up to the elements with no further treatment, you can treat the deck with Wood Life or another preservative labeled for wooden decks. It will give them a darker, richer color and less checking, or cracking along the grain, of the wood.

PATHS, STAIRS, AND PATIOS

31

Our paths, stairs, and patios are the structures on which we walk and live when we are outdoors in our landscapes. These paved areas of hardscape are the most important part of landscape design when it comes to establishing an environment in which people can enjoy the landscape. When I talk here about "paving," I am being inclusive to encompass any structures on which we walk, from cement paving to stairs and ramps to mulched pathways to compacted bare dirt paths.

As with all constructed elements in the landscape, there is one fundamental rule of design to remember for walks and patios: Blend with the environment and make it efficient. Design your walks and patios so that they blend with the environment and the other elements of your landscape. The challenge of landscape design is to install paths that follow the contour of the land and still serve as efficient routes from one place to another.

PATHS

A path begins to form if only one person walks over the land. You may have seen this phenomenon where the mailman crosses your property or where schoolchildren take a shortcut over your lawn. Foot traffic destroys the friable, aerated, well-drained soil that plants require to thrive. It causes soil compaction, which is conducive to pedestrian use but not plant growth. If such paths are taken regularly, plants grow smaller or less dense or will die. Paths can have a couple of different purposes.

Use paths to guide people along an approved route. If you want to keep people out of certain areas of the yard or garden, a path will make it clear where you do want them walking. Design your pathways to keep people out of planting beds and off roots. Paths also define space—yours for walking and recreation and your plants' for growing and blooming.

How you use your path will help determine its configuration. A modern practice for architects is to observe user-determined circulation patterns for several months before installing paving according to the routes that people took. Try self-determining circulation on your own property before installing hardened paths. Let the actual use patterns define your pathway. The well-beaten paths pedestrians have chosen to walk on are usually the most practical traffic patterns and the best way to decide where to put in your paths.

Since plants don't grow in straight lines, well-placed curved paths will blend naturally with the landscape. Straight walks give a more formal, clipped, or utilitarian feeling. Install a pattern of circulation that encourages meandering if you're interested in admiring the garden as you walk through it. A curved line or offset sections of paving have the effect of slowing movement, causing you to notice your surroundings. This path line would be appropriate for perennial, sculpture, water, or other gardens that invite closer scrutiny than just a quick glance.

When designing a circulation line solely to accomplish chores— such as taking out trash, tending the garden, walking the dog, or getting firewood—the walkway is better designed as a straight line. This invites rapid movement and gets you from point A to point B very efficiently.

Front walks are considered by most designers and architects as utilitarian and are generally installed as straight lines. But if a garden has been integrated with an entrance walk, paths with a subtle curve work nicely. If you use a curve, make sure it looks as if it is supposed to be there. You can do this with a mass of shrubs and flowerbeds within the curve, and maybe a sculptural element added as well. If you don't use this space, human nature takes over and people will heed their instinct to follow a straight line, the shortest distance between two points.

For areas where you want people to linger, you have a few options to slow people down. Remember that intersecting lines will cause the pedestrian to hesitate. Put in a flower bed or seating area where pathways intersect or where a walk goes off in a diagonal direction. Plant beds at the corners of paths that form a T intersection to keep people from cutting across the corner. You can also imply hesitation in a walkway by changing paving materials. Switching from dirt to mulch to paving are ways to provide hesitation in a straight path.

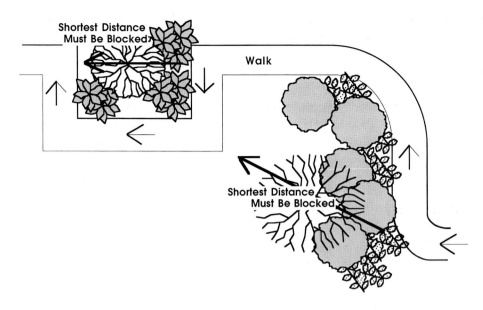

Planting Curves Use plantings to give a curve a reason to exist.

Once you have established the basic purpose and design of your walks, you will need to attend to the details regarding exact dimensions. Determine the minimum width of a path through the garden by basic needs. With the average human shoulder width at eighteen inches, a garden path, regardless of how informal, should be at least twenty-four inches wide for one person and twice that wide if it is to accommodate people passing in opposite directions. Paved walkways look best at thirty-six or forty-two inches wide. Forty-two inches is the minimum width you should use if a main walk is thirty feet or longer, such as the entry to your house or garden or a walk to the back shed or pool.

Walks that lead to main entrances and exits should be wide. Large homes could have walkways six to ten feet wide if they fit the proportion of the building. A path thirty feet or longer should be

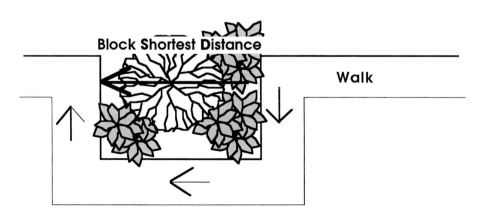

Planting Corners Plant at corners to stop cut-through traffic.

four to five feet wide to make it fit the space more comfortably. This keeps the buildings and the paving in the landscape around them in proportion to one another.

The minimum path size for people in wheelchairs is thirty-six inches, at least six inches wider than the thirty-inch vehicle. Sixty inches is usually sufficient for two-way traffic. At entries and gates, wheelchair paths should be a minimum of thirty-two inches wide. See chapter 11 for a complete discussion of designing for disabilities.

Walks need to drain, but that is seldom a problem because there is usually a difference in grade from point A at one end of your walk to point B at the other. The walk should also drain from side-to-side with at least a 1 percent grade across the surface. If the grade is more than 2 percent, it will start to show and your path will no longer look level from side-to-side. Ideally, your path should look level and still drain. If your grade is greater than 10 percent, you should consider putting in stairs or ramps.

STAIRS AND RAMPS

Almost every home will have the problem of getting people from one level to another on the property. Whether it's a step up to the front or back door, stairs to get up and down from a deck, or getting around a landscape with steep slopes and retaining walls, you will have to get people comfortably from point A to point B. The two options you have are stairs and ramps.

STAIRS

Make your steps part of your overall design so that they fit aesthetically and practically with the features that they connect, creating smooth relations and smooth circulation from one level to another. From a design standpoint, stairs are more than a ladder arrangement to get from a low point to a high point; they're an integral element of your landscape.

Consider a spiral staircase in your landscape if space is limited. This is a good looking and efficient mode of circulation to get from the upper to lower deck, while enhancing the surroundings. However, it is steep and may pose some safety issues for children, older individuals, and those with limited movement.

To fit the line of the landscape, use a curved staircase or stagger the steps to meander down a slope. Or soften the visual impact of the stairs in the landscape by tucking them into the walls. Don't stick them out in front of the retaining wall; put them through it.

Much of your attention regarding stairs will involve measurements and dimensions. Outdoor movement has a different flow than indoor movement, and the dimensions of your stairs should reflect this. Outdoor steps are wider and less steep than indoor steps.

Unless space is limited, design steps to *never have a higher riser than six inches or a narrower tread depth than fourteen inches.* If you need to use a riser height that is less than six inches, use this formula to determine the height of the riser: 2R(riser) + T(tread) = 26 inches. As an example, if you needed to have four-inch risers, you would figure 2(4) + T = 26 inches, for a tread of eighteen inches. This will give you steps that will allow for a comfortable gait through the landscape, if they will work into your design at those dimensions.

Handrails along stairs should be thirty-two inches high and extend eighteen inches before and beyond the steps. Use handrails whenever you have more than three steps.

Since there are so many safety issues involved with stairs, I have come up with a few tips on things you should avoid.

- Never put in more than ten steps without a landing.
- Never put in a single stair. In the landscape, it's a trip step, adding nothing but a potential hazard.
- Never make stairs narrower than three feet.
- Never have more than a 2 percent grade at the top or bottom of the stairs.
- Never have stairs in the dark. Light them from the top so you can see every step.

RAMPS

Ramps are becoming increasingly popular in landscapes, and their utility and design is covered in detail in chapter 11, Disabled Access Design. The ramp guidelines have been set by ADA standards, but ramps can be handy for many activities, including bicycle circulation, pulling a grocery cart, wheeling a lawn mower, pushing a baby carriage, wheeling a dolly for moving furniture and appliances, among numerous other wheeled activities. Consider a ramp where you might only have needed a couple of steps in a walk or at an entry. Or ramping over a curb is usually not too difficult because it is just a single step height. Use a maximum of an 8 percent grade (the one-for-twelve rule), 5 percent for wheelchair access.

While ramps are utilitarian features with the focus of getting from one place to another, they can also serve an ornamental purpose in the landscape. For instance, use a ramp to double as a bridge over a water feature or through some other interesting part of the garden.

Ramps can be used ornamentally for walkways in a staggered series of slopes that change grade gradually. Then stair sets of only about two to three steps each might be needed at several points between the long sections of walkways. To fit the normal human gait, a walk should run at least six feet between steps, and the step risers should be four to six inches. These designs, with the ramps separated by steps, are, of course, not wheelchair-accessible and would not be possible if you are designing for disabilities.

PATIOS

Patios are walks that have grown up—and out. Patios add functional space to your walking area for a multitude of purposes—dining, entertaining, relaxing in the sun, even sleeping.

Get ideas for what you want your patio to look like and where you want to site it by looking in your neighborhood, at public and private gardens, corporate and government office buildings, and even at your local mall. Design the patio to suit your needs. Think about what you will be using it for and work with that in mind (see chapter 2, Planning before Planting). I have designed many patios with sweeping lines because I like the way they fit the landscape, but that is a personal decision.

Decide how big to make your patio. I like to cite the guidelines of anthropologist Edward T. Hall, who offers suggestions for distances at which people are comfortable with one another. People are not comfortable with less than a four-foot buffer or "bubble

A patio with a curved edge fits into the landscape better than one with a squared edge.

space" between themselves and others, Dr. Hall found in his research. Therefore, allow four feet in every direction per person—which is 64 square feet—as the minimum size to make your patio for each person using it. This means that a patio built to accommodate five people should be approximately 320 square feet.

The most common consideration with shape is the ratio of one side to the other. We seldom build square patios. In architecture, a "golden rectangle"—with the ratio of sides 1 to 1.618 or approximately 3 to 5—is considered to be the perfect shape. Some patio measurements that fit this ratio are 10 by 16 feet (160 square feet), 12 by 20 (240 square feet) and 15 by 25 (375 square feet).

If possible, site your patio in a private part of the yard with a southeastern orientation, close to the house. Track the number of hours and movement of the sun over your yard to help determine the exact location.

Like paths, patios also have to drain. Patio surfaces should always be graded so water drains away from house walls. The grade should drop at least one inch per ten feet of paving. And don't block the existing drainage pattern in your yard. When building your patio, if it crosses a drainage swale, it might cut off the flow of storm water, causing puddling.

Now that you know the size, shape, and placement, let's look at the kinds of materials that are used to build walks and patios, and then I'll walk you through the steps to install your own patio or walkway.

PAVING MATERIALS

Any of a number of paving materials will work for your walks and patios, alone or in combination. But keep in mind the design principle of repetition when selecting your paving materials. (See chapter 1 for a full discussion of design principles.) Repeat similar elements to create comfort.

BRICK AND FLAGSTONE

Brick or flagstone will give you a somewhat classical appearance, what you would want for an English or colonial garden, for example. Mortared square- and rectangular-cut randomly sized flagstone presents a rich appearance. Square-cut flagstone gives a more formal look. Think about a mix of brick and flagstone, edging the flagstone with brick and repeating that pattern in patio and walks. Don't jumble the brick and flagstone together randomly, however.

Brick with wooden joints in between, such as railroad ties, is another attractive combination and there are numerous other options if repeated throughout the structure. How innovative can you get? What about flagstone within brick squares edged in wooden ties?

If you're using brick, whichever pattern you decide on, keep it consistent throughout your hardscape. Don't switch suddenly from

Brick edges offer clean, finished lines along flagstone.

herringbone to basket weave to running bond. Patterns can be changed successfully, but there must be a definite breakpoint, for example, a herringbone pattern with a running-bond edging could adjoin a running-bond walk. See next page for examples of brick patterns.

Flagstone that is mortared onto concrete gives the most finished and permanent look, but if you are installing paving yourself, I recommend a base of stone or stone dust or sand with no cement. With dry installation, you can lift the stone and move it around until you've got it right without the trauma of having to chisel your walk. Dry installation is also less expensive than mortared installation.

ASPHALT

Asphalt, a cement-like material, is rolled down as a solid sheet and provides some degree of permanence. It can be used in an attractive way if you design it with brick edging and brick joints, for example. However, asphalt can be tricky to install with brick or flagstone dividers. Talk with experts as you work on the design. Use steel or wooden ties for edging or build the soil up along the edge even with the surface of asphalt paving to give it far more longevity. Without something to hold it in place it deteriorates over time, cracking and sloughing off the edges.

Consider getting a professional to do your asphalt installation. Asphalt is more plastic than other paving materials are; you can

Brick Patterns

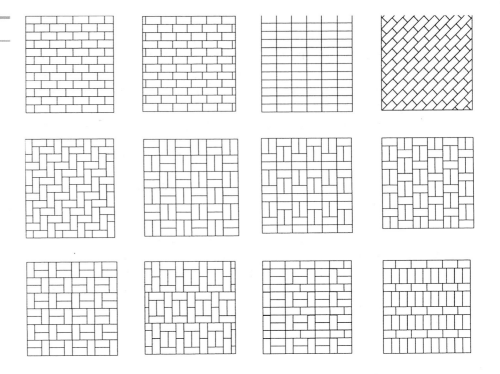

make it any shape you want, especially hot asphalt, which is the type to use. However, it's plasticity also means you have to be very experienced in working with it to end up with a perfectly flat surface that won't puddle.

Asphalt can be more ornamental than you might think. It can be painted, for example, for a completely different look. An example can be seen at Hillwood, the home of the famous hostess Marjorie Merriweather Post (now the Hillwood Museum and Garden, in Washington, D.C.). Mrs. Post wanted asphalt for her walkways because it provides better traction than slate or flagstone when wet, and she was concerned about the safety of her guests. But she was also concerned about aesthetics, so she painted the asphalt red to match the red flagstone paving of the patios.

ROCKS

Rocks are another material that can be difficult to fit into paving. Because rocks come in inexact sizes, it can be demanding and labor-intensive to lay them level. Set rocks in a thick sand or mortar base and use a level to keep checking the top surface as you lay them.

CONCRETE

Concrete is another option, and a solid poured concrete slab probably offers more longevity than any other paving surface. Modern technology offers more attractive concrete than in the past, with a technique to stamp a pattern on it or dye it so that it looks like brick or flagstone or cobblestone. Concrete can be found in many different colors. To find a reputable company in your area, call Bomanite, (800) 854-2094, or Patterned Concrete Industries, Ltd., (800) 252-4619.

CONCRETE PAVERS

Perhaps the wave of the future in paving is the new generation of concrete pavers that are on the market. Don't shy away from concrete pavers. These blocks, often interlocking, can make a fine-looking installation, often with the look of simulated brick, flagstone, or cobblestone. They are generally laid dry on sand or stone dust, which a do-it-yourselfer can accomplish.

LOOSE PAVING

Another class of paving materials consists of dry materials such as loose gravel, wood chips, or mulch. They call for a different set of installation guidelines.

Dry-laid interlocking block makes a comfortable patio for a small space.

Edge your loose paths with aluminum, steel, plastic, landscape timbers, old railroad ties, brick, or any number of other innovative types of edging materials. Edging can be any material that doesn't decay too quickly in-ground, will hold its shape, and will keep the loose wood chips or gravel on the path and out of the garden. Various types of edging materials are available from home and garden centers.

Mulch makes an attractive and comfortable path surface. If you use it in a woodland setting, it can just be spread on the ground with no edging and no fabric because it is organic material that will biodegrade. If you want to use a mulch path in a more formal setting, keep it in a neat line with an attractive edging.

Use landscaping fabric underneath nonorganic dry paving materials such as gravel or marble chips. The fabric allows you to gather up the materials and remove them, either for cleaning or relocating when they lose ornamental value.

Another loose material that is now being used for paths is rubber; for example, tires are ground up for playground surfaces and rubber mats that lock together like a jigsaw puzzle.

INSTALLING A PATIO OR WALK

Patio building takes many years of experience to truly master, and installation without mortar is the best style for beginners. With this type of dry installation, you can lift and re-lay your pieces until you get it right. A dry installation can yield a result that is as aesthetically pleasing and long-lived as a mortared installation. Follow these steps for a beautiful surface you'll enjoy for many years to come:

1. Dig out about five inches of soil in the area where you are going to build it. Its final grade should be about one inch above ground level.
2. Use edging to hold the patio or walk in place. There are paver edgers in heavy-duty poly, aluminum, steel, and wood.
3. Spread crushed gravel in the base of your excavation. This stone layer should be a minimum of two to three inches thick to take up the seasonal movement of soil. Use crushed gravel that is approximately three quarters to one inch in size.
4. Place a layer of stone dust (very fine, crushed gravel) one and a half inches thick on top of the course gravel as a leveling agent. The gravel and the stone dust are available in bulk or by the bag. You can find suppliers of crushed stone materials in the Yellow Pages under "Stone—Crushed." If

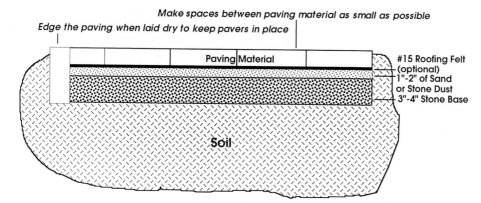

Make spaces between paving material as small as possible

Edge the paving when laid dry to keep pavers in place

Paving Material

#15 Roofing Felt (optional)
1"-2" of Sand or Stone Dust
3"-4" Stone Base

Soil

Patio Installation Using Stone and Stone Dust Base

you tell them your patio measurements and how thick you are laying the gravel base, they will help you calculate how many cubic feet, yards, or tons you'll need. Level the dust, sliding a board across the stone dust at a set height to create a perfectly flat surface. Roll the surface with a lawn roller or tamp and level again with a board to ensure that it is firm and level.

5. No. 15 roofing felt, available at home improvement centers, can be used for added strength.

6. Finally, lay your paving material on top. Use a two- to four-foot-long level as you lay the paving. That, more than any other tool, will assure that the finished product looks flat but it must not be perfectly level. It must drain at least one inch per ten feet, downhill away from structures. Make sure that the joints (points where bricks, flagstones, or other pavers touch) are as close together as possible when laid dry. If there are openings, sweep stone dust or sand between the joints to fill in all of the spaces.

DRIVEWAYS

32

Driveways serve a similar purpose as walkways—getting you from point A to point B efficiently and comfortably. Many of the same principles of design that I talked about in the previous chapter apply here, but there are a number of other issues important to driveways.

You can design your driveway to be both aesthetic and practical, but sometimes it takes some imagination. You may want to use your driveway as a way to enhance the other design elements in your landscape.

AESTHETIC CONSIDERATIONS

You want your landscape to shine, and cars in the landscape detract from it. So use your driveway to take the car out of easy view, to tuck it away in a carport or a garage or a parking space off to the side. Just remember when you are tucking your car away, not to take it so far that it makes it difficult for people to get from the car to the house. The best arrangement would be to have the luxury of getting your car to a handy location to enter your house, such as a side entry, without a harsh expanse of driveway paving across the front of the house.

Sometimes practicality and artistry may conflict. I had one client whose property seemed to offer two options: parking on the street in front of the house, fifty feet away, so they would have to carry packages and groceries from the vehicle to the house; or driving around the side of the house down a hill to the walkout basement level and entering the house from the back, climbing a long flight of steps to get to the living space.

This was my solution: a circular drive. It worked for them, and it can work for you. Put in a circular drive with a landing at the front door of the house, and soften the paved expanse with plantings between the house and the curve of the driveway. This will give you the opportunity to put in large attractive curved beds to blend with the house and driveway into the landscape. The advantage is that you can drive right up to the front door.

With another client, the fact that the property was on a corner offered the opportunity to conceal the driveway. If you have a corner property, consider bringing the driveway to the house from the side, so that you can design the full breadth of the front of your property without a lane cutting through the design.

MEASUREMENTS

Like for walks, many of the design considerations of your driveway concern specific measurements. To accommodate vehicular traffic, a straight single-car driveway must be at least nine feet wide. I prefer ten feet so you can open the car door with plenty of room to spare. Double the width if you want a two-car driveway.

If there is a curve in the driveway, make sure it is at least twelve feet wide. You need that extra width to be able to negotiate the curve and stay on the driveway. A curve in the driveway should be gentle. Make sure the inside radius to the curve is at least fifteen feet.

If your car is coming into a carport or garage, leave at least a twelve-foot-long straight expanse at the end of the drive as it enters the shelter, with no curves or turns. If you have to turn the wheel less than twelve feet from the garage, it will be difficult to negotiate and you'll risk running into the wall.

The maximum grade for a driveway is 12 percent. The area where you park or unload passengers should have a grade no greater than 2 percent.

If you will have a parking area off of your driveway, try to leave an area that is at least nine feet by eighteen feet for this purpose. This is a small, one-car parking area; if you drive a large car, you will be more comfortable in a ten-by-twenty-foot space.

The spot on your property where the driveway intersects the road is a place of potential danger if you don't take safety precautions. The driveway must intersect the road at a 90-degree angle (perpendicular) and not be angled off in one direction or the other. You don't want to have to make an acute turn in or out of your driveway from either direction. Visibility should be three hundred feet in each direction from the driveway up and down the street. This means no shrubs or other plantings should intercept the triangle of vision that you need as you approach the road. Unfortunately, people often do put plantings in this location, creating safety concerns.

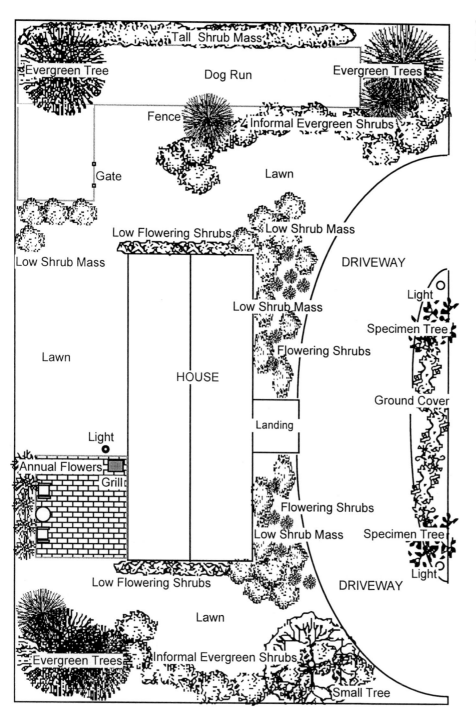

**Suggested Minimum
Driveway Dimensions**

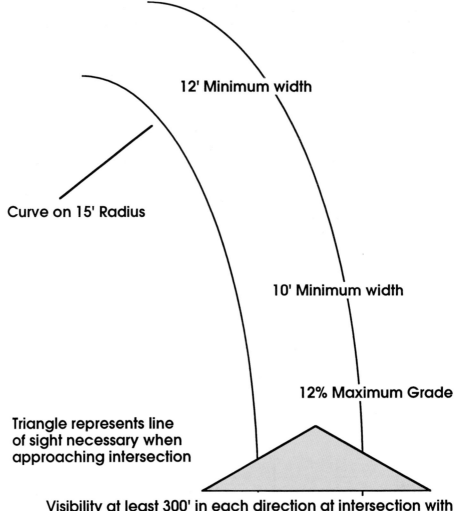

12' Minimum width

Curve on 15' Radius

10' Minimum width

12% Maximum Grade

**Triangle represents line
of sight necessary when
approaching intersection**

**Visibility at least 300' in each direction at intersection with
street**

Driveway must hit street at 90 degree angle

LOCAL APPROVAL

In virtually every home owner situation, your driveway will cross city or county property, and you need some kind of approval to cross that territory. Make sure you know all the regulations in your area before putting in a driveway. My own personal example is a good one. We lost our circular driveway four days before we settled on our home because it wasn't covered by permit.

When researching a drainage problem my new neighbor was having, a county official looked at the neighborhood plat and realized there was no circular driveway on the plan for the property we were buying. It had been put in without a permit fourteen years prior. In less than a day, the county had removed the part of the driveway that had been put in illegally, poured a curb across the area, put in soil, and planted grass.

Check with your state or county department of transportation when you are putting in a driveway. They can give you the proper specifications for building the apron, which is the ramped entrance to a driveway. They might need to approve the way your apron meets the road, the width of the apron, angle of approach, and other issues. If your plans differ from their regulations, you might need to apply for a variance and give a good reason why you need one to have it granted.

MATERIALS

In general, surfacing materials used for driveways are the same as those used for walks and patios, but with a thicker base. See chapter 8, Meeting a Budget, for a discussion on the costs of various building materials.

CONCRETE

For a concrete driveway, use a five-inch-thick base, with steel reinforcement (compared to three inches thick for a patio).

FLAGSTONE

If you are using flagstone for your driveway, make sure it is at least two inches thick, mortared solidly to a concrete base, so that it doesn't crack up.

BRICK

Brick can be tricky for driveways, but can be used successfully. When laying bricks, be very careful to make sure that the bed of mortar between the concrete base and the bricks is solid, so it can withstand the impact of vehicular traffic. The concrete should be reinforced and poured four to five inches thick under the brick. Use only paving bricks.

CONCRETE PAVERS

Concrete pavers can be as effective as concrete, more effective than brick and flagstone, and more ornamental than concrete or asphalt. Some of the state-of-the-art interlocking concrete pavers are better for driveway surfacing than classic flagstone, brick, or asphalt surfaces. They offer unity, evenness from one unit to another, and better longevity in some cases. The newest generation of pavers are blocks that lock together when laid and hold in place.

Lay pavers dry, on a stone base that is mixed with a fine stone dust leveled and tamped about three or four inches thick, rather than using mortar. Get exact specifications from the manufacturer before installation. You can find the materials you need at home improvement centers or yards that manufacture and supply block.

ASPHALT

Asphalt is often used for driveways, and its flexibility makes it very useful. As I pointed out with walks, however, its flexibility also means that you need to be experienced working with this substance in order to get a flat surface with no puddling. If you use edging or pack soil to edge the asphalt, it will have less of a tendency to crack off along the edges as it weathers.

TAR AND CHIPS

Tar and chips is another alternative for surfacing driveways. Asphalt companies are equipped to spread tar and roll the stone chips into the surface, which gives the appearance of a gravel driveway without having loose gravel being constantly pushed off of the driveway into the lawn and beds.

LOOSE GRAVEL

Loose gravel is often used for driveways, particularly in rural areas. Pay close attention to your gravel driveway and keep it groomed to prevent the washboard effect. Don't put it on too thick, or it will get kicked around and you will not have good traction.

SWIMMING POOLS AND WATER GARDENS

33

Swimming pools are a practical and enjoyable part of the landscape that is often ignored by home owners in their design plans. From a design standpoint, the pool is the most overlooked opportunity to make a statement, blending water with the landscape and utility with aesthetics.

All too often I have seen home owners buy a property, hire a pool builder who puts in the pool, and then hire a landscape designer to work around this big body of water that has been installed. However, in my years in the business, I have been happy to see a change in this pattern, and it is now much more common to see a more aesthetic treatment—for example, a pool designed around a waterfall feature or a rock structure.

It is far easier to integrate pools installed in the ground, whether made of concrete or a plastic liner. Aboveground pools present a large structure that you need to blend into the landscape. Large evergreen shrubs close to the pool might only serve to accent the feature. Screening aboveground pools is better achieved with evergreen trees planted some distance away.

SWIMMING POOLS

CHOOSING AND CONSTRUCTING

The shape you choose for your pool relates to how you will use it. Most people don't want and could never have an Olympic-sized pool on their property. But if you're interested in using your pool for working out and swimming laps, thirty-five feet is the minimum length practical. You will want your pool to be at least twenty feet wide. If you are going to use your pool for exercise, you will probably want a rectangular shape, or a curved shape should have a straight area with a thirty-five-foot continuous stretch.

If you are installing a pool for playing, splashing, and just cooling off, you can choose a more innovative shape. Possibilities include the classic kidney shape, oval, round, or even creek-like with an hourglass configuration where water will flow from one section to another through rock outcroppings with a whitewater effect.

If you are installing a pool, make sure an experienced pool installer is involved in your project, at least as a consultant. You can install a pool yourself, but this is a project that dare not have one hair out of place. A hairline crack in the concrete or a ding in the plastic is enough to undermine the whole project. The water in a pool must be perfectly level—any water on your landscape must be held in a perfectly level container. Installers know this, which is another reason to hire a professional. When selecting a professional, ask to see pools they've installed and get references.

Make sure the pool is accessible for cleaning. Pools must be cleaned, vacuumed, and treated on a regular basis. Depending on its position related to trees and other parts of the landscape, you may want to clean your pool every day. In some areas, it is common to screen pools to keep debris out; if this is done, it is important to keep the screen cleaned.

Drainage is very important around swimming pools. The surface of the site must drain away all the way around the edge, especially the pool deck, the walkway around your pool. This is critical to prevent washout of debris into the pool. Drain away water with at least a two-inch drop per ten-foot run.

While concrete and plastic are the two primary materials used to build pools, the cost of plastic liners has come down so much in recent years that these days concrete is only used in the most formal constructions. Plastic is also easier to repair and replace. There are a number of options you can choose among for your coping. For coping—the edging around your pool—use natural stone, flagstone, brick, or tile. Keep it ornamental and match your surroundings.

From a design standpoint, I advise against diving boards and sliding boards. They add nothing to the attractiveness of the pool or the landscape. Insurance companies do not like them either, but not for aesthetic reasons. These features are also great liabilities, and some insurance policies prohibit them.

TYING INTO YOUR LANDSCAPE

There are many ways to use a swimming pool to enhance the beauty of a landscape.

Waterfall

You can bring beauty to your landscape and fill a practical need at the same time. Build a rock structure along the edge of a pool and design the water circulation system so that your recirculating pump comes up though the rocks and flows water back into the pool in a waterfall. As a special touch, install a seat into the wall of the pool under the waterfall you have created with your recirculating system. The water will flow over you as you sit and relax. Increase the interest in the recirculation fountain with lights and changing colors. A flow of water and colored lights will create a captivating light show—don't be surprised to find guests stopping by on summer evenings.

Reflecting Lap Pool

The most functional of pools is a lap pool, designed for serious swimmers who swim laps for exercise. A client once challenged me to come up with a design for a lap pool that was as aesthetically pleasing as it was practical. I combined his lap pool with an Italian water sculpture garden. Fashioned after the canals of Venice, I designed a lap pool that fit the criteria for swimming laps—six feet wide by thirty-five feet long by four feet deep. The recirculation pump came up through a sculptural element, a woman with a pitcher. The pool deck was edged with a repeated planting of tall narrow evergreen columns that would reflect off the water when lit at night.

Paint It Black

Paint your pool a dark color, but light enough to see the bottom. From the landscape designer's perspective, the pool should be black, to give it depth, making it look more pondlike and natural. From a home owner's perspective, however, you will want to see any debris or wildlife lying on the bottom, and a black bottom would obscure this. Dark bottoms are more suited to water gardens than swimming pools.

Indoor Pools

Some architectural designs provide the opportunity for a pool's year-round use. If you are building a house on stilts or pilings, consider putting in a swimming pool on ground level with large ornamental sliding doors. Or build the pool as a separate room with a sliding ceiling that will open you to the outdoors in summer and slide closed to give you year-round swimming. In this arrangement, it is not the yard that houses the pool, but the house that does.

On a Smaller Lot

Many people would like a pool but think that their property is not large enough to accommodate one. You might be surprised. The smaller the property, the more the pool is likely to predominate, and the more need there will be for a design that coordinates it with the landscape and home. It may call for a Greek statue, formal urns, or an arbor and a stone bench, but a pool is certainly possible for a small space.

A pool will fit any size property. Even on a small lot, you can put in a little cool-off pool. Use a design with ornamentation that makes it look like you are crawling down into a hot spring. Use rock outcroppings and plantings to integrate it into the landscape.

For a rectangular pool in a rectangular space, soften it with an arbor or portico around the outer edge. This gives the space a very Moorish feel. Add some colorful mosaic tile as a pool coping to this arrangement, and you'll be developing a style similar to that seen in the Moorish gardens of the fifteenth century.

If you are putting a pool in a modest-sized suburban lot (six to ten thousand square feet), sometimes the best approach is to base the rest of the design on this dominant feature. Build your patio to the water's edge. Use brick or flagstone coping around the edge of the pool and use the same or complementary paving material on the pool deck. Continue this same paving theme with your patio. It will appear that the pool and patio were built as an integral unit, giving a very finished look.

A typical quarter-acre lot is eleven thousand square feet, and in lots beyond ten thousand square feet it becomes easier to separate the pool from the landscape. Create separate areas of the garden that don't relate to the swimming pool. On a quarter-acre lot, a pool can almost be a hidden garden. Perhaps it can be located on the other side of the kitchen garden, with a wall separating them. Or place the pool around the corner from your butterfly garden.

LANDSCAPING AN EXISTING POOL

We don't always have the luxury of designing and installing a swimming pool ourselves. Often when we buy a property, we inherit someone else's work. If you're stuck with a concrete deck and blue poly liner or blue painted concrete—a harsh expanse of water and concrete—there are steps you can take to make it look better.

Low walls or plants around pools with liners are sometimes a solution to screen the blue poly liner or the pool cover from view around the yard to help fit it into the landscape. Or consider replacing a concrete pool deck with a wooden walk to tie it into your wooden deck design and give the effect of a dock by the lake, which can be extremely aesthetically pleasing.

The deck around the pool sets it off and can soften its impact in the landscape. More practically, it provides walking space and an access area. The minimum width for a pool deck is three feet, and four will look better. Some asymmetry can lend interest to your design—think about making the pool deck three to four feet wide on one side and sweeping into a patio on the other. Plant a mix of perennials.

ABOVEGROUND POOLS

One of the more difficult challenges in contemporary landscaping is working aboveground pools into the landscape in an attractive way. A big, blue plastic container, a ladder up, a ladder down, a deck sticking up on stilts—it requires an innovative design approach to make it look like it belongs in the garden.

Alpine Pool

Design a mountain effect around an aboveground pool. Put in big boulders and evergreen trees on one side. Create the effect of a mountaintop lake.

Mountain Meadow

Build a soil berm several feel in front of your aboveground pool. Plant the berm with alpine wildflowers and create a mini-meadow around your pool. Lay a wildflower carpet, a sod of mixed wildflowers that are actively growing. All you have to do is lay and water it. Look for it at your garden center or ask a landscape professional.

Spring-Fed Pool

Set your aboveground pool into a hillside. Put a path up to a ledge in the hillside where you can sit by the pool's edge. Work in some rock outcroppings and give the space a spa-like quality.

Reflecting Pool

Just as with an in-ground pool, darker bottoms of an aboveground pool will provide reflection on the surface. The reflection of the trees, sky, and structures around the pool will have a tremendous aesthetic impact when trees or other plantings around it are objects that are perfectly mirrored on the surface of the pool.

POOL SAFETY

While pools are a wonderful source of recreation, entertainment, and relief from summer heat, they can be dangerous, especially to children. Make sure to keep the following guidelines in mind when constructing, maintaining, and enjoying your pool. The following guidelines are courtesy of the National Spa and Pool Institute. For complete safety guidelines, contact them at 2111 Eisenhower Ave., Alexandria, VA 22314; (800) 323-3996; www.nspi.org.

◎ Supervision—Constant adult supervision is the primary precaution for which there is no substitute. Never take your eyes off a child when he or she is in, or near, any body of water, even for a second. All other safety precautions should be used in addition to constant adult supervision.

◎ Fences and gates—Fencing should be at least four feet high. Check local regulations for specific requirements in your area. Fence gates should have latches that automatically close and latch securely. Windows and doors that open to the pool or spa area should all be self-latching. Many devices are available that attach to doors and gates that will sound a loud chime when opened and closed. Don't overlook placing alarms on sliding doors and windows that allow access to the pool or spa areas.

◎ Perimeter and motion alarms—Infrared detector beams are among high-tech safety options now available at very affordable prices. Infrared systems sound an alarm when the beam is crossed, and you can place them around the perimeter of a pool or spa. Water motion alarms are placed in the water along the edge of the pool and sound an alarm when the water is disturbed in any way.

◎ Safety covers—Get an impenetrable covering that completely covers the pool or spa, blocking access to water. Safety covers can be manual or automatic. Insist on a cover that has a label stating that it meets the ASTM F13-46 standard for pool and spa covers.

◎ Portable telephone—A cordless or poolside phone means parents don't have to leave children unattended while they answer the phone.

◎ Ropes, life rings, shepherd's crooks—Rope and float lines placed across the pool alert swimmers to the separation of the pool's deep and shallow ends. Rescue equipment such as life rings and shepherd's crooks can be used to pull someone in trouble to safety.

◎ Toys—Toys, tricycles, and other playthings should be stored away from the pool or spa area. A favorite toy left near the water can be a very strong attraction for a child.

◎ Substance-free—Never use a pool or spa while or after consuming alcohol or any drugs. Consult a physician if taking any medication on a regular basis prior to swimming or using a spa.

◎ Diving—Know the depth of the water prior to diving, and never dive into shallow water. Never dive into an aboveground pool. Learn safe diving from a local swimming instructor.

◎ Emergency procedures—Learning CPR, cardiopulmonary resuscitation, is a skill that may save a life. The local YMCA/YWCA, the Red Cross, and many local hospitals offer classes.

> "Never take your eyes off a child when he or she is in, or near, any body of water."

▲▲▲▲▲▲▲▲▲▲▲▲▲▲▲▲▲▲▲▲▲▲▲▲▲▲▲▲▲▲▲▲▲▲▲▲

OTHER WATER FEATURES

The variety of items that can integrate water into your property range from a large pond to the smallest spray. A formal or natural looking pond may become the central focus of your garden, or your water garden might be a small, free-standing feature that serves as a sculpture. A simple fountain or cascade will add the interest of sound, motion, and the play of light. Include plants, fish, and lighting, and a water garden will provide close to year-round interest, twenty-four hours a day.

Unless spring fed, most ponds, waterfalls, fountains, or other water features are self-contained. That is to say, they are watertight. They don't need constant replenishing from an outside source of water. You only need a hose to fill them when the water level drops due to evaporation, splashing, or after they are drained. And, you seldom need to drain in-ground ponds.

FOUNTAINS

In addition to beauty, fountains can also add sound to the water. They are available in fiberglass, metal, ceramic, stone, and concrete. Styles run simple to elaborate, rustic to formal, bubble to spray. And prices vary quite a bit, depending on size and construction. You can install one yourself or hire a specialist to design and put one in.

There are pre-built, ready-to-install features, such as the classic lion's head for a stone or brick wall or a cherub fountain. Create your own piece, made from rock, metal, or other material—it can be in any configuration you wish. You only need a basin to hold the water and a pump and hose to drive the flow. A pump with moderate to low flow rate—two to three hundred gallons per hour or less—can be all that's necessary for a small outdoor fountain.

When you are building a fountain, experiment with water delivery to achieve a certain stream or flow. Alter the shape of the outlet pipe to change the effect. Lay rocks in different places. Move the pipe around to try different angles of flow over the surface of the fountain.

But keep your design simple. If you dominate it with water features or sprays shooting in too many directions, you risk losing the beauty of the feature. For ideas, visit gardens and public spaces where there are fountains. Go to garden centers. Talk with specialists about installation to ensure maximum efficiency and proper water pressure.

PONDS AND LILY POOLS

Ponds and lily pools can be living ecosystems the year round. Place a pool in a sunny area so plants thrive. It should not collect an abnormal amount of leaves and debris. Add exotic flowering plants, fish, and other wildlife, and the aesthetic benefits double.

Almost all aquatic plants prefer to grow in calm water. Continuous movement should be very gentle if you want to have water lilies, lotuses, and irises, or you can separate the rush of water from the planted areas by placing them off to the side or tucked behind a rock in a still spot.

To bring the water garden into balance, plant the proper combination of aquatic plants to shade and oxygenate it, snails to clean it, and pumps to aerate, recirculate, and filter. The pump you should use to recirculate water in a pond depends on the height and size of the feature. Therefore, the ratings for pumps can run from 200 gallons per hour or less to 10,000 gallons per hour or more.

Install fish, either generic goldfish, which are usually very inexpensive, or more costly specialty ones, such as koi, that can be trained to eat out of your hand. And don't forget tadpoles. The interest factor is so high with a balanced water garden that you'll reap many hours of enjoyment. Complete information on installing and maintaining one can be obtained from a company specializing in fountains or ponds. They are listed under these headings in the Yellow Pages.

A SIMPLE WATER GARDEN

Building a pool can be a simple task. You can buy preformed fiberglass, install a liner, or have a concrete pool built. There are many possible variations.

Here are some guidelines for a very basic liner installation:

1. The top edge of the pool must be perfectly level. The ground surrounding the pool, however, needs to be graded down away from the brim so the water will drain away from the pool walls.
2. Dig it eighteen to twenty-four inches deep, in a configuration that fits your design. The soil you excavate could serve as a mounded planting bed and a way to create a cascade of water on an otherwise level site.
3. Put moist sand into the excavation. Smooth all sides of the hole with it.
4. Lay in a rubber pool liner, which can be bought at garden and home improvement centers, as well as water garden suppliers. To figure the size of a liner for a pool that is eight-

een inches deep, add five feet to width and five feet to length. This allows an extra twelve inches of liner to overlap the edge after smoothing the rubber sheet against the sand.

5. Fill the liner with water. Do not lay rocks in the bottom of the pool; they could puncture the liner.

6. Lay mortared or dry stone coping, or any choice of edging, to cover the top flap of the liner that is lying at ground level. The extra liner material at the top ensures that the entire unit remains watertight.

7. Purchase plants, snails, and a pump, which will help bring your pool into balance. Add fish.

The smallest flow of water can be dammed. You can use a waterfall, dripping ledge, quiet pool, splashing fountain, container of water, reflecting pool, basin, jar, tray, barrel, and a few dozen variations on each of these ideas. And you can add other features that add to the water garden: seating, patio, statuary, lighting, sculpted fountains, rocks, bridges, decking, plants, fish, frogs, turtles, and more. Depending on the type of water feature, consider its need for light and place it where debris won't tend to collect. As with most other constructions, check the regulations of your local jurisdiction to determine if there is a need for a permit to build a pond on your property.

ROCKS IN THE LANDSCAPE

34

Rocks are becoming increasingly popular in landscape design. They are probably one of the best hardscape elements to add to a garden when you want a natural look. Large rocks are the number one lowest maintenance element of the landscape, especially if they aren't stacked into a wall but just lying around in the beds.

The most important tip I can offer regarding landscaping with rocks is that they should always look like they belong in the landscape as a part of the natural surroundings. Achieve the natural look by spreading rocks through the area. But not too many—you aren't building a rock garden, but putting rocky accents into your landscape. Arrange a few rocks in a random fashion in a planting

These rocks have been designed to look like a natural part of the landscape.

Are these small rocks, or do they go deep below the surface? (Brookside Gardens, Wheaton, Maryland)

bed. Work at having the rocks complement the plantings so they both look like they belong there, adding some architectural value while being softened by flowers massed around their bases. Continue the theme in different beds throughout the garden. Repetition is an important design principle when landscaping with rocks. Even if you have a rock outcropping and it is the only natural section of rock in the neighborhood, get some more and repeat it here and there, not everywhere. Using just one rock in your landscape will not look natural.

Except for the glacial strewn look, most rocks occur in the landscape because they've had to stay—that is, they're trapped by the earth. Repeat this effect in your landscape. When using small rocks, make them appear as if they are jutting from the ground and there is more underground, simulating the outcropped look.

GETTING ROCKS

Most of the time, ornamenting your landscape with rocks is not something you can do on your own. A sitting rock could weigh two to three tons, so you'll need to bring in the professionals with heavy equipment to place them. When I order rocks for a landscape, they usually come in big boom trucks that include a self-contained crane to lift and place the rocks. You can estimate the weight of rocks at between fifty and one hundred pounds per cubic foot, depending upon its composition. Remember though, that rocks are very heavy and, therefore, pricey because of the expense involved in moving them.

Get your rocks from a local quarry. Check Yellow Page listings for quarries in your area. Some have showrooms, where they import and display rock from other parts of the country. But native rocks will fit the natural look well and will be far less expensive than rocks from somewhere else. Have a pretty good idea of the dimensions you are looking for when you go to the quarry. Some quarries will allow you to put on a hard hat and walk around and pick out what you want. Be as particular as you would be for plants. Look at color, texture, shape, size, etc.

The effort and expense of transporting and placing elements weighing several tons limits the use of ornamental rocks in the landscape. Nature has produced lava rock, which weighs a great deal less than regular rock and is much cheaper to transport. Lava rock, a very porous volcanic material, is significantly lighter than natural stone and available in a number of colors: blacks, browns, russets, grays. You should be able to find lava rocks at quarries, through landscape companies, garden centers, and you can get bags of small lava rocks at local home improvement stores.

Modern technology has stepped in with artificial rocks that look just like the real thing. Artificial rocks are composites of various materials, including fiberglass, reinforced plastic, and concrete. They are being used more and more—the National Zoo in Washington, D.C., installed a large display, and much of the garden was done with artificial rocks. They are much lighter than the real thing and can be fabricated to meet your exact specifications. Mixing artificial and real stone can be a good way to enhance your landscape. They are so realistic that large artificial rocks could be mixed with smaller pieces of the real thing and create a landscape design on your property—indoors or out—that would not have otherwise been possible. You can build waterfalls, cliffs, mountain scenes, and more. You're limited only by your imagination. Custom rock hardscapes are available from the companies that fabricate them; consult the Yellow Pages for companies in your area.

USES IN THE LANDSCAPE

I've discovered a lot of ways in which rocks can enhance the landscape. Be innovative in your thinking.

Use rocks for a natural or rustic effect. A stone wall is a charmingly rustic accent on your property, as is a rock coping around a natural water feature such as a lily pond.

Stonehenge-like monoliths add drama to this landscape. (Brookside Gardens, Wheaton, Maryland)

Plant rocks in the soil as steps. You can do this with big flat rocks in a way that is comfortable to follow up or down a slope. Also, smooth flat rocks make natural seats in the garden.

Another treatment with rocks is Stonehenge-type design work using six-foot-tall rocks with long smooth ends sticking up. This type of staggered wall of huge rock slabs can be used in gardens very effectively for partial screening and dramatic effect.

Water spraying through rocks lends a natural feel to the garden.

Rocks are a wonderful enhancement for water features. Water bubbling up over rocks, water falling down over rocks, rock fountains—these are just a few of the natural features we see and try to duplicate in our gardens. Artificial rocks work well in waterfalls.

Gather similar sized rocks and stack them for a stacked rock retaining wall. It only takes a few large rocks to get a sixteen- to eighteen-inch high wall, and low rock retaining walls are wonderful additions for giving a manicured look to a natural garden. Don't use artificial rocks for retaining walls. While they might be all right for a veneer, you need the heavier weight of real rock. See chapter 27 for more information about stone retaining walls.

STONE MULCH

Another use for rocks in the landscape is as an ornamental stone mulch. Stone mulches can be very colorful—grays, tans, pinks, blues, blacks, and other colors. They are available in a range of sizes, from pea sized to three to four inches, and they can be rounded stones or crushed chips. River and ocean gravel are rounded and smoothed by water and are my preference over crushed gravel for an ornamental mulch. Take advantage of the number of choices available. Atlantic Ocean gravel tends to be almost white. Along the eastern seaboard, ornamental gravel I have used are tan Potomac River gravel, brownish Susquehanna River gravel, gray Delaware River gravel, and a rich pink to blue granite based stone found along the Atlantic Ocean in Nova Scotia, Canada. All of these gravels are available everywhere. All other rivers and oceans have their own special colors and textures of stones, and you may want to take advantage of your local favorites and tie them into your landscape.

When installing stone mulch, always use a porous landscape fabric under the stone for air and moisture circulation. You will also be able to gather up the stone much easier when you re-landscape. In these times of security concerns, be careful where you place loose rocks. If you are placing a three- to four-inch stone mulch in a high traffic area, you might give some thought to the windows within throwing range that might be vandalized.

A stone mulch can get dirty, and it is difficult to clean. You can blow off the leaves and debris and freshen the mulch with new stone from your supplier. If you are going to use this maintenance technique of adding fresh stones annually, start with a fairly thin (one-inch) veneer because the thickness will grow over the years since rock doesn't decay.

There are good uses for ornamental stone mulch—and not so good uses. I generally don't recommend mulching planting beds with stone because of the difficulty of accessing the soil. It poses a very difficult maintenance situation and deprives plants of a continuing source of organic material in the soil. It can be effective, though, as a small buffer around trees or an edging around a bed, but you can't easily get compost into soil that has a rock coating over the surface.

Below are a few good places to use stone mulch. Try any of these, or be creative and come up with your own uses.

If you have a drainage swale, lay stone mulch to imply a riverbed. Covering the soil surface with a consistent aggregate material such as rounded river gravel will provide an effective and ornamental drainage medium.

Use stone as a mulch to cover a problem area; for example, a tramped-down area of compacted dirt or a pedestrian area. It is also good to put under a low deck to keep weeds and grass from growing up through the boards.

Use stone mulch to give a Southwestern feel to a portion of your garden. Mix it with sand, some larger rocks, and some cacti. Cacti, yuccas, agaves, and several other desert plants look good mulched with stone or coarse sand because they are meant to grow in that environment.

A variety of stone mulches can create a formal Italian pebble garden. Use imported crushed stones and rounded gravels for a variety of appearances. Set the stones in mortar or simply lay them in steel or aluminum frames. Another effective technique used in Italian pebble gardens is to have a layer of water four to eight inches deep flowing from a running fountain, covering some areas with water and leaving others dry.

The Well-Planted Landscape

THE WELL-PLANTED LANDSCAPE

35

Finally, we have come to the part of this book that everyone thinks of when they think of landscaping—the growing things, the plant material, the softscape. I think you can appreciate by now that softscape is only 50 percent of the formula.

Look back to chapter 4 for the discussion of preparing the soil with everything you need for your plants to thrive. But arranging them is part of the art of growing them, as well.

Again, I emphasize the importance of locating all of these softscape elements on a piece of paper—your design—before actually placing them in the garden. It is only by following a design that you will be sure you have everything just where you want it.

I am not a plant purist. I think all plants can and should be used together. In the perennial border, I would use shrubs, trees, and annuals, for example. Even a pure rose garden can have as accents lavender and artemisia, which serve as a wonderful foil for the leggy nature of roses and a nice complement for many of the colors available.

Trees are the most important elements of your softscape because they are the canopy of the garden. When your design is done and you begin its execution, start with the trees. Trees are the first plants to be installed, and they will eventually create shade in your landscape.

Ascertain the light requirements for all your plantings. This is even more important than soil preparation for the well-planted landscape. While many of the plants that we discuss, such as roses and lawns and edibles, require full sun to thrive, there are many plants that do well with less light.

The last chapter of this section is about pruning, and you will learn how tending your plants is an integral part of landscape design. Proper pruning enhances the landscape and the design, and I will discuss pruning—as well as espalier and topiary, which do not follow the natural growth pattern of plants.

> "I am not a plant purist. I think all plants can and should be used together."

TREES AND SHRUBS 36

Trees and shrubs, the woody landscape plants, are the first things you put in the ground when you begin to plant your landscape. The differentiation between trees and shrubs can blur sometimes, but generally shrubs grow to the ground, while trees are elevated off the ground with a fully visible trunk and branching habit. Many conifers, however, also grow to the ground. Generally, trees and shrubs together make up the woody plants that are used in landscaping. They are planted first because they are the slower elements of your landscape to establish and become ornamental. Locate your trees first as you begin to plant your landscape.

Think about all the ornamental characteristics of the plant and use them accordingly. Shrubs are important to consider for size, flower, berry, fall color, and screening from the ground up. They make perfect backgrounds for perennials or other plantings. Remember, though, that the distinction is not always clear. There are dogwoods—grown for flower, fruit, and fall color—that are shrubs and ones that are trees; crapemyrtles could be perennials, shrubs, or trees. This is true with many species.

Develop a concept of what you want when designing. Trees and shrubs occur in many forms, and the consideration of the plant forms is important. They can be vase shaped, globose, fan shaped, or many other forms. Don't be stuck on plant names—find a tree or shrub that will fit the leaf, flower, and other characteristics you are looking for, not a plant that you know the name of. Arrange them on paper first, as described in the chapter 3. Once you think you know exactly where you want the plants on your design, then you can get the plants and begin the work outside.

Be very careful about choosing your site and locating the plants on site. Stand back and look at them from every perspective. Have future vision. Think about what they will look like in three to four years, and longer. Only then will you really know the exact placement for planting, leaving plenty of room for trees and shrubs to grow and spread.

The most common error in planting by professionals and home owners is installing plants too close together and too close to structures. I've seen yews and junipers planted along a parking lot, just eighteen inches from the edge of the paving. These are shrubs that if sited properly can grow ten to fifteen feet tall and wide. Crowded against the pavement, they will never achieve their full ornamental potential. Remember, it's impractical to move trees and shrubs once they have established their roots. Without a vision of what this plant will look like in the future, it could lose its ornamental value within three to five years instead of becoming an absolute specimen in five to ten.

DECIDUOUS TREES

Trees give off oxygen, cool our environment, anchor the earth's mantle, provide food, and inspire poetry. While flower and fall color are considerations for trees, the branching habit should be its most important ornamental characteristic. Because a tree is a large part of the landscape, its shape and habit are very noticeable.

Trees come in many sizes, and from a landscape design perspective, size will be your first consideration in selecting a tree. Choose a small tree for a low garden for its handsome form, flowering value, and fall color. Use small trees massed in groupings of three or four in a common bed with other lower plantings or as a barrier. Medium trees can give flowering value and work as a canopy in small spaces, or they can stand as a lower layer of trees against taller trees. Just a few commonly seen examples of medium trees are the flowering pear, the kousa dogwood, and the red buckeye. Large trees stand as a tall canopy in your landscape and provide shade and screening and stateliness on your property. (See the plant lists in the appendices for information on specific trees.)

SMALL TREES

Locate a small tree off your patio as a source of shade. Although a small tree will seldom become a canopy because it only grows to about twenty-five feet in height, if located properly off a patio or deck, it can cast shade over a small area and allow sun to reach the flowers and other parts of the garden.

There are so many small trees to choose from, it's easy to overlook good specimens. Choose a kousa dogwood (*Cornus kousa*), a popular small tree, for its four seasons of interest. The kousas, with

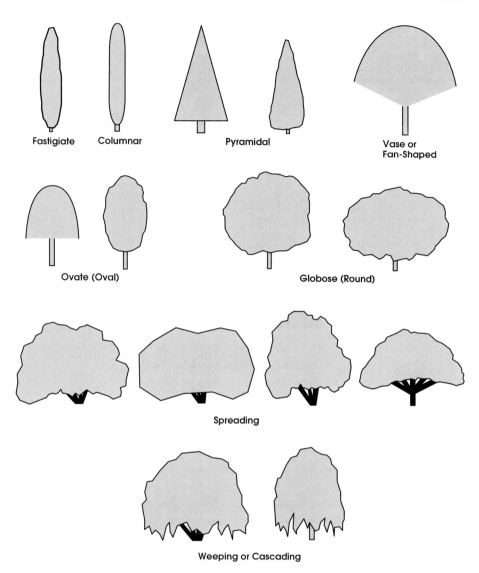

Fastigiate   Columnar   Pyramidal   Vase or Fan-Shaped

Ovate (Oval)   Globose (Round)

Spreading

Weeping or Cascading

Growth Habit of Trees These illustrations show the growth habits of trees. Using these terms will help professionals find you the type of tree you want in your landscape.

their lacy brown/light tan bark, provide an attractive look in winter and, as patio trees, give you a long season (two to three weeks) of late-spring flowers, edible fruits in autumn, and dependable maroon fall foliage.

Don't forget the small maples. We think of maples as big spreading trees or very expensive Japanese varieties, but there are many nice small maples like amur (*Acer ginnala*), trident (*A. buergerianum*), fullmoon (*A. japonicum*), paperbark (*A. griseum*)—one of my favorites for its cinnamon-colored papery bark. There are many others that provide a beautiful form and wonderful fall color.

The Japanese snowbell (*Styrax japonicus*) is a small tree that provides a wonderful, fine-textured, small canopy for the entry to a garden or just off your patio, for example. This is a tree that may

only grow as tall as a medium-sized shrub. Its daintiness and delicate growth habit, with white bell-shaped flowers in spring, make it attractive and welcome for a small space.

Stewartia is another tree that provides four seasons of interest with exfoliating bark, fall color, and summer camellia-looking flowers. There are several species available with differing barks and habits, but I couldn't recommend one over the other. Try one that you find appealing.

The white flowers of the downy serviceberry (*Amelanchier arborea*) are among the earliest spring flowers. Also called Juneberry, its edible berries are so attractive to birds that they may be gone before you get a chance to sample their tart sweetness in June. Depending on your climate, you may also see an orangish-maroon fall color.

Medium Trees

Medium-sized trees will fill another role in your landscape. On a small property, consider a medium tree. One that grows to about forty to sixty feet can provide a low canopy and intimate feeling. Also, small to medium-sized trees can be planted under utility lines without growing into them and needing topping, which ruins the ornamental value of the tree. Trees topping out at twenty-five to forty feet will probably not impede most power lines.

Some medium-sized trees can also have flowering value. Several of these include the saucer magnolia (*Magnolia* x *soulan-*

giana), the red buckeye (*Aesculus pavia*), and the ubiquitous Bradford pear (*Pyrus calleryana* 'Bradford'). Try one of the related varieties to 'Bradford', such as 'Redspire' or 'Whitehouse'.

LARGE SHADE TREES

Large trees are the aristocrats of the landscape. With their spreading canopies, they have the ability to give you the feeling of being in a cathedral. These ultimate shade trees live for hundreds, if not thousands, of years, forming the canopy over the final association of plants that have succeeded from the beginning of growth—mosses, lichens, grasses, flowers, and shrubs. Large shade trees are often deciduous or broadleaf evergreens. Conifers are usually full to the ground, thus they do not provide a canopy.

From a design standpoint, locate your big tree where you picture it becoming a venerable component of the landscape. Think big—a tree with a canopy spread of eight feet is already a mature specimen, but it may ultimately spread to fifty feet. Place it in a location that will do it justice.

Shade trees give you benefits besides their ornamental value. With three or four properly placed shade trees, you can cut up to 40 percent of your air-conditioning costs. Place the trees twenty-five to thirty feet off the east, west, and southwest walls of your house for best effect (see Energy Efficiency and Physical Comfort, chapter 13).

PLANTING AROUND LARGE TREES

Remember that all plantings in the area will evolve depending on the way that tree performs. When you are landscaping with big trees, whether you or someone from a previous generation started them, the rest of your job is to create a garden that will grow in their shade (see also chapter 18, Shade). No plant will grow in complete shade. It must have sun to photosynthesize, but shade is not the problem for growing things that many people think it is—you just have to find the right plants that thrive in partial sun. Trees will usually allow some light through the branches. There are many plants that tolerate lower light conditions well, as long as you are not trying to plant into a woody, tangled mass of roots. (Look for shade or partial shade designations in the plant lists in the appendices.)

Another difficulty you might face when planting around mature big trees is surface roots. When you are designing, make sure that you design under-story plants toward the drip line or outer branch spread of the tree to ensure enough light and less root competition. There is some debate about how planting over roots within the drip line will affect the health of the tree. I have not seen any detrimental effects to the tree or to the plants beneath from the practice of planting within the drip line, unless the tree was planted in a very poorly prepared site. When the only place a tree can get nutrients from is the top several inches of soil, trees and lower plantings will compete with each other for the same minerals and moisture. This usually occurs only because the soil is not deep and nutrient-rich enough. Amend the soil deeply with compost instead of leaving the area bare around under-story plantings.

WORKING WITH SHADE TREES

The U.S. was once well populated with American elms, one of the most regal specimens of large trees with its tall arching cathedral-like habit. The National Capitol Mall in Washington, D.C., and many of the main streets throughout the country were lined with magnificent arching specimens. Unfortunately most of these trees have been lost to Dutch elm disease.

The American liberty elm, a new and highly disease-resistant variety, is gradually taking the place of the lost elms in some communities (for more information, write the Elm Research Institute, Elm Street, Westmoreland, NH 03467, or call (800) FOR-ELMS). There are a number of new introductions of disease-resistant elms today. Search for them at your garden center. These new introductions include Frontier, Prospector, Patriot, Pathfinder, Valley Forge, and New Harmony.

Here's an important lesson we can learn from what happened to the elm: Don't plant in a monoculture, which means planting only one species. This is a tip that applies to city planners as well as home gardeners. Blights tend to strike selectively—you may have a problem such as gypsy moths, Dutch elm disease, oak blight, chestnut blight, or pear thrips. If you mix varieties, you'll never lose a whole stand of trees.

Rather than planting all of one type of tree, plant a variety of trees, but not too much of a variety. Use your designing skills, and the tips I have given you here, to avoid giving the appearance of a one-of-each type of collection. One way to do this is mass small trees together—for example, three dogwoods, then several eastern redbuds or hawthorns, and then group some crabapples in another part of the garden.

When planting shade trees, put in several varieties that have a similar shape, size, or texture to one another. If you want to replace the old vase-shaped elm you lost, use a zelkova (*Z. serrata*), which has a very tight, fan-shaped habit with many smaller branches growing to the inside of the tree. It doesn't quite achieve the effect of the elm, but it's a good substitute. Other shade trees that you can

"Dig wider but less deeply when planting trees. Trees should be put in slightly above the existing soil line and set on undisturbed soil so they don't settle."

plant with the zelkova to avoid planting a monoculture are red maple and katsuratree (*Cercidiphyllum japonicum*). You might even try one of the above listed elms at various locations on the property.

You can mix big shade trees with conifers to create a comfortable, open park-like setting, if your property is large enough. Ten thousand square feet is sufficient to establish a deciduous/evergreen woodsy area.

EVERGREEN TREES

Evergreen trees, or conifers, are a dominant part of the landscape across the country. Deciduous hardwood forests are a treat for fall colors and canopy, but the regal evergreens offer fragrant needles and tall screening elements. They tower over deciduous trees in the wild, growing to two and three hundred feet and taller.

Plant species of firs, pines, and spruces. I use conifers to screen the northwestern winter winds in groups of three to five or more. One will stand architecturally as a strong vertical element in the landscape. Plant them where they can mature and spread fifteen to twenty feet.

Many conifers grow with a pyramidal habit. The Japanese black pines, which have a handsome sweeping, windblown look are an exception to this rule. Design this windswept specimen for use in a Japanese style of garden or to mass as a windbreak. Japanese black pines (*Pinus thunbergii*) are a dependable conifer for most gardens.

Swiss stone pines (*Pinus cembra*) are slow-growing trees with tight blue-green bundles of needles that are valuable in the landscape as accent evergreens. They will fit into large beds with other plantings because they grow slowly and will spread only ten to fifteen feet wide and grow thirty to forty feet high. They will also stand alone as handsome specimens in the lawn, with their tight whorls of needles forming a dense tree.

Spruces and firs are widely used all across the northern part of the United States and in the South in higher elevations. They are naturally occurring in areas of severe climate conditions and seem to prefer high winds and low temperatures to warm, still air. Design them to complement large shade trees; use as a screen, or plant one of these regal pyramidal beauties individually in the lawn to set off the house and property. Several spruces with the widest range of hardiness are Norway (*Picea abies*), blue (*P. pungens* var. *glauca*), Oriental (*P. orientalis*), and Serbian (*P. omorika*). Firs usually like colder climates than spruces do. Two of the most adaptable to a wide range of climates are Nordmann (*Abies nordmanniana*) and white (*A. concolor*).

PLANTING TREES

When deciding where to plant, you'll most likely want to plant in the "golden section." The golden section is a theory of plant placement that has determined the best placement for plants or beds is about six-tenths of the distance (actually .618) from the house to the street or from one side of the lot to the other. The best composition is never dead center. You always want to offset your plantings slightly, perhaps a bed on one side, a shade tree on another.

The way trees are planted is important for their success—this is another lesson that we've learned from the disappearing elms. The elms lining Sixteenth Street in Washington, D.C., and in metropolitan areas around the country were planted a hundred years ago, before street paving had become widespread. As the streets were paved, the tree boxes became clay basins, and the trees were literally between a rock and hard place, between deep curbs and concrete walks.

Understand that for a big tree, the root zone is as important as the canopy in growth. The roots will spread as far or farther than the canopy. So they need a lot of room to stretch to allow the tree to achieve its full potential. Not only that, tree roots are very strong and may crack concrete walkways, foundation walls, and pipes as they reach for space underground.

This brings us to some tips for site preparation in planting trees. In general, follow the guidelines listed in chapter 4, but the necessity for widespread root growth entails some special measures for trees.

Dig wider but less deeply when planting trees. Trees should be put in slightly above the existing soil line and set on undisturbed soil so they don't settle. Prepare as wide a planting area for the root zone as possible, three to four feet or more. Backfill around a tree using existing soil from the site mixed with two to four inches of leaf mold or other compost. Using the native soil instead of importing topsoil helps a tree adapt to its new site.

Once trees are planted, there are several other maintenance areas you need to be aware of.

ROOT COLLARS

Keep the root collar exactly at the soil line. Find where the flare of the trunk of the tree meets its roots. That is called the root collar. Make this your top limit for soil or mulch against the tree. Piling soil or mulch against tree trunks will rot the bark and increase susceptibility to various fungi. In short, you'll lose the tree.

LEAF CLEANUP

Don't bother to gather up your fallen leaves. It has long been understood that a tree's leaves are its own best fertilizer, so let them lay to decay, except where they are smothering the lawn or other ornamental plantings. Until recently, professional and home gardeners raked and had all leaves hauled to the landfill. Professionals no longer recommend this, but you can certainly collect the major accumulations and compost them, returning them to the soil later.

TREE WRAP

Don't use tree wrap for general applications. Unless used while moving a tree or to repair damage, it probably kills more trees than it saves. While this thick paper wrap that comes in rolls does protect the tree for a couple of months in winter, the problems arise when it isn't removed after several months. Then it suffocates the tree and rots the bark.

STAKING

Stake a tree if it's planted with bare roots or has an insufficient root ball that might blow over in a storm. Remove the wires in one year. All too often, stakes and wires are left on the tree until the cambium layer (live wood) grows around the wire, impeding the normal flow of nutrients and opening the tree to insect and disease problems. Three stakes pounded equidistant from the tree and from each other, heavy gauge wire, and hose pieces are good staking materials. Leave some play in the wires. But don't stake or wire trees unless necessary. Research shows that trees establish better if their tops are allowed to blow in the wind without being staked and wired.

SHRUBS

A shrub is a woody deciduous or evergreen perennial plant that usually has more than one trunk. Shrubs—the plants most often thought of by the home owner after flowers—provide the vertical element of the landscape. Use shrubs for sequencing your design, as a steppingstone to fill the space between the low flower beds and groundcovers and the small and medium trees. They come in a variety of sizes and shapes, from vines to tree-like, and they fill a multitude of purposes. Shrubs can be used for screening, enclosure, flowers, or fragrance as hedges, informal masses, or single specimens. They are about the most versatile of the plants. Most can be hacked back and will return like loyal pets.

Like trees, shrubs are often divided into the low, medium, and tall categories. Of course, you're going to arrange them on paper first, as described in the design and planning chapters of this book (chapters 1 through 3). Low shrubs include low junipers like Andorra (*Juniperus horizontalis* 'Plumosa'), rockspray cotoneaster (*Cotoneaster horizontalis*), crimson pygmy barberry (*Berberis thunbergii* var. *atropurpurea* 'Crimson Pygmy'), Nikko deutzias, and Satsuki azaleas. For medium plantings, look to varieties such as dwarf-winged euonymus (*Euonymus alatus* 'Compactus'), nandina, winter flowering jasmine, or dwarf fothergilla (*Fothergilla gardenii*), azaleas, and barberries. In the large category, many viburnums will grow to eight by twelve feet. American boxwood (*Buxus sempervirens*) can get huge, as can arborvitae (*Thuja*) and yews (*Taxus*). These large shrubs need plenty of room to grow and make their best show.

Shrubs are often categorized as deciduous or evergreen. Of the evergreens, the broadleaf ones have colorful flowers and needled ones generally don't. Arrange flowering deciduous shrubs in mixed borders using several of each, perhaps with openings in between and a birdhouse or birdbath to add to the garden value and the wildlife or bird-attracting habitat.

Always place your shrubs where they can grow and mature and attain a size where their growth habit can be appreciated—at least five to eight feet apart. The oft-maligned forsythia has gotten a bad reputation because it is usually not grown properly and allowed sufficient space.

If you want a fast-growing screen, there are many deciduous and evergreen shrubs that will get there quickly and can be whacked back for easy control. Try photinias, yews, Japanese hollies, European cranberrybush (*Viburnum opulus*), forsythias, weigelas, or winged euonymus.

DECIDUOUS FLOWERING SHRUBS

There are so many attractive flowering shrubs that it's difficult to just recommend a few. Some of my favorites besides those mentioned in the tips below, that are good low maintenance, disease resistant shrubs for a deciduous flowering border, are flowering quince (*Chaenomeles*), weigela, pearlbush (*Exochorda*), and mock orange (*Philadelphus*).

Plant forsythia where you can allow the stems to grow long and full from the beginning of the season. This means a six- to eight-foot spread, perhaps at the rear of a perennial border. The forsythia

Flowering Deciduous Shrub Border

This shrub border uses the following plants:
A = *Amelanchier canadensis*
B = *Cercis canadensis*
C = *Chionanthus virginicus*
D = *Cornus sericea* 'Cardinal'
E = *Cornus sericea* 'Silver n' Gold'
F = *Fothergilla gardenii*
G = *Fothergilla major*
H = *Hamamelis mollis*
I = *Ilex glabra*
J = *Ilex verticillata*
K = *Itea virginica*
L = *Lindera benzoin*
M = *Magnolia virginiana*
N = *Rhododendron viscosum*
O = *Sambucus canadensis*
P = *Vaccinium corymbosum*
Q = *Viburnum dilatatum*

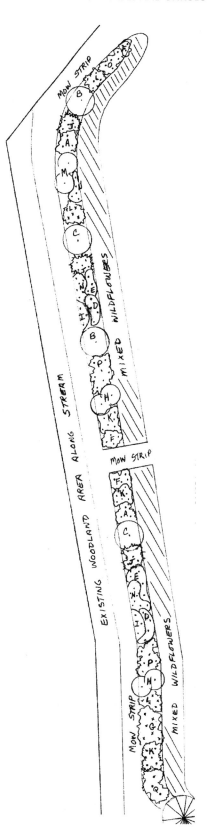

will flower profusely to a memorable point the next season. Just after flowering, prune them to less than a foot in length. Do not prune again for the entire growing season, and the long flowing stems will burst forth with new flowers in the spring.

Use the Nikko hybrid of deutzia, a low-growing deciduous shrub that only gets about four feet high and flowers white in mid-spring, in a mix with forsythia that you plant to prune to the ground right after flowering. The habits of the two shrubs will complement each other.

Plant lilacs, with their tall habit and high flowers, to the rear of a border. Keep them six to eight feet in height by keeping the thickest, tallest, and oldest wood cut out of the plant. Then you will have far less problems with borers in this southern European shrub, first cultivated in 1563.

Barberry is an excellent shrub to use as a background for your perennial border. This plant provides an interesting branching habit for birds to flit through in the winter, eating the berries and creating an object of interest in a season and area that would otherwise be devoid of interest since few perennials have any ornamental value in winter. If you use the crimson barberry (*B. thunbergii* var. *atropurpurea*), its foliage is deep red and beautifully contrasts with the green of other shrubs.

Harry Lauder's walking stick (*Corylus avellana* 'Contorta') is not a showy addition to the landscape until winter, when its curlicue stems are leafless. Then it's a veritable magnet for interest, which makes it a great perennial border complement. When fully in leaf, it looks like a handsome, globose eight-by-eight-foot shrub and is not particularly distinctive. In the winter, however, it loses its leaves and its contorted, corkscrewed branching habit strikes a singular note. The branches are a favorite for flower arranging and make it an object of immediate notice. In late winter, it forms long catkins, flowering bodies that droop like elongated dangles and disappear just before it comes back to leaf again.

EVERGREEN SHRUBS

Many people use evergreen shrubs for foundation plantings because they stay green year-round. There are many varieties of junipers, yews, and other needled evergreens because of all the hybrids that have been developed. I consider most of these shrubs to be boring, but they serve a purpose as year-round cover in front of your house.

Many people want to screen their home's foundation, but with today's new homes, this is often not necessary. Look at your foundation and decide if it needs screening. If it does, a common choice

Harry Lauder's walking stick displays its curlicue habit in the winter. (Brookside Gardens, Wheaton, Maryland)

for screening plants are evergreen shrubs. They will offer foliage twelve months a year. Use species that will stay low, such as weeping English yews (*Taxus baccata* 'Repandens'), Otto Luyken cherry laurels (*Prunus laurocerasus* 'Otto Luyken') or Helleri Japanese hollies (*Ilex crenata* 'Helleri').

Evergreen shrubs planted properly will grow into beautiful plants, but they must be planted and pruned to allow them to display their ornate characteristics. This means that you need to plant them far enough apart and will need to plant "filler" annuals, bulbs, and perennials and be patient for three or four years until the shrubs fill the area.

One of my favorite low evergreen shrubs is weeping English yew because of its billowy arching form and rich, dark green color. It will flow over a wall or mound slowly to about five feet in height with a six- to ten-foot spread. For the best spacing, plant them five to six feet apart. They must be planted in well-drained, acid soil, high in organic material, and they don't like standing in wetness. Be warned, though—deer love them.

Cherry laurels are underused plants, where they are hardy. As Zone 6 shrubs, they will survive to about -10°F. The cultivar 'Otto Luyken' has a compact habit, grows to only three or four feet without pruning, and has white, fragrant flowers in sun or shade. Plant them at least four feet apart.

There are low-growing Japanese hollies, but few have as interesting a growth habit as Helleri hollies. They stay low enough to plant against your foundation or use as an accent plant without the need for pruning. They have a handsome mounded and layered habit when not pruned. Plant them on three-foot centers in well-drained soil high in organic material and protected from the northwest wind, and they will survive to about -20°F.

Island Beds

If your foundation doesn't need covering, stop thinking in terms of foundation plants. Put in some low shrubs that won't hide the house and step out into the yard with an island bed that masses a sequence of interesting plantings that you can see from the house. You can use low and medium-sized flowering shrubs and small flowering trees in this arrangement.

Heirloom Shrubs

Until recently, the trend in American home landscaping, since the mid-1950s, was to use an increasing number of evergreen shrubs. Yews, junipers, Japanese hollies, arborvitae, azaleas, and rhododendrons—most maintained as clipped geometric shapes—had replaced many of the old-fashioned flowering shrubs. But these old-fashioned flowering shrubs are making a comeback, and you can find varieties of these "heirloom" plants in many garden centers and nurseries. I am happy to see these plants reappearing. Start with four or five plants and see how they perform. Get two or three of each variety, and mass them together. The following shrubs are ones I like and believe are worth trying around your home.

Glossy abelia (*Abelia* x *grandiflora*): This fragrant white-flowered Chinese evergreen, introduced in 1844, is in bloom from June and will flower until first frost. You can't beat it for dependable flower, evergreen leaves, and a medium growth habit of five to six feet tall and wide. Since it has long-blooming fragrant flowers, bees and other insects will frequent it all summer. Don't plant it near a sidewalk or an entrance to the house, unless you want to dodge flying insects as you walk past. It works well planted to the back of a perennial border.

Common boxwood (*Buxus sempervirens*): The aristocrat of heirloom shrubs, boxwoods were introduced from Europe, Africa, and Asia at varying times throughout recorded history. Legendary for their use in the formal gardens of kings, emperors, and wealthy citizens from many nations, they make a good evergreen shrub mass or hedge. Boxwoods look better placed together or planted as a single specimen. Plant no closer than five to six feet apart so each one will grow to its full size and display its billowy growth habit without need for shearing.

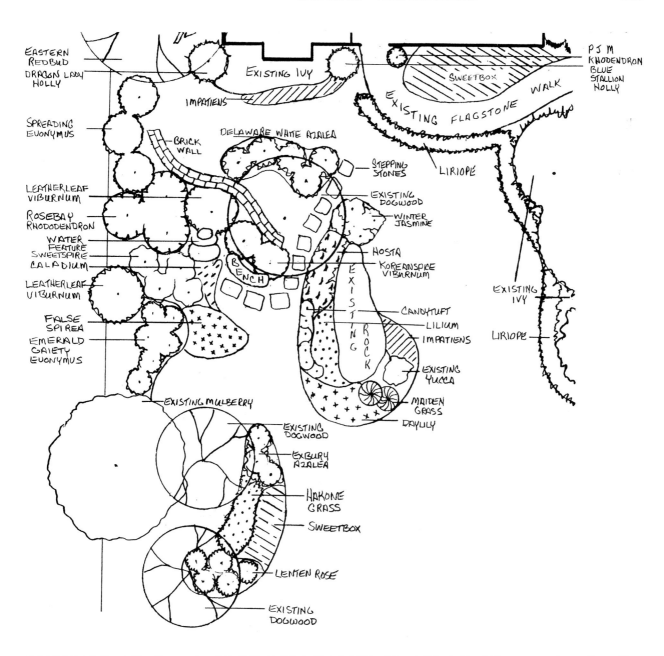

EASTERN REDBUD

DRAGON LADY HOLLY

SPREADING EUONYMUS

LEATHERLEAF VIBURNUM

ROSEBAY RHODODENDRON

WATER FEATURE

SWEETSPIRE

CALADIUM

LEATHERLEAF VIBURNUM

FALSE SPIREA

EMERALD GAIETY EUONYMUS

EXISTING IVY

IMPATIENS

BRICK WALL

DELAWARE WHITE AZALEA

STEPPING STONES

EXISTING DOGWOOD

WINTER JASMINE

BENCH

HOSTA

KOREANSPICE VIBURNUM

CANDYTUFT

LILIUM

IMPATIENS

EXISTING YUCCA

MAIDEN GRASS

DAYLILY

EXISTING ROCK

SWEETBOX

EXISTING FLAGSTONE WALK

PJM RHODENDRON

BLUE STALLION HOLLY

LIRIOPE

EXISTING IVY

LIRIOPE

EXISTING MULBERRY

EXISTING DOGWOOD

EXBURY AZALEA

HAKONE GRASS

SWEETBOX

LENTEN ROSE

EXISTING DOGWOOD

Island Beds

Chaste tree (*Vitex negundo*): George Washington grew this drought-tolerant plant at Mount Vernon. It was introduced in 1697 from Africa, Madagascar, Asia, and the Philippines. It grows as a handsome small tree or large shrub to about fifteen feet. The lavender flower spikes are welcome and showy, flowering in July and into August. It prefers well-drained soil in full, hot sun.

Slender deutzia (*Deutzia gracilis*): Use this plant in the mixed shrub border in front of taller plants, or use several together as a low hedge. Introduced from Japan in 1880, deutzia grows three to four feet tall and wide with pure white flowers in May.

Dwarf fothergilla (*Fothergilla gardenii*): This three- to five-foot-tall shrub is a nice complement to azaleas and rhododendrons, tolerates sun or shade, and likes wet feet. It has been available since 1765. It is pest free, with lightly scented flowers and very dependable reddish yellow fall foliage.

White fringe tree (*Chionanthus virginicus*): The fringe tree dates back to 1736. This native American large shrub or small flowering tree has white flowers in May that flow like an old man's beard, a name by which it's also known. Plant as a tree at the fringe of the woods, or as a fifteen-foot tall and wide shrub, and mix with lower growing shrubs in a deciduous border.

Japanese kerria (*Kerria japonica*): Best known for its bright yellow flowers that appear in early spring, kerria will flower dependably in sun or partial shade. Introduced from China in 1834, it has green zigzag stems and a fine-textured appearance. I don't know why this plant isn't used more extensively.

Mock orange (*Philadelphus coronarius*): This shrub from Europe and Asia was first introduced for landscaping in 1560. Growing from ten to twelve feet tall, it offers sweet scented white flowers, handsome shaggy orange-red bark, and is a reliable spring bloomer. If it gets leggy in old age, plant a lower-growing shrub such as deutzia or dwarf fothergilla in front of it.

Spiked or fragrant elaeagnus (*Elaeagnus pungens*): You will barely notice the silvery white fragrant flowers in fall, but its perfume will drench the air. You'll have fun watching visitors search for the fragrance. This disease-free plant was introduced in 1830 from Japan and is not for small gardens since it grows to ten feet or more. Plant as an accent along the path of a woodland garden. Several species are available that have white and gold variegated leaves. It is happy in shade, sun, moisture, and drought.

Hardy orange (*Poncirus trifoliata*): It came across the Pacific from China and Korea between 1823 and 1850. Grow this fully hardy citrus in sun or partial shade. Use its fruit as a garnish for drinks such as lemonade, tea and cocktails, or make it into a marmalade. If you need a barrier planting, a single shrub will form a thorny thicket up to fifteen feet in height.

"Old-fashioned flowering shrubs are making a comeback, and you can find varieties of these 'heirloom' plants in many garden centers and nurseries."

Summersweet shrubs are great for fragrance and flowers in summer.

Pearlbush (*Exochorda racemosa*): Introduced in 1849 from China, this member of the rose family is a tough plant that does well in sun or partial shade. It forms white flower buds at the ends of the branches that look like pearls in May and is good for a mixed shrub border.

Roses (*Rosa* species): Just as boxwoods have to be listed among heirloom plants, so do roses. Introduced from Asia pre-1600, roses are one of the first plants I think of when the word *heirloom* is mentioned. Literally thousands of different varieties have been bred in the past three to four hundred years.

Summersweet (*Clethra alnifolia*): A United States native, this deciduous shrub grows four to six feet tall and gets its common name for good reason. The fragrant summer flowers are a treat at a time when few shrubs are in flower. Introduced in 1731, it displays another season of interest with its russet-red fall foliage.

Virginia sweetspire (*Itea virginica*): This plant is a native of the eastern United States and was introduced for sale at garden centers in 1744. A low-growing, long-flowering plant, it has sweet smelling blooms and grows only two to four feet in height in sun or shade and in wet or dry soil. You get an extra dividend with its display of maroon fall foliage that holds for many weeks.

Common witchhazel (*Hamamelis virginiana*): Depending on how you prune it, this plant can qualify as a shrub or tree. A plant introduction that dates back to 1736, this United States native has yellow fragrant flowers that open in November and continue to bloom for about three weeks. This makes it the perfect complement to the fragrance of spiked elaeagnus. Fall leaf color is an outstanding yellow.

GROUNDCOVER

37

Groundcover plantings not only look good and are easy to maintain, but they also help stabilize the topsoil. Raindrop splash is the number one cause of soil erosion, and groundcovers alleviate this problem.

There are a number of ways to use them. You can use groundcovers in areas impossible to mow, such as slopes over a 25 percent grade that are too steep to safely walk on. Install plants that will form lush, flowering masses of low-maintenance green carpets. If you have shady areas where a lawn won't establish, try planting islands of lush evergreen foliaged groundcovers. And you can plant a meadow of wildflowers as groundcover on an acreage where mowing would leave time for little else (see chapter 42).

SELECTING GROUNDCOVER PLANTS

Some groundcovers are chosen for ornamental characteristics, while others are selected for their vigorous growth habit, depending on your priorities. I recommend that you take both characteristics into account, choosing plants that are aesthetically pleasing to your tastes and vigorous enough for quick cover. This will ensure the most desirable and lowest maintenance groundcover carpeting for your property. And unifying the garden with a single-species groundcover may be somewhat easier to care for than a specialty garden once it is established.

Choose groundcovers that have multiple seasons of interest. If selected properly, they can offer fragrance, flowers, berries, and fall color and are a natural controller of competing weeds. Wintergreen is a good example: The foliage and berries are fragrant, it has berries throughout the growing season, and the foliage is red in winter. It needs some shade and sandy soil.

273

St. John's wort forms a vigorous mass to use as a groundcover.

Look for plants ranging from four inches to four feet tall that will mass together to form a mat to make useful groundcover. The plants listed at the end of this chapter were chosen for this purpose, but any plant you know of that displays these characteristics will probably be a good groundcover. Your perennial gardens, mixed flower borders, rock gardens, or other plant collections are also groundcovers. These are viable options to hold soil. Each has its own cultural requirements, as explained in other chapters of this book. Keep your eyes open for possibilities already on your property—any vigorous low-growing plant that persists year after year and spreads like wildfire is an excellent candidate.

The most commonly installed groundcover in the landscape is lawn. Lawn seed or sod offers a quick green cover. Lawns will be covered in detail in the next chapter. Wildflowers are another groundcover that can be sown directly; they are discussed in detail in chapter 42.

Leaving an area to nature will also result in plants covering the ground. They'll do it voluntarily through self-seeding and wildlife activity. The forest is one example. It covers itself with leaf mulch annually, and up to a hundred species of flora will begin growing in an average acre. Cleared fields will automatically become covered with a wide mix of plants just by letting nature take its course. You then will have to manage the site to encourage the plants that you want to establish, such as raspberries, birches, butterfly weeds, and globe thistles, and to discourage the plants you don't want. Several of the undesirables might be multiflora rose, poison ivy, poison oak, poison sumac, and stinging nettle.

After you've selected the varieties you would like to plant, you'll need to determine if you will plant seedlings or sow seed. I usually recommend planting groundcovers from rooted cuttings or seedlings. They are more labor intensive to install than spreading seed, but many of the most desirable groundcovers would take far too long to grow from a sprout. And some do not even produce or set seed—English ivy and periwinkle (*Vinca minor*), for example.

SITE PREPARATION

If you prepare and design your site correctly, a lush and virtually maintenance-free carpet of plants will cover the area you have planted within three to five years. Site preparation is particularly important when installing groundcover because you won't have a second chance to go back in and dig more nutrients into the soil once the plants start growing together. Spring is generally the best time to install groundcovers from cuttings or young plants. You'll want to water them through the summer as they are establishing.

The following steps will guide you through the preparation of your site:

Get a soil test. Have your soil tested to determine what nutrients are needed for your choice of groundcover. A county extension service can usually do this, as explained in chapter 4.

Determine number of plants. Use the following guidelines to figure how many plants you'll need to cover the area you are planting, based on recommended spacing from your plant supplier:

- If you are planting eight inches apart, install 150 plants per hundred square feet.
- If you are planting twelve inches apart, install 100 plants per hundred square feet.
- If you are planting eighteen inches apart, install 45 plants per hundred square feet.
- If you are planting two feet apart, install 25 plants per hundred square feet.
- If you are planting three feet apart, install 11 plants per hundred square feet.

Spray a total weed killer. Apply weed killer in early spring prior to planting if weeds are a problem. In April, spray a glyphosate herbicide (Roundup, Finale, or Kleeraway) to control broadleaf weeds or grass when present and actively growing.

Add compost. At least ten days after last spraying with glyphosate, cultivate composted organic material (a one- to two-inch layer) and amendments (as indicated from the results of your soil test) into the top four to six inches of soil.

Plant. Rake area level and plant groundcover at the spacing recommended by the garden center or nursery. Make sure that the plants' roots are firmly anchored in soil, not mulch. This is of primary importance when planting groundcover. Depending on the size of the root ball, you may want to do what the professionals do: use a soil auger with a drill or a posthole digger to dig holes quickly.

Mulch with three inches of aged shredded hardwood bark. A shortcut is to mulch before planting and use a digging bar to punch holes through the top layer deeply enough to press the rooted cuttings into soil. It's a heck of a lot easier if you don't have to mulch around every little groundcover plant.

Water deeply. Newly established plantings should be watered thoroughly at time of planting. If you catch about an inch in a saucer under a sprinkler, that amount of water will penetrate to about a six-inch depth. Water this way about once a week during dry periods for the first couple of years. Weed as necessary.

MAINTENANCE

While groundcovers require a minimum of maintenance, there may be some upkeep necessary. Check with growers or garden center personnel about the characteristics of the plant material you have selected. Many groundcovers spread by rhizomes (underground plant stems that produce new plants) and stolons (horizontal branches that produce new plants from buds), and these can become invasive. You may wish to contain vigorous-growing groundcovers with edging. Also, some groundcovers can benefit from pruning now and then. Some may require it once or twice a year to be kept in bounds. For example, shearing or mowing renews English ivy, and some of the groundcover roses must be pruned to encourage fullness.

GROUNDCOVERS TO CONSIDER

FULL TO PARTIAL SUN

- Arnold dwarf creeping forsythia (*Forsythia* 'Arnold Dwarf'): Any soil; excellent bank cover; spring flower; sometimes good fall color. Plant three or more feet apart.
- Bergenia (*Bergenia cordifolia*): Well-drained humus; will take shade; pink flowers just above foliage in spring; bronze fall color; perennial. Plant twelve inches apart.

Weeping willowleaf cotoneaster is a rapid-growing prostrate shrub that will cover the ground quickly in full or partial sun.

- Compact Andorra juniper (*Juniperus horizontalis* 'Plumosa Compacta'): Most soils; low massing shrubs to eighteen inches; turning light purple to plum in winter; evergreen. Plant three feet apart.
- Flowering groundcover roses (*Rosa*): Most soil; low growing, long blooming; available in white, red, and pink flowers; may wish to cut back at end of season. Plant three feet apart.
- Plumbago (*Ceratostigma plumbaginoides*): Moist, well-drained soil; protected or eastern sun is best; deep blue flower all summer; red fall color; cut back in spring. Plant eight inches apart.
- St. John's wort (*Hypericum*): Any soil; blue-green foliage; invasive rhizome habit you may wish to contain; yellow flowers in summer; deciduous sub-shrub. Plant two feet apart.
- Snow-in-summer (*Cerastium tomentosum*): Any soil; silvery-green foliage; dense low grower; white flower spring and early summer; perennial. Plant twelve inches apart.
- Weeping willowleaf cotoneaster (*Cotoneaster salicifolius* 'Repens'): Moist, well-drained soil; vigorous prostrate shrub; maroon fall color; red berries into winter. Plant three feet apart.

PARTIAL TO HEAVY SHADE

- Creeping lily-turf (*Liriope spicata*): Any soil; green, twelve-inch-long evergreen grassy foliage; available with white variegation; excellent hedge against erosion in sun or shade; very invasive; plant only where it can grow into adjacent areas without harming other plantings. Plant twelve inches apart.

◉ English ivy (*Hedera helix*): Moist, well-drained humus; lush, deep evergreen foliage; many leaf textures and color variegations available; vine on structures. Plant eight inches apart.

◉ Wintergreen (*Gaultheria procumbens*): Sandy humus; some sun; fragrant fruit and foliage; berries throughout growing season; red in winter. Plant as pieces of sod.

◉ Pachysandra (*Pachysandra terminalis*): Moist well-drained humus; evergreen; handsome new growth; white spike flower in spring; easy to transplant. Plant eight inches apart.

◉ Periwinkle (*Vinca minor*): Moist, well-drained humus; blue or white flowers in spring; fine textured deep green; variegated cultivars available; evergreen. Plant eight inches apart.

◉ Sweet box (*Sarcococca hookeriana* var. *humilis*): Moist, well-drained humus; handsome dark green foliage; fragrant flowers; evergreen low shrub; slow to establish. Plant two feet apart.

◉ Wintercreeper (*Euonymus fortunei*): Moist well-drained humus; red margin on leaves; maroon fall coloration; evergreen; vigorous grower. Plant eight inches apart.

LAWN

38

Grass covers the earth, not only on our lawns, but in the fields of grain that feed our livestock and populations, and in a multitude of ornamental varieties that embellish our landscapes with their arching leaves and showy inflorescence. Grains, the agricultural grasses, are left to farmers, and we will talk about ornamental grasses in chapter 39. Turfgrasses are the grasses that make up our lawns, and that is what we'll focus on in this chapter.

I began in the landscaping business mowing lawns, and I've never lost my appreciation for the importance of the lawn in the landscape. Lawn is often a client's first concern—lawn installed around homes is usually the first element of the landscape and everything else in the softscape follows from the lawn. Too often, though, I find that people think either in terms of the absence of lawn, wanting to get rid of it, or they want a golf course. Both approaches are fairly unrealistic, as you need some lawn to set off your gardens or your home and no one has the time to keep his or her lawn looking like the front nine at St. Andrew's. Regardless of what size lawn you choose, there is nothing that can clean up the open space in a property better than manicured turfgrass with a sharp edge dividing lawn from planting beds.

Lawn is as low maintenance a groundcover as you can install. Instead of plucking the weeds, they can be mowed. It does not take long to mow a lawn, and mowing is the greatest improvement you can make to an urban lot. It adds organic material to the soil every time you cut and leave the trimmings. Your lawn will take an inexpensive initial investment of seed, digging, raking, and water. Then it requires attention (primarily mowing) about once a week during the growing season.

Don't make the decision to be without a lawn. There are many environmental benefits of lawn, including erosion and dust control,

> "Grass doesn't grow in shade, and you need at least six to eight hours of sunlight for a thick healthy lawn."

soil improvement, heat dissipation, temperature moderation, noise abatement, glare reduction, decrease of noxious pests, and reduced fire hazards. Grass offers health benefits, too—just 2,500 square feet of lawn will produce enough oxygen for a family of four. We also know through horticulture therapy programs and surveys by the National Gardening Association and Gallup Organization that there are social and mental health benefits of lawns, including social harmony, improved productivity, lower absenteeism from work, and more.

If you are trying to make a decision between some lawn and no lawn, your only consideration should be whether you can mow it weekly when it is growing. If you can mow or pay someone to have it mown, have some lawn. Don't make considerations based on fertilizer and chemical costs. The only other factor to consider is sunlight. Grass doesn't grow in shade, and you need at least six to eight hours of sunlight for a thick healthy lawn. If your entire yard is in shade, groundcovers will be a better choice than turfgrass (see chapter 37).

DESIGNING

When designing your lawn, determine how big an open grassy area you need by your personal preferences. Many landscape professionals (myself included) use the formula of two parts open space to one part mass in a landscape. Planting beds and shrubs make up your mass, while turf and patio are open spaces. I like to design sweeping lines to my lawns, for beds and patios. I don't generally recommend rigidly square type arrangements unless a client specifically requests it, usually for sports purposes. Don't forget to include these areas when you plan (see chapter 9, Athletic Activities). Turf is sports' greatest ally—you need it for many sports from croquet to football to golf to baseball to soccer. Whatever you play, you will need a big open grassy area to play it on.

SELECTING GRASS

There are several different ways you can plant your lawn, and a decision must be made about the variety of grass you use. Grasses are monocotyledons—they throw up a single leaf first, in contrast to broadleaf weeds that throw up two leaves. It comprises a massive family of plants, including grains, palm trees, and bamboo. Lawn grasses, called turf, are rather specialized members of this family. They must withstand regular cutting at heights of one to four inches, be perennial, stay green most of the year, and grow into a tight carpet that will withstand foot traffic. Turfgrasses that fit these criteria have been divided into two types, warm and cool season.

In general, cool-season grasses thrive in the spring and fall, when root and top growth is at its best, and have more root growth in winter than summer. Warm-season grasses are brown in winter and don't begin growing until average temperatures are over 60°F. Warm-season grasses have a coarser textured appearance and thicker leaf blades than cool-season grasses. The roots of warm-season grass will become massive and need to be thinned so that air can get through. The rhizomes (creeping underground roots) and stolons (creeping, aboveground stems) of cool-season grasses are not nearly as tough, do not knit as tightly, and are not near as dense in growth habit as warm-season varieties.

The choice between cool-season and warm-season grass depends on the plant hardiness zone you live in (see the USDA Zone Map on page 24). This is not always as clear-cut as it might seem, and the line of definition blurs where one can be grown and the other cannot. There are large overlapping areas and several different determinants. On a coast, for example, warm-season grasses are likely to do better farther north than toward the mountains, and cool-season grasses will flourish farther south toward the mountains but not on the coast. The map "Turfgrass Adaptation Zones" (page 282) shows which grasses should be used in which parts of the country. Count on your county Cooperative Extension Service (see the section "Free Information" in chapter 2) to help you make a final decision before putting in your lawn.

In the middle ground areas, where this is not definitive, you'll find cool and warm turf marketers competing for your lawn installation. Don't let the marketers make your decision for you—go to the local horticultural experts. You'll know that you have the wrong grass for your area if the grass stays brown at least six months of the year, as zoysia (warm season) does in Maryland and bluegrass (cool season) does in Florida.

When selecting and planting grass, avoid a monoculture, or all one variety of seed or grass. Mix varieties so that if one variety is hit with a disease or insect, your whole lawn won't be wiped out. Many bags of seed are combinations of a few types of seed, such as bluegrass, fescue, and ryegrass, which helps to establish the lawn quicker and to ensure against losing the entire lawn. Even if you want a stand of sure bluegrass, plant a blend of three to four varieties to lessen the chances of your whole lawn being killed.

COOL-SEASON GRASSES

Bluegrass

Fine fescue

Tall fescue

Rye

WARM-SEASON GRASSES

St. Augustine

Bahia

Zoysia

Bermuda

Centipede

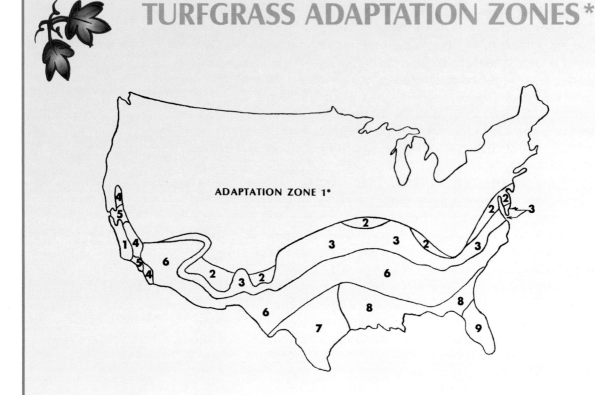

TURFGRASS ADAPTATION ZONES*

ADAPTATION ZONE 1*

Zone 1 = Bluegrass, fine fescue, bent grass, tall fescue, ryegrass (*includes southern Canada)
Zone 2 = Bluegrass, fine fescue, bent grass, tall fescue, ryegrass, Bermuda, zoysia
Zone 3 = Bermuda, zoysia, bluegrass, tall fescue, ryegrass
Zone 4 = Bermuda, dichondra, St. Augustine
Zone 5 = Bermuda, dichondra, St. Augustine, bluegrass
Zone 6 = Bermuda, zoysia, St. Augustine, centipede
Zone 7 = St. Augustine, Bermuda, zoysia, carpet grass
Zone 8 = St. Augustine, Bermuda, zoysia, carpet grass, centipede
Zone 9 = St. Augustine, Bermuda, zoysia, carpet grass, centipede, Bahia

*Used by permission of The Scotts Company, Marysville, Ohio.

COOL-SEASON LAWNS

Use a name-brand, improved variety of seed. It will be more disease resistant, more tolerant of insects, will grow denser, will contain fewer weed seeds, and is often bred for deeper green color. For example, if you are planting Kentucky bluegrass, buy seeds with names like Adelphi, Glade, Merion, or Vantage, not just plain old Kentucky blue.

Fine-textured bluegrass, fine fescue, and perennial rye are more prone to disease than coarse grasses, but they are softer to the eye and to touch. They can be mowed to a height of two-and-a-half inches and still maintain their lush appearance. For mixes of fine-bladed grasses, use bluegrasses, fine fescues, and ryes. I like a mix with approximately 40 percent bluegrass, 40 percent creeping red fescue, and 20 percent ryegrass. Try an already mixed selection, such as Blue Ribbon Shade for light shade (five to six hours of sun), Scotts All Purpose, Proscape Superior Sun and Shade, or find other named mixes. There are probably hundreds if not thousands of mixes on the market.

If you want a fast-growing lawn, plant ryegrass. Planted at the proper time in fall or spring, it will germinate in three days, and, given enough moisture, it will turn a bare area green in a couple of weeks. As with all grass seed, use a named variety, such as Penn-fine, Manhatten, and Citation. Do not plant annual or Italian rye for your lawn because it lives for only one growing season.

While ryegrass is a cool-season grass, annual ryegrass can be planted into a warm-season stand as an annual. If you have warm-season grass such as zoysia, it's brown when temperatures are under 60°F and green in the hottest part of summer. Seed an application of annual ryegrass over the warm-season grass in fall or early spring. It grows fast at 40 to 50°. The rye over the zoysia will yield green lawn during spring, summer, and fall.

With tall fescues, use compact-growing tall fescues (called dwarf tall fescues), or they will need to be mowed at a height of four inches. The improved varieties of tall fescues are not only disease resistant but also more compact, so they can be mowed at three inches. Don't mix tall fescues with bluegrass, fine fescue, and rye. Use a blend of compact-growing tall fescues, such as Compact Blend, Confederate, or another blend of three or more seed varieties. If you live in a cool-season grass area, choose between the tall fescues and the fine-leafed types, such as bluegrasses, fine fescues, and perennial ryes. Don't mix coarse-textured tall fescues and fine-bladed grasses.

WARM-SEASON LAWNS

As mentioned earlier, there are grasses that are adapted to warmer zones that grow better in the heat of the summer. When cool-season turf would go dormant or perish in hot conditions of the South, Southwest, and Southern California, warm-season grasses are thriving. They do best in temperatures between 80 and 90°F. Cool season grasses prefer 60 to 75°F.

"When cool-season turf would go dormant or perish in hot conditions of the South, Southwest, and Southern California, warm-season grasses are thriving."

There are many choices of warm-season turf. The most commonly planted species are Bermuda, zoysia, St. Augustine, centipede, Bahia, and carpet grass. As with all turf, always get a named variety. This means it's improved over the species in color, vigor, habit, disease, drought tolerance, or other more desirable characteristics.

Bermuda is grown throughout the South, from Florida to California. It's a native of Africa and was introduced in the United States around 1750. It will not thrive above the Mason-Dixon Line, stops growing at 60°F, and turns brown at 50°F. The further south it is, the better it will perform. Bermuda does not tolerate shade, poor drainage, or acidic soils, but is a popular sports turf because it will stand up to foot traffic and regrows fairly quickly. A couple of improved varieties to try are Cheyenne, Guyman, and Floratex. Tiflawn and Tifgreen have finer blades but are more invasive and will run into beds and paved areas. Mow about one inch high.

Zoysia has been hybridized to grow vigorously in colder climates. The most cold tolerant is Japanese zoysia, also called Korean zoysia. It's widely used in transition zones across the center latitude of the U.S., where neither cool or warm season turf does well. Zoysia will grow thick and keep any weeds from growing through. As a trade-off, the thick roots and stems create thatch that must be raked out, and once dethatched, zoysia is slow to renew. It also has high fertilizer needs in summer and is often brown for six months of the year. Try the hybrids El Toro or Emerald. Mow two inches high.

St. Augustine is a coastal grass in the warmest areas of the country. It's tolerant of salt spray and likes moist, fertile soil. It has a fast recovery but is probably the least tolerant of cold weather. Try Floratam, reportedly chinch bug resistant, or Bitter Blue, a fine-bladed hybrid with blue-green coloration. Mow one-and-a-half to three inches high.

Centipede grass is a low-growing native of China. Introduced here in 1919, it's not as tough a grass as Bermuda is, nor is it as tolerant of coastal conditions as St. Augustine. It's slow to establish but is seldom bothered by insects or diseases and it requires little maintenance due to its slow growth habit. The hybrid Centennial has better cold tolerance. Mow regularly at one to two inches high.

Bahia has a coarse growth habit and looks rough after it's mowed. This tropical American native has a yellow hue to the foliage. But work is being done to breed more desirable hybrids because it is drought and wear tolerant, insect and disease resistant, hardy from Zones 7 to 10, and very low maintenance. Named hybrids Argentine and Pensacola are superior to the species. Mow at two to three inches high.

Carpet grass is used because it will grow where no other turf-grasses survive. Growing in boggy, partially shaded conditions, carpet grass, a native of Central America, grows well in lowland areas from the Carolinas and south and west to Texas. It's insect and disease tolerant, but not drought tolerant. It does provide a green carpet for problem areas, such as swales or other waterways. There are no named hybrids; the species *Axonopus affinis* is all that you can get.

There are two native grasses that are best adapted to southern parts of the Great Plains and other semi-arid regions, buffalo grass and blue grama. They have a blue-green color and are slow growing and sparse in habit, but once established, you will have a lawn that only needs mowing two or three times a season. Because they are native and slow growing, these grasses are being tried in many regions of the country as a low-maintenance lawn. They will adapt to many drier areas of the country, but they do not do well in humidity. Hybrids of buffalo grass have been developed; try Prairie, Cody, or Topgun.

PLANTING YOUR LAWN

Plant cool-season lawns either by seeding or laying sod. Warm-season grass is planted by seeding, sprigging (spreading pieces of grass stolons over the surface), or by punching small plugs of it into the soil.

PREPARING THE SITE

The best way to treat a weedy lot that has not been cleared for months is to mow it level. In most jurisdictions, there are codes and covenants that dictate that you must mow your lawn, although a home owner involved in a legitimate wildflower meadow or woodland garden project may have a good argument for not mowing. To discourage regrowth of weeds, I often spray a glyphosate herbicide, such as Roundup or Kleeraway, after mowing and about ten days before overseeding or tilling and grading (see below).

A lawn that doesn't drain is useless. The area stays muddy so you can't use it, and turfgrass will die if it has wet feet. For optimum surface drainage, you should have at least a three-inch drop in grade over a ten foot run.

Check your pH with a soil test through your county extension service. They will tell you how to adjust the pH if needed. The optimum pH for a lawn is 6.5 to 6.8.

Whichever of the following planting methods you use, you need to prepare the site the same way. The soil in the lawn area should be tilled three to four inches deep with one inch of leaf compost and fifty pounds of lime per thousand square feet. The surface should be raked very level, but not turned into a powder. Remove rocks and leave a range of soil particles from a quarter-inch to an inch in diameter. This range of particle sizes will shade and hold seed and moisture in the lawn. Raking to a smooth dusty texture will tend to wash away and not hold moisture or seed, and moisture is crucial to seed growth.

SOD, SEED, SPRIGS, OR PLUGS?

Methods of planting all lawn grasses vary, but generally you can plant cool-season grasses from seeds, as discussed previously in this chapter, or you can sod. Sod is lawn that is grown on a farm and harvested when it is a thick mat of roots and can be moved like a carpet. You can buy it by the piece, which is usually three to four square feet. When laid tightly together on a properly prepared site, they will knit into a tight-growing, instant lawn.

Sodding

Plugging is a type of sodding that involves the planting of small blocks of sod approximately one foot apart on freshly prepared soil as discussed under the zoysia section above. More commonly, sodding is done with a thick mat of lawn and roots that are laid tightly together to become an instant lawn.

To sod, prepare the seed bed in the same manner as for seeding. Firm seed bed with a roller after final grading with a hard rake. Sod should not be laid on dry soil; the soil should be moist to a depth of six inches, but not saturated. Lay the sod pieces as you would lay brick, and fit them together as tightly as possible. Staggering the ends of the pieces of sod will prevent lines in the turf. Make sure the edges of the sod have good contact with each other but do not overlap. Roll or tamp to press it firmly against the soil.

Top-dress the surface of a newly sodded lawn with fine-textured soil or compost and work this into any cracks between sod pieces by dragging an upside-down wire or wooden rake over the surface. On steep slopes, sod should be held in place with wooden pegs or sod staples, inserted at right angles to the slope. When installing sod on steep slopes, the long dimension of the strip should be laid at right angles, rather than up and down the slope to prevent washing between the pieces.

After sodding is complete, irrigate deeply and continue to water well until the grass is established.

Seeding

Fall is the best time to spread cool-season grass seed. Make sure that the seed has good contact with the soil and good moisture so it will grow in the spring. Spring or summer is the best time to seed warm-season grasses. Follow the seeding directions on the package, as rates will vary depending on which type of spreader you use.

Plugging and Sprigging

Warm grasses, such as Bahia, Bermuda, and carpet grass, can be planted from sod or seed in the same way as cool grasses, but the time to plant them is just before their vigorous growth period. Therefore, plant in spring or summer. Warm-season grasses are also planted by two other methods because of their ability to sprout easily. Plugs or sprigs are commonly used for zoysia and St. Augustine. Plugs are pieces of sod cut into small, two inch squares or rectangles. You press them into holes about twelve inches apart, and they will establish in two to three years. Other grasses, such as rye, are often used as filler until the plugs establish.

Sprigging is the term used for spreading stem and root parts of warm-season grasses. Sprigs can be used in place of plugs. These broken or chopped up pieces of stolon and rhizome are about four to eight inches long. They are spread by machine or hand over a well-prepared lawn bed and should be rolled fairly deeply into the surface or planted in one- to two-inch-deep furrows. These sprigs will sprout roots and leaves to form new plants. They establish and spread most efficiently when mowed regularly.

WATERING

Different from irrigating sod, watering newly seeded lawns requires daily attention until seed germinates and grows several inches high. Begin watering the seeded area by sprinkling the top half-inch of soil; you can achieve this with a light spray of approximately an eighth-inch of water on the surface. You will know when it is moist enough by seeing that the soil is a darker color. As it dries and the soil color lightens, it should be sprinkled again, up to three times a day, if necessary.

As turf grows, watering frequency will be reduced—first to once a day as a greenish hue appears, then to every other day as blades extend to an inch or two in height. As soon as grass is high enough to be mowed, decrease watering to once a week and increase quantity of water to one inch on the surface. Measure this by placing a glass or other measuring device in the area of the spray. After the third or fourth mowing, your lawn is usually able to grow exclusively by rainfall, except in severe drought.

The latest research indicates that cool-season grass roots take their moisture in hot summers from the top one to two inches of soil. So for watering cool-season turf during scorching summers, lawns should be sprinkled three to four times a week with a quarter to half-inch of water. This keeps the necessary organisms vital that break down thatch, add fertility, and generally keep a lawn growing and healthy.

Maintaining Your Lawn

We are currently in an era where we understand that intensive use of insecticides, herbicides, fungicides, and fertilizers are not the best cultural practices to maintain the lawn. You should wait until there are problems to treat the lawn with pesticides, and just give it a shot of fertilizer in early spring and fall. Otherwise, the organic methods you'll find in this chapter are the way to go.

The ingredients for a healthy lawn are compost, nutrition, seed, and moisture. Here are some general tips for establishing and maintaining your lawn, whatever the variety of turfgrass.

Mowing

In season, lawns should be mowed weekly. Happy lawns could need mowing twice a week. The way to determine when to mow is by monitoring blade height and mowing when it's no more than a third of an inch above the desired height. Ideal blade length varies from one to three and a half inches.

There is some sentiment in the native plant movement, which is very popular today, to leave grasses growing for a natural environment that is hospitable to wildlife. I caution against this, though, particularly around your dwelling. Wildlife can be undesirable. Rabbits and squirrels aren't the only rodents of the city and suburbs, and manicured lawns offer no habitat to mice and rats. Ticks live in high grass, and regular mowing is one of the first things you do to control them.

Even in an overgrown area, establishing a defined area of mowed lawn is important. If you do want a wildflower meadow, keep it accessible by running a three- to four-foot mow strip in a meandering pattern through the meadow.

If you want wildlife habitats in your lawn, establish a corridor of trees and shrubs that the animals can follow with a mow strip somewhere through the center of that corridor. This will establish a low area you can see through clearly, to give you a view of the animal activity in the area.

DETHATCHING AND AERATING

Thin and aerate warm-season grasses with processes called dethatching and aerating. This should be done when the grass is actively growing to allow air and moisture down to the root system. Rent a dethatching machine or use a pointy-tined dethatching rake to drag through the grass and create openings. You can also rent an aerator to punch vertically into the soil for deeper penetration of air and moisture.

Generally, cool-season grasses, unless they are overfertilized, do not need as intensive a dethatching program, and aeration is usually enough. A plug aerator will achieve similar openings for air and moisture circulation as dethatching. Make several passes over the area for the most effective method of making openings in the lawn for air and moisture to penetrate. Make sure never to aerate when the lawn is wet. And don't use an aerator with solid tines. They allow penetration of water and nutrients but don't aerate. Solid tines actually *compact* the soil by pushing it together.

ADDING COMPOST

Condition the soil with compost that is fine textured enough to fill the aeration holes in the lawn. Sprinkle it about a half-an-inch thick over the holes, making sure that you don't cover the healthy growing turf. Your own compost is the best material to use. If you use commercial compost such as composted sewage sludge or recycled leaves, you might use as many as five bags per thousand square feet of turf if your lawn has a lot of bare areas, and as few as one or two per thousand if you already have a thick lawn.

> "In season, lawns should be mowed weekly. Happy lawns could need mowing twice a week."

FERTILIZING

Fertilize cool season grasses with dry material using a drop or broadcast spreader. Read the label on the bag for spreader settings and application rates. Use a fertilizer that is 40 to 50 percent organic with a percentage of slow release or water insoluble nitrogen (WIN). This allows the nitrogen to release slowly over months in the soil, and, since the fertilizer is organic, it will also add the extra value of humus. You should fertilize cool-season lawns three times during the growing season, in April, September, and October. If you can only fertilize cool-season grass once a year, September is the prime month to add nutrients. Cool-season grasses can use high nitrogen fertilizer in September because their leaves and roots grow vigorously between then and winter.

Fertilize warm-season turf when the grass is beginning to turn green and grow, in May, June, and July. Use at least two pounds per thousand square feet, or follow the directions on the bag.

It's also environmentally friendly to not catch your grass clippings, unless you want to use them for composting. Leave them where they lie and clippings, which are 4 percent nitrogen, will add organic nutrients to the soil.

OVERSEEDING

Overseed an already existing lawn with three to four pounds of seed per thousand square feet of lawn. Spring and fall are the best times to do this for cool-season turf, as grass seed does not germinate—or does not germinate well—in the warm temperatures of summer.

MIXING AMENDMENTS

After you aerate and spread the compost, fertilizer, and seed, ensure proper distribution of these amendments and break up the soil plugs taken from the holes in your lawn. Do this by walking an upside-down wire rake over the surface.

WATERING

Along with the sun, all of these lawn care practices must be combined with water. Without it, nothing grows. With a newly seeded lawn, when there is no rain, daily watering is necessary for establishment. To be sure your newly aerated and amended lawn is moist enough, irrigate with one inch of water. If dryness persists, sprinkle the area with a quarter inch of water when the surface appears dry. Measure depth of watering by placing a container under the sprinkler and measuring the water collected.

The latest research is beginning to show that lawn growth is a dynamic ongoing process, giving birth to new theories about watering your lawn. The old guideline that one inch of surface water once a week penetrates six inches into the ground has been replaced. When you water turf, do it more shallowly and more often. We have learned that for cool-season turfgrass, roots shorten from four inches to less than two inches in the hot summer, so regular watering of one-quarter inch on the surface every other day through heat and drought will keep the organisms working, breaking down the thatch. This will keep the grass growing and photosynthesizing.

Another option is to not water at all. Let the turf go dormant through a reasonable period of drought (two to four weeks) and the grass will start to grow again upon first moisture coming out of the drought. This is very environmentally friendly approach because it helps preserve water.

WEEDING AND KILLING PESTS

Weed killers, insecticides, and other toxic chemicals should be used with restraint on your lawn. Think of the environment, and tolerate some weeds and insects. Use pesticides on your property only when you see the pest and the damage from it. The pest could be weeds, diseases, or insects, but wait until it's a necessity to control them.

Weeds

When applying weed killer or herbicides, use formulations for specific grasses and weeds, especially to avoid damage to warm-season grasses. There are two classifications of weeds in a lawn: annual grasses such as crabgrass and goosegrass, and broadleaf weeds such as dandelions and plantain.

Control broadleaf weeds in the summer and fall with a pre-emergent weed killer labeled to keep the particular weed seeds you are trying to control from germinating. Broadleaf weeds tend to germinate and grow into the winter, so these treatments keep them from germinating.

In the spring, use postemergent weed killer. These are sold under a number of different commercial names and usually with fertilizer as a weed-and-feed. This is a good way to apply weed killer in early spring. Be sure to use a drop spreader and follow labeled instructions.

Diseases

Prepare in advance to avoid the necessity for a fungicide. The best hedge against lawn disease is good site preparation, good drainage, and proper air circulation. If you do all this and follow a sensible fertilization program and don't overfertilize, your lawn will rarely need a fungicide.

Insects

Treat for insect problems such chinch bugs, grubs, webworms, and others only when you see the damage and have an exact diagnosis. Again, the best vehicle for getting a diagnosis is your county extension service.

> "There are approximately 564,536,500 blades of grass in an acre of healthy turf!"

Before treating for grubs, be sure they are really the problem. Check by looking under dead sod for grubs; you should see six to eight per square foot if they are a problem. Treat with milky spore disease, and in two to three years the grub population will be almost eliminated and it won't come back. Milky spore disease is completely specific to the grubs, won't bother anything else, and is safe to the environment. A strain of nematodes (very small worms) that feeds on grubs is available. They work more quickly than milky spore disease and are supposed to reproduce and continue to control grubs indefinitely.

EVALUATING LAWN

Finally, how do you know if your lawn is as healthy as it should be? Here's a little exercise to help make that determination. Bend over and look at it. If it looks good, it's healthy. Or get scientific and count the blades—there are approximately 564,536,500 blades of grass in an acre of healthy turf!

Flowering Perennials and Biennials

39

Perennials

Perennials—the non-woody, herbaceous plants that will return year after year—can be used for the range of design styles in your garden, from meadow to natural informal to designed informal to formal. They usually come back from the roots after the tops freeze off during winter.

Perennials include bulbs, ornamental grasses, ferns, and some vegetables (asparagus, for example), as well as the ever-popular flowering materials most people think of as perennials—daylilies, black-eyed Susans, bleeding hearts, Shasta daisies, hostas, and some dianthus, to name just a few examples of the many perennials that thrive in our landscapes. You will find a list of the more popular perennials in appendix E.

You may think of perennials as established plantings, but one of the best things about them is the great flexibility they offer. Suppose you plant perennials somewhere and don't like the effect. Combinations may clash; one may move in on another; they may not flourish as you would like. If you don't like the placement of your perennials, dig them up and move them around. If you don't like them in the second place, dig them up and move them again. Most perennials give you the luxury of trial and error without sacrificing the plant.

Learn about the perennials that you plant. It's great that they grow and reproduce easily, but the downside of an easy-to-grow plant is that it can self-propagate and become a noxious weed in your garden. So learn about what you have planted through practical hands-on experience, and have no fear of getting rid of something if

293

You can achieve coordinated bloom with a mixed planting of astilbe, coreopsis, echinacea, and Jackman clematis.

it doesn't fit into your design plans. Be willing to take something out or move it to a place in your garden where you can allow it to totally take over.

Be patient. More than any other gardening, perennial gardening is an ongoing process. In the course I teach for the U.S. Department of Agriculture Graduate School on the use of landscape plants and principles of design, I advise that it takes a decade to develop the perennial garden you want.

BLOOM TIMES

Unlike annuals, which bloom all summer long, perennials have a season of bloom. Sometimes this season is quite lengthy. Plant your perennials in great enough numbers and coordinate them so that you have blooms all season long. Use long-blooming varieties such as Moonbeam coreopsis, Stella d'Oro daylily, or black-eyed Susan.

Long-Blooming Perennials

Name	Color	Height	Length of Bloom
Agastache foeniculum (anise hyssop)	Blue	30"	12 to 15 weeks
Coreopsis verticillata 'Moonbeam'	Yellow	12"	10 to 14 weeks
Echinacea purpurea (purple coneflower)	Purple	30"	10 to 14 weeks
Gaillardia x *grandiflora* (blanket flower)	Red/Yellow	24"	16 to 22 weeks
Heliopsis helianthoides (false sunflower)	Yellow	36"	12 to 16 weeks
Hemerocallis 'Stella d'Oro' (Stella d'Oro daylily)	Yellow	20"	10 to 14 weeks
Perovskia atriplicifolia (Russian sage)	Blue	36"	15 to 20 weeks
Scabiosa atropurpurea (pincushion flower)	Dark Red	36"	14 to 18 weeks
Verbena bonariensis (tall verbena)	Lilac	40"	18 to 24 weeks
Vernonia noveboracensis (New York ironweed)	Blue	30"	15 to 28 weeks

Use in Landscape

There are so many different ways to use perennials in your landscape that the possibilities are endless. Here are just a few suggestions.

Totally Informal Use perennials completely informally in a meadow. Many of the wildflowers that are naturally occurring native plants are perennials. Create your own version of a meadow in your perennial border. See chapter 42 for more about meadows.

Informal Groupings Stay informal with your perennials but in a more studied way. Place each plant in groupings rather than a shotgun method of establishment, perhaps with a path through them. But keep the arrangement informal and natural so they look like they sprouted where nature sowed them.

Plants with an open growth habit help to establish an informal look. Some examples are Japanese anemone, Russian sage (*Perovskia*), purple coneflower (*Echinacea*), and yarrow (*Achillea*). These plants have leaves that can sometimes be mistaken for weeds when they first begin to mature, and they flower at different heights.

For another informal arrangement, try a monoculture. Plant one species of perennial in a field as clumps and let it naturalize in a free-spreading fashion. Black-eyed Susan (*Rudbeckia*) colonizes very well that way. Astilbe in a shadier location gives the same shrubby massing effect. I've seen columbines (*Aquilegia*) seed themselves into colonies in cool, protected sites. Or try a clump of tall phlox in a protected area. Plant clumps of asters or butterfly weeds in full sun.

These informal plant groupings look as if they sprung naturally from the landscape.

Borders   Or plant perennials in a more organized fashion, along a sweeping bedline, sequenced by height, for example. Use a lower perennial such as candytuft (*Iberis*) and dianthus to the front. In the center, plant medium-height perennials such as peonies, lilies, bleeding hearts, and Autumn Joy sedums. In the rear, place your tall plants such as *Liatris,* New York ironweed (*Vernonia noveboracensis*), asters, *Boltonia,* and snakeroot (*Cimicifuga racemosa*).

An informal grouping of black-eyed Susans naturalizes and creates a vibrant monoculture.

Interesting Leaves   Many perennials are grown for their interesting leaves, such as hostas with showy variegated leaves and artemesias for their softly flowing, fragrant silver foliage. Autumn Joy sedum is another variety used for its attractive foliage throughout the season as well as for its flower. It grows about eighteen inches tall and is fleshy, with a succulent, light green leaf and large rounded flower heads. Its flowering foliage grows in a mass as a monoculture.

Foliage Patterns   Repeat plants in shade that have showy foliage. Mass the attractive leaves of one plant with the good-looking foliage of another to create a designed or patterned effect. For example, in shade, the silvery fronds of the Japanese painted ferns will blend with the silver markings on the leaves of lungwort (*Pulmonaria*). They can be placed to back up a groundcover of yellow archangel (*Lamiastrum*) in the foreground, which also has silvery markings on its leaves.

Formal Treatments   For formal beds, use plants with a low growth habit and tight foliage like santolina or germander (*Teucrium*). Plants with a handsome foliage and formal flower like Autumn Joy sedum or a clump of Siberian irises also work well in formal settings and precise geometric arrangements.

Planting Times

Perennials offer the greatest flexibility in time of planting. The time of year to plant perennials depends on when they bloom and the hardiness in your area. As a professional, I've planted perennials year-round. If you live in an area of marginal hardiness for the plant, you will want to plant in early spring before leaves emerge. Otherwise, fall and early spring are the time to move or divide your perennials.

Dividing

Perennials are among the easiest plants to propagate, much less labor-intensive and time-consuming than shrubs and trees because most of them are easily divided. A perennial that does well is an instant source of new plants. Plant enough variety, and you'll have

"A perennial that does well is an instant source of new plants."

a virtual nursery, which you can then use to trade with neighbors and friends to acquire new plants for your garden.

Most perennials can be divided and transplanted by the "quick and dirty" method. Just slice them into smaller root pieces with leaves on top and transplant. If you leave the parent plant rooted in the original space, it will continue to produce stock to divide from. Water divided perennials as you would any new plantings, when you're replanting and during dry periods.

There are, of course, specific guidelines for dividing each perennial. You should learn specifics for each plant, but don't be afraid to just give it a try. Here are a few guidelines for how to divide perennials:

- With the exception of hostas, hellebores, and a few other perennials that prefer to be undisturbed, many are happiest when they are divided every three to eight years.
- Established perennials should be divided in early spring when they are two to three inches high or in fall when foliage begins to die.
- Plants with dense clumps should be lifted out of the ground and pried apart into as many pieces as desired.
- Perennials with expansive root systems can be divided while in the ground by carefully slicing them into sections using a spade. To make the job easier, you may wish to cut back foliage if dividing in fall.
- Fibrous roots can be pulled apart with your hands.
- Woody roots should be divided with a sharp linoleum knife. Before dividing, clean soil from the clump to ensure that you can see what you're doing. This is as important for your safety as for the health of the plant.

Some perennials such as daylilies, irises, and peonies have fleshy roots, or rhizomes, and should be divided a little differently.

Dividing Daylilies   Daylilies grow in clumps. In the late summer to early fall, dig the entire clump out of the ground and pound or wash as much soil off the roots as possible. Divide the plant where the roots pull apart easily. Pull apart healthy roots that have at least three large eyes or buds on them.

Plant daylily divisions about three inches deep in full sun. Add liberal amounts of compost and a kelp/fish emulsion or other low-nitrogen growth stimulant. The divisions will leaf out in spring and should grow two to three scapes (flowering stems) by summer, with several flowers on each.

A "quick and dirty" method of dividing daylilies is to simply dig or cut off small clumps from the main root ball and transplant the pieces that you slice away from the parent plant. Plant them as described above, and they will thrive, but you won't get nearly as many plants per root ball as when you clean the roots and divide them into single pieces.

Dividing Irises   The four-foot high bearded iris, also known as German iris (*Iris germanica*), is one of the showiest of late spring flowers and many hybrids of all colors (except true red) are available. The healthiest bearded irises are ones that have been divided.

Bearded irises grow and bloom from shallow, fleshy roots, and when you dig them, the soil usually falls off the roots, and they divide rather easily. Keep only the one-year rhizomes (roots that are attached to the fan of leaves) and dispose of all older root pieces. This will keep your irises free of borers, the plant's most potentially devastating pest. The best time to divide and control the iris borer is in late summer after irises bloom—do not wait for fall.

The one-year rhizome you've divided for transplanting will be about three to four inches long and must have at least one large fan of leaves attached; a couple of smaller fans is also fine. Cut the fans in half, to about four inches in length, and transplant them to a new location in full sun, making sure that the eye or bud on the rhizome is at or within a half-inch of the soil surface. If not, it won't flower. Use a generous amount of compost.

Siberian irises (*I. sibirica*) grow from a tight mass or clump and are less particular about how you transplant them. They develop very showy and tight clumps of foliage that look good throughout the growing season and produce many flowers. Siberian irises do not need to be transplanted for their health, but if you want some to plant elsewhere, divide them in the fall, as they flower in spring.

If you wish to divide your Siberian iris to make more plants, dig the entire clump, which will be a tight mass. Knock as much of the soil off of the roots as you can. Look for natural divisions to get the most from your plant, but you may have to slice them apart. Use a curved-edge cutting tool such as a linoleum knife to separate tightly bound rhizomes. Transplant pieces that have at least three or four leaves on them and place in the soil at about the depth that the parent plant was growing.

Dividing Peonies   When peony foliage browns, move root pieces that are about four to five inches long and have four to six buds on each. Peonies have the same tendency as bearded irises—they will refuse to flower when the eyes on the root are planted too deeply, which is more than three-quarters of an inch.

Deadheading

Deadheading is a primary maintenance task for most perennials, and it's always good for the plant. When a flowering scape or stem fades, cut it down and keep the leaves. For plants where the flower comes up from the foliage, prune or pinch the flower off. It promotes healthier roots, fuller leaves, and you may get another flush of flowers with some perennials.

▲▲▲▲▲▲▲▲▲▲▲▲▲▲▲▲▲▲▲▲▲▲▲▲▲▲▲▲▲▲▲▲▲▲▲

BIENNIALS

**BIENNIALS TO GROW IN
PARTIAL SHADE***

Hollyhocks (*Alcea*)

Forget-me-nots (*Myosotis sylvatica*)

Violets

Hesperis

* five to six hours of sun

Biennials are sometimes misunderstood plants. At some garden centers they may be called annuals, while at others they may be labeled perennials, and sometimes their seeds can be hard to find. Biennials grow their leaves the first year and come back the second year to flower, seed, and die.

Pansies are an example. Seed pansies in the spring and they will grow their leaves and go into flowering mode late in the season, producing what is actually the following year's flower. In milder temperatures, they can bloom all winter and into spring. They might come back a third year, but they will be leggy and woody with smaller, sparser flowers. They can also be installed as started plants in autumn and will flower in fall and spring.

In general, biennials should be started from seed in July and August or as started plants from the garden center in spring. Seed catalogs are a good place to get biennial seeds. Several companies where you can order seeds are: Thompson & Morgan, (800) 274-7333; Shepherd's Garden Seeds, (860) 482-3638; Seeds of Change, (505) 438-8080, and W. Atlee Burpee, (800) 888-1447.

Biennials are not easily transplantable from the soil, so you should sow them where you ultimately want them to be growing. When planting, dig an inch of compost into the top two to three inches of soil, scatter the seeds lightly where you want them to grow, and very lightly slide an upside-down lawn or leaf rake over the planting bed to barely cover the seed. Sprinkle the seeds with water when planting and irrigate lightly three times a week through dry periods.

Or, to make transplanting easier, plant biennials in pots. When sown in pots, they can be moved to other locations after they are actively growing. Remember, seeding into pots does require keeping a close eye on moisture; seed in pots will dry out much faster than seed sown directly into the soil will. Biennials started in pots can be transplanted in spring or fall.

**BIENNIALS TO GROW IN FULL
SUN**

Foxgloves (*Digitalis*)

Larkspurs (*Delphiniums*)

Sweet Williams (*Dianthus barbatus*)

Poppies

Pansies

Protect the roots of the young plants in winter with a mulch of aged leaves or bark. If you are holding potted biennials over for planting in spring, you might want to put them into a cold frame, a low box that can be covered with Plexiglas or a thick plastic to keep temperatures even and to protect plants from freezes.

BULBS

Bulbs are the large food storage roots that grow the foliage of a plant. Nothing gives you spring flowers like bulbs, but many varieties also produce flowers in summer and fall. From a design standpoint, you can consider corms, rhizomes, tubers, and true bulbs in this category, and you can decide which of these bulbous plants you wish to coordinate through the growing season, just as you do for your mainstream perennials.

For blossoms from late winter into early spring, plant winter aconites (*Eranthis*), bluebells (*Hyacinthoides*), glories-of-the-snow (*Chionodoxa*), snowdrops (*Galanthus*), or crocuses. For spring blooms, plant daffodils, tulips, hyacinths, grape hyacinths, and early-blooming iris, such as *Iris reticulata*. For summer blooms, plant gladiolus, alliums, lilies, dahlias, daylilies, *Crocosmia*, irises, and cannas. Bulbs that will give you late-season blooms include autumn crocuses (*Colchicum*), fall-flowering crocuses (*Crocus*), naked ladies (*Amaryllis belladonna*), and sternbergias (*Sternbergia lutea*). Planting times are pretty easy to remember for bulbs: Plant spring-flowering bulbs in the fall and summer and fall-flowering bulbs in the spring.

Bulbs are best used in drifts of the same colors, as multiples of six or more of each variety that you use, and sixty is usually ten times better than six. Or you can mix colors in a sprinkled fashion, if that is your style, but sprinkle the colors evenly for the best effect.

Tulips are a wonderful example of classic spring-blooming bulbs.

Globose allium flowers create a focal point in early summer.

Since most bulbs will not hold their foliage throughout the season, grow perennials to mask the bulbs' yellowing foliage. Some interesting combinations are astilbe coming up as daffodils are fading, hostas growing to replace the leaves of tulips, or lilies as a filler for rose gardens.

After the bulbs have bloomed, you'll want to remove the dead foliage so the bulbs can come back next year. But you don't want to remove the foliage until it has completely yellowed or browned because the bulbs' nutrients are replenished by the green leaves and stored to help them grow next season.

With many bulbs, removing the yellowed foliage will be the only thing you need to do, except, of course, for maintaining the soil and other basic gardening tasks. They can be left in the ground to naturalize, that is, take hold and form a colony and reproduce and spread. Spring-blooming flowers to naturalize are daffodils, crocuses, and grape hyacinths. For summer, use daylilies, lilies, and *Crocosmia*. And in fall, naturalize autumn crocuses and naked lady amaryllises.

Gladiolus and cannas won't overwinter, so you must dig them up for replanting. Dig after the leaves fade but while you can still find them in the ground before the foliage disappears. This is only necessary in hardiness zones colder than Zone 8 (10 to 15°F). Store these bulbs in a cool, dry, dark place until you're ready to plant them the following spring.

ORNAMENTAL GRASSES

Ornamental grasses are used as a foliage plant as much for their architectural effect as for their flower, or inflorescence. Some have an outstanding inflorescence, the arrangement of their flowering parts on the stems. Some grasses will do well in shade, but you must use a tolerant variety. Most ornamental grasses need full sun.

Grasses have a somewhat specialized place in the garden. Don't use grasses as shrubbery because they don't have the same architecture as a woody plant. They lose structure as the leaves die and fall apart, By late winter, usually what you see is dead grass. It is very attractive to use ornamental grasses in conjunction with flowering shrubs and other perennials. The grasses provide an excellent point of accent, or focal point, within a mixed perennial deciduous shrub border.

When ornamental grasses are designed properly and perform well, the effects can be fascinating and varied. And, the habit of one grass can be very different from another. For example, the textures of grass with a strict habit, such as feather reed (*Calamagrostis* x *acutiflora*) and blue oat (*Helictotrichon sempervirens*) will make bold statements. Prairie cord grass (Spartina pectinata) planted in wet areas in drifts or groupings can appear to flow naturally, like a verdant river. Both design uses, formal and natural, are

The golden plumes and striped foliage of Japanese silver grass (*Miscanthus sinensis* 'Kaskade') brighten up a fall garden. (From *Continuous Bloom,* copyright © 2000 Pam Duthie. All rights reserved. Used by permission.)

low maintenance. The grasses just grow that way without much pruning, preening, or fertilizing. Blue fescues (*Festuca glauca*) and prairie dropseed (*Sporobolus heterolepsis*) are exceptional complements to a rock garden.

Use ornamental grasses for sweeps of color—the red foliage of Japanese blood grass (*Imperata cylindrica*), yellow of hakone grass (*Hakonechloa*), white of the variegated bird's foot sedge grass (*Carex ornithopoda* 'Variegata'), and golden speckles and other variegations of the many varieties of *Miscanthus sinensis*.

You can get some interesting design effects from ornamental grasses. In fairly heavy shade, the yellow of golden variegated hakone grass can be so brilliant that on a cloudy day it looks like the sun is shining. Japanese silver grass ('Kaskade') in full flower is a magnificent looking plant, and the inflorescence on it not only looks like silver feathers, but it holds its plumage into winter. Chinese fountain grass (*Pennisetum alopecuroides*) is one of the most beautiful two- to three-foot-tall arching grasses. It flowers dependably with black to purple inflorescence. It may also seed itself dependably, to your chagrin, and colonize an area, which would be all right if you want a colony. Otherwise, it's an extremely invasive pest.

Be wary of plants with extremely vigorous growth habits or those that produce prolific seed because they can take over a garden in short order and overrun your other plantings. Most literature and garden center personnel won't approach plant material from the perspective of what might become a problem because they want to sell you on their plants. So do I. You will only know these tendencies through practical hands-on experience. When you are unhappy with what you see, don't be averse to moving the plants, pulling them as weeds or, if necessary, spraying them with a glyphosate weed killer such as Roundup or Kleeraway.

Grasses need annual renewal, and when their leaves are dead, it's time to cut them to the ground and grind them for your compost. Cut down ornamental grasses when the winter wind starts to knock them apart. Some bigger heavier varieties, such as most species of Japanese silver feather grasses, may be knocked down before the winter winds and need to be tied together and staked for their ornamental value. One silver feather grass that is very self-supporting is *Miscanthus sinensis* 'Gracillimus'.

When it's time to cut it down, either in the fall or spring if you've decided to let the grass stand for winter interest, use an electric shears or hand hedge trimmer. Not surprisingly, some varieties can be tough. Remember that bamboo is a grass, but if you can, mow it with a lawn mower on its maximum height setting, or try a scythe or a machete. Make sure you do your cutting before the grasses start their growth in the spring.

ANNUALS

40

WHAT ARE ANNUALS?

Annuals are a large group of plants that complete their life cycle from leaf to flower to seed in one season and then die with the frost. Some, like ornamental cabbage or kale, will survive until a very hard frost. In a mild winter, they will live through winter and grow again in spring but will have lost ornamental value. Some hardy annuals—for example, dusty miller and snapdragons—will often overwinter a mild winter, but they will never display the same full foliage or be nearly as free flowering as they were the first year.

Some plants called annuals are really tender perennials, which means they are tropical and subtropical species that would live year-round in warmer climates. In the United States, except in the southernmost parts of the country, plants should be able to withstand a freeze to live year round. Otherwise, they should be considered annuals or houseplants.

Annuals give you the luxury of changing your mind from year to year about what you want to plant and where you want to plant it. If you don't like what you did for one growing season, by fall it's gone and you have the opportunity to start work again on a new blank canvas. However, remember that the temporal nature of annuals makes more installations necessary than for any other plant material except vegetables and some herbs. After years of installing annuals, it ends up costing considerably more than a perennial garden.

Another benefit is that annuals provide a full season of color. While you will have to wait for perennials to bloom for a limited time, annuals provide dramatic garden color as soon as you plant them. Nothing else will give you more color over a longer period

Annuals provide vibrant color that makes people take notice of your planting beds. This bed features wax begonias (left) and impatiens (center) under a cedar tree. (The Butchart Gardens Ltd., Victoria, British Columbia)

at less cost per installation. You can plant annuals in spring, after the last frost. See the chart below for when you can usually add these vibrant plants to your landscape. Microclimates and general variations in temperatures affect all areas. Be sure to check with your local extension office for accurate information for your particular locale.

There are two categories of annuals: hardy plants that tolerate mild frost and tender annuals that are damaged by frost. Keep the categories hardy (plants that tolerate frost) and tender (annuals damaged by frost) in mind when you are reading a catalog or ordering plants. You will want to ascertain whether your flowers will persist as late into the season as you want them to.

If you mass all of one type of plant in an area, such as impatiens, sweet alyssums, snapdragons, or pansies, your flowers might come back year after year by reseeding themselves. You'll get the excitement of seeing new colors, which will never be exactly the same as last year's colors because seed often reverts to sports, or varieties, that were used to hybridize the plants you bought.

To encourage this reseeding, grow impatiens, sweet alyssums, snapdragons, pansies, portulacas, or another flower in a soil rich in organic material (see Site Preparation, chapter 4). Don't deadhead; let the flower go to seed. Watch for seedlings to emerge in the spring. Be careful not to pull them as weeds in their early stages of growth. If a late freeze kills annual seedlings that started to grow, then you'll have to buy started plants after all danger of frost is past.

AVERAGE LAST SPRING FROST DATES

USDA Hardiness Zone	Last Average Frost Dates
Zone 10	February 10–15
Zone 9	February 28–March 10
Zone 8	March 30–April 15
Zone 7	April 20–30
Zone 6	May 1–15
Zone 5	May 15–30
Zone 4	May 30–June 5
Zone 3	June 1–15

DESIGNING WITH ANNUALS

Annuals are available in every size and configuration, providing an extensive array of possibilities for the way they can be used. Low, two- to six-inch plants such as lobelia or sweet alyssum; small marigolds, petunias, and wax begonias that grow to four to twelve inches high; foot-high cockscomb, salvia, tall marigolds, and zinnias; and vines such as morning glory, moonflower, Dutchman's pipe, and hyacinth bean that grow up to ten feet—these are all annuals. (See annuals list in appendix D.)

Go back to your design principles when putting annuals in your landscape, and pay particular attention to color. Annuals are the most static of all growing material in their appearance; you will see virtually the same color for the entire growing season. Blend them carefully. If they are in bloom at the garden center, hold the colors together to avoid clashes. Otherwise, use a color wheel for blending complementary colors. Recall that repetition is a strong unifier—use one type of annual to edge a bed. This will help blend the plantings together and make them flow visually from one to another.

Also consider annuals for their form. Annuals come in a variety of flower forms, from ruffly to smooth to spiky. Match forms and find the ones that will complement each other. Spiked blue flowers of salvia complement an edging of sweet alyssum and a background of black-eyed-Susans (*Rudbeckia hirta*)—an example of varying your heights with annuals and biennials.

As with perennials, there are countless ways to design annuals into your landscape, either in limited spaces or large expanses.

Annuals massed together for an island that flowers all summer long. The edging is white petunia; the center foreground is pink crested celosia (*C. cristata*) and the center background is plumed celosia (*C. plumata*). Also growing through the center of the bed are red, pink, and yellow snapdragons, and the plant with maroon foliage in the front is an amaranth.

ISLAND BEDS

Design an island bed with mixed annuals. Island beds are popularly used in all forms of landscape design and they work well for annuals because you can look across and see the lovely colors from all directions. Another thing I like about island beds is you can see them from the house without approaching them. I would not place a formal circle of plants out in the middle of the front yard with no background plants or other anchor. They should relate to an entry or another group of plantings.

In your island bed, for your edging use dainty low mounded fragrant sweet alyssums or a clean controllable plant like wax begonias, which provide a choice of red, pink, or white flowers and red or green leaves. Then cluster some blue or red salvias for a short spike to back up the alyssums or begonias. Toward the center of the bed, plant a grouping of tall snapdragons for a very dependable continuous season of bloom in full sun. Then, for some conversation pieces in the garden, cluster some cockscomb (*Celosia*). Finally, for the tallest plants in the center of the island, plant amaranths, a favorite of mine that grows four feet high with long flowing purple and white flowers and a variety of leaf colors (see photo).

GROUNDCOVERS

Use annuals to create beautiful temporary groundcovers. A good example for this use is petunias, which have floppy, spreading foliage, growing in a cascading habit across the ground. Another good groundcover is verbena, which is an annual in the northern half the country and a perennial in the southern. Portulaca, a succulent annual with small bright flowers that look a little like roses, is another low-growing, spreading annual that works well as a groundcover and will seed itself into the area and return year after year. If you are using annuals for groundcovers, plant them in mass for the best effect.

HANGING BASKETS AND CONTAINERS

Annuals also make spectacular hanging baskets for your patio, deck, or entry. Annuals and hanging baskets are a natural combination. At the end of the season, simply empty the basket and put it away. Many annuals are used well in hanging baskets, including verbenas, pansies, petunias, fuchsias, begonias, and impatiens.

Tubs or containers on patios or decks also work well filled with blooming annuals. For these larger containers, use plants with more architectural value than the flowers in hanging baskets. For example, put an edging of a low plant like begonia or dwarf marigold in a tub. In the center of the tub, use plants that will stand tall and make a greater impact with their color and their flower— zinnias, asters, strawflowers (*Helichrysum bracteatum*), or carnations (*Dianthus*) work well.

This striking grouping of hanging baskets is composed entirely of annuals. Note how the trailing habit of the ivy geraniums in the large center container hides the basket and looks like balls of flowers. (U.S. Botanic Gardens, Washington, D.C.)

Dried Flowers

Annuals can provide enjoyment well beyond the growing season if you dry them. The following steps will soon have you immortalizing your favorite blooms.

1. Cut freshly opened, full flowers on a sunny day with no moisture on the petals.
2. Place flowers into a receptacle containing a drying agent, such as silica gel. Make sure flowers are totally coated with your drying agent.
3. Place container in dry, dark area with good air circulation to retain maximum color on flowers.
4. Drying time will vary from several days to a week. Carefully check flowers after several days to see if they're dry.

Many annuals are good for drying, such as the following: asters, calendulas, crested celosias, chrysanthemums, cornflowers, dahlias, delphiniums, gypsophilas, pansies, scabiouses, statices, and strawflowers. Try some of these, and experiment with your own.

Fresh Cut Flowers

There are numerous annuals that offer a colorful array of flowers good for cutting. Many are planted primarily to be cut and brought inside for enjoyment. Plant snapdragons, strawflowers, marigolds,

Cleome arranged with grass for a natural setting.

zinnias, cockscombs, amaranths, statices, and many others for this purpose.

ACCENTS IN JOINTS AND WALLS

Plug annuals into walk joints or open areas in dry rock walls. Lobelia is a variety that works well for a rock joint, as do alyssum, a tiny variety of dianthus, and ageratum. Look for other little, rock accent plants.

COMPLEMENT STRUCTURES

Plant beds of annuals along walks or paths, fences, hedges, and walls. Mix annuals; don't make the bed a straight line that will accentuate the structure. Use the beds of annuals to create sweeps and tie the structures into the landscape.

ANNUALS IN NATURAL SETTINGS

Use annuals that will reseed themselves in wildflower or naturalistic settings, such as for meadows, banks, hillsides, or along your lane or roadside. Cosmos, cleomes, and poppies are annuals that will reoccur annually and can be used as wildflowers and are well suited to naturalistic settings. Brilliant red or orange poppies can be seen from great distances. Cosmos are also brightly colored and will compete with the grasses and pop up above them to get your attention. Cleomes are very tall, and you can see the white and purple flowers blowing in the breeze above other flowers and grasses. All of these are usually dependable seed producers that will come back for you annually.

SUCCESSION OF ANNUALS

Try succession planting of annuals for continual color from early spring to fall through winter. Depending on your climate, you might have to plant more than one kind of annual for continued flowering through the season. For example, pansies used as annuals are beautiful in spring, but they often flower poorly and lose their looks in the heat of summer. Ageratum in combination with annual phlox will take you through summer, and phlox is hardy enough to persist into fall, when you can plant ornamental kale and pansies that will overwinter and flower again next spring.

ROSES

41

Not only is the rose our national flower, but it's a bloom that has been treasured through history. It's a symbol for love in many cultures and can be found in ancient Egyptian tombs and in sacred rituals in ancient Greece and Rome. The Romans even developed hot houses to grow and force roses to bloom out of season, a practice common today.

Roses have long been thought of as difficult plants because of the diseases and insects they seem to attract. Despite that, requests from property owners for roses are on the rise. They can be used in a variety of ways, and these days I see them more as integral parts of the landscape than in the high-maintenance, pure rose gardens that were often grown in the past two centuries.

TYPES OF ROSES

Some roses need hardly any care and others demand a great deal more, depending on what you grow. The categories were developed according to the habit they displayed, but the lines between them blur more with each new variety that is introduced. There are now thousands of varieties, all of which developed from twelve original species. The greatest differences among them are how much they bloom and how big they get. The varieties I name are all disease resistant, but remember, no rose is immune.

SHRUB ROSES

Shrub roses are the hardiest and most disease-free roses. They have long arching canes and grow four to twelve feet in height and spread. Although they bloom less often than some other varieties,

313

they are the most dependable growers to form a hedge or ground-cover. Several of the best known shrub roses are 'Bonica' (pink), 'Carefree Beauty' (pink), and rugosa varieties (red and best to make rose hips jelly that's high in vitamin C).

Use them as a background in a perennial garden. Arrange problem-free shrub roses as a boundary planting. They will offer flowering value and a thorny barrier. Your neighbor will enjoy the flowers and added privacy, and so will you. Fill ugly corners with roses and you'll never think of the spots as ugly again. And you can use them to provide ornamental interest in the fall and winter in your garden. The bright red fruit on some shrub roses is beautiful in the cold months of the year and attracts birds.

GROUNDCOVER ROSES

Many lower-growing shrub roses—two to three feet tall—have been developed and are marketed as groundcovers, including 'Flower Carpet' and 'Meidiland', a popular variety. Plant these over a slope. Available at garden centers under various names, they are sold specifically to be planted in masses as groundcovers.

HYBRID TEA ROSES

Plant hybrid tea roses for fragrance and a wide range of colors. These are the most widely grown of all roses. Several time-tested,

---

MEIDILAND ROSE CULTIVARS

'Bonica', a pink that grows to five feet

'Alba', a white that grows to two and a half feet

'Pink', which grows to three feet

'White', which grows to two feet

'Scarlet', which grows to four feet

'Pearl', which grows to two and a half feet

'Red', which grows to two feet

Mixed hybrid tea roses make a fabulous garden. (Brookside Gardens, Wheaton, Maryland)

disease-resistant hybrid tea roses are 'Mister Lincoln' (red), 'Tiffany' (pink), and 'Touch of Class' (pink).

With hybrid tea roses, prune the stem that the flower bloomed on and a new bud will form. Cut it to the first strong leaf (five leaflets). They will bloom all summer until first frost. The growth habit is upright. They grow three to four feet tall and usually need regular attention to discourage leaf spot, aphids, and Japanese beetles. Powder or spray for fungi and insects on your hybrid tea roses every seven to ten days. However, the best fungus protection is good air circulation that will dry the foliage quickly.

FLORIBUNDA ROSES

Floribunda roses are a shorter, more compact derivation of the hybrid tea with flowers in clusters as opposed to individual blooms. Take advantage of the shorter form of floribunda roses to fit them into your landscape design with other landscape plants. They are excellent for creating a mass of color. Floribundas are considered easy to grow, but that doesn't necessarily mean they are disease resistant. They still must be treated with fungicide or insecticide if black spots or chewing damage begins to show on the leaves. Some disease-resistant varieties of floribunda are 'Europeana' (red), 'Iceberg' (white), and 'Sunsprite' (yellow).

GRANDIFLORA ROSES

Grandifloras are usually tall, slender plants with the grandest, largest flowers of all the roses. They usually grow from five to six feet and bloom on long stems. Design grandifloras to the rear of your shrub border or at your property line. They bloom in summer and will give you a second flush of bloom if you prune the flowering stems down to the first healthy leaf before the petals drop. Dependable, disease-resistant varieties include 'Gold Medal' (yellow), 'Queen Elizabeth' (pink), 'Tournament of Roses' (red). Fragrant grandiflora roses, such as the varieties 'Arizona', 'Olé', and 'White Lightnin', add a wonderful aroma along patios and drives.

CLIMBING ROSES

Roses that grow with very long arching canes are referred to as climbers. They don't actually climb, but rather grow long enough to look best trained on a fence, trellis, or arbor, as vines are trained. Attach the stems of the roses to the structure they are climbing with string or wire. Prune them to follow the supports to avoid a wild and weedy look. Climbers are good on fences, pergolas, and arbors where there is sun. Use climbing roses to frame a window or door, screen out an unwanted view on a trellis, or screen an ugly stump. Train climbing roses on the wall of a shed with flowers in a bed surrounding it for a cottage garden look. Or espalier climbing roses against brick, stone, or adobe walls as a vine that will give a formal feeling to your design.

Climbing roses will bloom two or three times by August and then you should prune them back to the main canes that form their framework. Leave these long canes; they grow from them the following year. Climbers that will give the best show and are hardy include 'Aloha' (pink), 'America' (orange), and 'Lady Banks' (white or yellow).

All roses are susceptible to winterkill, and climbing roses are more of a challenge to protect because their stems grow six to ten feet or longer. While they could be cut back and wrapped, I recommend protecting their roots with a generous layer of mulch, leaving the main canes to stand unprotected. In spring, cut back the winterkill and in a very short time they will put on new growth and be flowering right along with the rest of your roses. If you live in Zone 5 or colder, you might want to untie them and bury them in the soil or mulch, and tie them back up in early spring.

> "If you have an interest in history and tradition, incorporate old garden or old-fashioned roses into your landscape."

OLD GARDEN ROSES

If you have an interest in history and tradition, incorporate old garden or old-fashioned roses into your landscape. The American Rose Society recognizes old garden roses as those that were grown before 1867, the year the first hybrid tea was introduced. They are direct descendants of the original species roses and can be found in all the forms I have outlined above except the hybrid tea. Some of these antique groups are albas, damasks, mosses, and rugosas.

MINIATURE ROSES

Miniatures are diminutive forms of the rose that have been bred to mimic their full-sized counterparts. They are available as smaller versions of every form described above. Your miniature roses will require the same care as larger ones, but they take up less room. As with full-size roses, some have good disease resistance; others require regular treatments with fungicide and insecticide.

You will find many miniatures with the same names as larger, full-size roses, but they are designed into the garden differently. Use miniature roses as a low-edging for your planting beds. Mix them with perennials or herbs, mass them around your patio, or plant them in window boxes or other containers to put on your patio.

▲▲▲▲▲▲▲▲▲▲▲▲▲▲▲▲▲▲▲▲▲▲▲▲▲▲▲▲▲▲▲▲▲▲▲▲▲▲

USING ROSES

We've already discussed several uses for each type of rose, and here are some more suggestions that can be applied to all categories. The rose is unique as a shrub that gives you flowers on a vertical plane through the spring, summer, and fall. A couple of guidelines about growing roses remain true, no matter how you fit them into your landscape: First, plant roses only in full sun. Second, don't mix up your colors of roses. Instead, stick with one color in an area for a cohesive, consistent statement in the landscape. If you mix them, as in a bed of hybrid tea roses, pay attention to how the colors will blend using trial, error, and personal taste.

CONTAINERS

Use roses in a container outside your door. Nothing makes you feel better than stepping out your door to a container with a beautiful, fragrant rose growing in it. Floribundas are the best all-purpose roses. Plant some fragrant ones like 'Iceberg', 'Rose Parade', 'Saratoga', and 'Sunsprite'.

CUTTING GARDEN

Nothing gives you nicer cut flowers than roses. Mix colors in a rose cutting garden. From a landscape design standpoint, I recommend mixing colors in a sprinkled fashion, instead of putting all of one color together. A random distribution of the roses in the beds will keep colors balanced as you cut them. Hybrid tea roses are naturals for a cutting garden. You keep the flowers cut and they will continue blooming. Prune them to the closest healthy leaf, usually one with five leaflets.

MIXED GARDEN

Roses work well mixed with other flowers. Sweet alyssum is a wonderful, low-mounding groundcover to plant around roses. When your roses stop giving you their aroma, the sweet alyssum will add an extra touch of fragrance. Some other nice companions for roses are artemisia, lavender, and violets. When deciding on colors to use for accent and borders in a rose garden, think of blues and whites. They are the safest colors to use to avoid clashing with the roses.

▲▲

PLANTING AND CARE

In most areas, early spring is the best time to plant roses, but colleagues and I have moved roses whenever we've had to, anytime of the year. The important consideration when moving them is to capture all of the roots that spread out underground from the base of the rose than to dig a tight little root ball. To dig a root ball might require cutting many of the small roots that the rose needs. To capture all of these roots, go farther away from the base of the rose and pry away the soil around it to find the fine roots. Keep them intact, even if they come up without any soil on them. A large root ball capturing all roots is good, but if digging it involves cutting many roots, it is better to pry them up bare, keep them moist, and transplant them with most of their roots. To plant roses, prepare your bed deeply, at least eighteen to twenty-four inches, because they like rich, well-drained soil. Good drainage is crucial for healthy roses.

Roses like acidic soil, 6.0 to 6.5 pH, or even lower. This means that peat moss, while not commonly specified as a soil amendment these days, is one of the premier rose garden amendments because of its acidic nature coupled with the ability to hold moisture and keep the soil light in texture.

> "To plant roses, prepare your bed deeply, at least eighteen to twenty-four inches, because they like rich, well-drained soil. Good drainage is crucial for healthy roses."

Use commercial rose food or general purpose 10-10-10 fertilizer. Feed the modern repeat-bloom rose variety, such as hybrid tea roses, three times: in the spring right after blooming, when they have again developed flower buds, and then two months before the first frost in your area. Always monitor your roses for leaf spots and insects, and treat as soon as you see black spot or serious insect infestation.

Roses like low humidity and bright sun, but they also need regular watering. During a dry spell, water roses deeply once or twice a week. Morning is the best time for watering.

If you keep your roses pruned, deadheaded, and treated for diseases and insects, some varieties (i.e., the hybrid tea and floribunda roses) will provide flowers through the growing season, up until frost. Your climbing varieties will only give you one dependable period of blooming, although they might offer another flush of bloom at the end of the season.

All roses are susceptible to winterkill. Starting in November, protect against winterkill with mulch or straw and a burlap wrap.

Rose growers are a dedicated breed, and they and their organizations can be very helpful to anyone who has questions or wants to know more about growing roses. To pursue your interest, contact the American Rose Society, P.O. Box 300000, Shreveport LA, 71130; (318) 938-5402.

WILDFLOWER MEADOWS

Wildflower meadows—or prairie gardens, as they are called in the Midwest—can be a low-maintenance, long-lasting, and self-sustaining form of gardening to provide a coordination of bloom and seasonal interest for the home landscaper. The effect can be beautiful when the wildflower population comes into balance, but don't make the mistake of thinking this can be achieved without some work and forethought. You are mimicking nature's grassland association of plants, but she took fifteen to twenty-five years. You can do it in two to three years.

Wildflower gardening gives rise to one of my pet peeves: the "garden in a can." You'll do well to avoid the off-the-shelf mixed

A lone aspen stands among a mix of painted daisies, black-eyed Susans, and other naturally occurring wildflowers and grasses along a meadow path in Colorado.

wildflower seed that's sold to be sprinkled into the garden for, supposedly, instant beauty. Without proper site preparation, your efforts will yield, at best, one or two species and very possibly none. Wildflowers are a variation on landscaping with native plants, since the name implies plants that grow naturally in the wild. But it still takes proper timing and patience to create a balanced mixed wildflower or prairie garden. See the chart at the end of this chapter for a list of plants to use in a wildflower garden.

Site Preparation

For proper management of a wildflower garden, it's important to consider your site location, soil type and analysis, exposure to sun, weed growth, and other cultural considerations. And no wildflowers want weeds competing for the same soil. Allow yourself a year to properly prepare the site. Here's how to manage each of these considerations.

Sunlight

Locate your wildflower garden in full sun. These plants normally grow in open fields, and you should give them as much light as is possible.

These cosmos and rudbeckias are dependent only on sunlight and moisture to thrive year after year.

WEED CONTROL

Gain control of weeds before planting wildflowers. Spray glyphosate (Roundup or Kleeraway) three times (spring, summer, and fall), *but only when weeds are present and actively growing.* If you wish to control weeds without chemicals, spread black landscape fabric or plastic to mulch the area and keep it devoid of weeds for one year. The following spring, one year after beginning to prepare the site for a wildflower planting, spray again any weeds that have grown, unless you mulched with fabric instead. Let sit for ten more days.

SOIL

In the fall, ten days after the third herbicide spray, cultivate the following materials into the top four to five inches of soil: composted organic material (one- to two-inch layer), gypsum (eighty pounds per thousand feet square), and agricultural limestone (eighty pounds per thousand feet square). If you used fabric or plastic mulch, remove it to do preparation, then replace it until spring.

There are two theories on soil preparation. The first is listed above. But some experts feel that the soil should not be enriched. Unimproved soil is what wildflowers are native to, and most will flourish in it. This will also keep down the number of encroaching weeds, which are far more invasive in rich soil. You should kill all competing weeds, but leave the soil undisturbed until planting time.

SAMPLE WILDFLOWER MIX

The following mix would be for a short-grass meadow in dry soil, as recommended by Prairie Nursery, Westfield, Wisconsin. Note that this is only one of numerous possible mixes.

Wildflowers: lead plant, butterfly weed, sky blue aster, smooth aster, Canada milk vetch, lanceleaf coreopsis, pale purple coneflower, flowering spurge, western sunflower, roundhead bush clover, rough blazing star, lupine, dotted mint, beardtongue, purple prairie clover, prairie buttercup, black-eyed Susan, stiff goldenrod, showy goldenrod, spiderwort, hoary vervain.

Prairie nursery recommends the mix be planted with these grasses: little bluestem and sideoats grama.

SEEDING THE SITE

In late spring, around June 1, lift the fabric mulch. Ten days after the spring spraying (if you used herbicides), lightly scarify the soil surface a half-inch deep and seed with a mix tailored to your site. Purchase it from a supplier who can explain why one specified mix is better for your situation than another. If you wanted a wildflower mix on a south-facing clay slope, had a sandy plot with a western exposure, or were planting an area composed of shale, each would require a different seed mix. It would depend upon the soil and moisture requirements of the seeds in the mix. There can be twenty-five to fifty or more varieties of wildflowers and three to five prairie grasses in a seed mix.

On embankments, stake a fabric mesh to hold the seed in place. There are a variety of styles and materials, depending on how heavy-duty a fabric is needed and whether you will remove or leave it in place as growth begins. Look for erosion control blankets, mats, or netting materials at your garden or home improvement center.

I recommended that you plant a "nurse" grass with your wildflowers to provide a quick cover and to keep down competing weeds, so the slower germinating wildflowers have a chance to establish themselves. Annual ryegrass, hard fescue, and sheep fescue are great to use.

You don't want to disturb an area planted with germinating seed. It's better to leave a weed than disturb the many almost unnoticeable wildflowers that are growing around it.

Some wildflowers must be seeded annually by broadcasting them over the area in spring. Even though the parent plant dies with frost, some will seed themselves and grow back without having to buy more seeds every year. For example, blanket flower (*Gaillardia*), Queen Anne's lace (*Pimpinella major*), evening primrose (*Oenothera perennis*), and tickseed (*Coreopsis lanceolata*) will drop enough seed to grow back year after year.

Starting with Plants

You can use wildflowers in ways other than a broadcast seed mix. Wildflowers can also be tamed. You can take a wildflower and establish it as a plant in your garden. Think of it as a perennial or annual garden flower, not a wildflower. Many are sold as started plants at nurseries and garden centers, and you only need to select perennials one time. After that, they'll multiply on their own if they are meant to be growing there.

It's better to try other wildflowers to naturalize into an area if the first ones you plant fail. While amending a site can help plants, the idea of wildflowers, by definition, is that they'll grow maintenance free and thrive in the native soil.

Try arranging perennials in your garden, whether they are true wildflowers or not. Design a random enough pattern mixing low, medium, and tall plants including compact, open, and climbing growth habits (see Perennials, chapter 39).

You can get a mix of fifteen different species of wildflowers that have already grown together as a mat or sod. One of these products is available in five-square-foot pieces at garden centers under the name Wildflower Carpet.

Wildflower Selection Guide *

Common Name	Botanical Name	Height	Color	Bloom Time	Moisture	Soil	Sun
Red baneberry	Actaea rubra	1'–2'	White	June	Medium	Sand, loam, clay	Full sun, partial sun
Lavender hyssop	Agastache foeniculum	1'–3'	Purple	July–September	Dry, medium	Sand, loam	Full sun, partial sun
Nodding pink onion	Allium cernuum	1'–2'	White-pink	July–August	Medium, wet	Sand, loam, clay	Full sun
Leadplant	Amorpha canescens	2'–3'	Purple	June–July	Dry, medium	Sand, loam	Full sun
Angelica	Angelica atropurpurea	5'–10'	White	June	Wet	Sand, loam, clay	Full sun, partial sun
Columbine	Aquilegia canadensis	1'–3'	Red-yellow	May–June	Dry, medium	Sand, loam	Full sun, partial sun
Jack-in-the-pulpit	Arisaema triphyllum	1'–2'	Green	April–May	Medium, wet	Sand, loam, clay	Partial sun, shade
Red milkweed	Asclepias incarnata	3'–5'	Pink-red	June–July	Wet	Sand, loam, clay	Full sun
Common milkweed	Asclepias syriaca	2'–4'	Lavender	June–August	Dry, medium	Sand, loam, clay	Full sun
Butterfly weed	Asclepias tuberosa	2'–3'	Orange	June–August	Dry, medium	Sand, loam	Full sun
Butterfly weed for clay	Asclepias tuberosa var. clay	2'–3'	Orange	June–August	Medium	Loam, clay	Full sun
Sky blue aster	Aster azureus	2'–3'	Blue	August–October	Dry, medium	Sand, loam	Full sun, partial sun
Heath aster	Aster ericoides	1'–3'	White	August–October	Dry, medium	Sand, loam, clay	Full sun
Smooth aster	Aster laevis	2'–4'	Blue	August–October	Dry, medium	Sand, loam	Full sun
New England aster	Aster novae-angliae	3'–6'	Pink-purple-blue	August–October	Medium, wet	Sand, loam, clay	Full sun
Frost aster	Aster pilosus	1'–2'	White	August–September	Dry	Sand	Full sun

Continued

Wildflower Selection Guide [continued from page 323]

Common Name	Botanical Name	Height	Color	Bloom Time	Moisture	Soil	Sun
White aster	*Aster ptarmicoides*	1'–2'	White	August–September	Dry	Sand	Full sun
Canada milk vetch	*Astragalus canadensis*	2'–3'	Yellow	July–August	Dry, medium	Sand, loam	Full sun
Blue false indigo	*Baptisia australis*	2'–5'	Blue	June–July	Medium	Sand, loam, clay	Full sun, partial sun
Cream false indigo	*Baptisia bracteata*	1'–2'	Cream	May–June	Dry, medium	Sand, loam	Full sun, partial sun
White false indigo	*Baptisia lactea*	3'–5'	White	May–June	Dry, medium, wet	Sand, loam, clay	Full sun, partial sun
Pale Indian plantain	*Cacalia atriplicifolia*	4'–8'	White	July–September	Wet	Sand, loam	Full sun, partial sun
Poppy mallow	*Callirhoë triangulata*	1'–2'	Magenta	July–August	Dry	Sand	Full sun
Harebell	*Campanula rotundifolia*	1'–2'	Blue	June–September	Dry, medium	Sand	Full sun, partial sun
Partridge pea	*Cassia fasciculata*	1'–2'	Yellow	July–August	Dry	Sand, loam	Full sun
Wild senna	*Cassia hebecarpa*	4'–6'	Yellow	July–August	Medium, wet	Sand, loam, clay	Full sun
New Jersey tea	*Ceanothus americanus*	2'–3'	White	July–August	Dry, medium	Sand, loam	Full sun, partial sun
Lanceleaf coreopsis	*Coreopsis lanceolata*	1'–2'	Yellow	June–August	Dry, medium	Sand, loam	Full sun
Stiff coreopsis	*Coreopsis palmata*	2'–3'	Yellow	June–August	Dry, medium	Sand, loam	Full sun
Tall coreopsis	*Coreopsis tripteris*	6'–12'	Yellow	August–September	Medium, wet	Sand, loam, clay	Full sun
White prairie clover	*Dalea candida*	1'–2'	White	July–August	Dry, medium	Sand, loam	Full sun
Purple prairie clover	*Dalea purpurea*	1'–3'	Purple	July–August	Dry, medium	Sand, loam, clay	Full sun
Canada tick trefoil	*Desmodium canadense*	2'–5'	Purple	July–August	Medium, wet	Sand, loam, clay	Full sun
Shooting star	*Dodecatheon meadia*	1'–2'	White-pink	May–June	Medium	Sand, loam	Full sun, partial sun
Narrow-leaf purple coneflower	*Echinacea angustifolia*	1'–3'	Purple	June–July	Dry, medium	Sand, loam	Full sun
Pale purple coneflower	*Echinacea pallida*	2'–5'	Purple	June–July	Dry, medium	Sand, loam, clay	Full sun

Common name	Scientific name	Height	Color	Bloom time	Moisture	Soil	Light
Purple coneflower	*Echinacea purpurea*	3'–4'	Purple	July–September	Dry, medium	Sand, loam, clay	Full sun, partial sun
Rattlesnake master	*Eryngium yuccifolium*	3'–5'	White	June–August	Dry, medium	Sand, loam, clay	Full sun
Joe Pye weed	*Eupatorium maculatum*	4'–6'	Pink	July–August	Wet	Sand, loam, clay	Full sun
Boneset	*Eupatorium perfoliatum*	3'–4'	White	August–September	Medium, wet	Sand, loam, clay	Full sun
Sweet Joe Pye weed	*Eupatorium purpureum*	3'–6'	Purple	July–August	Medium	Sand, loam, clay	Full sun, partial sun, shade
Flowering spurge	*Euphorbia corollata*	2'–4'	White	July–August	Dry	Sand, loam	Full sun
Queen of the prairie	*Filipendula rubra*	4'–5'	Pink	June–July	Medium, wet	Sand, loam, clay	Full sun
Wild geranium	*Geranium maculatum*	1'–2'	Lavender	April–July	Medium	Sand, loam	Full sun, partial sun, shade
Prairie smoke	*Geum triflorum*	<1'	Red	April–May	Dry, medium	Sand, loam	Full sun
Sneezeweed	*Helenium autumnale*	4'–5'	Yellow	August–September	Wet	Sand, loam, clay	Full sun
Sawtooth sunflower	*Helianthus grosse-serratus*	6'–12'	Yellow	August–September	Medium, wet	Loam, clay	Full sun
Showy sunflower	*Helianthus laetiflorus*	3'–5'	Yellow	August–September	Dry, medium	Sand, loam, clay	Full sun
Downy sunflower	*Helianthus mollis*	4'–6'	Yellow	August–September	Dry	Sand	Full sun
Western sunflower	*Helianthus occidentalis*	2'–3'	Yellow	July–August	Dry, medium	Sand, loam	Full sun
Woodland sunflower	*Helianthus strumosus*	2'–5'	Yellow	August–October	Dry, medium	Sand, loam	Full sun, partial sun
Ox-eye sunflower	*Heliopsis helianthoides*	2'–5'	Yellow	June–September	Medium, wet	Sand, loam, clay	Full sun, partial sun
Wild iris	*Iris shrevei*	2'–3'	Blue	May–June	Wet	Sand, loam, clay	Full sun, partial sun

Continued

Wildflower Selection Guide *[continued from page 325]*

Common Name	Botanical Name	Height	Color	Bloom Time	Moisture	Soil	Sun
Blue flag iris	*Iris versicolor*	2'–3'	Blue	June–July	Wet	Sand, loam, clay	Full sun, partial sun
False boneset	*Kuhnia eupatorioides*	1'–3'	White	August–September	Dry, medium	Sand, loam	Full sun
Roundhead bush clover	*Lespedeza capitata*	2'–4'	White	August–September	Dry, medium	Sand, loam	Full sun
Rough blazing star	*Liatris aspera*	2'–3'	Purple-pink	August–September	Dry, medium	Sand, loam	Full sun
Meadow blazing star	*Liatris ligulistylus*	3'–5'	Purple	August–September	Medium	Loam	Full sun
Prairie blazing star	*Liatris pycnostachya*	2'–4'	Purple-pink	July–August	Medium, wet	Sand, loam, clay	Full sun
Dense blazing star	*Liatris spicata*	3'–6'	Pink-purple	August–September	Medium, wet	Sand, loam, clay	Full sun
Cardinal flower	*Lobelia cardinalis*	2'–5'	Red	July–September	Wet	Sand, loam	Full sun, partial sun
Great blue lobelia	*Lobelia siphilitica*	1'–4'	Blue	July–September	Medium, wet	Sand, loam, clay	Full sun, partial sun
Lupine	*Lupinus perennis*	1'–2'	Blue	May–June	Dry	Sand	Full sun, partial sun
Bergamot	*Monarda fistulosa*	2'–5'	Lavender	July–September	Dry, medium, wet	Sand, loam, clay	Full sun, partial sun
Dotted mint	*Monarda punctata*	1'–2'	Lavender	July–September	Dry	Sand	Full sun
Wild quinine	*Parthenium integrifolium*	2'–5'	White	June–September	Dry, medium	Sand, loam, clay	Full sun
Smooth penstemon	*Penstemon digitalis*	2'–3'	White	June–July	Medium	Sand, loam, clay	Full sun, partial sun
Slender penstemon	*Penstemon gracilis*	1'–2'	Lavender	May–June	Dry	Sand	Full sun, partial sun
Beardtongue	*Penstemon grandiflorus*	2'–4'	Lavender	May–June	Dry	Sand	Full sun

Common name	Scientific name	Height	Color	Bloom time	Moisture	Soil	Light
False dragonhead	Physostegia virginiana	1'–2'	Pink	August–September	Medium, wet	Sand, loam, clay	Full sun
Jacob's ladder	Polemonium reptans	1'–2'	Blue	April–June	Medium	Sand, loam	Full sun, partial sun, shade
Great Solomon's seal	Polygonatum canaliculatum	1'–4'	Green	May–June	Dry, medium	Sand, loam, clay	Full sun, partial sun
Yellow coneflower	Ratibida pinnata	3'–6'	Yellow	July–September	Dry, medium, wet	Sand, loam, clay	Full sun
Meadow rose	Rosa blanda	3'–4'	Pink-white	June–July	Medium	Sand, loam, clay	Full sun
Pasture rose	Rosa carolina	1'–2'	Pink	June–July	Dry, medium	Sand, loam	Full sun
Black-eyed Susan	Rudbeckia hirta	1'–3'	Yellow	July–September	Dry, medium	Sand, loam, clay	Full sun, partial sun
Green-headed coneflower	Rudbeckia laciniata	3'–6'	Yellow	August–September	Wet	Sand, loam, clay	Full sun, partial sun
Sweet black-eyed Susan	Rudbeckia subtomentosa	3'–6'	Yellow	August–October	Medium, wet	Sand, loam, clay	Full sun
Brown-eyed Susan	Rudbeckia triloba	2'–5'	Yellow	July–October	Medium, wet	Sand, loam	Full sun
Wild petunia	Ruellia humilis	1'–2'	Violet	June–August	Dry, medium	Sand, loam	Full sun
Royal catchfly	Silene regia	2'–4'	Red	July–August	Medium	Loam	Full sun
Rosinweed	Silphium integrifolium	2'–6'	Yellow	July–September	Medium, wet	Sand, loam, clay	Full sun
Compass plant	Silphium lacinatum	3'–10'	Yellow	June–September	Dry, medium	Sand, loam, clay	Full sun
Cup plant	Silphium perfoliatum	3'–8'	Yellow	July–September	Medium, wet	Sand, loam, clay	Full sun, partial sun
Prairie dock	Silphium terebinthinaceum	3'–10'	Yellow	July–September	Medium, wet	Sand, loam, clay	Full sun
Solomon's Plume	Smilacina racemosa	1'–2'	White	June	Medium	Sand, loam, clay	Partial sun, shade
Ohio goldenrod	Solidago ohioensis	3'–4'	Yellow	July–September	Medium, wet	Sand, loam, clay	Full sun
Stiff goldenrod	Solidago rigida	2'–5'	Yellow	August–October	Dry, medium	Sand, loam, clay	Full sun
Showy goldenrod	Solidago speciosa	1'–3'	Yellow	July–October	Dry, medium	Sand, loam	Full sun
Meadowrue	Thalictrum dasycarpum	3'–6'	White	June–July	Wet	Sand, loam, clay	Full sun, partial sun

Continued

Wildflower Selection Guide [concluded from page 327]

Common Name	Botanical Name	Height	Color	Bloom Time	Moisture	Soil	Sun
Ohio spiderwort	*Tradescantia ohiensis*	2'–4'	Blue	May–June	Dry, medium	Sand, loam	Full sun, partial sun
White Ohio spiderwort	*Tradescantia ohiensis–alba*	2'–4'	White	May–June	Dry, medium	Sand, loam	Full sun, partial sun
Blue vervain	*Verbena hastata*	2'–5'	Blue	July–September	Medium, wet	Sand, loam, clay	Full sun
Hoary vervain	*Verbena stricta*	2'–4'	Blue	June–September	Dry, medium	Sand, loam	Full sun
Tall ironweed	*Vernonia altissima*	5'–8'	Red-pink	August–September	Wet	Sand, loam, clay	Full sun, partial sun
Ironweed	*Vernonia fasciculata*	4'–6'	Purple	July–September	Wet	Sand, loam, clay	Full sun
Culver's root	*Veronicastrum virginicum*	3'–6'	White	July–August	Medium, wet	Sand, loam, clay	Full sun, partial sun
Bird's-foot violet	*Viola pedata*	<1'	Blue-purple	April–June	Dry, medium	Sand, loam	Full sun, partial sun
Heartleaf golden Alexanders	*Zizia aptera*	1'–2'	Yellow	May–June	Medium	Sand, loam	Full sun
Golden Alexanders	*Zizia aurea*	1'–2'	Yellow	May–July	Medium, wet	Sand, loam, clay	Full sun

CONTAINER AND BASKET PLANTING

Growing plants in containers can give you tremendous versatility in your landscape. Just about any plants that can be grown in the ground can also be grown in a container—annuals, perennials, vegetables, shrubs, and even trees. And virtually any object that will hold soil can be a container, from a bag of soil with holes punched for drainage to a traditional clay pot to an old wheelbarrow filled with soil.

Container planting can fill a number of different purposes. For example, you can use a container for a planting that you want to move around. Put a container on wheels or on a dolly to move it in or out of the sun, or from one location to another to fill various dec-

Impatiens can be tested in a shady location such as this before home owners commit to a full-scale planting.

329

orating or entertaining needs. This is an easy way to change your landscape effects periodically. Containers are also useful for trying something new on a small scale, to experiment without committing time and space. For example, if you have a shady area and want to see how things will do, put a few plants in pots in the area.

Containers can provide a garden spot in homes with no space for a traditional garden. Use them so that you can have plantings in places where you could not place a plant in the ground, as on a deck, patio, balcony, roof, or other hard surfaces. They can also create a variety of levels for your plantings. You can raise containers on pedestals, steps, or platforms, and you can lower them by sinking them into the ground. Or use containers of progressive sizes for a step effect.

Boxes and pots (on the left) provide places for plants where they couldn't ordinarily grow and provide greenery and flowers on multiple levels of this deck.

Containers are also perfect for overcoming cultural restrictions. You can overcome the problems of poor soil aeration and drainage by growing in pots or other holders. This approach can substantially expand the planting possibilities in some urban areas with very small yards and poor soil. It also makes possible the use outdoors of certain tender plants that can easily be moved indoors when the weather would ordinarily kill them.

Consider the value of a fully planted wagon or wheelbarrow, which can be rolled wherever you want it. Not only does it save you the strain of trying to lift a large pot, it also can add a very decorative element to your landscape, particularly if you want a rural or rustic look.

USING CONTAINERS

Designing with containers relates closely to the same principles that you use designing with plants in the ground. Containers vary in shape, color, and texture. Consider them as part of the landscape design. Relate and coordinate your containers with other parts of your landscape. If you have a contemporary patio with a contemporary concrete-and-chrome home, use contemporary fiberglass containers or perhaps chrome containers in pastel colors. If you live in a cedar shake home surrounded by split-rail fencing, use wooden tubs and farm implements as planters.

Designwise, most suburban homes would fall somewhere between the contemporary and rustic looks described above. In the case of a home with a less definitive style of its own, use the style of a container to help set the style of the garden. An old boot with flowers spilling out of it or a wooden bucket or tub on the patio, for example, will set a casual or rustic style. An ornate urn will give a formal and permanent tone. Just make sure to keep your style consistent. A very ornamental container may work best without any plantings, standing as ornamentation itself, like a sculpture. This is true of most urns, which often look best unplanted.

Plastic containers offer a number of advantages. They are lightweight, and therefore easy to handle and move around; and they also lower the evaporation rate of the moisture in the soil.

SUITABLE MATERIALS FOR CONTAINERS

Wood

Stone

Concrete

Ceramic

Fiberglass

Plastic

Fiber

Brass

Copper

Iron

Once you have established the style of your container, you will want to consider size. Use a container that is deep enough to allow for adequate root development for your plants. Consider the size that the mature plant will grow to when selecting a container. The size of your container will also dictate the types of plants you can use in it and the amount of watering they will need. The smaller the container, the more frequently you need to water. Containers come in all sizes. Standard sized clay pots, glazed or unglazed, can be found in two- to thirty-inch widths and even larger.

With large pots, you will sacrifice some mobility. When a large pot is filled with soil, it is extremely heavy and you won't be able to move it unless it's on wheels. To lighten your pots somewhat, instead of using terra-cotta pieces for drainage, use plastic peanuts, Styrofoam packing material, or perlite, and plant in plastic or fiberglass pots.

PLANTING

There are a few rules that are important to container planting.

Except for spring-flowering bulbs, when using containers, spring is usually the time to plant them. Because you'll be starting to grow in a somewhat unnatural growth situation, you want the sap to be flowing and active nutrient exchange occurring soon after planting. You want your plant to be dynamic from the time you plant it so that it will have the optimum chance to establish roots and survive.

If possible, allow a plant in a container a period to acclimatize before it is exposed to sun and wind. Hold in a shady location for a week or two, then gradually move it into the sun, except perhaps containers of annuals or perennials, which will acclimate much faster than trees, shrubs, or foliage houseplants.

Watering at planting time is essential. It's also a good idea to mist plants when first putting them in a container to keep them from transpiring, losing moisture through their leaves. Do not continue misting after transplanting. Once the plants are growing, humidity, is more important than misting.

Stake newly planted tall trees and shrubs, especially a tree that is planted bare root. In a container, you don't have the advantage of heavy soil holding the plant in place, as you do if planting into the soil. Continue staking through the root development period and possibly through the whole growing season. Attach the plant to the stake with a wire, with fabric or rubber hose protecting the stem of the plant.

GROWING

When growing plants in containers, the cultural needs become critical. This includes watering, fertilization, pest control, and root hardiness.

WATERING

Watering is critical to plants in containers. They are much more susceptible to drought than plants growing in the ground are. For less work, consider placing your container near a water source, within reach of your garden hose, or install a small drip irrigation system, available at garden centers. Make sure to never let the soil get so dry that it pulls away from the sides of the pot.

The material your container is made of will effect your plants' watering needs. Unglazed clay pots are porous, and water can more quickly evaporate through it than through plastic. While clay is more aesthetically appealing from a design standpoint, if you can find a plastic pot that looks like clay, it will be far better for holding moisture.

Using ornamental mulch will dress up your container, and it will hold extra moisture. Use aged shredded hardwood bark about an inch thick or pine bark nuggets. The pine bark nuggets will stay nicer for a longer period of time and can be easily shaved from the top and be reused at another time. Mulches also insulate the growing medium from sudden temperature changes. You can use as much as a two- to three-inch layer of pine bark nuggets on a big container.

Keep in mind the special needs of container plants exposed to wind and sun. Plants in containers that are exposed on all sides to the effects of wind and sun may need watering more than once a day.

The color of the container is also a consideration. In general, I recommend lighter-colored containers that reflect the heat. Darker colors absorb the heat, which will get seeds off to a quick start, but the soil will dry more quickly. Lighter-colored pots generally hold moisture for a longer period of time.

The other side of watering is drainage. Drainage is as critical to container planting as watering. Plants use water by absorbing microscopic particles that attach to soil particles. Excessive moisture produces root rots. Be sure your container allows for drainage. This can be as simple as making a hole if none is there. If you don't want to ruin a decorative pot with a hole, put a smaller pot inside. If you use a pot within a pot or a similar arrangement, make sure there is a buffer area. Don't let the pot sit directly in water or else the roots won't be able to breathe, won't be able to use the water, and will rot.

> "Using ornamental mulch will dress up your container, and it will hold extra moisture. Use aged shredded hardwood bark about an inch thick or pine bark nuggets."

Containers have gotten a practical helping hand from the super-absorbent gels that are now on the market. Use super-absorbent gels as a supplement to the planting medium in your containers. Gels such as Hydretain, TerraSorb, and Soil Moist reportedly absorb up to 400 times their weight in water, then slowly release it as the soil dries. Some of these materials are so absorbent that they can expand over the edge of the pot, so follow directions very carefully or you could end up with a gelatinous planting medium. Note that you must mix the dry gel with the planting medium before planting.

Test the soil in your container regularly by probing three to four inches with your finger into the pot to see if it is drying out. One of the most common causes of plant failure is overwatering or improper watering. The proper soil mix helps aid water absorption.

SOIL

You can make your own soil mix, but I recommend a soilless, pre-mixed, peat moss–based potting soil for growing in containers. It's sold at all garden and home improvement centers. Since peat moss tends to repel moisture until it is fully hydrated, soak it thoroughly before you begin planting. This means that you should add the water and mix it with your hands, like making a mud pie, to ensure that it is thoroughly wet. The downside of peat moss–based potting soil is that it tends to repel moisture when dry and wetting can take some time. This is a good reason to be sure to never let your container completely dry out. The potting preparation should always feel slightly moist to the touch.

SPACING AND PRUNING

Growing in containers is an easy and efficient way to control weeds. Since the need for weeding is minimal, there is no need to plant for access. Place herbaceous plants close together and let them spill over the edge of the container and grow together. When they are growing where you don't want them to be, simply pluck them from that spot, just as you would in the garden.

Non-cascading woody plants, such as trees and shrubs, however, need adequate spacing for trunks to grow. This is where root pruning and top pruning practices become very important. If you want to keep a woody plant growing year after year in a pot without transplanting to a larger container, you will need to root prune it within two to three years of planting.

A good rule of thumb for pruning is take about one to two inches off the roots all the way around and open up the top growth, taking off no more than one-third of the top. The best time to do this is in early spring before growth begins.

TRANSPLANTING

The alternative to root pruning is increasing the size of your container. Move to a container approximately two inches larger in diameter than the previous one. When you make your transfer, if the plant's roots are bound together and twisted around the container, trim them by slicing through the root-bound material. If you don't wish to root prune and want to watch your plant grow larger, plan to transplant up to a larger container every two to four years.

FERTILIZING

Fertilization is another important element of successful container planting, and there are several options available. If you want to use dry fertilizer, choose a 5-10-5 mix and sprinkle it over the soil surface of the container. Or you can use manufactured fertilizer stakes (similar to tree stakes) and just stick them in the soil. They will fertilize as you water. Some of the premixed soil preparations come with nutrients plugged in, but they have little staying power. You should still supplement with a fertilizer. The best one you can use is a material that's labeled for your particular plant, such as rose or tomato food.

> "Fertilizing container plantings with a water-soluble fertilizer every other watering is the easiest."

In my experience, fertilizing container plantings with a water-soluble fertilizer every other watering is the easiest. My choice is a well-balanced food for flower, foliage, fruit, or whatever you are growing. It's called Peters Plant Food and can be put right into a watering jug or can.

There are a group of growth stimulants and plant vitamins emerging on the market that are fertilizer supplements and will stimulate growth tremendously on virtually any plant in any type of soil. Many are composed of humic acid, fish/kelp/seaweed, and/or vitamin B complex. Two such materials that I have seen incredible results from are Superthrive, manufactured since 1940 by the Vitamin Institute in North Hollywood, California, and Dyna-Gro K-L-N Rooting Concentrate, made by Dyna-Gro.

Know when to fertilize. You can add root growth stimulants when planting, but wait about two weeks to a month after planting to add fertilizer. Fertilizing too early overstimulates or can burn the roots. The plant doesn't need the fertilizer until it has feeder roots growing in the medium in the container. Fertilize trees and shrubs after new growth in the spring and monthly thereafter during peak growth season. As you go into the winter, always err on the side of too little fertilizer because new growth is vulnerable.

TEMPERATURES

In some of the finest gardens in Europe and the U.S., you will see orangeries, large atriums built to house plants in winter that would not overwinter otherwise. These were named for their original purpose in France, where they were built to house potted orange trees through the winter.

Because entire containers will easily freeze in sub-freezing temperatures, only the hardiest of plants growing in containers will make it through the winter, except in very mild climate zones. To keep a marginally hardy plant alive, have a provision to move it indoors for the winter. You can add months to the lives of your container plants and extend the harvest or bloom season by moving them indoors when the weather grows cold. Don't think of your outdoor/indoor container plants as house plants—for the most part, they won't last forever. But you can extend their lives before they start to get scraggly looking and you finally decide to get rid of them. Bring your tender deciduous trees and shrubs indoors in September or October, well before the first frosts and begin their acclimatizing before you need full-time heat in your house. Let the soil dry between waterings and fertilize no more than once a month, if at all. Wait until all danger of freezing passes before moving these tender plants outdoors again. People often jump the gun on this. The exact time of year depends on your region. It's usually sometime between May and June.

Unlike typical houseplants that need indirect sunlight, most potted plants that have been growing in full sun will require the same conditions inside. Place indoors where they will receive maximum sunlight. Container plants moved indoors may need supplemental lighting. Consider grow bulbs, either fluorescent or incandescent.

Don't forget that your plant needs humidity indoors. If your house is dry, as is almost every house with a heating system, set the containers in shallow pans filled with stones, with water to the top of the stones. The water rising in its gaseous form in the air around the plant gives it the humidity it needs. Or place pots of water over the heater vents.

Hardier deciduous plants can overwinter outdoors, if you take special steps to protect them. The ends of roots that reach the edge of the container and touch the walls of the container might just as well be touching the outside air, and they need special attention. If you intend to keep your container outside over the winter, mulch it

TEMPERATURES AT WHICH ROOTS WILL DIE IF PLANTED IN CONTAINERS

The following list of selected shrubs and groundcover is from research conducted by Dr. Francis A. Gouin at the University of Maryland. There are many other plants not listed that can be container grown; experiment on your own and try others. The plants here are listed in order of hardiest to least hardy when in containers.

Common name	Botanical name	°F
PJM rhododendron	*Rhododendron* 'PJM'	−9
Bush cinquefoil	*Potentilla fruticosa*	−9
Serbian spruce	*Picea omorika*	−9
White spruce	*Picea glauca*	−9
Catawba rhododendron	*Rhododendron catawbiense*	0
Carolina rhododendron	*Rhododendron carolinianum*	0
Douglas creeping Juniper	*Juniperus horizontalis* 'Douglasii'	0
Mountain pieris	*Pieris floribunda*	5
Fetterbush	*Leucothoë fontanesiana*	5
Wintercreeper euonymus	*Euonymus fortunei* 'Coloratus'	5
American arborvitae	*Thuja occidentalis*	10
Hinodegiri azalea	*Rhododendron* 'Hinodegiri'	10
Gibraltar azalea	*Rhododendron* 'Gibraltar'	10
Oregon grapeholly	*Mahonia aquifolium*	10
Yew	*Taxus* x *media* 'Nigra'	12
Single-seed juniper	*Juniperus squamata*	12
Andorra juniper	*Juniperus horizontalis* 'Plumosa'	12
Shore juniper	*Juniperus conferta*	12
Praecox cotoneaster	*Cotoneaster adpressus* var. *praecox*	12
Periwinkle	*Vinca minor*	15
Purple Gem rhododendron	*Rhododendron* 'Purple Gem'	15
Royal azalea	*Rhododendron schlippenbachii*	15
Japanese pieris	*Pieris japonica*	15
Japanese spurge	*Pachysandra terminalis*	15
Mountain-laurel	*Kalmia latifolia*	15
Baltic ivy	*Hedera helix* 'Baltica'	15
Carrierei wintercreeper	*Euonymus fortunei* 'Carrierei'	15
Red leaf Japanese maple	*Acer palmatum* var. *atropurpureum*	15
Koreanspice viburnum	*Viburnum carlesii*	15
Goldenrain tree	*Koelreuteria paniculata*	16
Inkberry	*Ilex glabra*	16

TEMPERATURES AT WHICH ROOTS WILL DIE IF PLANTED IN CONTAINERS

Common name	Botanical name	°F
Warminster broom	*Cytisus* x *praecox*	16
Hicks yew	*Taxus* x *media* 'Hicksii'	17
Japanese cryptomeria	*Cryptomeria japonica*	17
Rockspray cotoneaster	*Cotoneaster horizontalis*	17
Exbury azalea	*Rhododendron* Exbury hybrid	17
Cutleaf stephanandra	*Stephanandra incisa*	18
Winged euonymus	*Euonymus alatus*	19
Hino-Crimson azalea	*Rhododendron* 'Hino-Crimson'	19
Doublefile viburnum	*Viburnum plicatum* var. *tomentosum*	20
Plumleaf azalea	*Rhododendron prunifolium*	20
Skogholm cotoneaster	*Cotoneaster dammeri* 'Skogholm'	20
Star magnolia	*Magnolia stellata*	22
San Jose holly	*Ilex* x *aquipernyi* 'San Jose'	22
Spreading euonymus	*Euonymus kiautschovicus*	22
Flowering dogwood	*Cornus florida*	22
Laland scarlet firethorn	*Pyracantha coccinea* 'Lalandei'	23
Leatherleaf mahonia	*Mahonia bealei*	23
Saucer magnolia	*Magnolia* x *soulangiana*	23
Nellie Stevens holly	*Ilex cornuta* 'Nellie Stevens'	23
American holly	*Ilex opaca*	23
Meserve hybrid holly	*Ilex* x *meserveae*	23
Stokes holly	*Ilex crenata* 'Stokes'	23
Hetzii holly	*Ilex crenata* 'Hetzii'	23
Helleri holly	*Ilex crenata* 'Helleri'	23
Convex holly	*Ilex crenata* 'Convexa'	23
St. John's wort	*Hypericum* species	23
Vegetus euonymus	*Euonymus fortunei* var. *vegetus*	23
Rose daphne	*Daphne cneorum*	23
Bearberry cotoneaster	*Cotoneaster dammeri*	23
Dazzler holly	*Ilex crenata* 'Dazzler'	25
Pyrenees cotoneaster	*Cotoneaster congestus*	25
Boxwood	*Buxus sempervirens*	27

with bales of straw packed tightly around and over the container. Get double duty from the straw in the spring as mulch for your vegetable garden.

To overwinter hardy evergreen plants in a container, move the container from an exposed site to an area free of excessive sun and wind by November (in most zones). Hardy evergreens shouldn't be kept in a heated area. Mulch well, pile bales of straw around the container, and continue the watering until the soil freezes.

For your container plants that will be spending the winter outdoors, water until the soil in the container begins to freeze in late fall. Then begin watering again as soon as the soil thaws in spring. If you bring your hardy evergreen to a garage or basement, where temperatures stay above freezing, water it whenever it dries out. It probably won't need much. In the garage or basement, the temperature should not exceed 40 to 45°F, or the evergreen will begin to sprout new growth.

In the spring, gradually introduce the plants back into the landscape. Don't put them back out in full wind and sun exposure all at once. Give them a chance to acclimate for best growth.

Bulbs work well in containers and are an exception to the spring planting rule. Plant your spring flowering bulbs in containers in the fall and mulch them. Plants will show growth in spring when soil temperatures warm. It's best to protect containers in a garage or shed at about 40°F, if possible.

Ornamental grasses are another perennial that you can plant effectively in containers. While the plant dies and winter robs it of its chlorophyll, the structure of the leaves will stand into February or March, depending on the wind. Then cut the dead leaves back and growth will begin again from the base. Do not move indoors.

HANGING BASKETS

Among the most popular and attractive containers for planting are hanging baskets. Use hanging baskets outdoors as an attractive and useful way to decorate walls, lampposts, trellises, and balconies. They are a great way to get colorful arrangements at a height where you normally wouldn't find flowers. Also, if you have limited space on a deck or patio, they hang up off the floor and out of your way. Another nice thing about them is that you can plant them yourself if you enjoy creating your own combinations, or you can buy them already planted and ready to hang. Gardening can't get any easier than that!

A couple different types of baskets are on the market—moss or natural fiber and plastic. Moss and natural-fiber baskets are made

> "Moss and coco baskets are more upscale and add a lot of beauty to the planting."

by lining a wire basket with moss or coco fiber, and you can find kits to make these or buy them already assembled. Moss and coco baskets are more upscale and add a lot of beauty to the planting. But if you have plants that trail over the basket and hide it from view, then plastic is a cheaper option, since no one can see the container. Baskets eight to nine inches in diameter will hold two to three annuals such as sweet alyssum, begonias, or impatiens.

Wire baskets are not practical for indoor use because they can drip for hours after watering. Hanging baskets with solid sides, drain holes, and attached saucers are more appropriate for indoor use; simply fill with soil mix and plant them. There are a wide variety of flowering and cascading plants sold at garden centers already potted and ready for hanging.

Hanging baskets might require watering every day during the summer, especially if they are in the sun. And natural-fiber baskets will require watering more than the same plant in a plastic basket since water will evaporate through the fibers. You could install a drip line that with a tube leading from a water source that can be put on a timer to water the plants automatically. All other soil and fertilizer requirements for hanging baskets follow the same rules as for other types of containers.

EDIBLE LANDSCAPE 44

Design for all your senses, including taste. Originally, the term *gardening* referred chiefly to cultivating edible plants, and for many people the vegetable garden or fruit orchard is the focus of their horticultural activities. When I talk about the edible landscape, though, I am not talking about rows of beans and corn, but about the creative ways you can incorporate tasty morsels into your environment as part of your landscape design. But you can also incorporate some of the basic principles of design into your conventional vegetable garden.

THE VEGETABLE GARDEN

Throw away your preconceived notions of what a vegetable garden should look like and design it to be ornamental as well as utilitarian. It doesn't have to be strictly rectangular, and it doesn't have to be just vegetables. Add some flowers. Colorful edging rows of marigolds, for example, not only look good but also have insect repellent properties.

Don't just plant your vegetables in rows, but in hills, beds, or other groupings. This may even be a more efficient method of gardening than a standard vegetable garden arrangement. Consider a "three sisters" mound with squash, beans, and corn. In one mound, squash vines are planted to crawl along the ground under the corn. It shades the soil, holds moisture, and controls the weeds. Planting pole beans to climb the corn stalks creates an extremely efficient and ornamental method of gardening.

Keeping the last chapter in mind, try combining vegetable and flowering plants in a container. Set off your tomatoes in a large container with dwarf marigolds, wax begonias, or alyssum around the edge.

Now let's look at some ways you can bring edibles out of your garden and use them to enhance the landscape.

341

Cherry tomatoes are the perfect hanging basket or window box ornaments.

- Use summer squash as a groundcover on a sunny slope with taller tomato vines staked above them, perhaps gracing a serpentine walkway.
- Train pole beans or peas onto a trellis to create privacy around a porch in summer.
- Strawberries make a great edible groundcover.
- Grow dill to soften a bare wall and cucumbers to cover a fence. Harvested together, you can make dill pickles.
- Plant creeping thyme (*Thymus* species) in spaces between paving material that was laid dry on a stone dust or sand base. It grows in most soils; best in full sun. When walking on it, its fragrance is released. It's great for cooking or mixing into your salad dressing.
- Use dill and asparagus if you want a light, ferny foliage in your landscape. Dill must be replanted annually. Asparagus will come back for years. Both are handsome additions to a garden. And once established, you'll get asparagus spears every spring and fall.

EDIBLE FLOWERS

Volumes have been written about edible flowers, but these aren't your "run of the mill" edibles. So, here are some general safety tips related to eating flowers, according to Cathy Wilkinson Barash's book *Edible Flowers*:

- Not all flowers are edible; some, in fact, are poisonous. One rule of thumb is that if the fruit is edible, its flowers are.
- Eat only flowers that you are positive are edible and then only from organically grown plants.
- If you have hay fever, asthma, or allergies, don't eat flowers, as they'll only aggravate your allergies and cause a potentially serious reaction.
- Don't eat flowers picked along a road where particulate pollution, and possible pesticides, abound. Eat your own or others that you know are pesticide free.
- Eat only flower petals.
- Introduce flowers to your diet in small amounts at first.

You can use flowers as accents to your meals, as garnishes, for spice, and for color in a dish. The flowers from your crabapples are edible, as are flowers from daylilies, nasturtiums, and many others. They'll make colorful highlights to salads and desserts. And you can pick a handful of violets and use them in sauces, omelets, pastries, and candies.

OTHER EDIBLES

In the past two decades, interest in the edible ornamental landscape has grown. Here are some specific ideas about edible ornamentals that I like to use. Blueberry and currant bushes blend well with ornamental shrubs, and raspberries and blackberries fit beautifully in the natural landscape. You can get double duty from your shade trees by planting nuts. Butternut, English walnut, and Chinese chestnut trees will give you a canopy of shade and baskets full of edible nuts.

Hardy kiwi (*Actinidia arguta*) is a tough, woody, entwining vine that needs a solid support. Plant two, a male and female, in order to get clusters of small, grape-sized fruit. It's perfect grown along a deck or on a trellis by the patio so you can harvest it with ease as fruits ripen. It requires sun for fruit, but the vine is very shade tolerant.

Corneliancherry dogwood (*Cornus mas*) not only offers edible red berries, but it's also one of the first trees to flower in spring. The berries ripen in July and can be used in tarts, as syrup, or for cranberry sauce. This shaggy barked tree is virtually disease free, and its low, rounded habit makes it good as a screening plant, an ornamental tree for a mixed shrub border, or planted as a hedge. It grows to about twenty feet high in a sunny location.

If you want to attract birds to your garden, plant a downy serviceberry (*Amelanchier arborea*). The purplish black semisweet

> "You can get double duty from your shade trees by planting nuts."

berries of this small early-flowering native tree are so attractive to birds that you have to pick them quickly before the birds devour them. The berries ripen in June, and they are so good you can eat them right off the tree or make jellies and pies. This white-flowering tree is shade tolerant, but it will bear more flowers and fruit in sun. Plant it on the edge of woods or by your patio or deck for a low-branching privacy tree with fall color.

I find that the jujube (*Ziziphus jujuba*), a hardy, late-flowering, drought-tolerant tree, is the perfect snack tree. The upright habit, which grows to about twenty feet tall, doesn't create a lot of shade, so you can group it with other flowers and edible plants. Harvest fruit in the fall after the skin browns. Used as a dessert in Europe, the jujube fruit has a sweet custard flavor and a texture that is very appealing to the palate.

The kousa dogwood (*Cornus kousa*) is a small, flowering tree with year-round interest. In winter, the bark is a lacy, peeling texture that colors brown to ivory on the trunk. It flowers from late April well into May. The meat of the fruits is edible and very sweet, as they soften and turn red, and the foliage colors maroon in autumn. Kousa is resistant to the dogwood anthracnose that is killing native varieties. It grows well in sun or shade, but fruiting is always enhanced in sun. Design in groupings with flowering shrubs and edible perennials or groundcovers, or use as a single specimen in the lawn.

Trifoliate hardy orange (*Poncirus trifoliata*) is a fully hardy citrus that grows in sun or partial shade. Use its fruit as a garnish for drinks such as lemonade, tea, and cocktails, or make it into marmalade. If you need a barrier planting, this shrub will form a thorny thicket up to fifteen feet high that no one would walk through or hide in without first wearing armor.

Houttuynia (*Houttuynia cordata* 'Chameleon'), sometimes called hot tuna, is a problem-free, vigorous-growing groundcover with edible greens and roots. It loves wet spots and will fill the area with salad greens and ginger-flavored roots. Don't plant other low ornamental groundcovers with it. The low, red, white, and green variegated foliage and fleshy stems need room to grow, especially in full sun and moisture.

FOR MORE INFORMATION

There is a mail-order company for edible ornamental plants called Edible Landscaping. Their catalogue is available by calling (800) 524-4156. It is as much an excellent resource for information about edible landscape plants as it is a source for acquiring them.

EDIBLE PLANTS FOR LANDSCAPE USE

Edible parts are listed next to the plant name. Please read the entire chapter on edible plants before eating any of the plants on this chart.

Trees

Apple (*Malus*)—fruit
Apricot (*Prunus*)—fruit
Ash, mountain (*Sorbus*)—berry
Birch (*Betula*)—sap, twigs
Butternut (*Juglans*)—nut
Cherry (*Prunus*)—fruit
Chestnut (*Castanea*)—nut
Crabapple (*Malus*)—fruit
Dogwood, kousa (*Cornus*)—fruit
Dwarf fruit trees—fruit
Elderberry (*Sambucus*)—berry
Hawthorn (*Crataegus*)—berry
Hazelnut (*Corylus*)—nut
Honeylocust (*Gleditsia*)—
young seed
Larch (*Larix*)—young shoots
Linden (*Tilia*)—leaf bud, flower
Maples (*Acer*)—sap
Mulberry (*Morus*)—berry
Nectarine (*Prunus*)—fruit
Oaks (*Quercus*)—acorn
Pawpaw (*Asimina triloba*)—fruit
Peach (*Prunus*)—fruit
Pear (*Pyrus*)—fruit
Persimmon (*Diospyros*)—fruit, leaf
Pines (*Pinus*)—young shoots, needles
Plum (*Prunus*)—fruit
Redbud (*Cercis*)—flower, young pod
Sassafras (*Sassafras*)—root
Serviceberry (*Amelanchier*)—berry
Spruce (*Picea*)—young shoots, sap
Sweetgum (*Liquidambar*)—sap
Swiss stone pine (*Pinus cembra*)—nut
Sycamore (*Platanus*)—sap
Walnut (*Juglans*)—nut

Shrubs and Vines

Blackberry (*Rubus*)—fruit
Blueberry (*Vaccinium*)—fruit
Currant (*Ribes*)—fruit
Grape (*Vitis*)—fruit, young leaf
Honeysuckle (*Lonicera*)—fruit
Lemon verbena (*Aloysia*)—leaf
Kiwi (*Actinidia*)—fruit
Quince (*Pseudocydonia*)—fruit
Raspberry (*Rubus*)—fruit
Rosemary (*Rosmarinus*)—leaf
Rose (*Rosa*)—hips
Spicebush (*Benzoin*)—fruit
Strawberry (*Fragaria*)—fruit
Wintergreen (*Gaultheria*)—
fruit, leaf
Yucca (*Yucca*)—ripe fruit,
flower petals

Perennials and Bulbs

Allium (*Allium*)—bulb
Amaranth (*Amaranthus*)—leaf, seeds
Anise (*Pimpinella anisum*)—root, fruit
Asparagus (*Asparagus*)—stalk
Bee balm (*Monarda*)—flower
Daylily (*Hemerocallis*)—tuber, flower, bud
Houttuynia—all parts
Hyacinth (*Hyacinthus*)—bulb
Hyssop (*Hyssopus*)—leaf, flower
Jerusalem artichoke (*Helianthus*)—tuber
Lily (*Lilium*)—bulb
Mint (*Mentha*)—leaf
Pineapple sage (*Salvia*)—leaf
Purslane (*Portulaca*)—stem, leaf, seed
Tarragon (*Artemesia dracunculus*)—leaf
Thistles (*Onopordum*)—stem, leaf
Thyme (*Thymus*)—leaf
Violet (*Viola*)—young leaf, flower

FRAGRANCE

Don't leave your nose out of your landscape design. Aromatic flowers and plants, and the oils extracted from them, have been used as ornament, medicine, food, and in cultural traditions and religious rites throughout history. While most of us are aware of the lovely smells of flowers like lilacs, hyacinths, and roses, there are many other creative ways you can bring fragrance to your garden. Both the flowers and foliage of many plants can perfume your environment.

As you can tell by the plant listings in this chapter, fragrant plants abound. Use them to add fragrance to your landscape design. I have selected several to write about further and offer tips that you might not have considered when planning your fragrant garden.

FRAGRANT PLANTS

SPICEBUSH

For what I call guerrilla fragrance, plant a spicebush (*Lindera benzoin*) or two. The foliage of this plant, which is native to the mid-Atlantic region, imparts a spicy fragrance that you will find if you grab and bruise a leaf. Then its sweet spiciness will perfume the air.

SWEET ALYSSUM

Plant a window box or hanging basket by your front door with alyssum (*Lobularia maritima*) to get a sweet aroma every time you walk by. Its low billows of foliage are almost hidden by small, white, fragrant flowers in spring and fall. They tend to fade in the hot summer sun, but in protected sun, flowers and foliage persist and cascade over the edge of a basket or window box.

Spiked Elaeagnus

You will barely notice the silvery white fragrant flowers of spiked or fragrant elaeagnus in fall, but its perfume will drench the air. You'll have fun watching visitors search for the fragrance. This disease-free plant is not for small gardens since it grows to ten feet or more. Plant as an accent along the path of a woodland garden. It's happy in shade, sun, moisture, and drought.

Virginia Sweetspire

Virginia sweetspire (*Itea virginica*) is a native of the eastern United States and was introduced for sale at garden centers in 1744. A low-growing, long-flowering plant, it has sweet-smelling blooms and grows only two to four feet high in sun or shade and in wet or dry soil. Its display of maroon fall foliage can hold for weeks.

Witchhazel

Common and Chinese witchhazels (*Hamamelis virginiana* and *H. mollis*) both have yellow fragrant flowers. The common witchhazel opens in November and will continue to bloom for three weeks; the Chinese opens in February and can persist into spring. Depending on how you prune them, these plants can qualify as shrubs or trees.

Fragrant Herbs

Herbs are a wonderful way to add fragrance to your landscape.

Lavender

Edge a flower bed with herbaceous lavender (*Lavandula angustifolia*) to fill the air with a saccharine bouquet on a summer day, especially when it grows over the edge of the planting bed and brushes your leg as you walk past. The foliage will offer the fragrance twelve months a year if you pinch the plant to encourage the oils to escape into the air.

Mint

Mint (*Mentha*) might be too invasive to grow among other ornamentals, but there are ways to contain it. Golden mint works wonderfully as a perennial container planting, and Corsican mint—only a half-inch high and with a strong peppermint fragrance—thrives in any nook or cranny you might find in the garden, a rock wall, between patio steps, or in a knothole.

THYME

Thyme (*Thymus*) is available in over four hundred species, and once you experience its strong fragrance, you will want to collect them. Lemon thyme, caraway thyme, camphor thyme, and creeping thyme are just a few examples. They can be planted in spaces between walls, walks, and patios.

BASIL

Highly valued as a culinary herb, basil also offers a number of varieties that can scent different areas of your garden. It gives off a pleasant fragrance when bruised. Purple basil (*Ocimum basilicum* 'Dark Opal') gives the added bonus of rich purple foliage in a perennial garden. Plant basil along a walkway, allowing it to spill onto the path.

ROSEMARY

Use fragrant rosemary (*Rosmarinus officinalis*) to soften the sharp line of a wall, steps, or patio. This evergreen shrub will flop and cascade over a wall or rock or can be sheared into a low hedge. Not overly invasive, it will grow to form a cluster of fragrant foliage for almost twelve months, and it flowers for the summer.

FRAGRANT FOLIAGE

Shrubs and Trees

Bayberry (*Myrica*)

Lemon verbena (*Aloysia*)

Rosemary (*Rosmarinus officinalis*)

Spicebush (*Lindera benzoin*)

Sweetbrier (*Rosa eglanteria*)

Perennials

Anise (*Pimpinella anisum*)

Basil (*Ocimum*) (an annual)

Lavender (*Lavandula*)

Lavender cotton (*Santolina chamaecyparissus*)

Lemon balm (*Melissa*)

Mint (*Mentha*)

Pineapple-scented sage (*Salvia rutilans*)

Scented geranium (*Pelargonium*)

Southernwood (*Artemesia abrotanum*)

Tarragon (*Artemesia dracunculus*)

Thyme (*Thymus*)

Wormwood (*Artemesia absinthium*)

HYPOALLERGENIC GARDENING

While technically not part of a fragrant garden, people generally associate their allergies with fragrant flowers. Whether your allergies are triggered or not depends not on how a flower smells, but rather on how it's pollinated. So you really can enjoy sniffing certain types of flowers without triggering your hay fever.

The term *hay fever* refers to allergic reactions people have to pollen that travels by air to pollinate the female flowers. Pollen is a microscopic round or oval particle, usually coming from a male plant finding its way to the female flowers. Plant allergies are an immune system disorder. However, if you have the gene for it, something must happen, such as continuous exposure to airborne pollen, to stimulate an allergic response in you. Even if you don't have hay fever, you could develop it. Or you could have plant allergy symptoms and not know it, like itching and watering eyes, runny nose, coughing, sneezing, and a raw throat at specific times during the growing season. According to the U.S. Department of Health and Human Services' Public Health Service, National Institutes of Health, airborne pollen allergies affect millions of Americans every growing season. People become more sensitive to these allergens as exposure increases.

What people need who react to plant pollen are hypoallergenic landscape designs. One of the main components necessary is a lot of hardscape, such as patios, decks, gazebos, covered porches, and walkways. Replace lawn with these structures, and then install a variety of plants that are pollinated by insects, not wind, in the spaces where you designed beds.

Plants to avoid are those that have dry pollen that looks like dust when you brush a branch. These wind-pollinated plants include lawn grasses, many trees, and some wildflowers and weeds. Try to distance yourself from nut trees, including the green pollen from the oak trees that cover cars and walks in spring. Pines, junipers, and yews are evergreens to avoid. In spring, pollen rises from them every time the wind blows or you walk past. White pines drop a yellow dust onto the landscape.

This may sound like you need to avoid a lot of plants, but it's the showy, flowering trees, shrubs, perennials, and annuals that pose no problems for allergy sufferers—probably the exact opposite of what people would normally assume. So this still allows for a great deal of flora.

Most fruit trees depend on insect pollination. You can plant flowering cherry, apple, plum, pear, and peach. Other trees include dogwood, fringetree, magnolia, serviceberry, and stewartia. Yellowwood (*Cladrastis kentukea*) and buckeye (*Aesculus hippocastanum*) will make showy, flowering hypoallergenic shade trees.

The showiest flowering shrubs are usually fine for planting. Many of them are completely dependent on insects because of their sticky pollen that doesn't blow around in the wind. Azalea, butterfly bush, camellia, hydrangea, lilac, rose, rhododendron, and viburnum are several woody ornamentals that bear showy, insect pollinated blossoms.

Your perennial and annual border can include many desirable plants. Begonia, bleeding heart, crocus, daffodil, daylily, hibiscus, iris, Japanese anemone, peony, phlox, salvia, snapdragon, verbena, and clematis on a trellis are a few suggestions.

I prefer to install gardens with lots of organic material and use landscape fabric to cover the areas that aren't planted to control

> "Whether your allergies are triggered or not depends not on how a flower smells, but rather on how it's pollinated."

weeds that might contribute to discomfort. Pull weeds before flowering, especially ragweed. Ragweed blooms from late summer to fall and presents perhaps the greatest stumbling block for the perfect hypoallergenic garden. Three-quarters of all people who display sensitivity to pollen-producing plants are allergic to ragweed. Ten to 20 percent of the population in this country is allergic to ragweed. It is the most-common cause of hay fever, and once the pollen of one of the seventeen species that grow in this country takes to the air, it continues until first frost. Incredibly, ragweed is a long-distance traveler that has been measured four hundred miles into the ocean and two miles up into the atmosphere. So you can't escape it.

If pollen allergies are severely debilitating during the growing season, here are some steps that you should take to stay as comfortable as possible. The suggestions come from the Asthma and Allergy Foundation of America, The American Academy of Allergy and Immunology, and the U.S. Department of Health and Human Services.

- Wash pollen off of plants and hardscape regularly.
- Keep house doors and windows closed and use an air conditioner with a high-efficiency particulate air filter attachment if the pollen count is high.
- Keep car windows closed.
- Wear a surgical mask outside when pollen count is high.
- Wash hair and clothing after being outdoors.
- Don't dry laundry on a line.
- Brush pets regularly.
- The closer to the ocean, the lower the pollen counts. Take a cruise during pollen season.
- Dust furniture and vacuum regularly.
- Other environmental conditions, such as vehicle emissions, smoke, other air pollutants, and high humidity put more demands on your respiratory system. Avoid them.

Track pollen counts in your area by watching local weather or call (800) 9-POLLEN for the numbers in your area. They are indicators when you can be most comfortable outdoors. Ragweed pollen is worse between 10:00 A.M. and 3:00 P.M. than at other times of the day, weather permitting.

A fine book on the subject is *Allergy-Free Gardening* by Thomas Leo Ogren (Ten Speed Press, 2000). You can also find more information about asthma and allergies on the Internet at www.aafa.org.

WILDLIFE IN THE GARDEN

Increasing numbers of people are choosing to walk on the wild side, so to speak, by installing natural gardens as part of their landscape. You don't need to prune, preen, and putter as much as in a formally designed space. And then there's the excitement of the fauna.

It's like the philosophy in the well-known baseball film *Field of Dreams:* "If you build it . . . they will come." If you install flora, wildlife will appear. And more than birds will show up. You might see butterflies, bees, chipmunks, rabbits, turtles, frogs, snakes, and deer—maybe too many.

There are three requirements for animals: food, water, and shelter. If you want animals to remain as part of the garden, provide long-term shelter and protection for their offspring. Often, these criteria are different for each animal. We'll look at a few of the more popular animals here, and if you want to attract a creature not listed, check at your local garden center or library for how to lure them.

BIRDS

Food sources for birds are diverse. Common flickers, for example, feed on crawling insects and a variety of berries; purple martins live almost exclusively on flying insects. But all birds need some type of cover to nest and raise their young. Planting a shrub or tree is a big step toward creating that shelter. Plug in the element of water, usually shallow like a birdbath, to give birds a need to visit your garden, especially during dry weather.

By installing plants that are native and have berries, you've added a strong incentive for birds to visit your home. Some native bird-attracting shrubs and trees are most species of serviceberries, spicebushes, inkberry hollies, bayberries, viburnums, and dogwoods—which alone attract eighty-six aviary species.

I recommend plants to attract birds to urban and suburban gardens, as opposed to installing bird feeders. I've heard many stories about rodent problems because the seed drops to the ground and the unwanted creatures are drawn to it.

HUMMINGBIRDS

The hummingbird is a different sort of creature. It has no natural enemies because of its speed. Flapping its wings up to eighty strokes per second, it can fly backwards, eat while hovering, and feed on nectar and insects all day long. Its heart beats so fast that it emits a faint humming. Because of its metabolism, this native of the Americas drops its heart rate and body temperature and puts itself into a state of suspended animation every evening so it won't starve.

Hummingbirds, which nest in the same area every year, migrate and can be spotted along the same migratory paths of hawks and monarch butterflies. As nectar feeders, they count on tubular flowers, mostly ones with red blooms. The ruby-throated hummingbird is the only one that nests east of the Mississippi River. Out west, there are more than a dozen. They will often come to anything red to feed, even a shirt.

They are fearless enough to feed from a flower in your hand once they get used to feeding around you. The following are some plants that hummers prefer:

- Wild columbine (*Aquilegia canadensis, A. formosa*)
- Honeysuckle (*Lonicera*)
- Cardinal flower (*Lobelia cardinalis*)
- Penstemon (*Penstemon*)
- Trumpet vine (*Campsis radicans*)
- Bee balm (*Monarda*)
- Red-flowering salvias (*Salvia*)

BEES

Along with the birds come the bees, the world's most beneficial insect pollinators. One-third of the world's food crops depends on them. In fact, melons and cucumbers depend entirely on the honeybee for pollination. One honeybee does a lot of work for little return. It pollinates as many as five thousand plants yet produces about an eighth of a teaspoon of honey in its lifetime. The nectar-producing plants that attract hummingbirds and butterflies will also be magnets for honeybees.

To learn more about beekeeping, honey, honeybees, and for over five hundred links to other bee-related Web sites, go to Beekeeping: The Beekeepers Home Pages at http://ourworld.compuserve.com/homepages/Beekeeping/right.htm.

BUTTERFLIES

There are 670 species of butterflies in the United States and Canada, and, in their short life as butterflies, they visit hundreds to thousands of flowers to drink nectar and pollinate plants. They are harmless, and only one of their larvae, called caterpillars, might be considered a crop pest. The cabbage butterfly lays its eggs on young plants in the cabbage family, and the larvae feed on the heads as they form. Virtually all other feeding is harmless to the plants.

There are many flowers from which butterflies drink nectar, and there is a host plant on which each butterfly hatches, feeds, and pupates from egg to caterpillar into an adult. You should grow flowers and host plants if you want their life cycle to be self-sustaining.

This Eastern tiger swallowtail butterfly is enjoying the verbena planted along a walkway.

Of course, the first type of plants that everyone wants are the flowering ones, but without the caterpillars' habitats, you'll have no butterflies. In our yard, the host plants happened to be there already, so we just had to plant their favorite flowers and supply puddles for water and small flat rocks for sunning and relaxation.

Following are the nectar-producing flowers that will keep butterflies occupied all summer long:

- Black-eyed Susan (*Rudbeckia*) is Maryland's official state flower. Its golden yellow flowers will feed butterflies throughout the summer.
- Butterfly bush (*Buddleia*) is a flowering shrub with purple or white spiked flowers in summer and fall. It grows tall and wide. To keep it as a low shrub, prune back to twelve inches before it leafs out in spring.
- Butterfly weed (*Asclepias*) has gained popularity because it attracts butterflies. I also know it as milkweed and, in my many years as a landscape professional, have removed it as a weed. Plant it in a natural, moist setting.
- Cosmos has the distinction of being an annual that seeds itself dependably and grows back annually, just like you want the butterflies to do.
- Goldenrod (*Solidago*) has gotten a bad rap because its showy golden flowers open at the same time as ragweed, to which many people are allergic. Goldenrod gets blamed as the allergen, but it's not. What it does do is attract butterflies.
- Joe Pye weed (*Eupatorium*) likes moist sites and has a tall (five to six feet) coarse-textured habit. It will flower in August and September and is best used to the back of the perennial border.
- Lantana grows in hot sunny locations. This free-flowering, drought-tolerant, butterfly-attracting plant must be replaced annually, but it's worth it for a whole summer of flowers.
- Lavender (*Lavandula*) stays green in winter and offers flowers that we like for sachet and butterflies love for nectar.
- Mint (*Mentha*) has leaves for our tea and flowers for butterflies' nectar. It's a perfect match.
- Purple coneflower (*Echinacea*) will cure the common cold, according to the latest medicinal herb information. Butterflies act as if it has curative qualities for them, too.
- Sage (*Salvia*) offers a low blue to purple spiked flower for the front of your perennial border in summer. The cultivar 'Mainacht' has kept the butterflies busy in our garden.
- Thyme works well as a groundcover cascading over walls or as a filler in joints of walls and patios. It'll keep your "winged

flowers," butterflies, flitting at your feet and hanging on your retaining walls.

- Verbena is the most butterfly-attracting plant I have experienced. Every butterfly in our yard loves its purple rounded clusters of flowers that last all summer until first frost.

Without host plants to help butterflies complete their life cycle, they would be faced with extinction. Some of them need one specific host. For example, the monarch butterfly will hatch and grow only on milkweed, and as I wrote in the above flower listing, I've been controlling it as a weed for over a quarter of a century. We need to make an effort to maintain the habitat of this incredible long-lived butterfly. The winter generation of the monarch lives for up to six months. They migrate a thousand to two thousand miles to the mountains of Mexico and rest on the branches of fir trees, then fly back in spring, mating along the way. The next generation will often complete the journey home. Think about that the next time you spot their orange wings with black edges and white dots decorating your garden. If you see them late in the season, they're probably the ones that are about to go on vacation in Mexico. And it must have milkweed as a host or it will become extinct.

The following are several other plants that serve as hosts for butterflies:

- Daisies and asters attract the painted lady and pearly crescentspot.
- Oak will host the gray hairstreak.
- Plum and wild cherry hosts the coral hairstreak.
- Spicebush or sassafras will provide a home to the spicebush swallowtail.
- Willow, apple, and cherry are used by the viceroy.
- Fennel, dill, parsley, and rue are preferred by the eastern black swallowtail.
- Verbena and snapdragon will host the buckeye butterfly.
- Willow, ash, and cherry offer habitats to the tiger swallowtail.

To ensure a habitat that butterflies will thrive in, locate garden in a sunny area. Plant nectar-producing flowers that you have seen attracting butterflies in your area. Single flowers (one row of petals) are more accessible to butterflies than doubles. Plant as a coordination of bloom throughout the growing season. Install host plants, as described above. Be sure to include shallow puddles for drinking and small flat rocks so they can bask in the sun. It's also very important not to use pesticides in or near a butterfly garden, as you'll be harming the very creatures you are drawing to your landscape.

> "Without host plants to help butterflies complete their life cycle, they would be faced with extinction."

Finally, get a good book and learn which butterflies frequent your area and the flowers that they prefer.

REPTILES AND AMPHIBIANS

Some of my fondest childhood memories with wildlife are catching toads and box turtles. It seems like there were more of them back then, but given the right habitat, their populations will increase again.

Toads and turtles are valuable assets to the home landscape, not just for ambiance but because they are voracious slug and insect eaters. Their appetite for insects is legendary and well earned. The American toad, for example, will eat about two hundred insects a night. They need clean in-ground water, thick grasses, and boggy areas in which to live. Turtles must have shallow water with gradually sloping rocks and a soft forest floor or beach for burying eggs, and cover plants for foraging and shelter.

Some of the more-maligned beneficial garden animals are snakes. Few are poisonous, and all eat insects and rodents. Habitat is the main determinant for attracting them to your garden. Areas of moist woods or grassy areas with hollow logs and rocks will attract them.

For planning, planting, and certification of your backyard as a habitat, call the National Wildlife Federation about their Backyard Wildlife Habitat and Schoolyard Habitat programs; their number is (703) 790-4434.

ATTRACTION OR PEST?

But where is the line between wildlife attraction and wildlife pest? Nothing could be cuter than rabbits and chipmunks on your property, provided they aren't digging up the garden. Rabbits are also capable of nibbling every one of your emerging flowers and vegetables to the ground. And deer damage is so common that the expression has become cliché.

Raccoons, while cute, can be destructive. Foxes are beautiful, and it's exciting to see one run across your lawn, as long as it doesn't have rabies. If these animals are approaching you, especially in the daytime and acting aggressive or strangely, play it safe by calling the animal control authority in your local jurisdiction.

REPELLING DEER

I was raised in Lebanon, Pennsylvania, where deer season meant the first day of hunting food for the winter. At Lebanon High, missing class for the first day of hunting season was an excused absence.

This is a topic for landscape design because deer season is all year long for many gardeners and landscape professionals. Nurseries in New York estimate their annual deer damage in excess of $50 million. They are by far the most-prominent mammal in our lives, with virtually no natural predators. Deer prefer fertilized and irrigated plants, and the more accustomed they are to people, the better the chance they'll eat your ornamentals. And if they're hungry, they'll eat almost anything.

Since 1942, the deer population in the United States has gone from five hundred thousand to an estimated 27 million. So any plant that has foliage or fresh green edible stems in winter, such as azaleas, roses, and yews, are about to be mowed down as a food source by fifty-four times as many deer as during World War II.

Deer control theories begin with basic common sense. Keep them away from your plants. You can do this with a fence that's too high for them to jump, eight to ten feet. Many county codes only allow six- to seven-foot fences; therefore, in addition to a fence that would meet code, widen the horizontal distance the deer must jump. Plant tall, spreading shrubs along both sides of the fence. But the extra width is a deterrent only if you choose deer-resistant shrubs.

The latest in deer fencing is a stiff plastic mesh material that comes in rolls. It can simply be wrapped around and drawn between trees for support in woodland areas, and you don't need to stake it. It's generally seven to eight feet high, black, and not extremely visible as it blends with the woods. See-through mesh netting is also available; I've seen it sold under the name Invisible Mesh Barrier and is sold at an eight-foot height. Check with your local garden or home improvement center and look in gardening catalogs. If your local government considers these mesh materials as fences, the height might not be permitted without filing for a variance with your jurisdiction.

Another possible barrier is an electric fence that runs off of house current, a battery, or solar power and comes complete with bait. The idea here is to bring the deer to the wire for a "safe" jolt that will train them to stay away. It sounds good in theory.

The only shortcoming of all of these fences is that they don't look good, and my job is to help you aesthetically enhance your

This deer looks cute from afar, but not to the person whose plants are being eaten!

property. Purely utilitarian fences must be tucked into the woods or hidden by shrubbery. This can limit the possibilities for vistas or smooth circulation patterns through your landscape. In which case, I recommend a combination of deterrents.

In addition to fences, another physical means that has been created for controlling deer is a motion-activated sonic warning device. This is a big speaker that emits a high-pitched sonic blast to scare off any intruder crossing its path. There are several on the market, but it has been reported that deer won't scare as easily when they get used to the noise.

Some people hang strobe lights on a deer fence to scare them. I'm skeptical that strobe lights will do the trick, and when I think about the number of them needed to cover an area, it might be counterproductive, especially if it makes the garden inhospitable for you as well.

How about a water blast from a heat- and motion-activated automatic sprinkler called a Sensor Controlled Animal Repeller? You can mount it in the garden and connect it to a hose. The sensors work off of a nine-volt battery. The downsides are that you can't use it in winter, and I question the effectiveness of a blast of water from a sprinkler head. If someone would invent a sprayer with the force of a fire hose, they might have something. The upsides are that the plants get watered whenever deer wander through, and it might effectively startle them.

Another physical control is to drape netting over the deer's favorite plants. It's effective for the inside foliage, but they'll still eat all the leaves they can reach.

Creating repellents so the deer won't want to eat the plants is another theory. It is based on the fact that deer are herbivores, eating only vegetable matter, and avoid all products that smell or taste like animals. According to this theory, any animal product that you put around or on your greenery, especially if it smells like a predator, will keep deer away.

Many are products that everyone has at home. Home remedies include human hair in a wool bag hung onto the plant; bar soap, such as Ivory, rubbed and strung onto shrubs and trees; and suet that, when used in conjunction with bird seed, will repel one type of wildlife while attracting others. These should be hung on or applied to the stems and leaves of plants that deer eat in order to determine if these products of animal derivation will work.

Commercial spin-offs of deer-repelling products based on the deer's distaste for goods made from animals range from putrescent eggs to animal urine. Several you might try are the egg-based Deer Guard, Hinder, a deer and rabbit repellent made of ammonium salts of fatty acids, or Coyote Urine.

Another class of deer repellent is made from products that simply make the plants taste bad or create discomfort when eaten. Bad-tasting home remedies are garlic, Tabasco, and other spicy sauces spread or sprayed onto the leaves of the plants. Castor oil is known to make plants taste bitter and has been a successful deterrent for other wildlife as well as deer. And the *Guinness Book of World Records* states that "the most bitter substance know to man" is trademarked Bitrex. It's used in the deer deterrent product Tree Guard. These types of items are available from virtually every garden and home improvement center. But remember that all natural powders and liquids are chemicals, so always follow labeled instructions.

If all else fails, try a dog. Provided you can train it to stay on your property, a dog is a predator that deer are supposed to fear. I'm sure it will also offer its share of canine urine on your plants as a further deterrent.

There are also certain types of plants that deer don't like to eat. Generally, these are plants that have sticky or hairy leaves, thick, leathery foliage, medicinal uses, or minty or lemony fragrance. The following evergreen shrubs and trees have the best chance of surviving deer browsing intact: firs, hollies, junipers, pines, spruces, boxwoods, cherry laurels, mahonias, nandinas, pyracanthas, rhododendrons, and viburnums.

> "Nurseries in New York estimate their annual deer damage in excess of $50 million."

XERISCAPE DESIGN 47

Xeriscape is the term used for landscaping in dry conditions, as is necessary in many areas of this country such as the Southwest, Southern California, and Florida. I prefer to use the term *water-efficient landscaping,* which everyone should practice, no matter what the water conditions in the area where you live. Xeriscape design must be coordinated with irrigation, which is covered in chapter 14 of this book. Fifty percent or more of residential water consumption is for irrigation—the application of one inch of water on a thousand square feet consumes six hundred gallons.

There are several basic principles of xeriscaping.

MULCHING

Use mulch, which is any material that can be laid in the beds to act as a protective covering over a bed to hold in moisture. It will reduce evaporation, prevent erosion, and control weeds that compete for moisture. It can be compost, straw, salt hay, ground corn cobs, pine bark nuggets, cocoa bean hulls, shredded hardwood bark, licorice root, wood chips, newspaper, landscape fabric, stone, and even shredded tires. I personally prefer organic, partially composted materials laid two to four inches thick.

Mulch is a way to conserve water, but mulching only goes so far. Large mulched areas won't effectively conserve water unless plantings will ultimately cover and protect at least 75 to 80 percent of the area.

COMPOSTING

Use compost as an amendment in the soil to hold in moisture. Compost enriches the soil and helps it to drain as it holds moisture. Lay it two to four inches thick, and till it into the top eight to twelve inches of soil. Composting is covered in detail in chapter 10.

ZONING

An important element of xeriscaping is a concept called zoning the plants. This is, essentially, grouping in beds plants that have similar water needs. This allows you to "zone" your watering practices so that plants are only watered as needed, not on an arbitrary schedule, with minimum waste. When zoning your landscape take into the account the differences between cool and shady areas of your property. Sun and shade orientation affect the plants' need for water. South-facing slopes dry fastest, so they may require closer attention. Low-lying drainage areas or areas near downspouts are best used for plants with high water needs. And try to confine plants that require a lot of water to zones where they are easily accessible to a water source.

WATERING

Since xeriscaping is concerned with efficient use of water, there are certain principles to follow so your irrigation efforts yield maximum results. Avoid using a sprinkler that just throws a fine mist into the air. You want droplets to douse your plant, a drenching solid stream to the plant. A mist into the air loses too much to evaporation to be efficient. You can save water by using low-volume and low-pressure drip or bubbler emitters to irrigate shrubs and trees individually, and groundcovers and perennial beds. A drip irrigation system can save up to 60 percent of all water used in the lawn and garden areas.

If you choose to use a sprinkler, keep track of how much water is distributed during a sprinkling session. To get the best results, place the sprinkler in the desired location and collect water in a saucer under the spray. The time it takes for an inch of water to accumulate in the saucer is how long you should water shrubs. How deep that amount of water will penetrate depends on the type of soil. You can figure percolation at four inches for clay, eight inches for silt or loam, and eighteen inches for sandy soil.

Regardless of your watering system, you should check for soil moisture at varying depths to make sure you have gotten to the base of the roots of the plants without watering too deeply. Use a dowel, screwdriver, or other implement that might indicate the wetness level. The probe should be moist at least six inches deep after watering. It should stay evenly wet but not muddy after several days; if it doesn't, you may have drainage problems. You will also want to use a rain gauge to keep track of how much natural precipitation your landscape has received. You'll have a better idea of when you need and don't need water without checking the soil.

Raise the water-efficiency of your soil with the addition of a state-of-the-art gel, such as Hydretain, TerraSorb, and Soil Moist. These water-holding polymers allow the soil to use moisture more efficiently. Be sure to follow labeled instructions.

Here are a few other quick tips for efficient watering:

- Water in the morning. If you water later in the day, much of the water evaporates, and watering at night increases the risk of fungus growth.
- Don't water during hot, windy, or rainy weather.
- Repeat water cycles are especially important on slope sites and areas where soil percolates poorly.
- In the winter, soak the root zones of plants monthly if there has been no winter precipitation and if the soil is not frozen.
- Remember that even drought-resistant plants need to be watered while they are establishing.

LAWNS

An excellent planting for conserving water is turfgrass. Theories about lawn watering are somewhat controversial, and I don't agree with the need to water constantly. Turf can make it through a long, dry period without watering. This means as long as three weeks to a month of drought. After three weeks, you will want to consider starting an irrigation program (see chapter 14), if it will save you from reinstalling a lawn.

Water lawn areas separately from tree and shrub beds because they have different water requirements. You can also help a lawn retain moisture by leaving grass clippings on the lawn when you mow. For maximum water efficiency, aerate your lawn. Do it in the spring and fall to ensure maximum take-up of surface water. Aerate with a plug aerator (see chapter 38 for details).

Groundcovers are an excellent alternative to lawns. They also conserve moisture and require less maintenance than a lawn does (see chapter 37).

Pink dianthus (top) and blanket flowers (*Gaillardia*) (bottom) are examples of long-blooming, drought-tolerant perennials.

SELECTING PLANTS

When choosing which plants to use in your landscape, keep in mind that xeriscaping involves efficient water use. Plants with high water requirements that need moist soils will be harder to maintain than will be plants with more modest needs. Not only will these plants perform better during times of drought, but you will save a fortune when your water bill comes due. Since many communities regulate water use during dry stretches, you may find it impossible to give some plants the water they need to thrive.

The following charts list several excellent plants that are tolerant of dry conditions. This is not exhaustive, so experiment on your own and ask for suggestions at your local garden center.

DROUGHT-TOLERANT TREES AND SHRUBS

Amur maple (*Acer ginnala*)

Black haw viburnum (*Viburnum prunifolium*)

Cinquefoil (*Potentilla* species)

Cockspur hawthorn (*Crataegus crus-galli*)

Common hackberry (*Celtis occidentalis*)

Fiveleaf aralia (*Eleutherococcus sieboldianus*)

Fragrant elaeagnus (*Elaeagnus pungens*)

Goldenrain tree (*Koelreuteria paniculata*)

Green ash (*Fraxinus pennsylvanica*)

Hedge maple (*Acer campestre*)

Japanese barberry (*Berberis thunbergii*)

Juniper (*Juniperus* species)

Kentucky coffeetree (*Gymnocladus dioica*)

Lacebark elm (*Ulmus parvifolia*)

Lydia broom (*Genista lydia*)

Northern bayberry (*Myrica pensylvanica*)

Panicled dogwood (*Cornus racemosa*)

Privet (*Ligustrum* species)

Russian olive (*Elaeagnus angustifolia*)

Sage leaf rock rose (*Cistus salviifolius*)

Saltspray rose (*Rosa rugosa*)

Scotch broom (*Cytisus scoparius*)

Smoke tree (*Cotinus coggygria*)

Sumac (*Rhus* species)

Thornless common honey locust (*Gleditsia triacanthos* f. *inermis*)

Turkish filbert (*Corylus colurna*)

Vernal witchhazel (*Hamamelis vernalis*)

White pine (*Pinus strobus*)

DROUGHT-TOLERANT PERENNIALS

African iris (*Dietes bicolor*)
Autumn fern (*Dryopteris erythrosora*)
Blanket flower (*Gaillardia*)
Butterfly weed (*Asclepias tuberosa*)
Candytuft (*Iberis sempervirens*)
Cast-iron plant (*Aspidistra elatior*)
Catmint (*Nepeta* x *faassenii*)
Coneflower (*Rudbeckia*)
Coreopsis (*Coreopsis grandiflora*)
Cottage pinks (*Dianthus plumarius*)
Daylily (*Hemerocallis* species)
Evening primrose (*Oenothera*)

False indigo (*Baptisia*)
Fortnight lily (*Dietes vegeta*)
Gaura (*Gaura*)
German iris (*Iris germanica*)
Golden marguerite (*Anthemis*)
Mullein (*Verbascum*)
Salvia (*Salvia pitcheri*)
Snow-in-summer (*Cerastium tomentosum*)
Spurge (*Euphorbia*)
Wormwood (*Artemisia*)
Yarrow (*Achillea*)

DROUGHT-TOLERANT ANNUALS

African daisy (*Arctotis*)
Bachelor's button (*Centaurea cyanus*)
Blackfoot daisy (*Melampodium paludosum*)
Blanket flower (*Gaillardia pulchella*)
California poppy (*Eschscholzia californica*)
Cape leadwort (*Plumbago auriculata*)
Celosia (*Celosia*)
Chinese forget-me-not (*Cynoglossum amabile*)
Cosmos species
Creeping zinnia (*Sanvitalia procumbens*)
Flossflower (*Ageratum houstonianum*)
Garden verbena (*Verbena* x *hybrida*)

Gazania (*Gazania rigens*)
Globe amaranth (*Gomphrena globosa*)
Gloriosa daisy (*Rudbeckia hirta*)
Joseph's coat (*Amaranthus* species)
Marigold (*Tagetes*)
Moss rose (*Portulaca grandiflora*)
Narrowleaf zinnia (*Zinnia angustifolia*)
Perilla (*Perilla frutescens*)
Pinks (*Dianthus* species)
Snow-on-the-mountain (*Euphorbia marginata*)
Spider flower (*Cleome hassleriana*)
Wax begonia (*Begonia* x *semperflorens-cultorum*)

YEAR-ROUND INTEREST

48

Twenty years ago, academia was teaching twelve-month interest as a basic tenet of landscape design, and today home owners are increasingly demanding it in their landscapes. Year-round interest can be achieved in a number of ways—from a single plant that offers many interesting characteristics (for example, long bloom, berries, fall color, handsome winter form, interesting bark) to combinations of plants with blooming times staggered throughout the season to garden art and other outdoor objects integrated into the design.

HARDSCAPE

Many of the same items that you use in your landscape to add summer interest will also serve for added interest throughout the year. Try any or all of these to give your property pizzazz all year long.

- Paint a mural on a blank wall. Design your plantings to complement the painting.
- Plant in a wheelbarrow. When the plants need light, wheel it into the sun; when entertaining, wheel onto the patio; when freezing temperatures threaten, wheel into the sunroom; when time to replant, wheel to the compost bin, dump, refill with potting soil or compost, and start again.
- Garden sculptures of steel, bronze, stone, wood, and other weatherproof material are elements that can change the personality of a garden with a change in the weather. One of the most innovative sculptures I've seen is built like a stringed instrument and involves the interplay of wind and light to create harmony and reflections. It's built of steel, titanium, and quartz crystal to create a perfectly balanced,

tuned sculpture called a wind harp, built by Ross Barrable of SoundScapes International, Pagosa Springs, Colorado, www.soundscapesinternational.com.

- Build a greenhouse or solarium, and grow indoors. You'll have greenery and flowers every month!
- A bird feeder and a heated birdbath are fun for spectators and birds year-round.
- Install trellis, arbors, gazebos, ornate well covers, or other outdoor structures that will stand on their own as ornamental features without plants and double as plant supports during the growing season.
- Rocks can provide interesting shapes and patterns in the snow.
- Wind chimes chime every time the wind blows. Wind kites sail every time the wind blows.
- Landscape lighting extends the opportunity for enjoyment of the garden to twenty-four hours a day, all year long (see Lighting, chapter 20).

A unique and elegant work of art, a wind harp can be music to your ears—and eyes. (Copyright © 1996 SoundScapes International. All rights reserved. Used by permission.)

Long after the water garden is frozen over, this trellis will draw people's eyes, especially as the green stands in contrast to the coming winter snow. (Copyright © 1997 Walpole Woodworkers. All rights reserved. Used by permission.)

HOME GREENHOUSES

A large portion of the United States sees harsh winter conditions, and many plants would never survive without our assistance. There are a variety of ways to protect these plants, from plant wraps and cold frames to sophisticated indoor and outdoor structures—anything that can control temperature, light, moisture, soil, and other conditions essential for plant growth. Not only will they protect the plants, but they will also give you a way to garden all year long, even when a foot of snow is on the ground.

A greenhouse, sometimes called a hothouse, enables you to grow anything you want all year and is the ultimate in year-round interest. Grow vegetables, flowers, shrubs, and trees from seeds or cuttings, if you wish; raise exotic flora from warmer zones; store the containers from your patio planted with figs and other tropicals. Many people think of a greenhouse as a building separate from their main house. It is in some cases, but not all. Greenhouses come in myriad sizes and shapes, using a wide variety of colors and materials. One style can have a very different climate than another. I have seen greenhouses created inside solaria not larger than a bay window. They can be something as simple as a sunroom, an enclosed swimming pool, or indoor patio—any controlled environment can serve as a hothouse.

Let's first look at traditional greenhouses. You can find very handsome, restored greenhouses dating from the 1920s to the 1940s through Ward Greenhouses in Concord, Massachusetts, (978) 369-1354. Owner Mark Ward specializes in finding, buying, and restoring older greenhouses, which are made of better materials than can be found today, and placing them on new properties. These are very ornate and pricey additions at twenty thousand to eighty thousand dollars each, plus a fancy stone or brick knee wall as a foundation and all of the necessary equipment to control the climate. Add benches, floors, insect screens, and climate controls—including heating, cooling, ventilation, fans, water, and shades—and such a unit will return decades of pleasure.

If you do not wish to spend that kind of money, but want a greenhouse on your property, there are prefabricated units for much less. Some of these are designed to attach to a house where the house wall serves as one of the walls for the greenhouse.

Generally, greenhouses are built of glass, polyethylene, polycarbonate or fiberglass. They can be transparent or translucent, depending on the location of the structure and the season. Glass is preferred by far, and it should be glazed, meaning it should have a finish applied and tempered to make it harder. Fiberglass, polyethylene, and polycarbonate are also used when cost is a factor. It will reduce the price considerably, and you can find these types of inexpensive greenhouses starting at about fifteen hundred dollars.

The floor needs a liberal layer of gravel for drainage and a wooden or other raised walk for a dry walking surface. Finer greenhouses have concrete or other masonry surfaces for more permanence than wood, and floor drains and proper drainage are carefully designed and installed to control irrigation runoff.

Ventilation—the exchange of outside air through vents, windows, and fans—is crucial to plant health. They can be regulated automatically depending on outside wind, rain, and, primarily, temperature. It can get hot in a greenhouse, hot enough to twist metal. If you have ever left anything plastic in a car in summer, you know how hot it can get under glass and can guess how important temperature control is.

Air circulation is also critical. You want humidity, molecules of water suspended in the air, but not large droplets of water hanging on surfaces, including plants and tools, inside the greenhouse. Whether vents are open or not, condensation shouldn't form on the windows or plants; it promotes disease. Internal circulating fans will mimic wind and keep down on liquid in the air.

Some method of shading the windows during the hottest periods could be required, depending on the surrounding trees and other structures. Shades are often used. A removable paint will serve the same purpose, provided you have a glass greenhouse.

Since greenhouses are meant to protect plants from winter and must be heated and humidified with cool moisture, you will also need a heat source for winter. Regardless of whether you heat with oil, gas, or electricity, this dries plants and makes it necessary to add humidity to the atmosphere. You can use a humidifier to supplement in winter.

Irrigation of plants depends entirely on the type of growing you are doing. There are tubes that will drip the water onto the planting medium in whatever way you want it delivered, by spray or dripping directly into the soil. Or you could simply use a hose for delivery.

Just as there is a choice of watering, you have a choice of supplemental lighting. You might consider grow lights in a greenhouse a contradiction in terms. But there are times when you might want them, such as to extend the growth period so a tropical plant can fruit or flower when days get shorter. Or you might just need to supplement a low-light situation, but try to site your greenhouse so this isn't necessary. Various types of light sources and methods of mounting are used. Hotter bulbs must be placed further away from plants or they will burn the leaves.

Benches are an important tool for holding pots and keeping everything drained, watered, and at a comfortable working height.

> "A greenhouse, sometimes called a hothouse, enables you to grow anything you want all year and is the ultimate in year-round interest."

You will find these and all the other furnishings and accessories through the same companies offering greenhouses.

A less expensive way to protect your plants is using a cold frame. You can make one with an old window and some bricks, blocks, or rocks, or they are available commercially. Sometimes cold frames, when heated from below by composting manure or electrical cables, are referred to as hotbeds. They were used for hundreds of years to propagate and protect tender seedlings and rooted cuttings.

For more information, see the Hobby Greenhouse Association Web site at www.orbitworld.net/hga, or check out Cold Frames and Greenhouse Growing at http://gardening.about.com/homegarden/gardening/cs/msub43/index.htm.

SOFTSCAPE

Now lets look at some specific plants and how they can keep your garden interesting throughout the year. The right mix of plants is what you need to provide color and interest all year long. See appendix N, Coordinating Plants for Twelve-Month Interest, to make the most of blooms, fruit, and foliage and keep your landscape interesting year-round.

FOUR SEASONS

Four seasons, one plant. A small to medium kousa dogwood (*Cornus kousa*), a tree reaching twenty to thirty feet in height, offers twelve-month interest. It flowers white for several weeks in spring and has gorgeous form and summer foliage. It bears edible fruit in autumn and then the leaves turn a deep red. The mature bark exfoliates (peels) to reveal a patchwork of beige, tan, and brown, giving the trunk a lacy appearance for the winter landscape.

THREE SEASONS

Three seasons (spring, summer, and fall), two plants. Titillate your senses throughout the growing season by training two perennial vines onto a lattice trellis—Boston ivy (*Parthenocissus tricuspidata*) interplanted with Jackman clematis (*Clematis* x *jackmanii*). The leaves of the ivy are red when emerging in early spring. The violet or blue flowers of the clematis will bloom through the ivy from early summer into fall. As the clematis blooms fade in fall, the ivy turns maroon for a final splash of color before winter.

Plants with Multiple Seasons of Interest

Note: Always determine mature size and growth habits of all plants before planting.

Deciduous Trees

Yellowwood (*Cladrastis kentukea*)—Fall color, flower, fragrance.
Autumn flowering cherry (*Prunus subhirtella* 'Autumnalis')—Fall color, flower spring and fall, graceful habit.
Enkianthus (*Enkianthus campanulatus*)—Fall color, flower, small (six feet) specimen
Franklin tree (*Franklinia alatamaha*)—Fall color, flower, handsome bark and foliage.
Baldcypress (*Taxodium distichum*)—Color changes spring, summer, and fall.
Golden larch (*Pseudolarix kaempferi*)—Fall color, colorful needles, attractive cones.

Deciduous Shrubs

Bush cinquefoil (*Potentilla fruticosa*)—Flower all summer, interesting foliage.
Fothergilla (*F. gardenii*)—Fall color, flower, fragrance.
Winterberry holly (*Ilex verticillata*)—Showy winter berries, summer shrub screen.
St. John's wort (*Hypericum frondosum*)—Flower, attractive foliage, exfoliating bark for winter interest.
Linden viburnum (*Viburnum dilatatum*)—Fall color, flower, heavily berried, attractive.

Evergreen Trees

Lacebark pine (*Pinus bungeana*)—Lacy bark, specimen, year-around interest.
Red pine (*Pinus resinosa*)—Colorful bark, specimen, year-around interest.

Evergreen Shrubs

Longstalk holly (*Ilex pedunculosa*)—Attracts birds, berry display, rustles in wind all year.
Heavenly bamboo (*Nandina domestica*)—Spring color, flower, berries, fall and winter color.

Groundcovers

Meidiland rose (*Rosa* cultivar)—Spring, fall, and summer flower.
Fragrant sumac (*Rhus aromatica*)—Fall color, flower, fragrant.
Wintergreen (*Gaultheria procumbens*)—Fall color, fragrant foliage, flower, berries summer through winter.

Vines

Boston ivy (*Parthenocissus tricuspidata*)—Spring and fall color, summer cover, deciduous.
Jackman clematis (*Clematis x jackmanii*)—Long flowering season, can be June through November.
Japanese wisteria (*Wisteria floribunda*)—Flower fragrance, pods, interest with and without leaves.

Perennials and Grasses

Coreopsis (*Coreopsis verticillata* 'Moonbeam')—Four- to six-month flowering period.
Leatherleaf sedge grass (*Carex buchananii*)—Bronze foliage for almost twelve months.
Gaillardia (*Gaillardia* x *grandiflora*)—Four- to six-month flowering period.
Lily-turf (*Liriope muscari*)—Flowers August through September, foliage holds color for ten months.
Silver grass (*Miscanthus sinensis* 'Gracillimus')—Ornamental grass four to seven feet high, silver-plum flower September through October, handsome into winter.
Fountain grass (*Pennisetum alopecuroides*)—Three-foot-high arching habit, reddish spiked flower.

Boston ivy clinging to a wall makes the perfect trellis to support the entwining Niobe clematis.

TWO SEASONS

Two seasons (spring and fall), one plant. Add resurrection lily (*Lycoris* species) to your perennial border for a plant that makes you remember it every other season. It leafs out in spring and you say, "Oh, that's right. I forgot I had that planted there." Then the leaves dry and fade in summer and you forget about it just as flowers spring from the ground on bare stems in autumn and make a magnificent, although leafless, display.

THE WINTER GARDEN

People always ask me for designs for winter, thinking this is the most difficult time to create an interesting garden. It's not that hard. Choose plants for form, winter berries, colorful bark, bark with interesting patterns, winter flowers, or any other interesting features you can identify. Here are some specific plant suggestions for the winter garden.

STEMS AND BARK

Bark is an element of winter interest that can extend a plant's aesthetic appeal by months. Trees with smooth, exfoliating, shaggy,

Yellow-twigged dogwood blends with winterberry hollies for winter interest. (Brookside Gardens, Wheaton, Maryland)

striped, checkered, or other patterned bark offer extra seasons of interest.

- Red-twigged and yellow-twigged dogwood (*Cornus sericea*) will give you twigs of shrubs colored deep red or yellow when dormant, adding color to the winter landscape.
- With coral bark Japanese maple (*Acer palmatum* 'Sango Kaku'), the name says it all. Red/orange coral-colored bark in winter is always an attention-grabber.
- Scotch broom (*Cytisus scoparius*) can be cut and used as a broom, and the fine spray of green stems makes a noticeable contrast to the color of most plants in winter.
- Winterberry holly (*Ilex verticillata*) comes alive in winter. Deciduous in most areas, it's flush with brilliant red berries after loosing its leaves. This is a plant that can't be missed in the woods in winter.
- The pure white exfoliating (peeling) bark of the white birch (*Betula papyrifera*) says "winter." Groves of the bright white bark can be found all over the northern United States. In milder climates, landscape designers specify an insect-resistant birch with gray to tan exfoliating bark, the heritage river birch (*B. nigra* 'Heritage').
- A rich brown to reddish brown exfoliating bark is the reason paperbark maple (*Acer griseum*) gets the award for the most noticed tree in winter against winter snow. The bark begins to exfoliate on young wood, and the entire tree has a rich cinnamon color, especially noticeable in winter.

> "Choose plants for form, winter berries, colorful bark, bark with interesting patterns, winter flowers, or any other interesting features you can identify."

FLOWERS

- Winter jasmine (*Jasminum nudiflorum*) is a hardy jasmine that withstands freezing temperatures and wants to drape over rocks and walls. It has yellow forsythia-looking flowers in February and, weather permitting, blooms into April.
- Vernal witchhazel (*Hamamelis vernalis*) is a durable witchhazel that tolerates shady sites and still flowers dependably for up to a month from February to March. The Chinese witchhazel (*H. mollis*) has fragrance too. The colors are red to yellow.
- Hellebores (*Helleborus* species) are amazing woodland plants that never tire of growing. They don't like being moved, but once established, they make a low evergreen mass of maroon-to-pink and white-to-chartreuse flowers that begin as early as January and can persist into April.

The number one reminder that winter is waning is the winter flowering crocuses (*Crocus tommasinianus*). A good companion for this lavender to purple crocus is *Crocus flavus*, an early flowering yellow/orange. In conjunction with these well-known bulbs are several other late-winter bloomers, such as snowdrops (*Galanthus*), winter aconites (*Eranthis*), and bluebells (*Hyacinthoides*)

HABIT

In general, you can add interest to your winter landscape with shape and form. Plants with contorted growth, a weeping habit, or handsome bark can be more interesting in winter than in summer. These characteristics can make a tree a specimen that will stand out against a bare winter landscape.

Harry Lauder's walking stick (*Corylus avellana* 'Contorta'; see page 267 for a photograph) and dragon's claw willow (*Salix matsudana* 'Tortuosa') are plants with a contorted habit of the branches that makes them stand as leafless curlicues in winter, giving them tremendous ornamental impact. Twigs of these trees are favorites for use in cut flower arrangements as well as specimens in the garden.

Some evergreens also have a shape that is striking in the winter. Weeping blue spruce (*Picea pungens* 'Glauca Pendula'), weeping Norway spruce (*Picea abies* 'Pendula'), and weeping white pine (*Pinus strobus* 'Pendula') are tall-growing evergreen trees with weeping habits that are magnificent in winter. They are especially effective when standing under a full moon with snow on the branches.

Trees with Interesting Bark

The following trees are just a few examples of trees featuring different types of bark. There are many more available for each one. If you are looking for a certain effect, consult with your local nurseries to find the trees that are best for your home.

Type of Bark	Type of Tree
Smooth	Serviceberry (*Amelanchier arborea*), American hornbeam (*Carpinus caroliniana*)
Exfoliating	Japanese stewartia (*Stewartia pseudocamellia*), Chinese quince (*Pseudocydonia sinensis*)
Shaggy	Corneliancherry (*Cornus mas*)
Striped	Striped maple (*Acer pensylvanicum*)
Checkered	Persimmon (*Diospyros virginiana*)
Lacelike	Lacebark pine (*Pinus bungeana*), lacebark elm (*Ulmus parvifolia*)

PRUNING AND TRAINING

49

Nothing is more important to the continued success of your landscape than pruning. Proper pruning makes or breaks the ornamental value of a plant. If you neglect your plant, it can become weedy and overgrown. If you sheer it into gumdrops, it will become stunted with its natural habit destroyed. But, with proper placement, planting, and pruning, you will be able to attain the effects you want.

I've been pruning plants for over forty years, and it's one of my favorite landscape activities because it makes such a difference ornamentally. When you've elevated and cleaned out the branches of a tree and made it fit its space, and then you stand back and look at it, you receive instant gratification. Then, if you've done your job right, it will grow into an absolute specimen to give you pleasure for years to come.

In my years of landscaping and design, I've seen styles and philosophies of pruning change. The "less is best" philosophy has come to dominate horticulture. This values the integrity of your plantings and is the reason some of these tips will tell you how not to prune your plants.

TREES

The best thing you can do for your trees is to site them properly when you plant them. If you give them enough space to grow and mature and take on their natural growth habit, you will get more flowers, more berries, and more leaves with a minimum of pruning. Make sure not to plant tall trees under power lines. And don't them. Topping (removing the tops of the central trunk and the main branches of a tree) destroys their form, stimulates them to grow

> "If you give trees enough space to grow and mature and take on their natural growth habit, you will get more flowers, more berries, and more leaves with a minimum of pruning."

weak and spindly, opens them to insects and diseases, and aids in the formation of dead wood. Roots are also injured by these practices, and the new, young limbs more easily snap off in a storm.

Plant your evergreens (conifers) where they can grow full to the ground and have enough growing space so they won't need pruning. In most cases you don't want to prune your evergreens at all. If you wish to control the shape, you should prune the new growth that emerges in the spring (called the candle). You can cut half the candle, and your tree will grow tighter and slower. However, you should be aware before you begin that this is a very tedious process and a commitment once it is started. Another alternative to pruning conifers is to remove the entire candle—all of the new growth—in the spring. The will cause your tree to grow larger very, very slowly.

Give deciduous trees attention every four or five years. Clean out their inside and crossing branches, cut off dead wood, and prune the lower limbs of large shade trees if you can't comfortably walk underneath the branches. As a guideline, you should be able to stand back, look at a newly pruned shade tree, and see approximately the same size and shape as when you started, but with more sky showing through.

Don't prune flush with an adjoining branch or leave long stubs. When you cut, leave only the branch collar of the limb you are pruning. The collar is the flared nub at the base of a branch that is about one-quarter to three-quarters of an inch long and wider than the rest of the stem. This wider flared area occurs at the base of every branch, and it's where the healing of the cut occurs.

With newly planted trees, prune no more than 15 percent of the top growth of the tree. Pruning any more wood than that causes stress, and the young tree may not be sturdy enough to handle it. Wait for the tree to grow and get hardier before undertaking any more extensive pruning.

Don't use pruning paint. Pruning paint is of no value as a one-time treatment. If the tree is pruned properly, the wound will heal more effectively without paint. Paint eventually cracks and allows moisture in, and the area between the paint and the wood becomes a perfect habitat for insects and diseases. Use pruning paint only as a fix for special cases, such as painting rose canes to protect against disease.

SHRUBS

Like trees, shrubs should be pruned selectively. The exceptions are in the case of hedging or topiary, which will be discussed later in this chapter.

Use selective pruning for your shrubs to follow the line of the shrub's ornamental appearance. Selective pruning means that you select out approximately one-third of the growth of the shrub, concentrating on the longest branches or branches growing where you don't want them to grow. Leave everything else in your shrub the same and all the flowers that were forming will grow. For example, if you have a Koreanspice viburnum growing along the edge of the walk to your house, you will want to keep it sufficiently contained so that it doesn't overflow the walk, but at the same time allowing it to continue to flower and provide a wonderful fragrance as you enter your house. Prune the longest stems of the plant, leaving the shortest to grow. Over the course of the season, flowers will form on the ends of the shorter branches that you left alone. If you had pruned all the branch tips, you wouldn't get any flowers.

Avoid persistent shearing of your shrubs except in the case of topiary, discussed below, or hedging, when selective pruning would be far too labor intensive. Shearing—cutting everything back to the same length—creates an unhealthy layer of suckering growth and spindly small growth, not the healthy branching a shrub should have. It creates a form in which air circulation and sunshine can't get to the inside of the plant. After a few years of shearing, you'll end up with a plant with only one to three inches of foliage on the outer edge and nothing but bare branches on the inside.

Outer shearing can serve a purpose for a couple of years on fast-growing deciduous and some evergreen shrubs. Sometimes you can shear regularly, and if the plant renews itself vigorously, you can cut it back hard every four to five years to allow it to begin again from the inner growth, ensuring good air circulation and a healthy, open-branching habit. Some evergreen shrubs such as arborvitae (*Thuja*) and Leyland cypress (X *Cupressocyparis leyandii*) should be sheared annually to control their size and keep them from losing leaves on lower limbs. Prune them to be tapered on top to allow sun to reach the lower branches so they will maintain their value as screening plants.

Some shrubs can be pruned back to eight to twelve inches and will come back from the base as a whole new shrub. This is usually for renewal, but some quick-growing plants can be cut this way every year. The best example is forsythia. It would be cut back right after blooming. Slower-growing plants such as flowering quinces, weigelas, abelias, and winter flowering jasmines can be cut back hard every three to five years.

Other shrubs might need renewal pruning every five to ten years or less. Examples of shrubs that need only occasional renewal pruning are euonymus, hollies, azaleas, yews, and boxwoods. These can be pruned from as big as four to six feet down to eighteen inches in February, just before the end of the winter before any growth begins.

> "Avoid persistent shearing of your shrubs. After a few years of shearing, you'll end up with a plant with only one to three inches of foliage on the outer edge and nothing but bare branches on the inside."

Prune cautiously. Cut away the hard, big wood over a three-year period, a third of the wood each year. With this process, you can leave enough green so there is some foliage each year.

VINES

For woody vines such as grapes and wisterias, you'll need more specialized pruning methods. When pruning woody vines, don't be afraid to prune hard back to the main cane. After flowering, cut hard back to a main cane or wherever the main network of canes is in the case of three or four canes coming off a main base. What about side shoots? When you cut back the side shoots, leave three to five spur buds about six to eight inches long, where the big whips were. Cutting back vegetative growth will encourage flowering and fruiting.

But I recommend a different approach for herbaceous vines. Let herbaceous perennial vines like clematis and Boston ivy grow because that's their nature. Often at the end of the growing season they defoliate and will leaf out again from the same wood in spring. Just cut them back when they are overgrown or in an area where you don't want them to be.

Annual vines, such as morning glory, moonflower, hyacinth bean, and Dutchman's pipe, die at the end of the growing season and should be cut back. Some will reseed themselves and sprout and grow as new vines in spring.

ROSES

Roses require specialized pruning. Prune hybrid teas right after flowering to keep them budding and flowering throughout the growing season. Prune each flower down to a five-leaflet cluster (the first healthy leaf) right after flowering. Shrub and groundcover roses can be cut back on an as-needed basis. For more information about pruning roses, see chapter 41.

ESPALIER

Espalier is a pruning technique that makes a vine out of a plant that is not normally a vine or trains a tree or shrub that would normally stand alone to grow on a trellis. Think of it as making something that grows in three dimensions fit into a two-dimensional plane.

The French took this technique to its most sophisticated level as an intensive method of growing fruit trees.

The basic, logical, and somewhat oversimplified approach to espalier is to cut off the back and front branches. Beyond that, select the branches that you want to have growing in certain areas and remove the branches that you don't want growing.

For a formal espalier, start with a very young whip and train it from its initial growth. You can train it in any of a number of forms that have been recognized—for example, a fan or fishbone pattern—or customize it to espalier your initials on the wall of your house, a heart over your doorway, or any design you wish.

Many vigorous growing vines and other plants can be trained as espalier because they will throw shoots on the wall. One of the best uses I've ever seen for the southern magnolia (*M. grandiflora*) tree is as an espalier on a trellis.

TOPIARY

Topiary is the art of turning living plants into architectural and sculptural elements. The basic concept is to form designs that are ordinarily unnatural growing shapes for plant material. It is usually seen in formal arrangements. For an example of topiary, shear an evergreen shrub into a dove sitting on a nest. Or, more simply, just shear a formal hedge so tightly that it appears as a wall.

Some forms of topiary, such as this man walking a dog, add a light touch to a garden. (Ladew Topiary Gardens, Monkton, Maryland.)

Use topiary if you want to include a whimsical touch in your landscape. A wonderful example of the whimsy of topiary can be seen at Ladew Topiary Gardens in the northern Maryland hunt country. As you drive in the entry, you are greeted by a topiary rider on a topiary horse chasing topiary dogs chasing a topiary fox. Another of my favorites is a topiary man with a topiary dog on a leash.

Topiary is achieved by doing what I preached against at the beginning of this chapter—shearing on a single plane and turning the plant into a sculptural element. Shearing a shrub on a single plane for topiary should only be done once a year on evergreen shrubs, or the plant will not have a chance to grow and stay healthy. It needs the annual new growth to stay vital. For the most successful topiary, use the finer-textured evergreens that can make a smooth line. These include Japanese hollies, boxwoods, yews, junipers, and hemlocks. Fast-growing shrubs are the easiest to start shaping up. Specialized tools are available for trimming shrubs.

Another form of topiary uses a framework that is more artificial than the actual body of the shrub. For what I call the "Chia Pet style of topiary," take a wire frame that has the shape you want, fill it with sphagnum moss, then plant it with any of a number of plants. Creeping fig is used commonly, especially indoors, and I have seen mondo grass done very cleverly. Flowers and groundcovers are also planted this way. Disney offers enchanting examples of topiary done in this fashion. They have incorporated movement and bubbles and the appearance of steam coming from their topiary cast of characters.

APPENDIX A

COMMON NAME–BOTANICAL NAME CROSS-REFERENCE

COMMON NAME	BOTANICAL NAME	COMMON NAME	BOTANICAL NAME
Abelia, glossy	*Abelia* x *grandiflora*	Aster	*Aster novae-angliae*
Abelialeaf, Korean	*Abeliophyllum distichum*	Aster, China	*Callistephus chinensis*
		Aster, Stokes	*Stokesia*
Actinidia, kolomikta	*Actinidia kolomikta*	Aucuba, Japanese	*Aucuba japonica*
Akebia, fiveleaf	*Akebia quinata*	Avens	*Geum*
Alder, white	*Alnus incana*	Azalea	*Rhododendron*
Alternanthera	*Alternanthera*	Baby's breath	*Gypsophila paniculata*
Alyssum, sweet	*Lobularia maritima*	Bachelor's buttons	*Centaurea cyanus*
Amaranth, globe	*Gomphrena globosa*	Baldcypress, common	*Taxodium distichum*
Amaranthus	*Amaranthus*	Balloon flower	*Platycodon grandiflorus*
Ampelopsis, porcelain	*Ampelopsis brevipedunculata*	Barberry, crimson pygmy	*Berberis thunbergii* 'Crimson Pygmy'
Anemone, Japanese	*Anemone* x *hybrida* 'Honorine Jobert'	Barberry, Japanese	*Berberis thunbergii* 'Atropurpurea'
Anise tree, Florida	*Ilicium floridanum*	Barberry, Korean	*Berberis koreana*
Aralia, fiveleaf	*Eleutherococcus sieboldianus*	Barberry, mentor	*Berberis* x *mentorensis*
		Barberry, paleleaf	*Berberis candidula*
Arborvitae, American	*Thuja occidentalis*	Barberry, wintergreen	*Berberis julianae*
Arborvitae, giant	*Thuja plicata*	Barrenwort	*Epimedium*
Arborvitae, Oriental	*Thuja orientalis*	Basket of gold	*Aurinia saxatilis*
Ardisia, Japanese	*Ardisia japonica*	Bayberry, northern	*Myrica pensylvanica*
Artemisia, silvermound	*Artemisia schmidtiana*	Bayberry, southern	*Myrica cerifera*
		Bearberry	*Arctostaphylos uva-ursi*
Ash, flowering	*Fraxinus ornus*		
Ash, green	*Fraxinus pennsylvanica*		

COMMON NAME	BOTANICAL NAME
Beard tongue	*Penstemon*
Bear's foot	*Helleborus foetidus*
Beautyberry, Japanese	*Callicarpa japonica*
Beauty bush	*Kolkwitzia amabilis*
Bee balm	*Monarda didyma*
Beech, American	*Fagus grandifolia*
Beech, European	*Fagus sylvatica*
Begonia, hardy	*Begonia grandis*
Begonia, tuberous	*Begonia x tuberhybrida*
Begonia, wax	*Begonia x semperflorens-cultorum*
Bellflower	*Campanula*
Birch, Chinese paper	*Betula albosinensis*
Birch, paper	*Betula papyrifera*
Birch, river	*Betula nigra*
Bittersweet, American	*Celastrus scandens*
Black-eyed Susan	*Rudbeckia fulgida* 'Goldsturm'
Black-eyed Susan vine	*Thunbergia alata*
Blanket flower	*Gaillardia x grandiflora*
Bleeding heart	*Dicentra formosa* 'Luxuriant'
Bleeding heart, old-fashioned	*Dicentra spectabilis*
Blue star	*Amsonia*
Bluebeard	*Caryopteris x clandonensis*
Bluebells, Virginia	*Mertensia virginica*
Blueberry, high-bush	*Vaccinium corymbosum*
Blueberry, rabbit-eye	*Vaccinium ashei*
Boltonia	*Boltonia asteroides*
Boxwood, common	*Buxus sempervirens*
Boxwood, littleleaf	*Buxus microphylla*
Browallia	*Browallia speciosa*
Brunnera, heartleaf	*Brunnera macrophylla*
Buckeye, bottlebrush	*Aesculus parviflora*
Buckeye, red	*Aesculus pavia*
Bunchberry	*Cornus canadensis*

COMMON NAME	BOTANICAL NAME
Butterfly bush	*Buddleia davidii*
Butterfly weed	*Asclepias tuberosa*
Caladium	*Caladium*
Camellia, Japanese	*Camellia japonica*
Camellia, sasanqua	*Camellia sasanqua*
Candytuft	*Iberis sempervirens, Iberis umbellata*
Cast-iron plant	*Aspidistra elatior*
Castor-aralia	*Kalopanax pictus*
Catmint	*Nepeta*
Cedar, atlas	*Cedrus atlantica*
Cedar, deodar	*Cedrus deodora*
Cedar of Lebanon	*Cedrus libani*
Centaurea	*Centaurea*
Cherry, bell-flowered	*Prunus campanulata*
Cherry, higan	*Prunus subhirtella*
Cherry, Kwanzan flowering	*Prunus serrulata* 'Kwanzan'
Cherry, purpleleaf sand	*Prunus x cistena*
Cherry, sargent	*Prunus sargentii*
Cherry, yoshino	*Prunus x yedoensis*
Chestnut, Chinese	*Castanea mollissima*
Chestnut, red horse	*Aesculus x carnea*
Chrysanthemum	*Chrysanthemum*
Cinquefoil	*Potentilla*
Cinquefoil, bush	*Potentilla fruticosa*
Cinquefoil, spring	*Potentilla tabernaemontani*
Clematis	*Clematis*
Cockscomb	*Celosia argentea* var. *plumosa*
Coffeetree, Kentucky	*Gymnocladus dioica*
Coleus	*Coleus hybridus*
Columbine	*Aquilegia*
Coneflower, purple	*Echinacea purpurea* 'Magnus'
Coral bells	*Heuchera*
Coreopsis, threadleaf	*Coreopsis verticillata* 'Moonbeam'
Cornflower	*Centaurea cyanus*
Cosmos	*Cosmos bipinnatus*

COMMON NAME	BOTANICAL NAME
Cotoneaster, bearberry	*Cotoneaster dammeri*
Cotoneaster, cranberry	*Cotoneaster apiculatus*
Cotoneaster, creeping	*Cotoneaster adpressus*
Cotoneaster, hedge	*Cotoneaster lucidus*
Cotoneaster, rockspray	*Cotoneaster horizontalis*
Cotoneaster, spreading	*Cotoneaster divaricatus*
Cotoneaster, willowleaf	*Cotoneaster salicifolius*
Crabapple, flowering	*Malus* (many species)
Cranesbill	*Geranium*
Crapemyrtle, common	*Lagerstroemia indica*
Creeper, Virginia	*Parthenocissus quinquefolia*
Crossvine	*Bignonia capreolata*
Cryptomeria, Japanese	*Cryptomeria japonica*
Currant, Alpine	*Ribes alpinum*
Cypress, Leyland	X *Cupressocyparis leylandii*
Cyrilla, swamp	*Cyrilla racemiflora*
Dahlia	*Dahlia*
Daisy, English	*Bellis perennis*
Daphne, fragrant	*Daphne odora*
Daylily	*Hemerocallis*
Delphinium	*Delphinium*
Deutzia, Nikko	*Deutzia gracilis* 'Nikko'
Deutzia, slender	*Deutzia gracilis*
Devil's-walkingstick	*Aralia spinosa*
Dogwood, Corneliancherry	*Cornus mas*
Dogwood, flowering	*Cornus florida*
Dogwood, kousa	*Cornus kousa*
Dogwood, red osier	*Cornus sericea*
Dove tree	*Davidia involucrata*
Dragon lady	*Ilex* x *aquipernyi*
Dusty miller	*Senecio cineraria*
Dutchman's pipe	*Aristolochia macrophylla*

COMMON NAME	BOTANICAL NAME
Elm, lacebark	*Ulmus parvifolia*
Enkianthus, redvein	*Enkianthus campanulatus*
Euonymus, Japanese	*Euonymus japonicus*
Euonymus, winged	*Euonymus alatus*
Euonymus, wintercreeper	*Euonymus fortunei*
False blue indigo	*Baptisia australis*
False spirea	*Astilbe, Astilbe* x *arendsii* 'Fanal', *Astilbe simplicifolia* 'Sprite'
False sunflower	*Heliopsis*
Falsecypress, hinoki	*Chamaecyparis obtusa*
Falsecypress, Japanese	*Chamaecyparis pisifera*
Falsecypress, Lawson's	*Chamaecyparis lawsoniana*
Fatshedera	X *Fatshedera lizei*
Fatsia, Japanese	*Fatsia japonica*
Fetterbush	*Leucothoë fontanesiana*
Fig, climbing	*Ficus pumila*
Filbert, Turkish	*Corylus colurna*
Fir, common China	*Cunninghamia lanceolata*
Fir, Douglas	*Pseudotsuga menziesii*
Fir, Fraser	*Abies fraseri*
Fir, white	*Abies concolor*
Firethorn, scarlet	*Pyracantha coccinea*
Flax	*Linum*
Fleece flower	*Polygonum aubertii*
Flossflower	*Ageratum houstonianum*
Foamflower	*Tiarella*
Forsythia, Arnold dwarf	*Forsythia* 'Arnold Dwarf'
Forsythia, border	*Forsythia* x *intermedia*
Fothergilla, dwarf	*Fothergilla gardenii*
Franklin tree	*Franklinia alatamaha*
Fringeflower, Chinese	*Loropetalum chinense*

COMMON NAME	BOTANICAL NAME
Fringetree, white	*Chionanthus virginicus*
Fuchsia	*Fuchsia* x *hybrida*
Gayfeather	*Liatris spicata*
Georgia plume	*Elliottia racemosa*
Geranium	*Pelargonium* x *hortorum*
Ginkgo	*Ginkgo biloba*
Globe thistle	*Echinops*
Globeflower	*Trollius europaeus*
Goldenchain tree	*Laburnum* x *watereri*
Goldenrain tree, panicled	*Koelreuteria paniculata*
Grapeholly, Oregon	*Mahonia aquifolium*
Guava, pineapple	*Feijoa sellowiana*
Gum, black	*Nyssa sylvatica*
Hackberry, common	*Celtis occidentalis*
Hawthorn, cockspur	*Crataegus crusgalli*
Hawthorn, Washington	*Crataegus phaenopyrum*
Heath, spring	*Erica carnea*
Heather, Scotch	*Calluna vulgaris*
Heavenly bamboo	*Nandina domestica*
Heliotrope	*Heliotropium arborescens*
Hemlock, Canadian	*Tsuga canadensis*
Hemlock, Carolina	*Tsuga caroliniana*
Holly, American	*Ilex opaca*
Holly, Chinese	*Ilex cornuta*
Holly, common winterberry	*Ilex verticillata*
Holly, English	*Ilex aquifolium*
Holly fern, Japanese	*Cyrtomium falcatum*
Holly, Foster's	*Ilex* x *attenuata* 'Fosteri'
Holly, inkberry	*Ilex glabra*
Holly, Japanese	*Ilex crenata*
Holly, longstalk	*Ilex pedunculosa*
Holly, Meserve hybrid	*Ilex* x *meserveae*
Holly, Nellie R. Stevens	*Ilex* x 'Nellie R. Stevens'

COMMON NAME	BOTANICAL NAME
Honeylocust	*Gleditsia triacanthos* var. *inermis*
Honeysuckle, goldflame	*Lonicera* x *heckrottii*
Honeysuckle, winter	*Lonicera fragrantissima*
Hop tree	*Ptelea trifoliata*
Hops, golden	*Humulus lupulus* 'Aureus'
Hophornbeam, American	*Ostrya virginiana*
Hornbeam, American	*Carpinus caroliniana*
Hornbeam, European	*Carpinus betulus*
Horsechestnut, common	*Aesculus hippocastanum*
Huckleberry, box	*Gaylussacia brachycera*
Hyacinth bean	*Dolichos lablab*
Hydrangea, climbing	*Hydrangea anomala* ssp. *petiolaris*
Hydrangea-vine, Japanese	*Schizophragma hydrangeoides*
Hyssop, anise	*Agastache*
Impatiens	*Impatiens wallerana*
Incensecedar, California	*Calocedrus decurrens*
Inkberry	*Ilex glabra* 'Compacta'
Iris	*Iris*
Ivy, Boston	*Parthenocissus tricuspidata*
Ivy, English	*Hedera helix*
Jacob's ladder	*Polemonium*
Jasmine, cape	*Gardenia jasminoides*
Jasmine, common white	*Jasminum officinale*
Jasmine, Confederate	*Trachelospermum jasminoides*
Jasmine, winter	*Jasminum nudiflorum*
Jessamine, Carolina	*Gelsemium sempervirens*
Joe Pye weed	*Eupatorium*
Juniper, creeping	*Juniperus horizontalis*

COMMON NAME	BOTANICAL NAME
Juniper, Japanese garden	*Juniperus procumbens*
Juniper, Pfitzer Chinese	*Juniperus chinensis 'Pfitzeriana'*
Juniper, Rocky Mountain	*Juniperus scopulorum*
Juniper, shore	*Juniperus conferta*
Katsuratree	*Cercidiphyllum japonicum*
Kerria, Japanese	*Kerria japonica*
Lamb's ears	*Stachys*
Larch, European	*Larix decidua*
Larch, golden	*Pseudolarix amabilis*
Larch, Japanese	*Larix kaempferi*
Laurel, Alexandrian	*Danaë racemosa*
Laurel, common cherry	*Prunus laurocerasus*
Lavender	*Lavandula angustifolia*
Lavender cotton	*Santolina chamaecyparissus*
Leadwort	*Ceratostigma plumbaginoides*
Lenten rose	*Helleborus orientalis*
Leopard's bane	*Doronicum*
Leucothoë, coastal	*Leucothoë axillaris*
Lilac, Chinese	*Syringa x chinensis*
Lilac, common	*Syringa vulgaris*
Lilac, cutleaf	*Syringa laciniata*
Lilac, Japanese tree	*Syringa reticulata*
Lilac, Meyer	*Syringa meyeri*
Lilac, Persian	*Syringa x persica*
Lily	*Lilium*
Lily of the Nile	*Agapanthus*
Lily-turf, blue	*Liriope muscari*
Lily-turf, creeping	*Liriope spicata*
Linden, littleleaf	*Tilia cordata*
Linden, silver	*Tilia tomentosa*
Lobelia	*Lobelia erinus, Lobelia cardinalis*
Locust, black	*Robinia pseudoacacia*
Lungwort	*Pulmonaria*

COMMON NAME	BOTANICAL NAME
Lupine	*Lupinus*
Maakia, amur	*Maakia amurensis*
Magnolia, cucumbertree	*Magnolia acuminata*
Magnolia, saucer	*Magnolia x soulangiana*
Magnolia, star	*Magnolia stellata*
Magnolia, sweetbay	*Magnolia virginiana*
Mahonia, creeping	*Mahonia repens*
Maple, amur	*Acer ginnala*
Maple, fullmoon	*Acer japonicum*
Maple, hedge	*Acer campestre*
Maple, Japanese	*Acer palmatum*
Maple, paperbark	*Acer griseum*
Maple, red	*Acer rubrum*
Maple, Shantung	*Acer truncatum*
Maple, sugar	*Acer saccharum*
Maple, tatarian	*Acer tataricum*
Maple, trident	*Acer buergerianum*
Marguerite, golden	*Anthemis tinctoria*
Marigold	*Tagetes*
Marigold, cape	*Dimorphotheca sinuata*
Marigold, pot	*Calendula officinalis*
Mock orange, sweet	*Philadelphus coronarius*
Monkey flower	*Mimulus x hybridus*
Monkshood	*Aconitum carmichaelii*
Moss rose	*Portulaca grandiflora*
Mountainash, European	*Sorbus aucuparia*
Mountainash, Korean	*Sorbus alnifolia*
Mountain-laurel	*Kalmia latifolia*
Nasturtium	*Tropaeolum majus*
Nemesia	*Nemesia strumosa*
New Guinea hybrids	*Impatiens*
Oak, blue Japanese	*Quercus glauca*
Oak, chestnut	*Quercus prinus*
Oak, Chinese evergreen	*Quercus myrsinifolia*

COMMON NAME	BOTANICAL NAME	COMMON NAME	BOTANICAL NAME
Oak, columnar English	*Quercus robur* 'Fastigiata'	Phlox, garden	*Phlox paniculata* 'David'
Oak, English	*Quercus robur*	Photinia, Chinese	*Photinia serrulata*
Oak, live	*Quercus virginiana*	Photinia, Fraser	*Photinia* x *fraseri*
Oak, pin	*Quercus palustris*	Photinia, Japanese	*Photinia glabra*
Oak, red	*Quercus rubra*	Pieris, Japanese	*Pieris japonica*
Oak, sawtooth	*Quercus acutissima*	Pieris, mountain	*Pieris floribunda*
Oak, scarlet	*Quercus coccinea*	Pincushion flower	*Scabiosa columbaria* 'Butterfly Blue'
Oak, shingle	*Quercus imbricaria*	Pine, Austrian	*Pinus nigra*
Oak, water	*Quercus nigra*	Pine, bristlecone	*Pinus aristata*
Oak, willow	*Quercus phellos*	Pine, eastern white	*Pinus strobus*
Oleander	*Nerium oleander*	Pine, Himalayan	*Pinus wallichiana*
Olive, Russian	*Elaeagnus angustifolia*	Pine, Japanese black	*Pinus thunbergii*
Orange, hardy	*Poncirus trifoliata*	Pine, Japanese red	*Pinus densiflora*
Osmanthus, Fortune's	*Osmanthus* x *fortunei*	Pine, Japanese white	*Pinus parviflora*
Osmanthus, holly	*Osmanthus heterophyllus*	Pine, Korean	*Pinus koraiensis*
		Pine, lacebark	*Pinus bungeana*
Pachysandra, Allegheny	*Pachysandra procumbens*	Pine, limber	*Pinus flexilis*
Pachysandra, Japanese	*Pachysandra terminalis*	Pine, Macedonian	*Pinus peuce*
Pagodatree, Japanese	*Sophora japonica*	Pine, mugo	*Pinus mugo* var. *mugo*
Pansy, garden	*Viola* x *wittrockiana*	Pine, red	*Pinus resinosa*
Parasol tree, Chinese	*Firmiana simplex*	Pine, Swiss stone	*Pinus cembra*
Parrotia, Persian	*Parrotia persica*	Pink, China	*Dianthus chinensis*
Partridge berry	*Mitchella repens*	Pinks	*Dianthus*
Paxistima, Canby	*Paxistima canbyi*	Pistachio, Chinese	*Pistacia chinensis*
Pea shrub, Chinese	*Caragana sinica*	Pittosporum, Japanese	*Pittosporum tobira*
Pea shrub, Siberian	*Caragana arborescens*	Plantain lily	*Hosta*
Pear, Bradford	*Pyrus calleryana* 'Bradford'	Plum, cherry	*Prunus cerasifera*
		Podocarpus, Chinese	*Podocarpus macrophyllus* 'Maki'
Pear, Chinese sand	*Pyrus pyrifolia*	Poplar, Japanese	*Populus maximowiczii*
Pear, ussurian	*Pyrus ussuriensis*	Poppy, California	*Eschscholzia californica*
Pearlbush, common	*Exochorda racemosa*	Poppy, Oriental	*Papaver orientale*
Peony	*Paeonia*	Primrose	*Primula*
Periwinkle (annual)	*Vinca*	Privet, amur	*Ligustrum amurense*
Periwinkle, common	*Vinca minor*	Privet, border	*Ligustrum obtusifolium*
Periwinkle, large	*Vinca major*		
Petunia	*Petunia* x *hybrida*	Privet, Japanese	*Ligustrum japonicum*
Phlox	*Phlox*	Quince, Chinese	*Pseudocydonia sinensis*
Phlox, annual	*Phlox drummondii*		

COMMON NAME	BOTANICAL NAME
Quince, common flowering	*Chaenomeles speciosa*
Redbud, Chinese	*Cercis chinensis*
Redbud, eastern	*Cercis canadensis*
Red-hot poker	*Kniphofia*
Redwood, dawn	*Metasequoia glyptostroboides*
Rhaphiolepis, yeddo	*Rhaphiolepis umbellata*
Rhododendron	*Rhododendron*
Rose	*Rosa*
Rose of Sharon	*Hibiscus syriacus*
Rose, Meidiland	*Rosa* 'Meidiland'
Rose, memorial	*Rosa wichuraiana*
Rosemary	*Rosmarinus officinalis*
Rubber tree, hardy	*Eucommia ulmoides*
Sage	*Salvia*
Sage, Russian	*Perovskia atriplicifolia*
Sage, yellow	*Lantana camara*
Salvia	*Salvia*
Sandmyrtle, box	*Leiophyllum buxifolium*
Sapphireberry	*Symplocos paniculata*
Scotch broom	*Cytisus scoparius*
Sea thrift	*Armeria maritima*
Sedge	*Carex*
Serviceberry, downy	*Amelanchier arborea*
Silverbell, Carolina	*Halesia tetraptera*
Silverberry	*Elaeagnus commutata*
Silvervine fleece flower	*Polygonum aubertii*
Skimmia, Japanese	*Skimmia japonica*
Smoke tree, common	*Cotinus coggygria*
Snakeroot	*Cimicifuga racemosa*
Snapdragon	*Antirrhinum majus*
Sneezeweed	*Helenium*
Snowbell, Japanese	*Styrax japonicus*
Snow-in-summer	*Cerastium tomentosum*
Soapweed, small	*Yucca glauca*
Solomon's seal	*Polygonatum*
Sourwood	*Oxydendrum arboreum*

COMMON NAME	BOTANICAL NAME
Speedwell	*Veronica, Veronica* x 'Goodness Grows'
Speedwell, creeping	*Veronica peduncularis* 'Georgia Blue'
Spicebush	*Lindera benzoin*
Spider flower	*Cleome hassleriana*
Spirea, Bumald	*Spiraea bumalda*
Spirea, Japanese white	*Spiraea albiflora*
Spruce, Colorado	*Picea pungens*
Spruce, Norway	*Picea abies*
Spruce, Oriental	*Picea orientalis*
Spruce, Serbian	*Picea omorika*
Spruce, white	*Picea glauca*
St. John's wort	*Hypericum*
St. John's wort, Aaron's beard	*Hypericum calycinum*
St. John's wort, golden	*Hypericum frondosum*
St. John's wort, shrubby	*Hypericum prolificum*
Statice	*Limonium sinuatum*
Stephanandra, cutleaf	*Stephanandra incisa*
Stewartia, Japanese	*Stewartia pseudocamellia*
Stewartia, mountain	*Stewartia ovata*
Stonecrop	*Sedum*
Strawflower	*Helichrysum bracteatum*
Sumac, flameleaf	*Rhus copallina*
Sumac, fragrant	*Rhus aromatica*
Sumac, staghorn	*Rhus typhina*
Summersweet	*Clethra alnifolia*
Sun rose	*Helianthemum nummularium*
Sweet box	*Sarcococca hookeriana* var. *humilis*
Sweetgum, American	*Liquidambar styraciflua*
Sweetshrub, common	*Calycanthus floridus*

COMMON NAME	BOTANICAL NAME
Ternstroemia, Japanese	*Ternstroemia gymnanthera*
Tickseed	*Coreopsis grandiflora*
Toad lily	*Tricyrtis*
Tobacco, flowering	*Nicotiana alata*
Treasure flower	*Gazania rigens*
Trumpet creeper, common	*Campsis radicans*
Turtlehead	*Chelone lyonii*
Umbrellapine, Japanese	*Sciadopitys verticillata*
Verbena	*Verbena bonariensis,* *Verbena* species
Viburnum, arrowwood	*Viburnum dentatum*
Viburnum, Burkwood	*Viburnum* x *burkwoodii*
Viburnum, Chindo	*Viburnum awabuki* 'Chindo'
Viburnum, Conoy service	*Viburnum utile* 'Conoy'
Viburnum, doublefile	*Viburnum plicatum* var. *tomentosum*
Viburnum, European cranberrybush	*Viburnum opulus*
Viburnum, Japanese	*Viburnum japonicum*
Viburnum, Judd	*Viburnum* x *juddii*
Viburnum, Koreanspice	*Viburnum carlesii*
Viburnum, leatherleaf	*Viburnum rhytidophyllum*
Viburnum, linden	*Viburnum dilatatum*
Viburnum, nannyberry	*Viburnum lentago*
Viburnum, Siebold	*Viburnum sieboldii*
Viburnum, wayfaringtree	*Viburnum lantana*

COMMON NAME	BOTANICAL NAME
Viburnum, withe-rod	*Viburnum cassinoides*
Violet, Labrador	*Viola labradorica*
Waxbells, yellow	*Kirengeshoma*
Weigela, old-fashioned	*Weigela floribunda*
Windflower	*Anemone*
Wingnut, caucasian	*Pterocarya fraxinifolia*
Wintergreen, creeping	*Gaultheria procumbens*
Winterhazel, fragrant	*Corylopsis glabrescens*
Wintersweet, fragrant	*Chimonanthus praecox*
Wishbone flower	*Torenia fournieri*
Wisteria, Japanese	*Wisteria floribunda*
Witchhazel, Chinese	*Hamamelis mollis*
Witchhazel, common	*Hamamelis virginiana*
Witchhazel, hybrid	*Hamamelis* x *intermedia*
Witchhazel, vernal	*Hamamelis vernalis*
Woadwaxen, common	*Genista tinctoria* 'Plena'
Yarrow	*Achillea* x 'Coronation Gold'
Yaupon	*Ilex vomitoria*
Yellowroot	*Xanthorhiza simplicissima*
Yellowwood, American	*Cladrastis lutea*
Yellowwood, Japanese	*Cladrastis platycarpa*
Yew, Anglojap	*Taxus* x *media*
Yew, Japanese	*Taxus cuspidata*
Yew, weeping English	*Taxus baccata* 'Repandens'
Zelkova, Japanese	*Zelkova serrata*
Zinnia, garden	*Zinnia elegans*

DECIDUOUS GROUNDCOVERS

BOTANICAL NAME	COMMON NAME	HARDINESS ZONE	LIGHT	CHARACTERISTICS AND/OR USE
Cornus canadensis	Bunchberry	2–6	Partial shade or shade	Fall color, fruit for birds
Cotoneaster adpressus	Creeping cotoneaster	4–7	Sun	Fruit, use in rock gardens
Cotoneaster apiculatus	Cranberry cotoneaster	4–7	Sun	Fruit, will cascade over wall, bank cover
Cotoneaster horizontalis	Rockspray cotoneaster	5–7	Sun	Low massing
Cyrtomium falcatum	Japanese holly fern	8	Shade	Foliage, true fern
Forsythia 'Arnold Dwarf'	Arnold dwarf forsythia	5–8	Sun	Low habit, vigorous spreader
Genista tinctoria 'Plena'	Common woodwaxen	4–7	Sun	Green stems in winter, yellow flowers
Parthenocissus tricuspidata	Boston ivy	4–8	Shade	Fall color, spring color
Potentilla tabernaemontani	Spring cinquefoil	4–7	Sun	Mat forming, summer yellow flowers
Rhus aromatica	Fragrant sumac	3–9	Sun	Fragrant, fall color, fast growing
Rosa 'Meidiland'	Meidiland rose	4–5	Sun	Groundcover, repeat bloomer, disease resistant
Rosa wichuraiana	Memorial rose	5–8	Sun	Long prostrate canes, large banks
Xanthorhiza simplicissima	Yellowroot	3–9	Sun	Dense, handsome foliage

Evergreen Groundcovers

BOTANICAL NAME	COMMON NAME	HARDINESS ZONE	LIGHT	CHARACTERISTICS AND/OR USE
Arctostaphylos uva-ursi	Bearberry	2–6	Sun or shade	Salt tolerant, fall color
Ardisia japonica	Japanese ardisia	8–9	Shade	Tall dense mat
Berberis candidula	Paleleaf barberry	6–8	Sun	Dense, spine tipped
Calluna vulgaris	Scotch heather	4–6	Sun or partial shade	Summer flowers, mass
Cotoneaster dammeri	Bearberry cotoneaster	5–7	Sun	Fast growing, glossy carpet
Cotoneaster salicifolius	Willowleaf cotoneaster	6–7	Sun	Cascading habit, good over walls
Erica carnea	Spring heath	5–7	Sun	Winter/spring flowers, mass
Euonymus fortunei	Wintercreeper euonymus	5–9	Sun or shade	Wall covering, low hedge
Gaultheria procumbens	Creeping wintergreen	3–5	Partial shade	Fragrant leaves, winter color
Gaylussacia brachycera	Box huckleberry	5–7	Partial shade	Dwarf, use under rhododendron and pine
Hedera helix	English ivy	4–9	Shade	Lush green, heavy shade, vigorous grower
Hypericum calycinum	Aaron's beard St. John's wort	5–8	Sun	Semi-evergreen, summer yellow flowers
Iberis sempervirens	Candytuft	4–8	Sun	Early white flowers
Juniperus conferta	Shore juniper	6–9	Sun	Seashore, poor soils

BOTANICAL NAME	COMMON NAME	HARDINESS ZONE	LIGHT	CHARACTERISTICS AND/OR USE
Juniperus horizontalis	Creeping juniper	4–9	Sun	Many forms, blues, greens, and yellows available
Juniperus procumbens	Japanese garden juniper	4–8	Sun	Dwarf plant, handsome
Liriope muscari	Blue lily-turf	6–9	Sun or shade	Broad-leaved, arching habit, low maintenance
Liriope spicata	Creeping lily-turf	4–9	Partial shade	Vigorous spreader in all light and soil
Mahonia repens	Creeping mahonia	5–7	Partial shade	Green in summer, purple in winter
Mitchella repens	Partridge berry	3–9	Shade	Very low to ground
Pachysandra procumbens	Allegheny pachysandra	5–9	Shade	Wide leaves, bluish color
Pachysandra terminalis	Japanese pachysandra	4–8	Shade	Handsome under trees
Paxistima canbyi	Canby paxistima	3–7	Sun or partial shade	Border planting around shrubs
Sarcococca hookeriana var. *humilis*	Sweet box	6–8	Partial shade	Fragrant flowers, dense groundcover
Vinca major	Large periwinkle	6–9	Sun or shade	Blue flowers, large leaves
Vinca minor	Common periwinkle	3–8	Sun or shade	Blue flowers, lush shade carpet

ANNUALS

BOTANICAL NAME	COMMON NAME	LIGHT	CHARACTERISTICS AND/OR USE
Ageratum houstonianum	Flossflower	Partial shade	Blue, white, edgings, flower border
Alternanthera	Alternanthera	Sun to partial shade	Foliage, carpet beds, take shearing well
Amaranthus	Amaranthus	Sun	Brilliant foliage, good background plant
Antirrhinum majus	Snapdragon	Sun to partial shade	Many bright colors, mixed border or background
Begonia x *semperflorens-cultorum*	Wax begonia	Sun to partial shade	Foliage and flower color, bushy mass
Begonia x *tuberhybrida*	Tuberous begonia	Partial shade to shade	Brilliant colors
Browallia speciosa	Browallia	Sun to partial shade	Blues, whites, cascades, hanging baskets, window boxes
Caladium	Caladium	Partial shade to shade	Colorful foliage, good for containers
Calendula officinalis	Pot marigold	Sun	Apricots, yellows, oranges and reds
Callistephus chinensis	China aster	Partial shade	Many colors, for cut flowers, borders
Celosia argentea var. *plumosa*	Cockscomb	Sun	Vivid colors, feathery flower, for cut flowers
Centaurea cyanus	Cornflower, bachelor's buttons	Sun	Blue, pink, white, red, flowers freely, for cut flowers

BOTANICAL NAME	COMMON NAME	LIGHT	CHARACTERISTICS AND/OR USE
Cleome hassleriana	Spider flower	Sun	White, pink, purple, "spidery" flowers, continuous bloomer
Coleus hybridus	Coleus	Shade	Colorful foliage, pinch flowers to keep plant bushy
Cosmos bipinnatus	Cosmos	Sun	White, pink, red, good for mixed borders
Dahlia	Dahlia	Sun	Extremely showy flowers
Dianthus chinensis	China Pink	Sun	Fringed edge, good for front of border and containers
Dimorphotheca sinuata	Cape marigold	Sun	Large daisylike flowers, likes cool summers
Dolichos lablab	Hyacinth bean	Sun	Fast growing vine, purple or white flowers, purple pods
Eschscholzia californica	California poppy	Sun	Variety of colors, naturalizes well, drought tolerant
Fuchsia x hybrida	Fuchsia	Partial shade to shade	Colorful pink, red, purple, white flowers, good in hanging baskets
Gazania rigens	Treasure flower	Sun	Daisy-type flowers, tolerates heat and wind
Gomphrena globosa	Globe amaranth	Sun	Purple, rose, pink, or white flowers, good for drying
Helichrysum bracteatum	Strawflower	Sun	Excellent for drying, retain color
Heliotropium arborescens	Heliotrope	Sun	Fragrant, purple, blue, or white flower, good for containers
Iberis umbellata	Candytuft	Sun	Edging, masses, rock garden
Impatiens	New Guinea hybrids	Sun	Large flowers, colorful foliage, use for containers, accents
Impatiens wallerana	Impatiens	Shade	Variety of colors, use for hanging baskets, edging, shrub effect
Lantana camara	Yellow sage	Sun	Interesting flower form, tolerates poor soil
Limonium sinuatum	Statice	Sun	Excellent cut and dried, tolerates heat and salt spray
Lobelia erinus	Lobelia	Sun to partial shade	Many shades of blue, use for hanging baskets, edging
Lobularia maritima	Sweet alyssum	Sun to partial shade	Fragrant, use for ground-cover, edging, rock gardens

BOTANICAL NAME	COMMON NAME	LIGHT	CHARACTERISTICS AND/OR USE
Mimulus x *hybridus*	Monkey flower	Partial shade to shade	Yellow and red bicolor, showy flowers, tolerates wet areas
Nemesia strumosa	Nemesia	Sun to partial shade	Floppy habit, good for baskets or window boxes
Nicotiana alata	Flowering tobacco	Sun to partial shade	Red, pink, white flowers, fragrant, mass for showy display
Pelargonium x *hortorum*	Geranium	Sun to partial shade	Showy, use for hanging baskets, border, edging
Petunia x *hybrida*	Petunia	Sun to partial shade	Many colors, use for baskets and containers
Phlox drummondii	Annual phlox	Sun	Clip faded blooms to keep full, use in rock gardens
Portulaca grandiflora	Moss rose	Sun	Very colorful, low plant, tolerates heat and drought
Salvia	Salvia	Sun to partial shade	Spiked colorful flowers, mass together, use for containers, accent
Senecio cineraria	Dusty miller	Sun to partial shade	Silver gray foliage, mounded form, use for edging
Tagetes	Marigold	Sun	Yellows to reds, ferny foliage, long-blooming, use for edging
Thunbergia alata	Black-eyed Susan vine	Sun to partial shade	Light petals, dark centers, use for trellises, hanging baskets
Torenia fournieri	Wishbone flower	Shade	Bicolor flowers, pansy looking, good in deep shade
Tropaeolum majus	Nasturtium	Sun	Classic trailing plant, edible leaves and flowers
Verbena bonariensis	Verbena	Sun	Purple flowers, good for edging, attracts butterflies
Vinca	Periwinkle	Partial shade to shade	Good flower and foliage, shrublike
Viola x *wittrockiana*	Garden pansy	Sun to partial shade	Many colors, use in mass, cool season bloomer
Zinnia elegans	Garden zinnia	Sun	Bright colors, mass, long bloomer, deadhead, use in borders

PERENNIALS

Many species and hybrids are available with most perennials. They vary widely in size and habit, and new ones are being introduced in the market almost daily. Determine plants' habits before purchasing and installing them. The species that have hybrid names listed are ones that have performed well for our company or can be commonly found.

BOTANICAL NAME	COMMON NAME	HARDINESS ZONE	LIGHT	CHARACTERISTICS AND/OR USE
Achillea x 'Coronation Gold'	Yarrow	3–8	Sun	Yellow flowers, fernlike foliage, for cut or dried flowers
Aconitum carmichaelii	Monkshood	3	Sun or partial shade	Dark blue flowers late summer, all parts poisonous
Agapanthus	Lily of the Nile	7–10	Sun	Trumpet-shaped flowers on scapes, mostly blues, summer
Agastache	Anise hyssop	5–9	Sun	Spiked flowers, many colors available, attracts butterflies
Amsonia	Blue star	3–9	Sun or partial shade	Spring flowers, fall color
Anemone	Windflower	3–8	Partial shade	Spring- to fall-blooming varieties available
Anemone x *hybrida* 'Honorine Jobert'	Japanese anemone	5–7	Partial shade	Fall white flowers, tall, very popular
Anthemis tinctoria	Golden marguerite	5–7	Sun	Yellow flowers, continuous bloom, for cut flowers

BOTANICAL NAME	COMMON NAME	HARDINESS ZONE	LIGHT	CHARACTERISTICS AND/OR USE
Aquilegia	Columbine	3–8	Sun or partial shade	Variety of colors, spring flowers, attracts hummingbirds
Armeria maritima	Sea thrift	4–8	Sun	Showy flowers, bed edging, salt tolerant
Artemisia schmidtiana	Silvermound artemisia	3–8	Sun	Interesting silver foliage and mounded habit
Asclepias tuberosa	Butterfly weed	4–9	Sun	Tall, orange flowers, late summer, attracts butterflies
Aster novae-angliae	Aster	4–8	Sun or partial shade	Fall blooms
Astilbe	False spirea	4–8	Partial shade or shade	Many colors, habits, and bloom times
Astilbe x arendsii 'Fanal'	False spirea	4–9	Partial shade or shade	Red summer flowers, fernlike foliage, popular
Astilbe simplicifolia 'Sprite'	False spirea	4–8	Partial shade or shade	Light pink flowers, low growing, for edging, popular
Aurinia saxatilis	Basket of gold	3–7	Sun	Early spring fragrant yellow flowers, use in rock gardens
Baptisia australis	False blue indigo	3–9	Sun or partial shade	Spring blue flowers, attractive foliage, attracts butterflies
Begonia grandis	Hardy begonia	6–9	Partial shade or shade	Pink or white flowers, summer into fall, reseeds
Bellis perennis	English daisy	4–10	Sun or partial shade	Spring flowers, use in rock gardens
Boltonia asteroides	Boltonia	4–9	Sun	Late summer daisy flowers
Brunnera macrophylla	Heartleaf brunnera	3–7	Partial shade or shade	Tiny blue flowers in spring above heart-shaped foliage
Campanula	Bellflower	3–8	Sun or partial shade	Many sizes and habits, blue, pink, or white bell-shaped flowers
Carex	Sedge	5–9	Sun or partial shade	Grass-type foliage, large color range, some evergreen
Centaurea	Centaurea	3–8	Sun	Bloom late spring into summer, for cut flowers

BOTANICAL NAME	COMMON NAME	HARDINESS ZONE	LIGHT	CHARACTERISTICS AND/OR USE
Cerastium tomentosum	Snow-in-summer	2–7	Sun	White spring flowers, silvery foliage, fast growing groundcover
Ceratostigma plumbaginoides	Leadwort	5–8	Sun or shade	Blue flowers in summer, red foliage fall color, groundcover
Chelone lyonii	Turtlehead	3–7	Sun or partial shade	Summer pink flowers, for cut flowers
Chrysanthemum	Chrysanthemum	3–9	Sun	Many colors, habits, bloom times, showy flowers, for cut flowers
Cimicifuga racemosa	Snakeroot	3–7	Partial shade or shade	White flowers late summer
Coreopsis grandiflora	Tickseed	4–9	Sun	Yellow flowers, many compact growing hybrids
Coreopsis verticillata 'Moonbeam'	Threadleaf coreopsis	4–9	Sun	Dainty yellow flowers in summer, fine-textured ferny foliage
Delphinium	Delphinium	3–7	Sun or partial shade	Spiked flowers, many sizes and habits available
Dianthus	Pinks	3–10	Sun	Low growing, some evergreen, use in rock gardens, edging, for cut flowers
Dicentra formosa 'Luxuriant'	Bleeding heart	2–8	Partial shade or shade	Repeat bloomer with cherry-red flowers, heat tolerant
Dicentra spectabilis	Old-fashioned bleeding heart	2–8	Partial shade or shade	Heart-shaped flowers, beautiful in early spring
Doronicum	Leopard's bane	4–7	Sun or partial shade	Early bloom, yellow daisylike flowers
Echinacea purpurea 'Magnus'	Purple coneflower	3–8	Sun	Rosy-purple daisy flowers midsummer to frost, attracts butterflies
Echinops	Globe thistle	3–7	Sun	Blue flowers, prickly foliage, attracts butterflies, for cut flowers
Epimedium	Barrenwort	4–8	Partial shade or shade	Yellow, red, pink, or white flowers in spring, beautiful foliage
Eupatorium	Joe Pye weed	4–9	Sun or partial shade	Tall, coarse texture, flowers late, attracts butterflies, use in moist areas

BOTANICAL NAME	COMMON NAME	HARDINESS ZONE	LIGHT	CHARACTERISTICS AND/OR USE
Gaillardia x *grandiflora*	Blanket flower	2–9	Sun	Red, yellow, and orange flowers, long blooming, attracts butterflies, for cut flowers
Geranium	Cranesbill	3–8	Sun or partial shade	Many colors and habits, fragrant foliage, use in rock gardens
Geum	Avens	4–7	Sun	Bright flowers in spring, good fall color
Gypsophila paniculata	Baby's breath	3–9	Sun	Tiny pink or white summer flowers, airy foliage, for cut flowers
Helenium	Sneezeweed	3–8	Sun	Good late summer bloom for cut flowers, can be invasive
Helianthemum nummularium	Sun rose	5–7	Sun	Blooms spring to mid-summer, evergreen, cascade over walls
Heliopsis	False sunflower	3–9	Sun	Yellow sunflower-type flowers midsummer
Helleborus foetidus	Bear's foot hellebore	5–9	Partial shade or shade	Blooms winter into early spring, lobed evergreen foliage
Helleborus orientalis	Lenten rose	4–9	Partial shade or shade	Blooms winter into early spring, leathery evergreen foliage
Hemerocallis	Daylily	3–9	Sun	Many colors and bloom times, attractive foliage
Heuchera	Coral bells	3–8	Sun or partial shade	Wide foliage selection, some evergreen, tiny flowers
Hosta	Plantain lily	3–8	Partial shade or shade	Many sizes, leaf shapes, and colors, edging plant
Hypericum	St. John's wort	5–7	Sun or partial shade	Yellow flowers, attractive foliage, some evergreen, groundcover
Iberis sempervirens	Candytuft	3–8	Sun or partial shade	Profuse white flowers spring, low growing, evergreen, edging
Iris	Iris	3–9	Sun or partial shade	Many forms, sizes, colors, and bloom times, showy flowers
Kirengeshoma	Yellow waxbells	5–8	Partial shade or shade	Yellow flowers late summer, large maple leaf foliage

BOTANICAL NAME	COMMON NAME	HARDINESS ZONE	LIGHT	CHARACTERISTICS AND/OR USE
Kniphofia	Red-hot poker	5–8	Sun	Orange, red, yellow flowers summer, attracts hummingbirds, for cut flowers
Lavandula angustifolia	Lavender	5–9	Sun	Entire plant fragrant, evergreen silver-gray foliage, for dried flowers
Liatris spicata	Gayfeather	3–9	Sun	Purple or white flower spikes summer, attracts butterflies, for cut flowers
Lilium	Lily	3–9	Sun or partial shade	Many colors, heights, and bloom times
Linum	Flax	4–8	Sun or partial shade	Commonly available with blue flowers in spring, use in rock gardens
Lobelia cardinalis	Lobelia	2–9	Sun or partial shade	Red summer flowers, attracts butterflies and hummingbirds
Lupinus	Lupine	4–6	Sun or partial shade	Showy spiked flowers, variety of colors, for cut flowers, borders
Mertensia virginica	Virginia bluebells	3–9	Partial shade or shade	Blue flowers in spring, with other perennials, dormant in summer
Monarda didyma	Bee balm	3–7	Sun or partial shade	Summer flowers, variety of colors, attracts butterflies and hummingbirds
Nepeta	Catmint	3–8	Sun or partial shade	Blue and lavender flowers summer, silver to gray foliage, masses
Paeonia	Peony	3–8	Sun or partial shade	Shrublike, many colors, fragrant showy flowers
Papaver orientale	Oriental poppy	2–7	Sun	Beautiful pinks, reds, oranges, whites in spring
Penstemon	Beard tongue	3–8	Sun	Many colors, habits, and bloom times, tubular flowers, for cut flowers
Perovskia atriplicifolia	Russian sage	5–9	Sun	Blue flowers mid-summer to frost, fine-textured foliage
Phlox	Phlox	4–9	Sun or partial shade	Variety of colors, habits, and bloom times

BOTANICAL NAME	COMMON NAME	HARDINESS ZONE	LIGHT	CHARACTERISTICS AND/OR USE
Phlox paniculata 'David'	Garden phlox	4–8	Sun	White summer flowers, fragrant, mildew resistant
Platycodon grandiflorus	Balloon flower	3–8	Sun or partial shade	Mid-summer blooms in blues, white, pinks, saucer-shaped flowers
Polemonium	Jacob's ladder	3–7	Sun or partial shade	Attractive foliage, blue to white summer blooms, use in rock gardens
Polygonatum	Solomon's seal	3–9	Partial shade or shade	Woodland, varied sizes and foliage colors, nodding spring blooms
Potentilla	Cinquefoil	3–7	Sun	Good forms available for groundcover and rock gardens
Primula	Primrose	3–8	Sun or shade	Many colors, bloom times vary spring to summer
Pulmonaria	Lungwort	3–8	Partial shade or shade	Interesting foliage, pink, blue, or white flowers early spring
Rudbeckia fulgida 'Goldsturm'	Black-eyed Susan	3–9	Sun	Yellow flowers from mid-summer to fall, use in borders
Salvia	Sage	4–8	Sun	Good range of colors, habits, and bloom times, spiked flowers
Scabiosa columbaria 'Butterfly Blue'	Pincushion flower	3–9	Sun	Light blue flowers spring until frost
Sedum	Stonecrop	3–9	Sun	Many sizes, habits, and colors, various uses
Stachys	Lamb's ears	3–8	Sun	Silver-gray woolly foliage, groundcover
Stokesia	Stokes' aster	5–9	Sun	Summer daisy flowers, variety of colors, for cut flowers, borders
Tiarella	Foamflower	3–8	Partial shade or shade	Unusual leaves, some patterned, spring blooms
Tricyrtis	Toad lily	4–8	Partial shade or shade	Graceful arching foliage, many colors available, late summer
Trollius europaeus	Globeflower	3–7	Sun or partial shade	Yellow flowers in late spring, use in moist areas
Verbena	Verbena	7–10	Sun	Flowers all summer, vigorous growth habit, attracts butterflies

BOTANICAL NAME	COMMON NAME	HARDINESS ZONE	LIGHT	CHARACTERISTICS AND/OR USE
Veronica	Speedwell	3–8	Sun or partial shade	Many sizes, habits, and bloom times, use in border, edging
Veronica peduncularis 'Georgia Blue'	Creeping speedwell	6–8	Sun or partial shade	Blue flowers, fall color, spreading low habit
Veronica x 'Goodness Grows'	Speedwell	3–8	Sun or partial shade	Blue flowers all summer, masses
Viola labradorica	Labrador violet	4–8	Partial shade or shade	Diminutive plant with purple foliage and violet blooms in spring

APPENDIX

F

VINES

BOTANICAL NAME	COMMON NAME	HARDINESS ZONE	LIGHT	CHARACTERISTICS AND/OR USE
Actinidia kolomikta	Kolomikta actinidia	4–8	Sun	Large leaves, fast grower
Akebia quinata	Fiveleaf akebia	6–8	Partial shade	Good vine for structures
Ampelopsis brevipedunculata	Porcelain ampelopsis	4–8	Sun	Ornamental fruit, train on trellis
Aristolochia macrophylla	Dutchman's pipe	4–8	Partial shade	Screen on trellis
Bignonia capreolata	Crossvine	6–8	Sun	Flowers red/purple in cold
Campsis radicans	Common trumpet creeper	4–9	Sun	Quick cover, orange trumpet flowers
Celastrus scandens	American bittersweet	3–8	Sun	Cut branches, container or very large spaces
Clematis	Clematis	3–8	Sun	Beautiful long-season flowers
X *Fatshedera lizei*	Fatshedera	8	Shade	Large-leaved climber
Ficus pumila	Climbing fig	8–10	Sun	Mats onto structure
Gelsemium sempervirens	Carolina jessamine	6–9	Sun	Bright yellow flowers, cascading habit
Humulus lupulus 'Aureus'	Golden hops	4–8	Sun	Golden leaves, fragrant flowers
Hydrangea anomala ssp. *petiolaris*	Climbing hydrangea	4–7	Shade	Winter flowers, good climber
Lonicera x *heckrottii*	Goldflame honeysuckle	5	Sun	Ever-blooming

BOTANICAL NAME	COMMON NAME	HARDINESS ZONE	LIGHT	CHARACTERISTICS AND/OR USE
Parthenocissus quinquefolia	Virginia creeper	3–9	Shade	Quick cover, fall cover
Parthenocissus tricuspidata	Boston ivy	4–8	Shade	Fall color, spring color
Polygonum aubertii	Silvervine fleece flower	4–7	Partial shade	Vigorous with good foliage
Schizophragma hydrangeoides	Japanese hydrangea-vine	5–8	Partial shade	Hybrid 'Moonlight' has silver mottling
Trachelospermum jasminoides	Confederate jasmine	8	Sun	Fragrant
Wisteria floribunda	Japanese wisteria	4–9	Sun	Heavy wood, excellent fragrant flowers

DECIDUOUS SHRUBS (THREE TO TEN FEET)

BOTANICAL NAME	COMMON NAME	HARDINESS ZONE	LIGHT	CHARACTERISTICS AND/OR USE
Abeliophyllum distichum	Korean abelialeaf	5–8	Sun or partial shade	Early white fragrant flowers
Aesculus parviflora	Bottlebrush buckeye	4–8	Sun or partial shade	Specimen or mass
Berberis koreana	Korean barberry	3–7	Sun or partial shade	Berries, flowers, barrier
Berberis x *mentorensis*	Mentor barberry	5–8	Sun or partial shade	Hedge, barrier
Berberis thunbergii 'Crimson Pygmy'	Crimson pygmy barberry	4–8	Sun	Low growing, reddish leaves, most common barberry
Berberis thunbergii 'Atropurpurea'	Japanese barberry	4–8	Sun	Foliage color, barrier
Buddleia davidii	Butterfly bush	5–9	Sun	Summer flowers, attracts butterflies, for cut flowers
Callicarpa japonica	Japanese beautyberry	5–8	Sun or partial shade	Attractive fruit in autumn, perennial in the north
Calycanthus floridus	Common sweetshrub	4–9	Sun or shade	Fragrant flowers, open natural habit
Caragana arborescens	Siberian pea shrub	2–7	Sun	Adaptable to extremes of climates and soils
Caragana sinica	Chinese pea shrub	5–7	Sun	Early flowers, fragrant bark
Caryopteris x *clandonensis*	Bluebeard	6–9	Sun or partial shade	Blue flowers late summer, aromatic

BOTANICAL NAME	COMMON NAME	HARDINESS ZONE	LIGHT	CHARACTERISTICS AND/OR USE
Chaenomeles speciosa	Common flowering quince	4–8	Sun or partial shade	Gorgeous flowers, good barrier
Chimonanthus praecox	Fragrant wintersweet	7–9	Sun or partial shade	Fragrant flowers, winter-early spring
Clethra alnifolia	Summersweet	4–9	Sun or partial shade	Fragrant white summer flowers, shrub border
Cornus sericea	Red osier dogwood	2–7	Partial shade	Red or yellow stems, winter interest
Corylopsis glabrescens	Fragrant winterhazel	5–8	Sun or partial shade	Early spring fragrant flowers
Cotinus coggygria	Common smoke tree	5–8	Sun	Purplish leaves, prune as tree
Cotoneaster divaricatus	Spreading cotoneaster	4–7	Sun or partial shade	Attractive summer and fall foliage
Cyrilla racemiflora	Swamp cyrilla	6–11	Sun or partial shade	Good fall color, fragrant flowers
Cytisus scoparius	Scotch broom	5–8	Sun or partial shade	Green stems, tolerant of poor soil
Deutzia gracilis	Slender deutzia	4–8	Sun or partial shade	Hedge, mass, graceful habit
Deutzia gracilis 'Nikko'	Nikko deutzia	4–8	Sun or partial shade	Low growing, white spring flowers, use in front of bed
Euonymus alatus	Winged euonymus	4–8	Sun or shade	Fall color, specimen, mass
Exochorda racemosa	Common pearlbush	4–8	Sun or partial shade	Flowers white, mass with other shrubs
Fatsia japonica	Japanese fatsia	8–10	Shade	Large, tropical-looking leaves
Forsythia x *intermedia*	Border forsythia	4–8	Sun	Early flowers
Fothergilla gardenii	Dwarf fothergilla	5–8	Sun or partial shade	Disease free, shrub mass, interesting flowers
Hamamelis x *intermedia*	Hybrid witchhazel	5–8	Sun or partial shade	Early flowers, yellows and reds
Hamamelis mollis	Chinese witchhazel	5–8	Sun or partial shade	Fall color, long-lasting early fragrant flowers
Hamamelis vernalis	Vernal witchhazel	4–8	Sun or partial shade	Long-lasting winter flowers and good fall color
Hibiscus syriacus	Rose of Sharon	5–8	Sun or partial shade	Summer flowers, large areas in mass

BOTANICAL NAME	COMMON NAME	HARDINESS ZONE	LIGHT	CHARACTERISTICS AND/OR USE
Hypericum frondosum	Golden St. John's wort	5–8	Sun or partial shade	Summer yellow flowers, exfoliating bark
Hypericum prolificum	Shrubby St. John's wort	4–8	Sun or partial shade	Low hedge, bed edging, yellow flowers
Jasminum nudiflorum	Winter jasmine	6–10	Sun or shade	Winter yellow flowers, good cascading plant
Kerria japonica	Japanese kerria	4–9	Partial shade	Yellow flowers through growing season, tough
Kolkwitzia amabilis	Beauty bush	4–8	Sun	Pink flowers in spring, plant alone
Lagerstroemia indica	Common crapemyrtle	7–9	Sun	Specimen for bark and blooms during summer
Lindera benzoin	Spicebush	4–9	Sun or partial shade	Fragrant plant, spring flowers, fall color
Lonicera fragrantissima	Winter honeysuckle	4–8	Sun	Early fragrant flowers
Myrica pensylvanica	Northern bayberry	3–6	Sun or partial shade	Salt tolerant, massing
Philadelphus coronarius	Sweet mock orange	4–8	Sun or partial shade	Fragrant flowers
Potentilla fruticosa	Bush cinquefoil	2–6	Sun	Low border, yellow flowers all summer
Pyracantha coccinea	Scarlet firethorn	6–9	Sun	Outstanding berries, espalier plant
Rosa (many species)	Rose	4–8	Sun	Formal beds or thickets of thorns
Spiraea albiflora	Japanese white spirea	4–8	Sun	White flowers, edging shrub
Spiraea bumalda	Bumald spirea	3–8	Sun	Flowers throughout summer, massing
Stephanandra incisa	Cutleaf stephanandra	4–7	Sun or partial shade	Fall color, low mass or hedge
Syringa meyeri	Meyer lilac	3–7	Sun	Smaller than common lilac, cleaner habit
Syringa x *persica*	Persian lilac	3–7	Sun	Small lilac, lavender fragrant flowers
Vaccinium ashei	Rabbit-eye blueberry	8–9	Sun or partial shade	Fruit, southern climates
Vaccinium corymbosum	High-bush blueberry	3–7	Sun or partial shade	Fruit, shrub border
Viburnum x *burkwoodii*	Burkwood viburnum	5–8	Sun or partial shade	Fragrant, semi-evergreen, tough

BOTANICAL NAME	COMMON NAME	HARDINESS ZONE	LIGHT	CHARACTERISTICS AND/OR USE
Viburnum carlesii	Koreanspice viburnum	5–7	Sun or partial shade	Fragrant and beautiful flowers
Viburnum cassinoides	Withe-rod viburnum	3–8	Sun or partial shade	Fall color, showy fruit
Viburnum dilatatum	Linden viburnum	5–7	Sun or partial shade	Attractive manageable hedge
Viburnum x *juddii*	Judd viburnum	4–8	Sun or partial shade	Fragrant flowers, disease resistant
Viburnum plicatum var. *tomentosum*	Doublefile viburnum	5–7	Sun or partial shade	White flowers, specimen
Weigela floribunda	Old-fashioned weigela	5–8	Sun	Deciduous border, flowers

H

DECIDUOUS SHRUBS/HEDGES (FIVE TO FIFTEEN FEET)

BOTANICAL NAME	COMMON NAME	HARDINESS ZONE	LIGHT	CHARACTERISTICS AND/OR USE
Acer campestre	Hedge maple	5–8	Sun	Small lawn tree, can be pruned into hedge
Cotoneaster lucidus	Hedge cotoneaster	4–7	Sun or partial shade	Tall narrow habit, good for hedge or screen
Eleutherococcus sieboldianus	Fiveleaf aralia	4–8	Sun or shade	Pollution tolerant, low maintenance
Elliottia racemosa	Georgia plume	6–8	Sun	White flowers
Euonymus japonicus	Japanese euonymus	7–9	Sun or shade	Fast grower, tolerates salt spray
Ilex verticillata	Common winterberry holly	3–9	Sun or partial shade	Berries persist without leaves, mass plantings
Jasminum officinale	Common white jasmine	8–10	Sun	Fragrant flowers, deep green foliage
Ligustrum amurense	Amur privet	4–7	Sun or partial shade	Withstands heavy pruning, pollution tolerant
Ligustrum obtusifolium	Border privet	4–7	Sun	Use in mass or hedge
Poncirus trifoliata	Hardy orange	5–9	Sun	Yellow fruit, thorny barrier, hedge
Quercus glauca	Blue Japanese oak	8–9	Sun	Large, dark green foliage, slow growing
Ribes alpinum	Alpine currant	2–7	Sun or shade	Good hedge

BOTANICAL NAME	COMMON NAME	HARDINESS ZONE	LIGHT	CHARACTERISTICS AND/OR USE
Symplocos paniculata	Sapphireberry	4–8	Sun or partial shade	Attracts birds, can prune as tree
Syringa x *chinensis*	Chinese lilac	3–7	Sun	Fragrant flowers, graceful habit
Syringa laciniata	Cutleaf lilac	4–7	Sun	Fragrant flowers, lacy leaves, low mounded habit
Syringa vulgaris	Common lilac	3–7	Sun	Flowers most fragrant and showiest of lilacs
Viburnum dentatum	Arrowwood viburnum	3–8	Sun or partial shade	Hardy hedges
Viburnum japonicum	Japanese viburnum	7–9	Sun	Dense, narrow screen
Viburnum lantana	Wayfaringtree viburnum	4–7	Sun or partial shade	Backgrounds, hedges, massing
Viburnum lentago	Nannyberry viburnum	3–7	Sun or shade	Background plant, attracts birds
Viburnum opulus	European cranberrybush viburnum	3–8	Sun	Beautiful flowering shrub
Viburnum sieboldii	Siebold viburnum	4–7	Sun	Specimen, groupings, use for large buildings

Deciduous Specimen Trees (Under Forty Feet)

BOTANICAL NAME	COMMON NAME	HARDINESS ZONE	LIGHT	CHARACTERISTICS AND/OR USE
Acer buergerianum	Trident maple	5–8	Partial shade	Fall color, specimen
Acer campestre	Hedge maple	4–8	Sun	Specimen, fall color
Acer ginnala	Amur maple	2–8	Sun	Small specimen, container
Acer griseum	Paperbark maple	5–7	Sun	Fall color, peeling bark
Acer japonicum	Fullmoon maple	5–7	Sun	Fall color
Acer palmatum	Japanese maple	5–8	Sun	Specimen, many forms
Acer tataricum	Tatarian maple	3–8	Sun	Specimen
Acer truncatum	Shantung maple	4–8	Sun	Fall color, lawn
Aesculus x *carnea*	Red horse chestnut	3–7	Sun	Red showy flowers
Aesculus pavia	Red buckeye	4–8	Sun	Showy red flower panicles
Amelanchier arborea	Downy serviceberry	4–9	Sun	White flowers, fall color
Aralia spinosa	Devil's-walkingstick	4–9	Sun	Pollution tolerant, thorny
Betula albosinensis	Chinese paper birch	5–6	Sun	Orange bark, specimen
Betula nigra	River birch	4–9	Sun	Large birch, borer resistant

BOTANICAL NAME	COMMON NAME	HARDINESS ZONE	LIGHT	CHARACTERISTICS AND/OR USE
Betula papyrifera	Paper birch	2–6	Sun	White bark, fall color
Carpinus caroliniana	American hornbeam	3–9	Shade	Wet soil, shade
Cercis canadensis	Eastern redbud	4–9	Partial shade	Flowers early, good in natural setting
Cercis chinensis	Chinese redbud	6–9	Partial shade	Extremely showy flowers
Chionanthus virginicus	White fringetree	3–9	Sun	Specimen or groupings
Cladrastis platycarpa	Japanese yellowwood	5–8	Sun	Showy flowers, disease free
Cornus florida	Flowering dogwood	6–9	Partial shade	Specimen patio tree
Cornus kousa	Kousa dogwood	5–8	Sun	Specimen, good near house
Cornus mas	Corneliancherry dogwood	4–8	Partial shade	Early flowers, mass together
Crataegus crusgalli	Cockspur hawthorn	3–7	Sun	Fall color, two-inch thorns
Crataegus phaenopyrum	Washington hawthorn	3–8	Sun	Fruit, fall color, specimen
Davidia involucrata	Dove tree	6–8	Shade	Specimen, flowers
Elaeagnus angustifolia	Russian olive	2–7	Sun	Gray foliage, salt tolerant
Enkianthus campanulatus	Redvein enkianthus	4–7	Partial shade	Specimen, flowers, fall color
Firmiana simplex	Chinese parasol tree	7–9	Sun	Very large leaves
Franklinia alatamaha	Franklin tree	5–8	Sun	Specimen, fall color, flowers
Halesia tetraptera	Carolina silverbell	4–8	Sun	Natural settings
Hamamelis virginiana	Common witchhazel	3–8	Sun or partial shade	Fragrant fall flowers
Koelreuteria paniculata	Panicled goldenrain tree	5–9	Sun	Patio tree, yellow flowers in summer
Laburnum x *watereri*	Goldenchain tree	5–7	Partial shade	Sun but protected, flowers
Maakia amurensis	Amur maakia	4–7	Sun	Flowers late summer
Magnolia x *soulangiana*	Saucer magnolia	4–9	Sun	Early showy flowers, specimen
Magnolia stellata	Star magnolia	3–8	Sun	Earliest magnolia flower specimen

BOTANICAL NAME	COMMON NAME	HARDINESS ZONE	LIGHT	CHARACTERISTICS AND/OR USE
Magnolia virginiana	Sweetbay magnolia	5–9	Partial shade	Fragrant flowers, wet areas
Malus (many species)	Flowering crabapple	3–8	Sun	Flowers, many growth habits
Ostrya virginiana	American hophornbeam	3–9	Partial shade	Graceful, city use
Oxydendrum arboreum	Sourwood	5–9	Partial shade	Summer flowers, fall color
Parrotia persica	Persian parrotia	4–8	Sun	Pest free, specimen
Pistacia chinensis	Chinese pistachio	6–9	Sun	Nice fall color and habit
Prunus campanulata	Bell-flowered cherry	6–9	Sun	Fall color, flowers
Prunus cerasifera	Cherry plum	3–8	Sun	Red leaves, fragrant flowers
Prunus x *cistena*	Purpleleaf sand cherry	2–8	Sun	Hardy purple leaves
Prunus sargentii	Sargent cherry	4–7	Sun	Flowers, fall color, large
Prunus serrulata 'Kwanzan'	Kwanzan flowering cherry	6–8	Sun	Flowers
Prunus subhirtella	Higan cherry	4–8	Sun	Graceful, flowers
Prunus x *yedoensis*	Yoshino cherry	5–8	Sun	Made Washington, D.C., famous for cherry blossoms
Pseudocydonia sinensis	Chinese quince	5–6	Sun	Fragrant fruit, peeling bark
Ptelea trifoliata	Hop tree	3–9	Partial shade	Small, low-branching habit
Pyrus calleryana 'Bradford'	Bradford pear	4–8	Sun	Flowers, dense, shiny leaves
Pyrus pyrifolia	Chinese sand pear	5–8	Sun	Large, good flowering display
Pyrus ussuriensis	Ussurian pear	3–8	Sun	Large hardy specimen
Quercus myrsinifolia	Chinese evergreen oak	7–9	Sun	Small garden tree, evergreen
Rhus copallina	Flameleaf sumac	4–9	Sun	Fall color, specimen
Rhus typhina	Staghorn sumac	4–8	Sun	Fragrant stem, good in natural setting
Sorbus alnifolia	Korean mountainash	4–7	Sun	Excellent for flowers and fruit

BOTANICAL NAME	COMMON NAME	HARDINESS ZONE	LIGHT	CHARACTERISTICS AND/OR USE
Sorbus aucuparia	European mountainash	3–6	Sun	Handsome fruit, many diseases
Stewartia ovata	Mountain stewartia	5–9	Partial shade	Good flowers, bark, and fall color
Stewartia pseudocamellia	Japanese stewartia	5–8	Partial shade	Good flowers, bark, and fall color
Styrax japonicus	Japanese snowbell	5–8	Sun	Flowers, specimen
Syringa reticulata	Japanese tree lilac	3–7	Sun	Specimen tree

SHADE TREES OVER FORTY FEET

BOTANICAL NAME	COMMON NAME	HARDINESS ZONE	LIGHT	CHARACTERISTICS AND/OR USE
Acer rubrum	Red maple	3–9	Sun	Excellent fall color
Acer saccharum	Sugar maple	3–8	Sun	Excellent fall color, not for cities
Aesculus hippocastanum	Common horsechestnut	3–7	Sun	Flowers, large spaces
Alnus incana	White alder	2–7	Partial shade	Cold, wet areas
Carpinus betulus	European hornbeam	4–7	Partial shade	Fall color
Castanea mollissima	Chinese chestnut	4–8	Sun	American chestnut replacement
Celtis occidentalis	Common hackberry	3–8	Sun	Good in wind and dry soils, Midwest
Cercidiphyllum japonicum	Katsuratree	4–8	Sun	Fall color, large specimen
Cladrastis lutea	American yellowwood	3–8	Sun	Showy flowering shade tree
Corylus colurna	Turkish filbert	4–7	Sun	Few pests, lawn, city, nice habit
Eucommia ulmoides	Hardy rubber tree	4–7	Sun	Pest free, Midwest
Fagus grandifolia	American beech	3–9	Sun	Specimen, large areas
Fagus sylvatica	European beech	4–7	Sun	Specimen, prune as hedge
Fraxinus ornus	Flowering ash	5–6	Sun	Showy fragrant flowers
Fraxinus pennsylvanica	Green ash	3–9	Sun	For tough-to-grow areas, Midwest

BOTANICAL NAME	COMMON NAME	HARDINESS ZONE	LIGHT	CHARACTERISTICS AND/OR USE
Ginkgo biloba	Ginkgo	3–8	Sun	Good city tree and fall color
Gleditsia triacanthos var. *inermis*	Honeylocust	3–9	Sun	Casts light shade
Gymnocladus dioica	Kentucky coffeetree	3–8	Sun	Interesting large-space tree
Kalopanax pictus	Castor-aralia	4–7	Sun	Large-leaved shade tree
Liquidambar styraciflua	American sweetgum	5–9	Sun	Fall color, lawn tree, large areas
Magnolia acuminata	Cucumbertree magnolia	3–8	Sun	Large leaves, large areas
Nyssa sylvatica	Black gum	3–9	Sun	Specimen, fall color
Populus maximowiczii	Japanese poplar	3–9	Sun	Broad-spreading leaves, Midwest
Pterocarya fraxinifolia	Caucasian wingnut	5–8	Sun	Medium specimen shade tree
Quercus acutissima	Sawtooth oak	6–9	Sun	Medium size, flowers
Quercus coccinea	Scarlet oak	4–9	Sun	Dark green in summer, scarlet fall color
Quercus imbricaria	Shingle oak	4–8	Sun	Good in Midwest, can be used as hedge
Quercus nigra	Water oak	6–9	Sun	Wet areas
Quercus palustris	Pin oak	4–8	Sun	Nice pyramidal habit, residential landscape
Quercus phellos	Willow oak	5–9	Sun	Clean, good lawn tree
Quercus prinus	Chestnut oak	4–8	Sun	Drought resistant, poor soils
Quercus robur	English oak	4–8	Sun	For large areas
Quercus robur 'Fastigiata'	Columnar English oak	4–8	Sun	Excellent narrow tree can grow to sixty feet tall
Quercus rubra	Red oak	4–8	Sun	Fast-growing shade tree
Quercus virginiana	Live oak	7–10	Sun	Specimen shade tree, larger properties
Robinia pseudoacacia	Black locust	3–8	Sun	Grows in any soil
Sophora japonica	Japanese pagodatree	4–8	Sun	Flowers late summer, city tree
Tilia cordata	Littleleaf linden	3–7	Sun	Can prune into hedge
Tilia tomentosa	Silver linden	4–7	Sun	Heat and drought resistant
Ulmus parvifolia	Lacebark elm	4–9	Sun	American elm replacement
Zelkova serrata	Japanese zelkova	5–8	Sun	Elm substitute, fall color

EVERGREEN SHRUBS
(THREE TO TEN FEET)

BOTANICAL NAME	COMMON NAME	HARDINESS ZONE	LIGHT	CHARACTERISTICS AND/OR USE
Abelia x *grandiflora*	Glossy abelia	6–9	Sun or partial shade	Fragrant, flowers all summer, attracts insects
Aspidistra elatior	Cast-iron plant	7–9	Partial shade or shade	Shrub edging for beds
Aucuba japonica	Japanese aucuba	7–10	Shade	Variegated leaves available, dense shade
Buxus microphylla	Littleleaf boxwood	6–9	Sun or shade	Hedge, formal garden
Buxus sempervirens	Common boxwood	5–8	Sun or shade	Hedge, specimen
Camellia japonica	Japanese camellia	7–9	Partial shade	Flowers in late fall, specimen
Camellia sasanqua	Sasanqua camellia	7–9	Partial shade	Flowers in early fall, specimen
Danaë racemosa	Alexandrian laurel	8–9	Shade	Graceful habit, cut branches for indoor use
Daphne odora	Fragrant daphne	7–9	Partial shade or shade	Fragrant long-lasting flowers, temperamental
Gardenia jasminoides	Cape jasmine	8–10	Sun or partial shade	Fragrant flowers, specimen
Ilex glabra 'Compacta'	Inkberry	5–9	Sun	Disease resistant, shear for hedge
Ilex x *meserveae*	Meserve hybrid hollies	5–7	Sun or partial shade	Specimen, many cultivars and sizes
Ilex pedunculosa	Longstalk holly	5–6	Sun or partial shade	Attracts birds, specimen, leaves rustle in wind

BOTANICAL NAME	COMMON NAME	HARDINESS ZONE	LIGHT	CHARACTERISTICS AND/OR USE
Ilicium floridanum	Florida anise tree	6–9	Partial shade or shade	Fragrant foliage
Kalmia latifolia	Mountain-laurel	4–9	Sun or shade	Showy flowers, good for woods
Lavandula angustifolia	Common lavender	5–8	Sun	Fragrant flowers and foliage, edging for walks
Leiophyllum buxifolium	Box sandmyrtle	5	Sun or partial shade	Low rock garden plant
Leucothoë axillaris	Coastal leucothoë	4–6	Shade	Deep green, rhododendron companion
Leucothoë fontanesiana	Fetterbush	4–6	Shade	Colorful leaves, woodland plant
Ligustrum japonicum	Japanese privet	7–10	Sun or shade	Glossy foliage, can shear
Loropetalum chinense	Chinese fringeflower	7–9	Sun or partial shade	Masses, varied foliage colors available
Mahonia aquifolium	Oregon grapeholly	5–7	Partial shade	Fragrant yellow flowers, blue berries
Myrica cerifera	Southern bayberry	7–9	Sun or partial shade	Fragrant foliage, salt tolerant, bayberry candles
Nandina domestica	Heavenly bamboo	6–9	Sun or shade	Foliage, berry clusters through winter
Nerium oleander	Oleander	8–10	Sun	Showy flowers, pollution tolerant, toxic plant
Osmanthus x *fortunei*	Fortune's osmanthus	7–9	Sun or partial shade	Hedge or specimen
Osmanthus heterophyllus	Holly osmanthus	7–9	Sun or partial shade	Hedge or specimen
Pieris floribunda	Mountain pieris	4–6	Partial shade	White fragrant flowers, low habit
Pieris japonica	Japanese pieris	5–7	Partial shade	Beautiful flowers, specimen
Pinus mugo var. *mugo*	Mugo pine	3–7	Sun	Low pine shrub
Pittosporum tobira	Japanese pittosporum	8	Sun or shade	Good massing shrub
Prunus laurocerasus	Common cherry laurel	6–8	Partial shade	Hedge, mass, fragrant flowers
Rhaphiolepis umbellata	Yeddo rhaphiolepis	8–10	Sun or partial shade	Low massing shrub
Rhododendron (many species)	Azalea	5 & south	Partial shade	Spring flower color

BOTANICAL NAME	COMMON NAME	HARDINESS ZONE	LIGHT	CHARACTERISTICS AND/OR USE
Rhododendron (many species)	Rhododendron	4 & south	Shade	Colorful, coarse, natural habit
Rosmarinus officinalis	Rosemary	6–8	Sun	Fragrant needlelike foliage, low hedge
Santolina chamaecyparissus	Lavender cotton	6–9	Sun	Good edging shrub, silver-gray foliage
Skimmia japonica	Japanese skimmia	7–8	Partial shade or shade	Red fruit, low mass
Taxus baccata 'Repandens'	Weeping English yew	5–7	Sun or partial shade	Low mass, weeping habit
Taxus cuspidata	Japanese yew	4–7	Sun	Deep green foliage, massing
Ternstroemia gymnanthera	Japanese ternstroemia	7–10	Partial shade or shade	Accent, attractive foliage, screening
Viburnum utile 'Conoy'	Conoy service viburnum	6–8	Sun or partial shade	Compact growth habit, disease resistant
Yucca glauca	Small soapweed	4–8	Sun	Sharp, sword-shaped leaves, spiked flowers

Evergreen Shrubs/Hedges (Five to Twenty-five Feet)

BOTANICAL NAME	COMMON NAME	HARDINESS ZONE	LIGHT	CHARACTERISTICS AND/OR USE
Berberis julianae	Wintergreen barberry	6–8	Sun	Good barrier hedge, long thorns
Calocedrus decurrens	California incensecedar	5–8	Sun	Handsome, formal
X *Cupressocyparis leylandii*	Leyland cypress	6–10	Sun	Fast growing
Elaeagnus commutata	Silverberry	4–6	Sun	Silver leaves
Feijoa sellowiana	Pineapple guava	8–10	Sun	Foliage and flowers
Ilex x *aquipernyi*	Dragon lady	6–9	Sun	Specimen, foliage, berries
Ilex cornuta	Chinese holly	7–9	Sun	Winter berries, hedge
Ilex crenata	Japanese holly	5–6	Sun	Good hedge and texture
Ilex glabra	Inkberry holly	5–9	Sun or partial shade	Hedge or shrub mass
Ilex vomitoria	Yaupon	7–10	Sun	Persistent berries, narrow spreading habit
Juniperus chinensis 'Pfitzeriana'	Pfitzer Chinese juniper	4–9	Sun	Many forms, available in blue, yellow, green
Juniperus scopulorum	Rocky Mountain juniper	3–7	Sun	Very blue, good in Midwest
Photinia x *fraseri*	Fraser photinia	7–10	Partial shade	Smaller than Chinese photinia
Photinia glabra	Japanese photinia	7–9	Partial shade	Smaller than Fraser photinia

BOTANICAL NAME	COMMON NAME	HARDINESS ZONE	LIGHT	CHARACTERISTICS AND/OR USE
Photinia serrulata	Chinese photinia	6–9	Sun or partial shade	New growth red, takes shearing
Podocarpus macrophyllus 'Maki'	Chinese podocarpus	8–10	Sun	Deep green foliage
Taxus x *media*	Anglojap yew	4–7	Sun	Dense spreading habit, mass or screen
Thuja occidentalis	American arborvitae	3–7	Sun	Narrow hedge, accent
Thuja orientalis	Oriental arborvitae	6–11	Sun	Narrow hedge
Viburnum awabuki 'Chindo'	Chindo viburnum	7–9	Partial shade	Rich dark green leaves, handsome habit
Viburnum rhytidophyllum	Leatherleaf viburnum	5–7	Partial shade	Large leaves, rhododendron companion

Evergreen Trees over Fifteen Feet

Please note that trees marked with an asterisk (*) are deciduous and not evergreen.

BOTANICAL NAME	COMMON NAME	HARDINESS ZONE	LIGHT	CHARACTERISTICS AND/OR USE
Abies concolor	White fir	4–7	Sun	Specimen, blue spruce substitute
Abies fraseri	Fraser fir	4–7	Sun	Specimen, Christmas tree substitute
Cedrus atlantica	Atlas cedar	6–9	Sun	Specimen
Cedrus deodora	Deodar cedar	7–8	Sun	Specimen
Cedrus libani	Cedar of Lebanon	5–7	Sun	Specimen
Chamaecyparis lawsoniana	Lawson's falsecypress	5–7	Sun	Drooping, branching habit, specimen
Chamaecyparis obtusa	Hinoki falsecypress	5–8	Sun	Specimen
Chamaecyparis pisifera	Japanese falsecypress	4–8	Sun	Golden varieties available
Cryptomeria japonica	Japanese cryptomeria	5–8	Sun or partial shade	Specimen
Cunninghamia lanceolata	Common China fir	7–9	Partial shade	Specimen, mass
Ilex aquifolium	English holly	6–9	Sun or partial shade	Berries, specimen
Ilex x *attenuata* 'Fosteri'	Foster's holly	6–9	Sun	Pyramidal habit, heavy fruit in winter

BOTANICAL NAME	COMMON NAME	HARDINESS ZONE	LIGHT	CHARACTERISTICS AND/OR USE
Ilex x 'Nellie R. Stevens'	Nellie R. Stevens holly	6–9	Sun or partial shade	Dense, vigorous growing, large red berries
Ilex opaca	American holly	5–9	Sun or shade	Winter berries, specimen
*Larix decidua**	European larch	3–6	Sun	Deciduous conifer, fall color, screen
*Larix kaempferi**	Japanese larch	4–7	Sun	Ornamental for large areas
*Metasequoia glyptostroboides**	Dawn redwood	4–8	Sun	Deciduous conifer, fast-growing for large areas
Picea abies	Norway spruce	3–7	Sun	Graceful habit, windbreak
Picea glauca	White spruce	2–6	Sun	Hardy, specimen
Picea omorika	Serbian spruce	4–7	Sun	Weepy stems, specimen or groupings
Picea orientalis	Oriental spruce	4–7	Sun	Deep green, specimen
Picea pungens	Colorado spruce	3–7	Sun	Stiff habit, specimen
Pinus aristata	Bristlecone pine	4–7	Sun	Specimen, rock garden
Pinus bungeana	Lacebark pine	5–7	Sun	Peeling bark, specimen
Pinus cembra	Swiss stone pine	3–7	Sun	Handsome bluish foliage
Pinus densiflora	Japanese red pine	3–7	Sun	Specimen, orangish bark
Pinus flexilis	Limber pine	4–7	Sun	Handsome and hardy
Pinus koraiensis	Korean pine	3–7	Sun	Specimen, groupings
Pinus nigra	Austrian pine	3–7	Sun	Specimen, windy locations
Pinus parviflora	Japanese white pine	4–7	Sun	Hardy, specimen
Pinus peuce	Macedonian pine	4–7	Sun	Specimen
Pinus resinosa	Red pine	2–5	Sun	Gorgeous tree for habit and bark
Pinus strobus	Eastern white pine	3–7	Sun	Can be sheared, fine texture
Pinus thunbergii	Japanese black pine	5–8	Sun	Salt tolerant, windy areas
Pinus wallichiana	Himalayan pine	5–7	Sun	Long graceful needles
Pseudolarix amabilis	Golden larch	5–7	Sun	Deciduous conifer, specimen, cones
Pseudotsuga menziesii	Douglas fir	4–6	Sun	Specimen, windbreak

BOTANICAL NAME	COMMON NAME	HARDINESS ZONE	LIGHT	CHARACTERISTICS AND/OR USE
Sciadopitys verticillata	Japanese umbrellapine	5–7	Sun	Fleshy needles, unusual texture, specimen
Taxodium distichum*	Common baldcypress	4–11	Sun	Deciduous conifer, specimen
Thuja plicata	Giant arborvitae	5–7	Sun	Specimen, hedge
Tsuga canadensis	Canadian hemlock	3–7	Partial shade	Graceful, excellent hedge
Tsuga caroliniana	Carolina hemlock	4–7	Partial shade	Whorled needles, rigid habit

Coordinating Plants for Twelve-Month Interest

There are many varieties of each plant listed in the chart on the following pages that are available in a wide selection of flower colors, habits, and foliage. Timing is based on Hardiness Zones 6 to 7. Blooming times are approximate and depend on weather conditions from year to year. The blooming times shown are dependent on your particular microclimate and the specific variety of plant used.

The colorful exfoliating bark of kousa dogwood, sycamore, paperbark maple, Chinese elm, and lacebark pine all year, most evident during winter months.

A star (*) before the plant name indicates that there are many varieties of this genus, which, when considered together, bloom during the entire time frame. For example, you can have windflowers that bloom in spring (*Anemone sylvestris*) and ones that will bloom in fall (*A.* x *hybrida*). Together they offer four to five months of interest.

Research all plant material before installing in your garden to be sure you achieve the desired effect.

JANUARY	FEBRUARY	MARCH	APRIL	MAY	JUNE

Conifers (evergreen foliage) → →

Holly (*Ilex*) berries →

Witchhazel (*Hamamelis*) in bloom → → →

Lenten rose (*Helleborus*) → → → → →

Snowdrop (*Galanthus*) → → →

Winter aconite (*Eranthis*) → → →

Japanese pieris (*Pieris japonica*) → → → → → →

Pussy willow (*Salix*) → → → → → →

Winterhazel (*Corylopsis*) → → → → → →

Winter jasmine (*Jasminum nudiflorum*) → → → → → →

Crocus → →

Bluebell (*Hyacinthoides*) → → → → →

Scilla → → → → → → →

Azalea → → → → → → → → → → → →

Corneliancherry (*Cornus mas*) → → → → → → → →

Crabapple → → → → → → → → →

Dogwood (*Cornus florida*) → → → → →

Flowering cherry → → → → → → → → → → →

Flowering pear (*Pyrus calleryana*) → → → → → → → → →

Flowering quince (*Chaenomeles speciosa*) → →

Forsythia → →

Fothergilla (flower) → → → →

Korean rhododendron (*R. mucronulatum*) → → → → → → → →

PJM rhododendron (*R.* 'PJM') → → → → → → →

Saucer magnolia (*M.* x *soulangiana*) → → →

Star magnolia (*M. stellata*) → → → → → →

Barrenwort (*Epimedium*) → → → → →

Candytuft (*Iberis*) → → → → → →

Foamflower (*Tiarella*) → → → → → →

Forget-me-not (*Myosotis*) → → → → → → → →

Lungwort (*Pulmonaria*) → → → → → →

Pasque flower (*Pulsatilla*) → → → → → →

Periwinkle (*Vinca minor*) → → → → → →

*Phlox → → → → → → → → → → → → → →

Violet → → → →

*Windflower (*Anemone*) → → → → → → → →

*Daffodil → → → → → → → → → → →

Fritillary (*Fritillaria*) → → → → →

Grape hyacinth (*Muscari*) → → → → → →

Snowflake (*Leucojum*) → → → → → → → →

Tulip → → → → →

JULY	AUGUST	SEPTEMBER	OCTOBER	NOVEMBER	DECEMBER
			(evergreen foliage) → → → → → → → →		
					(berries) → →
		(fruit)	(maroon foliage)		
→ →					
→ → → → → → → →					
			(yellow/orange foliage)		
→ → →					
→ → →					
→ → → → → → → → →					
→ → →					
→ → → → → → → → → → → → → → →					
→ → →		Windflower (*Anemone*) → →			

JANUARY	FEBRUARY	MARCH	APRIL	MAY	JUNE
					Kousa dogwood (*Cornus*
				Dove tree (*Davidia involucrata*) → →	
				Lilac	
				Mountain-laurel (*Kalmia*)	
				Rhododendron → → → → →	
				*Rose → → → → → → → →	
				Tree peony (*Paeonia*	
			*Viburnum → → → → → → → → → → → → →		
				*Bleeding heart (*Dicentra*)	
				Columbine (*Aquilegia*) → → →	
				*Coral bells (*Heuchera*) → → →	
				*Cranesbill (*Geranium*) → → →	
				*Daylily → → → → → → → → → →	
				Heartleaf brunnera → → → → →	
					Peony (*Paeonia*) →
				*Pinks (*Dianthus*) → → → → →	
				Solomon's seal (*Polygonatum*)	
			*Primrose → → → → → → → →		
			*Sage (*Salvia*) → → → → → → →		
				Hardy orchid (*Bletilla*) → → →	
			*Iris → → → → → → → → → → → →		
				Lily-of-the-valley → → → → →	
				*Lily → → → → → → → → → → →	
					Fringetree
					Goldenrain tree
					Maakia (*Maakia*
					Southern
					Pyracantha
					Arrowwood
					Linden
					Bellflower
				*Clematis → → → → → → → →	
					False
					Foxglove
				Globeflower (*Trollius*)	
					Lavender
					Leadwort
					Ligularia
				Primrose (*Primula*) → → → →	
					Purple
					Stokes'

JULY	AUGUST	SEPTEMBER	OCTOBER	NOVEMBER	DECEMBER
kousa) → → → → → → →					
→ → → → → →					
→ → → →					
→ →					
suffruticosa) → → →					
→ → →		(fruit & foliage) →			
→ →					
→ → →					
→ → → → → → → → → → →					
→ →					
→ → → → → → → → → → → → → → → → → → → →					
→ →					
→ → → → → → → → → → → → → → → → →					
→ → → → → → → → → → →					
→ → → →					
→ →					
→ → →					
→ → →					
→ → → → → → → → → → → → → →					
(*Chionanthus*) → → →					
(*Koelreuteria*) → → → → → → →					
amurensis) → → → → → → →					
magnolia →					
(flower) →		(fruit) →			
viburnum (*V. dentatum*) → → → → →		(fruit) →			
viburnum (*V. dilatatum*) → → → → → →		(fruit) →			
(*Campanula*) → → → → → → → → → → → → →					
→ →					
spirea (*Astilbe*) → → → →					
(*Digitalis*) → → → → → → → →					
→ → → →					
(*Lavandula*) → → → → → → → → → → → → → → → → → → →					
(*Ceratostigma*) → → → → → → → → → → → → → → (red foliage) → →					
→ → → → → → → → → → → →					
→ → → →					
coneflower (*Echinacea*) → → → → → → → → → →					
aster → → → → → → → → → →					

JANUARY	FEBRUARY	MARCH	APRIL	MAY	JUNE
					Tickseed
					Verbena → → →
					Potentilla
					St. John's wort
					Baby's
					Bee balm
					Blanket flower
					Dahlia →
					Golden
					*Speedwell (*Veronica*)
					*Stonecrop (*Sedum*)
					Yarrow

JULY	AUGUST	SEPTEMBER	OCTOBER	NOVEMBER	DECEMBER

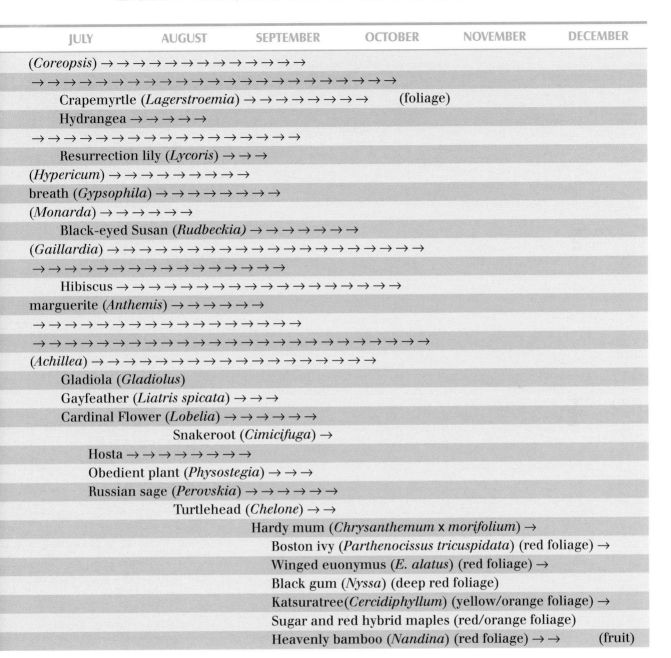

(*Coreopsis*) → → → → → → → → → → → → →

→ →

Crapemyrtle (*Lagerstroemia*) → → → → → → → → →   (foliage)

Hydrangea → → → → →

→ → → → → → → → → → → → → → → → → → → →

Resurrection lily (*Lycoris*) → → →

(*Hypericum*) → → → → → → → → → →

breath (*Gypsophila*) → → → → → → → → →

(*Monarda*) → → → → → →

Black-eyed Susan (*Rudbeckia*) → → → → → → →

(*Gaillardia*) →

→ → → → → → → → → → → → → → → → → →

Hibiscus →

marguerite (*Anthemis*) → → → → → →

→ → → → → → → → → → → → → → → → → → →

→ →

(*Achillea*) →

Gladiola (*Gladiolus*)

Gayfeather (*Liatris spicata*) → → →

Cardinal Flower (*Lobelia*) → → → → → →

Snakeroot (*Cimicifuga*) →

Hosta → → → → → → → →

Obedient plant (*Physostegia*) → → →

Russian sage (*Perovskia*) → → → → → →

Turtlehead (*Chelone*) → →

Hardy mum (*Chrysanthemum* x *morifolium*) →

Boston ivy (*Parthenocissus tricuspidata*) (red foliage) →

Winged euonymus (*E. alatus*) (red foliage) →

Black gum (*Nyssa*) (deep red foliage)

Katsuratree(*Cercidiphyllum*) (yellow/orange foliage) →

Sugar and red hybrid maples (red/orange foliage)

Heavenly bamboo (*Nandina*) (red foliage) → →   (fruit)

BIBLIOGRAPHY

Adams, George. *Birdscaping Your Garden.* Emmaus, PA: Rodale Press, 1998.

Armitage, Allan M. *Herbaceous Perennial Plants.* 2nd edition. Champaign, IL: Stipes Publishing, 1997.

Barash, Cathy Wilkinson. *Edible Flowers: From Garden to Palate.* Golden, CO: Fulcrum Publishing, 1993.

Brickel, Christopher and Judith D. Zuk, editors-in-chief. *The American Horticultural Society A–Z Encyclopedia of Garden Plants.* New York: Dorling Kindersley Publishing, 1997.

Buchanan, Rita, and Frances Tenenbaum, editors. *Taylor's Guide to Herbs.* New York: Houghton Mifflin, 1995.

Carpenter, Jot D., editor. *Handbook of Landscape Architectural Construction.* Washington, DC: The Landscape Architecture Foundation, 1976.

Clausen, Ruth Rogers and Nicolas H. Ekstrom. *Perennials for American Gardens.* New York: Random House, 1989.

Dirr, Michael A. *Manual of Woody Landscape Plants.* 5th edition. Champaign, IL: Stipes Publishing, 1998.

Duthie, Pam. *Continuous Bloom.* Batavia, IL: Ball Publishing, 2000.

Giles, Floyd. *Landscape Construction.* Champaign, IL: Stipes Publishing, 1999.

Harper, Pamela J. *Time-Tested Plants.* Portland, OR: Timber Press, 2000.

Hart, Rhonda Massingham. *Deer-Proofing Your Yard & Garden.* Pownal, VT: Storey Books, 1997.

Heath, Brent and Becky Heath. *Daffodils for American Gardens.* Washington, DC: Elliott & Clark Publishing, 1995.

Hudak, Joseph. *Gardening with Perennials Month by Month.* 2nd edition. Portland, OR: Timber Press, 1993.

Keville, Kathi. *Herbs: An Illustrated Encyclopedia.* New York: Friedman/Fairfax Publishing, 1999.

Kress, Stephen W. *National Audubon Society Birder's Handbook.* New York: Dorling Kindersley Publishing, 2000.

Mikula, Rick. *The Family Butterfly Book.* Pownal, VT: Storey Books, 2000.

Nash, George. *Wooden Fences.* Newtown, CT: Taunton Press, 1999.

Ogren, Thomas Leo. *Allergy-Free Gardening.* Berkeley, CA: Ten Speed Press, 2000.

Proctor, Rob and David Macke. *Herbs in the Garden.* Loveland, CO: Interweave Press, 1997.

Provey, Joe and Kris Robinson. *Better Lawns Step by Step.* Upper Saddle River, NJ: Creative Homeowner Press, 1999.

Roth, Sally. *The Backyard Bird Feeder's Bible.* Emmaus, PA: Rodale Press, 2000.

Rothert, Gene. *The Enabling Garden.* Dallas: Taylor Publishing, 1994.

Ruggiero, Michael A. and Tom Christopher. *Annuals with Style.* Newtown, CT: Taunton Press, 2000.

Smiley, Beth and Ray Rogers, editors. *Ultimate Rose.* New York: Dorling Kindersley Publishing, 2000.

Smith, Michael D., editor. *The Ortho Problem Solver.* 5th edition. Des Moines, IA: Better Homes and Garden Books, 1999.

Snyder, Tim. Decks. Emmaus, PA: Rodale Press, 1991.

Still, Steven M. *Manual of Herbaceous Ornamental Plants.* 4th edition. Champaign, IL: Stipes Publishing, 1994.

INDEX

ABOUT JOEL M. LERNER

Joel M. Lerner is founder and CEO of Environmental Design, Capitol View Park, Maryland, a company specializing in landscape consulting, design, and seminars. Catering to residential and commercial clientele for thirty years, he is creator of Lernscaping™, a unique system of design that matches personalities to properties.

Joel writes "Green Scene," a weekly landscape and garden column in *The Washington Post.* He hosted *The Garden Show* on WWRC-AM in Washington, D.C., for five years, appears on *Fox Morning News* as a contributor, and was featured in a four-part homeowner series on TBS, Lifetime's *Our Home,* televised public service announcements for the Outdoor Power Equipment Institute, and as a national spokesperson for the Toro Company.

A past president and board member of the Association of Professional Landscape Designers, Joel is a certified professional landscape designer and author of six critically acclaimed books and numerous articles and columns for professional and homeowner publications. He is a member of the Garden Writers Association of America. His articles and designs have been published in *American Nurseryman, Better Homes and Gardens, Garden Design, Architectural Designs, Gardens,* and *Early American Life.*

Chair of the USDA Graduate School Advisory Committee on Horticulture and Landscape Design, Joel received its 1994 USDA Director's Award, held an appointment to the American Institute of Architects Committee on the Environment, was profiled in *Landscape Design* magazine and named Designer of the Month in *Home Mechanix* magazine.

He teaches seminars on landscape design and has lectured at the U.S. National Arboretum, American University, Smithsonian Institution, Missouri Botanical Garden, George Washington University, Illinois Nurserymen Association, Minnesota Nursery and Landscape Association, Montana Association of Nurserymen, professional landscape and nursery associations, flower shows, and others.

Joel's books include *101 Townhouse Garden Designs* (HPBooks, 1985), *101 Designs with Houseplants* (SANJO Press, 1987), *101 Home Landscape Ideas* (HPBooks, 1988), and *The Complete Home Landscape Designer* (St. Martin's Press, 1992; revised and updated 1995).

For information about Joel Lerner's design services, lectures, or seminars, please write or call: Environmental Design, P.O. Box 15121, Chevy, Chase, MD 20825; (301) 495-4747; fax (301) 589-0059; e-mail: info@gardenlerner.com

Don't miss Joel's Green Scene column in the real estate section of the *Washington Post* every Saturday: www.washingtonpost.com.